The Laxdœla Saga

UNC | COLLEGE OF ARTS AND SCIENCES
Germanic and Slavic Languages and Literatures

From 1949 to 2004, UNC Press and the UNC Department of Germanic & Slavic Languages and Literatures published the UNC Studies in the Germanic Languages and Literatures series. Monographs, anthologies, and critical editions in the series covered an array of topics including medieval and modern literature, theater, linguistics, philology, onomastics, and the history of ideas. Through the generous support of the National Endowment for the Humanities and the Andrew W. Mellon Foundation, books in the series have been reissued in new paperback and open access digital editions. For a complete list of books visit www.uncpress.org.

The Laxdœla Saga
Its Structural Patterns

A. MARGARET ARENT MADELUNG

UNC Studies in the Germanic Languages and Literatures
Number 74

Copyright © 1972

This work is licensed under a Creative Commons CC BY-NC-ND license. To view a copy of the license, visit http://creativecommons.org/licenses.

Suggested citation: Madelung, A. Margaret. *The Laxdœla Saga: Its Structural Patterns*. Chapel Hill: University of North Carolina Press, 1972. DOI: https://doi.org/10.5149/9781469657851_Madelung

Library of Congress Cataloging-in-Publication Data
Names: Madelung, A. Margaret Arent.
Title: The laxdœla saga : Its structural patterns / by A. Margaret Arent Madelung.
Other titles: University of North Carolina Studies in the Germanic Languages and Literatures ; no. 74.
Description: Chapel Hill : University of North Carolina Press, [1972] Series: University of North Carolina Studies in the Germanic Languages and Literatures. | Includes bibliographical references.
Identifiers: LCCN 73158284 | ISBN 978-1-4696-5784-4 (pbk: alk. paper) | ISBN 978-1-4696-5785-1 (ebook)
Subjects: Laxdæla saga. | Sagas — History and criticism. | Rhetoric, Medieval.
Classification: LCC PT7269 .L5M3 1972 | DCC 839/.63

TO

SNORRI

and

ELIZABETH MARY WILKINSON

PREFACE

This monograph was first conceived in 1958 and grew out of work done in preparation for an English translation of *Laxdœla saga*. During the intervening years and since its presentation as part of a Ph. D. dissertation, the study presented here has undergone revision in format. The content, the examples and their interpretations, however, have through the years of maturation proved themselves, hence whatever development has taken place there consists rather in a sharpening of the concepts and in further substantiation.

The reading and rereading of the original text, indispensable to both translation and commentary, revealed a striking number of parallels in the saga; the narrative abounds in repetitions and formulae. Curiously enough, when it comes to close observation of vocabulary choices or recollection of where an unusual or previously used word has appeared, a non-native reader of a language sometimes has an advantage. Recognition of these parallels and linguistic similarities led to discernment of the structural patterns of *Laxdœla saga* and revealed a master design that unifies the saga into an artistic whole.

In many respects such a detailed commentary on a single saga may seem too tedious for the non-specialist. But in order to demonstrate how deftly and tightly structured the saga is on all levels, illustration in every instance has been preferred to unsubstantiated statement. And since repetition and interweaving of the structural forms distinguish the content and style of the saga, a certain amount of duplication has proved unavoidable. I trust that the ample documentation will aid rather than impede aesthetic appreciation of this particular saga, and that the results obtained will encourage others to evaluate the creative prose of the saga genre on the basis of close internal analysis of individual texts.

During the rewriting for publication of the final chapter "Literary Perspectives," which summarizes the broader conclusions reached, I stumbled — some ten years after the inception of the whole idea — upon something totally unexpected. A solution emerged that was farthest from any preconceived notions I had entertained, but which in a strange way converged with the original experiment I had set out upon, namely to demonstrate that the saga was a work of art deliberately so created. The serendipitous discovery — the saga metamorphoses into a *roman à clef* — is based solely on the internal evidence of the saga, and its validity rests on the accuracy and cogency of the aesthetic analysis. Verification from external sources has been undertaken in part in my article appearing in the Festschrift for Lee M. Hollander (*Saga og språk: Studies in language and literature* [Austin, Texas]), now in press. Since of necessity this monograph is limited to treatment of the saga as a closed unit, only a glimpse of the direction and promise that the aesthetic method holds when used in conjunction with comparative studies of other texts in the genre can be indicated. Much of the old romanticism surrounding the sagas will no doubt thereby have been lost, but something far more valuable will surely be gained. The aesthetic method may prove salutary in coming to grips with other Icelandic sagas and a welcome alternative for medievalists who deal with similar questions of oral origins, folk traditions, linguistic formulae and patterns, and anonymous works.

For scholars in adjacent disciplines, who would encounter difficulty with the Icelandic quotations, I have added English renderings, except in those places where the meaning can be gathered from the context or from preceding quotations. The Icelandic forms which illustrate the author's use of similar linguistic configurations have been italicized. All quotations from the *Laxdœla saga* both in the text and in the notes (chapter reference being given in small roman letters and page number in arabic numerals) are from the edition of Einar Ólafur Sveinsson, Vol. V of "Íslenzk fornrit" (Reykjavík, 1934).

For their splendid guidance and inspiration during the initial stages of this work as a Ph. D. thesis, I am most grateful to Professors Gösta Franzén and George J. Metcalf of the University of Chicago.

My appreciation also goes to the United States Educational Foundation in Iceland (Fulbright) and to the Board of Foreign Scholarships for the study grant to Iceland in 1958—59 that made this work possible. For their helpfulness and encouragement during those "Winter Nights" I give public thanks to Donald Wilson and Mildred B. Allport of the USIS in Reykjavík at that time. To Sigurður Nordal, Professor Emeritus of the University of Iceland, I am indebted for the reading of the preliminary manuscript and for his support of the project. And to my Icelandic friends Egill and Katrín Jacobsen, whose hospitality I enjoyed in Reykjavík and who sustained me in every sense of the word, I should like to offer my sincerest gratitude and friendship.

The training in aesthetic method which brought this work to life I owe to Elizabeth Mary Wilkinson of University College, London, who opened the door to poetry. To her and to Snorri's grand duplicity this work is dedicated.

Oak Park, Illinois   A. Margaret Arent Madelung

March, 1971

CONTENTS

Introduction 1
   Problems of Saga Research 1
   Previous Studies on *Laxdœla saga* 5
Chapter I: Foreknowledge 15
   The General Plan of the Saga 15
   Dreams, Curses, Premonitions, and Prophecies 18
   Anticipation in Retrospect 26
Chapter II: Repetition 47
Chapter III: Comparison: Parallels and Contrasts 65
Chapter IV: Triplets and Quadruplets: Contrapuntal Variation . . 97
   The Parties 97
   The Goadings 100
   The Killings 105
   The Drownings 110
   The Sales of Land 113
   Quadruplets 118
Chapter V: Recurrence 123
Literary Perspectives 147
   The Historical Illusion 148
   The Oral Heritage Re-evaluated 150
   Written Sources 154
   The Social and Moral Order 158
   Destiny 160
   The Characters 162
   The Epic Base 164
   The Dramatic Presentation 166
   Style and Tone 167
   Rhythm and Time 173
   The Age of the Sturlungs: Authorship and Date of the Saga . . . 183
Notes 197
Appendix I: Genealogical Tables 236
Appendix II: Manuscripts of *Laxdœla saga* and Abbreviations 238
Bibliography 239
Index of Topics and Concepts 245
Index of Personal Names 255

INTRODUCTION

Problems of Saga Research

In the more than three centuries since their discovery by the outside world, the *Íslendingasögur* (Sagas of Icelanders or Family Sagas) have for the most part been neglected by literary criticism, the discipline which would be proper to their essence and which could supply the methodology commensurate with their intent. The formal, artistic nature of these sagas has been eclipsed by philological, historical, and folkloristic interests. Although the sagas have often been extolled for their unique prose style, their singular aesthetic merit has tended to be avowed rather than demonstrated.

Neglect by the literary critic can be attributed in part to the fact that these thirteenth-century Icelandic writings have been beset with problems extraneous to art as such.[1] When the Icelandic literature first came to the attention of scholars outside of Iceland, toward the end of the sixteenth century, it was assumed to contain historical accounts of the remote prehistory of Scandinavia (*Fornaldarsögur* or Mythological Sagas), of the kings of Norway (*Konungasögur* or Kings' Sagas), of Iceland during the period of Settlement (*Íslendingasögur*). The Sagas of Icelanders, of which *Laxdœla* is one, deal with events of the tenth and eleventh centuries, were apparently composed and written down in the thirteenth century, and are known today from vellum and paper manuscripts of the fourteenth century. Since only a few fragmentary manuscripts can be assigned to the thirteenth century, we therefore are dependent on copies or even copies of copies. One of the major tasks of saga scholarship has been to establish critical texts for these sagas, an undertaking and achievement which has provided us with the indispensable "Íslenzk fornrit" series, of which many volumes are still to come. In addition, the fact that these manuscripts are anonymous and undated has prompted through several centuries of scholarship no little speculation concerning their origin and chronology.[2]

When these manuscripts first came into the hands of scholars, it was almost inevitable that the sudden discovery of such wealth of new material relating to

1

the mythology, history, and earliest culture of the North would overwhelm the Scandinavian world. Acquisition of these texts coincided with both an awakened antiquarian interest and a rising feeling of nationalism and competition among the Scandinavian countries. Indiscriminate perusal of the manuscripts, particularly the *Fornaldarsögur*, for facts about the prehistory of the North engendered such faith in the reliability of the sagas that two centuries passed before that notion, at least in respect to the *Fornaldarsögur*, was corrected.

With the sharpening of critical acumen and historical method, the attempt was gradually made to sift fact from fancy. In the early nineteenth century P. E. Müller (1776—1834) produced his epoch-making *Sagabibliothek* (Vols. I—III, Kiøbenhavn, 1817—1820), which divided the sagas according to content into the three general groupings still recognized today. The *Fornaldarsögur* could not stand against the *Konungasögur* and the *Íslendingasögur* in reliability. The former were frankly imaginative, the latter "obviously realistic" and therefore of historical content, although Müller was aware that even here degrees of reliability were possible. Müller was one of the first to connect development of the saga genre with cultural circumstances. Tacitly the faith in historicity had rested on the assumption of accuracy in the transmission of the events related in the sagas. Anonymity spoke for oral transmission; the straight-forward, objective presentation pointed to factual recording. To account for such a remarkably long, accurate, oral tradition certain exceptions had to be granted. Cultural and social conditions peculiar to Iceland were pressed into service, as well as implicit, preconceived notions concerning the nature and excellence of folk (oral) literature. Although most of Müller's assumptions had been anticipated here and there during the two previous centuries, it was with his *Sagabibliothek* that the oral theory on the origin, development, and chronology of the sagas became hopelessly entangled with the arguments for historical reliability.

The late eighteenth and early decades of the nineteenth century saw the rise in Germany of the Romantic School with its lively interest in folklore. Müller's chronology can be said to rest, implicitly at least, on Romantic premises of the priority of oral traditions. The more "oral traits" any given saga contained, the older the saga. Likewise, the concomitant Romantic tenets concerning the priority of folk poetry in respect to its genuineness and perfection found their way into discussions of the Icelandic sagas and merged with the age-old conviction of their historical value.[3] Authenticity in the sense of genuine folk tradition and folkloristic style all too frequently became synonymous with the reliability demanded by a critical historical discipline.

This "unhappy marriage," as Theodore Andersson dubs it,[4] between oral transmission and historical reliability reached its most complete formulation in the writings of Andreas Heusler (1865—1940)[5] who took the lead among the Free-prosaists, as he himself labeled the adherents to this theory. After P. E. Müller, Finnur Jónsson (1858—1934), Knut Liestøl (1881—1952), and Rudolf Meissner (1863—1948), among others, held individually modified versions concerning fluid or rigid oral transmitting, the artistic superiority or primitiveness of folk poetry, the degree to which the sagas are historically reliable, the amount of influence to be attributed to oral tradition, redactors, or authors. Heusler was, at first, the most extreme, insisting in one breath upon exact transmission, historical intent, and literary excellence of the sagas. Müller had postulated the chronological priority of oral sagas but had never insisted on the superiority of folk poetry and tradition. Heusler, like most of the others, was constrained to hedge on these points, admitting that oral transmission was subject to variants, that the "pure" saga (that is, the oral saga in its pristine perfection), since it was told artfully, became more than chronicle, and that degrees of "bookishness" had to be reckoned with. It is curiously ironic to watch how among the proponents of the Free-prose school arguments consistently rest on aesthetic judgments: only folk poetry can be so naively realistic, objective, succinct in expression, full of dialogue; the best sagas are the earliest; and so forth. Yet at no time does the great lacuna in knowledge concerning the existence of an oral substratum ever prompt critics to turn to the written sagas themselves.

Thus, until recently, investigations surrounding the Sagas of Icelanders have taken the form of checking and verifying historical data, of demonstrating the validity of genealogies from outside sources, even of excavating for the famed burnt house of *Njáls saga*. Stylistic studies have on the whole been directed toward singling out "genuine oral elements" or toward discovering "bookish traits" that would point to later manipulation and hence to a decline from pure saga style and from truthful account. The results of these endeavors, based as they are on unproved assumptions, have yielded disappointing results. The inner chronology of the sagas cannot stand up against the dating from historical annals, nor can many of the details about the persons be substantiated, and indeed quite a few of the saga characters themselves are unverifiable. The discrepancies attending this line of thought invited a fresh approach.

In the early years of the twentieth century a change in attitude was initiated by Björn M. Ólsen's (1850—1919) evaluation of *Gunnlaugs saga ormstungu* and somewhat later by Sigurður Nordal's introduction to *Egils saga* in the "Íslenzk fornrit" series and by his study of *Hrafnkels saga*.[6] Scholars began to feel that the sagas warranted attention less as possible sources for history or as reflexes of an oral tradition and more in themselves as literary works of merit. These Book-prosaists, as they became called, among them Ólsen, Nordal (who emerged as leader of the Book-prose school), Walter Baetke, Einar Ólafur Sveinsson, and Gabriel Turville-Petre, considered artistic excellence to be indicative of a later rather than early origin. Sagas that formerly were assigned an early place in a relative chronology because of unified composition, simplicity, vigor of language and so on were transposed to a point diametrically opposite in the time scale. All the special excellences previously thought to be the prerogatives of oral, folk art, all the "obviously" oral traits, could be shown to be the highly sophisticated techniques of written compositions. For the new school, literary progression spans an ascending gradient from primitive, less developed, artistic forms to more masterful presentations.[7] Accordingly, artistic features are primarily attributable to scribes, redactors, or authors, depending upon the degree of departure from the notion of an oral substratum. Having come into being as a school of opposition, the Book-prosaists have had to devote their efforts mainly to correcting former ideas. The more cautious and less extreme members of the two schools share many points. The Free-prosaists, for their part, have had to admit to degrees of reliability and to influence from scribes and redactors. Many Book-prosaists, while on the one hand emphasizing the role of authors and written records in the composition of the sagas, on the other hand admit to some kind of oral sources. While there continue to be some die-hards in respect to belief in the historical reliability of the sagas and in the accuracy of oral traditions, the Free-prose school need no longer feel incumbered by such extreme views.[8] Walter Baetke, sensing the ambivalance of the new school, has advocated a clean break with the past, with all notions of a substratum, making a plea for an appraisal of each saga as a literary work of art, self-contained as an aesthetic whole.

Even if it is conceded that the sagas as we know them are literary productions in the strictest sense of the term, written in the thirteenth century, it is nonetheless counter to logic and all historical-literary progression to assume that they came into being *ex nihilo*. The art of writing came to Iceland following the introduction of Christianity (A. D. 1000) and the subsequent establishment of church schools. To the Book-prosaists, Nordal and E. Ó. Sveinsson, belongs credit for the abandonment of the theory that the sagas are survivors in the form of written transcriptions from the age of oral composition and for promulgating the view that saga writing was an art that developed in the thirteenth century.[9] Literary development, however, is always a continuum; the preliterate past and its probable achievements should not be totally dropped from sight. These roots cannot have been cut off entirely by the advent of writing, since many of the techniques of oral composition would naturally have been accommodated to the new written medium. Indeed, such remnants can be detected, even though, in the narrower sense, they are now literary devices. A comparison of the components which the sagas hold in common can in particular be expected to throw light on traditional origins. Of great interest in this regard are the earlier sources for the Kings' Sagas and the *Heimskringla*. Furthermore, the learned training of the Church and hagiographic literature played a prominent role in stimulating saga writing and deserve more careful attention. Acquaintance with the total body of Icelandic writing during this prolific period would be desirable before firm judgments are pronounced.

The pinnacle of saga writing reached in the thirteenth century has almost three centuries of written learning behind it and so lies far removed from the preliterate age. What remnants from the past age of poetry still remain, what marks the sagas as unique compositions with the stamp of individual authors, can best be assessed if the sagas are analyzed each on its own merits, as Baetke urges. Then only will it be meaningful to draw comparisons, to ferret out sources and borrowings from among the extant texts, and to search for identifiable authors.

Previous Studies on Laxdœla saga

Scholarly investigation of *Laxdœla saga* has in general reflected the attitudes and theories which have governed saga scholarship as a whole. One of the earliest detailed treatments of the saga is contained in A. W. Bååth's *Studier öfver kompositionen i några isländska ättsagor* (Lund, 1885). Proceeding from the general assumption that the sagas were composed of short, individual episodes that existed in the oral tradition as *þættir* and that these *þættir* were at a later period joined together by particularly gifted redactors or authors to form larger wholes, Bååth concluded that sagas having the most *þættir* were the oldest; the more the *þættir* were amalgamated, the more unified and later the work. An aesthetic principle was thus also his guide to a chronology.

Bååth thought that he could discern the *þættir* divisions in the first twenty-seven chapters of *Laxdœla saga* more readily than in the last fifty-one where a thread of fated occurrences pointed to a conscious, thought-through reworking by a redactor or author.[10] A preconceived notion about the origin and composition of the sagas, however, led Bååth to draw the wrong conclusions from his observations. Also, in many instances, Bååth's insights derive from mistakes in the 1826 edition, the only one available to him at that time. In tracing chapter by chapter the links between episodes Bååth was following the method of the author without being aware of it. So intent was he upon finding an "afdelnings början," that he missed the import and aesthetic function of these links. When he speaks incidentally of "the recalling and fulfillment of something previously introduced,"[11] without recognizing it, he has stumbled upon one of the major structural and formal devices employed by the author of the saga. For Bååth, however, the recalling of what was previously written marked only the beginning of a new *þáttr*.

Some fifty years later Johannes van Ham followed Bååth's divisions into *þættir*[12] but did not accept Bååth's theory that the idea of fate was the prime factor that gave the saga its literary character. The notion of fate, van Ham states, is used with "aesthetiese overwegingen" and is an "aestheties middel van hoge werking"; it cannot, however, be considered unique, for it is common property and belongs to the general "volksbezit." On the other hand, van Ham feels that historical inaccuracies, fictional characters, litotes, superlative epithets, and the appearance of type characters point rather toward the literary quality of the work than toward historical purpose. Furthermore, van Ham believes that these literary qualities were already present in the oral saga. He assumes that the saga writer received the material "in min of meer volledige vorm van de volksoverlevering," but that the final redactor took some liberty with the text.[13]

Since he has not disencumbered himself from the notion of an oral saga, van Ham dwells more on the folk origin for these aesthetic devices than on their special function within the saga. Their precise artistic value he misses for lack of perception as to the overall design of the saga. It suffices him to say:

> Maar de wijze waarop ze in de saga wordt aangewend, de effeckten die er mee worden bereikt, de overeenstemming van deze stijlwendingen in karakter met de hoogtepunten van het verhaal en met de tekening der personen, maken voor ons duidelik op welke kunstzinnige wijze van deze natuurlike middelen is gebruik gemaakt.[14]

Nevertheless van Ham has some good insights into one of the basic stylistic qualities of *Laxdœla saga*: the vacillating between the two extremes of overstatement (superlative epithets) and its opposite, understatement (litotes and euphemism). He rightly senses the stereotyped character of much that is in the saga and realizes that the technique, particularly that of understatement, has been applied with greater individuality and variation by the author (narrator or writer) so that one must be sensitive to the slightest nuances.

A decade later Margrit Schildknecht-Burri applied to *Laxdœla saga* categories prescribed in Andreas Heusler's *Die altgermanische Dichtung* in an attempt to determine to what extent the saga had been corrupted by later bookish traits.[15] In her discussion she accepts Heusler's assumption that the oral saga sets the norm for what is "sagegemäß" or best. Yet she often demonstrates with what superb skill the saga author handles these bookish traits, thereby vitiating Heusler's contention that younger characteristics indicate a decline from excellence. Unfortunately, the examples she chooses neither illustrate the point she sets out to make, nor do her conclusions follow from her points. Occasionally she refers to parallels within the saga but disregards the evidence in order to agree with Heusler: "Es ist sonst nicht üblich, solchen Zusammenhängen in der Saga nachzugehen."[16] She then concludes that there is no red thread running through the saga, and that its "episodic" character justifies the judgment that it is uneven, "von ungleichen Formgefühlen."[17] In addition she finds the first forty-three chapters of the saga closest to the older, chronicle style of the better sagas, the middle portion (Chapters xliv-lvi) "später, aber noch vorzüglicher Sagastil," and the final chapters (lvii-lxxviii) the most bookish and thus indicative of the "jüngere Merkmale" which she has set out to find.[18]

Her dependency upon preconceived notions of the oral saga is further evident in the following passage:

> Es ist vor allem die buchmäßige Sprache, die Wortwahl und der Satzbau, welche die Laxd. zusammen mit der Vatnsd. von allen anderen Sagas unterscheidet. Hier hat nicht, *wie sonst oft, ein Sagaerzähler die Saga einem Schreibenden diktiert,* sondern der Schreibende selbst, ein Gebildeter, ein Geistlicher, hat die Saga, während er sie in das Kleid seiner gewählten Sprache hüllte, neu durchformt.[19]

Recent investigations on *Laxdœla saga* include studies by Rolf Heller and Peter Hallberg. The first of Heller's studies, *Literarisches Schaffen in der Laxdœla saga*,[20] is aimed primarily at demonstrating the historical unreliability of parts of the saga, especially of the Melkorka incident and the genealogy of Kjartan. The saga account, Heller says, "wird in verschiedener Hinsicht fragwürdig."[21] Although Heller disproves the realistic function of several incidents in the story, for example the price paid for Melkorka as a bondwoman, he misses their poetic justification.

In addition, Heller points out some striking parallels in content and wording between *Sturlunga saga*, the *Konungasögur*, and *Laxdœla saga*, and concludes that contemporary writings were used as source material to a much greater extent than heretofore surmised and that the author of *Laxdœla* did some borrowing.[22] Heller has recently cited parallelisms in the *Morkinskinna*, *Heimskringla*, *Knýtlinga saga*, *Steins þáttr Skaptasonar*, Odd's *Óláfs saga* (AM 310), *Páttr Egils Siðu-Hallssonar*, and *Piðranda þáttr ok Þórhalls* (originally part of a lost *Óláfs saga Tryggvasonar* by the monk Gunnlaug) which are closely related to passages in *Laxdœla*.[23] In themselves and taken at face value, the conjectures in respect to plausible trains of thought which would incline the *Laxdœla* author to incorporate these passages in his own work appear reasonable. In some instances a "rittengsl" is no doubt to be suspected, especially if thematic similarities can be established besides isolated phrases, for the traceable source itself may represent elements more common and current than the parallelisms in the compared works might at first indicate. Against the borrowing of isolated phrases some doubts can be raised, unless it can be shown that the same text was used as source in other respects. Generally in the medieval period borrowing was of a broader and more thematic nature. Such literary "rittengsl" as are discovered also require close scrutiny to determine in which direction the borrowings go. Especially gratifying are Heller's remarks that the *Laxdœla* author has completely transformed the materials borrowed to suit his own purpose.[24]

Heller's other studies along this line include source finding in the *Biskupasǫgur* ("Laxdœla saga und Bischofssagas") and in the *Knýtlinga saga* ("Laxdœla saga und Knytlinga saga").[25] Here again, particularly in the case of the *Knýtlinga saga*, many more factors need to be weighed in order to determine the direction of borrowing. Nonetheless his investigations are far more fruitful in establishing connections between the sagas than are the statistical studies attempted by Peter Hallberg.[26] To demonstrate that Óláf hvítaskáld Thórdarson is the author of both *Laxdœla* and *Knýtlinga* Hallberg has sifted the vocabulary of the latter within limited grammatical categories (adjectives and adverbs, personal and collective designations, verbs and verbal constructions, abstracts) and compared these words over against the vocabularies of five other sagas (*Eigla*, *Laxdœla*, *Eyrbyggja*, *Njála*, *Grettla*). Whichever saga (in this case *Laxdœla*) shared with *Knýtlinga* the greatest number of "parord" (pairwords, that is, words occuring in two of the sagas but in no others) was deemed of common authorship. Not only are the criteria according to which the "parord" are selected faulty (limiting the selection to certain sectors of the vocabulary, including or excluding compound forms with negative prefix, accepting or rejecting verbs with or without their idiomatic prepositional combinations, to name a few of the arbitrary factors), but also the fact that the evidence is not held up against all possible texts and authors arouses serious misgivings. All pair-words which were found in the *Heimskringla*, for instance, were automically stricken from the list, and Sturla Thórdarson's *Íslendinga saga* is not represented and neither is *Hrafnkatla*. A most serious objection must be voiced against the tacit assumption in all such quantitative analyses that the language of any given saga represents an "at random" mode of expression, an uncalculated, freely written prose, flowing from the author's subconscious, hence revealing his idiosyncracies, his favorite words. While each writer or poet may have his private, distinctive linguistic world, as an artist often has his individual palette, some poets and artists may be capable of varying their materials and their vision and likely do not write as they talk. In any case the poet or artist is best recognized qualitatively rather than quantitatively. And as with *Laxdœla* or *Hrafnkatla* where the prose is deliberately contrived or repetitions consciously calculated, lexical-statistical results would be invalid from the outset.

These same criticisms can be levelled at the work of Marina Mundt, whose *Sturla Þórðarson und die Laxdæla saga* offers a rebuttal against Hallberg's demonstration that Óláf Thórdarson is the author of *Laxdœla*.[27] Entering his own bailiwick, while avoiding some of his pitfalls, she applies the statistical method substituting for the "parord" the concept of plus and minus words. Plus words or favorite words are selected on the basis of their more frequent occurence in *Laxdœla* than would be normal for the same amount of text in other sagas; minus words are those that are strikingly absent or less frequent than would be expected. It is at once obvious that the system will break down in the case of *Laxdœla*, for she maintains that any word must be used three times in *Laxdœla* to qualify as a favorite word, and this is precisely one of the structural and stylistic features of the saga, hence repetitions in threes quantitatively will tell us little about the author's favored, unconscious linguistic world. The *Laxdœla* author deliberately repeats and restricts his vocabulary toward an aesthetic end. Not in quantity does the author reveal himself but in the handling of his linguistic units, in his design for the whole saga and in his style. These are qualities that cannot be measured mechanically. M. Mundt recognizes herself the deficiencies in claiming authorship on the basis of statistical studies alone, for how great the numerical correspondences between two texts must be in order for them to be identified as from the same hand remains an arbitrary decision, especially since the numerical count, in view of differences in the length of the texts compared, must be adjusted as proportional ratios. And precisely here her method shows its weakness in that she takes Sturla's two works together as one unit (*Hákonar saga* and the *Íslendinga saga*) in order to reach a more favorable result for Sturla over against Óláf's *Knýtlinga*:

> Wenn ich schließlich beide Werke in der Regel als eine einheitliche Textmasse behandelte, so aus der Überlegung heraus, daß bei zwei so ungleichen Texten es umso schwerer fallen sollte, günstigere Werte als für die Knytlinga zu bekommen, jedenfalls solange es darum geht, der Textmenge entsprechend, einen Ausdruck regelmäßig öfter oder seltener als andere zu gebrauchen. Denn da genügte es ja gewöhnlich nicht, wenn Sturla nur in dem einen oder in dem anderen Werk das betreffende Wort etwa genau so oft oder genau so selten wie der Verfasser der Laxdæla verwendete.[28]

This loading of the deck and the admission here and elsewhere that texts from the same author can be utterly different discredit the endeavor. One can only ask, would the lexical-statistical method reveal Sturla to be the author of the two works attributed to him? M. Mundt remarks that this point is worth an individual study, and, indeed, by the results of it the method would stand or fall. Furthermore, she herself criticizes Hallberg for not including in the test series all possible authors, yet she, too, limits the candidates. It is by no means a foregone conclusion that *Laxdæla*'s author must be either Óláf or Sturla. One only gets answers to the questions asked. If the right question is withheld, one is sure to get a wrong answer.

Since the statistical method breaks down at so many points, a close look at each saga for its internal structure and aim seems called for and past due. From there one might be able to launch investigations into external matters with more assurance of success. The design, style, and spirit of each saga must be analyzed, and against this internal evidence all else must be measured and assessed. Only in the Chapter entitled "Miscellen" [sic] does M. Mundt touch upon some of the singular stylistic phrasing which the *Íslendinga saga* and *Laxdæla* seem to share. The relationship between these two sagas, however, still remains somewhat of an enigma. Instead of pointing to the same author the similarities lexical or otherwise, which both Heller, Mundt and others have discovered, may represent borrowings, where it is by no means a simple matter to reach even a tentative conclusion as to which served as source for the other.

The statistical studies of Hallberg and Mundt to ascertain the authorship of *Laxdœla*, the source findings of Heller that serve also the avowed purpose of identifying the author will remain problematical and inconclusive as long as the internal evidence is disregarded. Knowledge of sources, the *Stoffgeschichte* of the saga, unfortunately leaves the saga just as much a patchwork as did the old *þættir* hypothesis. Source studies may throw light on the author and his working methods, but they fail to bring the analyzed elements into a synthesis. The approach reflects the negative aspect of the Book-prose theory, namely to disprove the oral origin and historical reliableness of the sagas and to demonstrate the use of written source material. The problems dealt with are thus peripheral to the study of the saga as an example of a literary work of art, which in itself forms a unit greater than the sum of its parts or sources.

As the present study was nearing completion, Heller's article, "Studien zu Aufbau und Stil der Laxdoela Saga,"[29] appeared and corroborated some of my findings and strengthened my conviction that the method I had followed in preparing the translation of the saga was indeed imperative.[30] Heller adopts the premises of the Book-prosaists that the sagas are purely literary productions and that the unity of the work as well as the problem of authorship can best be demonstrated by looking at the language of any individual saga. He asserts, as Bååth had long before him, that *Laxdœla saga* was composed according to a "wohlüberlegter Plan," and that the saga author exhibits a decided preference for certain words and phrases — his "Lieblingsausdrücke" — and has used repetition as one way of emphasizing certain points for his audience.

Heller sets up categories of repeated words and expressions that: (1) follow closely upon one another and are related in content; (2) are close together but unrelated in content; and (3) are both spatially far apart and unrelated to one another. These groupings leave much to be desired in conception and interpretation of the data. Distance of separation is an irrelevant factor; many important examples are omitted; and many of those included are inappropriate or erroneously elucidated. As Heller himself admits, they represent but "ein Sammeln und erstes Sichten eines vielgestaltigen Materials."[31]

In addition, Heller discusses various repeated scenes and motifs in the saga. The relationship of these and other repetitions to the author's "wohlüberlegter Plan" is never suggested and the individual examples never crystallize into a systematic whole but remain isolated curiosities — "Besonderheiten" — of the saga. Indeed, Heller's avowed purpose is to discover through examination of individual characteristics not the unified structure of the saga but the peculiarities of the author:

> Die Sagas müssen also als Spiegelbilder für Dichterpersönlichkeiten gesehen werden. ... Ich bin der Ansicht, daß sich durch die Beobachtung solcher Besonderheiten am ehesten Eigenheiten des Verfassers — etwa hinsichtlich seiner Bildung oder seiner Interessen — oder Abhängigkeiten von Sagas untereinander feststellen lassen.[32]

Thus these studies contribute little to the understanding of *Laxdœla saga* as a work of art and lead outside rather than into the composition.[33]

A similar systematic cataloguing, in effect a concordance of words and phrases made for tranlation of the saga, led me to a hypothesis of its aesthetic structure. Hence the presuppositions for the formulation of my categories depart basically from those of Heller. In the subsequent chapters, I shall discuss the various devices employed by the author in composing his saga. These structural and formal elements will be considered under five aspects: Foreknowledge, Repetition, Comparison (Parallels and Contrasts), Triplets and Quadruplets, and Recurrence. The examples under these categories will attest to the skill of the author in carrying out his design and point up the kind of world he is symbolizing: a sphere limited by predestination and a prescribed ethical code. Most importantly, the internal sphere of the saga sets up an analogue to the social and ethical demands of the action in that the concrete features of the linguistic medium have been seized upon to function as an abstraction and have been selected to create of themselves a word-picture of the implications behind the saga's events. It is with this word-pattern that the author is most concerned, not with the discursive reference of his language "as a medium." His language is "an event," to use the terms of W. F. Bolton,[34] and its reference remains always intrinsic, being unconcerned with any use or origin that the words or phrases may have outside the saga. Thus the emphasis in this literary analysis is consistently placed on the components of the narration and the linguistic patterns that make them recognizable. The focus remains on the text itself and ignores the problems which encompass the saga literature in general. External circumstances of development or authorship, historical facts or cultural influences are considered only incidentally in the final section Literary Perspectives and in the footnotes at times. A literary study of this sort, although dissociated from these external questions, might well be of aid in finding a solution to them.

After Gest has listened attentively to Gudrún's narration of her four dreams, he tells her: "What I have to say will seem very much of a piece, for

I intend to interpret all of them in very much the same way." So it is with *Laxdœla saga* and so with its interpretation. It is all "very much of a piece," and the various aspects of it are parts of one organic whole. For the task at hand, we must look to the saga itself and let it speak.

I

FOREKNOWLEDGE

The General Plan of the Saga

Laxdœla saga is one of the Sagas of Icelanders and tells the story of the lives of the descendants and kin of Ketil Flatnose.[1] Although the saga relates how many kinsmen and others came to Iceland and settled there, the opening chapters focus attention upon two branches of his household, that of his son, Bjorn the Eastman, and of his daughter, Unn the Deep-minded. Upon arriving in Iceland Bjorn and Unn, each in turn, find their new dwelling places marked for them by the drifting ashore of the high-seat posts, the *ǫndvegissúlur*.[2] The fact that the *ǫndvegissúlur* are mentioned only in reference to these two characters would indicate that the coincidence should not be regarded as arbitrary. Rather, here at the very beginning of the story, fate sets the course for each side of the house, for Bjorn and Unn, and all their kin. And as the saga unfolds, it gradually shows Unn's two great-great-great-grandsons, Kjartan Óláfsson and Bolli Thorleiksson, and Bjorn's great-great-granddaughter, Gudrún Ósvífsdóttir, to be the central figures in a love triangle that leads the family to feud and tragedy.

A sequence of ill omens, curses, prophetic dreams, and premonitions foretells the lives and fates of Kjartan, Bolli, and Gudrún. Supernatural powers contained in two swords control Kjartan's life and death. One, called Footbiter and owned by Kjartan's beloved foster brother Bolli, carries a curse that it will be the death of that one in the family whose loss would be hardest to bear. Kjartan's own sword, Konungsnaut (King's Gift) carries a blessing and the prophecy that Kjartan will never feel a weapon's fatal sting so long as he bears it. Through the curse and the blessing the swords are juxtaposed and their powers pitted one against the other. Gest Oddleifsson, who is gifted with second sight, discloses what will happen: Bolli will kill Kjartan and through so doing bring about his own death. Thus fate has decreed that the foster brothers who are bound to each other in affection and kinship are also to be each other's bane. Their quarrel arises over Gudrún and their love for her.

Four dreams reveal to Gudrún the course of her life, and they are interpreted for her by Gest. She is to have four hubands: the first, symbolized by an ill-fitting headdress, she will not love and will cast off; the second, symbolized by a silver arm band, she will love much but lose by drowning; the third, symbolized by a gold arm band, she will not love the more, although gold is more precious than silver. This husband will be killed largely through her carelessness. A helmet set with gems and almost too heavy for her to bear symbolizes the fourth. The helmet topples from her head into the Hvammsfjord, indicating that she will lose this husband, too, by drowning. When Gest finishes with interpreting her dreams, Gudrún remarks wistfully and somewhat ironically: "There is certainly much to look forward to if all this is to come to pass."

Similarly, throughout the saga prophecies provide a framework for the structure and an outline for the central action. In the action three interlinked and mutually dependent parts can be discerned. The introduction (Chapters i-xxxi), with slow epic pace, lays before us the world of the saga and sets its temper and tone. Specifically, it describes Unn's side of the house, generation by generation, each somewhat more illustrious than the one before, until the family is seen to reach a new height in the two radiant youths, Kjartan and Bolli. Yet, that this height is merely the setting for the tragic events of the next section is indicated by Óláf's dream about his ox Harri, which closes Part I.

In the second part (Chapters xxxii-lvi) with the entrance of Gudrún and her family, the main action begins. Chapters xxxii and xxxiii, like an oracle, boom forth portents of the events which the following chapters present. The lives and fates of the three main characters become intertwined. Gudrún's first two marriages take place in rapid succession. Attention is drawn to Kjartan's and Gudrún's love for each other, to Bolli's friendship with Kjartan in spite of underlying envy, and finally to the surprising turn of events when Bolli marries Gudrún. Emotions become strained, passions run deep, and an open breach between the friends and kinsmen results. As foreshadowed by Footbiter's curse, the ensuing enmities lead to Bolli's killing of Kjartan, then to the death of Bolli in accordance with the demands of honor and revenge. The central theme develops quickly and dramatically to full pitch and fury through whiplash retorts, bursts of anger, and spiteful goadings, and ends in the din of clashing weapons as hostilities bring doom and disaster.

In the final section (Chapters lvii-lxxviii) the remaining prophecies are fulfilled. As predicted by Helgi Hardbeinsson, revenge for Bolli is accomplished; and Gudrún's fourth marriage takes place in accordance with the fourth dream. In the final chapters tensions and dissonances are gradually resolved and fade off in softer and less violent reechoings of earlier themes.

At no time do the adumbrations of future events compromise suspense in the saga, for the prophecies thoughout are veiled in dreams, hunches, premonitions, and curses and are characterized by ambiguity and uncertainty. Both the characters in the story and the reader feel apprehension and doubt whether predictions will come true, how all will happen, and when.

Although it never acts as a *deus ex machina,* an omnipresent fate determines the action. The people of the saga, however, are not passive puppets of this power; they are true agents and are integral to the action. Yet only through conversations or actions do we know what is going on in their minds. There is no soliloquizing; no introspective reasoning. It is clear that the inner will of the characters in an inextricable manner suggestive of classical Greek linking of fate and character corresponds to the predeterminate will of destiny, and vice versa.[3] This compelling force renders them incapable of thwarting or averting what is ineluctable and, unlike the main agents in *Njáls saga* or *Gunnlaugs saga ormstungu,* Kjartan and Gudrún do not even try. So Óláf Peacock's attempts for peace are abortive, and Snorri's conciliatory measures come to naught.

Throughout the saga, fate is thus seen as a determining power promoting a sequence of events which comes about as a result of individual action rather than external manipulation. Any misfortune or luck experienced by the agents is part of destiny's complex pattern. The author skillfully weaves together significant ethical and religious notions: (1) a code of honor which exacts revenge, demands like for like, and by so doing sets off a chain of killing and retaliation; and (2) belief in a mysterious unseen force compelling toward doom and death. Social code and supernatural power thus inscrutably work together toward the same end.[4] In this way an inevitability hangs over the affairs of men. The course of destiny is unalterable; so, too, the strict causality of the ethical code is irreversible.

Three characters express this determinism. After Gest has seen Kjartan and Bolli swimming, tears stream down his face, and he says to his son Thórd the Short:

"*Þarfleysa er at segja þat*, en eigi nenni ek at þegja yfir því, er á þínum dǫgum mun fram koma; en *ekki kemr mér at óvǫrum*, þótt Bolli standi yfir hǫfuðsvǫrðum Kjartans, ok hann vinni sér þá ok hǫfuðbana" (xxxiii, 92: "It will do no good to say it, but I cannot be silent about what is certain to come to pass in your own day; it will be no surprise to me if some day Bolli stands over Kjartan's body and thereby also reaps his own death").

Upon Kjartan's departure from Norway, King Óláf Tryggvason sadly comments: " 'Mikit er at Kjartani kveðit ok kyni hans, ok *mun óhœgt vera atgǫrða við forlǫgum þeira*' " (xliii, 132: " 'Much is augured for Kjartan and his kin, and it will not be easy to ward off their destiny' "). When Kjartan rides down the valley toward ambush and death, Thorkel of Hafratindar and his shepherd see both parties. When the boy wishes to give Kjartan warning, Thorkel dissuades him: " 'Þegi skjótt.... *Mun fóli þinn nǫkkurum manni líf gefa, ef bana verðr auðit?*' " (xlix, 152: " 'Hold your tongue! ... Are you fool enough to think you can save a man's life if he be doomed to die?' "). No good can come from knowing, telling, or trying to prevent what is fated to happen, for nothing can change it.

Dreams, Curses, Premonitions, and Prophecies

Both the storyteller and his audience wholeheartedly accepted and believed in dreams, fetches, portents, curses, visions, and hunches. These natural means of foreshadowing therefore constituted a valuable artistic device for introducing into the narrative prophetic pronouncements or subtle presentiments without disturbing the chronological sequence or lessening the suspense.

I shall consider individually forewarnings and prophecies associated with the central action. For example, we have been told that Óláf Peacock loves Kjartan best of all his sons (xxviii, 77: "Óláfr unni mest Kjartani allra barna sinna"). While Óláf is abroad in Norway, he meets Geirmund, who decides to take passage with him to Iceland. Óláf, however, has misgivings:

"Eigi myndir þú fara á mínu skipi, ef ek hefða fyrr vitat, því at vera *ætla ek* þá munu *nǫkkura* á Íslandi, at betr gegndi, at þik sæi aldri" (xxix, 78: "You wouldn't be going on my ship now, had I known of this before, for I suspect there will be some in Iceland who would be better off if they never set eyes on you").

Óláf's hunch refers specifically to his daughter Thuríd, who in her marriage with Geirmund makes a bad match. Through the unspecific *nǫkkura* it also, however, forewarns of the general misfortune Geirmund will occasion for the house of Óláf, for in coming to Iceland he brings with him the sword Footbiter. Geirmund deserts Thuríd, and she retaliates by stealing the sword from him, whereupon Geirmund pronounces this curse:

> "Ekki happ mun þér í verða at hafa með þér sverðit.... Þat læt ek þá um mælt...at þetta sverð verði þeim manni at bana í yðvarri ætt, *er mestr er skaði at*, ok óskapligast komi við" (xxx, 82: "No good luck will come of your having this sword in your keep....I now lay a curse that this sword will be the death of that man in your family whom it would be hardest to lose, and this shall come about most atrociously").

The reader may bear in mind that Kjartan is the most loved and by implication the one whose loss would be hardest to accept. Thuríd gives the ill-fated sword to Bolli.

Óláf's dream about his slaughtered ox Harri intensifies the foreboding. The woman in the dream admonishes Óláf:

> "Son minn hefir þú drepa látit ok látit koma ógørviligan mér til handa, ok fyrir þá sǫk skaltu eiga at sjá þinn son alblóðgan af mínu tilstilli; skal ek ok þann til velja, er ek veit, *at þér er ófalastr*" (xxxi, 84—85: "You have had my son [the ox Harri] killed and sent him back to me mutilated and for that you shall have to see your son drenched in blood at my instigation; I shall also choose the one I know you would least like to lose").

The last doubt about which son is meant is removed by Gest's words as he watches Óláf's sons swimming. Óláf has asked which one will likely make the most of himself, and Gest replies: "'Þat mun mjǫk ganga eptir ástríki þínu, at *um Kjartan mun þykkja mest vert, meðan hann er uppi*'" (xxxiii, 92: "'It will be in keeping with your fondest love that Kjartan will be most highly esteemed, for as long as he lives'").[5] The predictions that the beloved son of greatest promise will meet an untimely death and the certainty that this son is Kjartan give the words *meðan hann er uppi* the ring of tragedy.

These omens are preparatory, and upon them rest both Gest's prohecy that Bolli will be Kjartan's slayer and Óláf Tryggvason's apprehensions concerning the fate of Kjartan and his kin. Yet we cherish a faint hope that ill destiny may be averted, for the Norwegian king has given Kjartan a sword with protective powers: "'Láttu þér vápn þetta fylgjusamt vera, því at *ek vænti þess, at þú verðir eigi vápnbitinn maðr, ef þú berr þetta sverð*'" (xliii, 132: "'Let this sword ever be at your side, for I venture to say that you will never feel a weapon's sting so long as you bear this sword'"). With what dismay then do we learn later that the sword has been stolen. Alternating between hope and fear, we are relieved when the sword is returned, only to discover that Kjartan's pride in the king's gift has been injured because its sheath has not been recovered. He wraps it in a cloth and stores it in a chest. Nothing could be more convincing psychologically than the desire to lay away a cherished item after it has been spoiled in some way. Thus the natural course of events plays into the hands of the supernatural and coincides with what has been fated. Kjartan does not have the protective sword when his life is at stake: "Síðan brá Kjartan sverðinu — ok hafði eigi konungsnaut" (xlix, 152-153: "Then Kjartan drew his sword — but he did not have Konungsnaut").

Just before Kjartan's fateful ride into the ambush in Svínadal, another forecasting of death deepens the ominous shadows. Kjartan, Án the Black, and Thórarin have been making merry at Hól with Aud, when Án the Black has a bad dream in which a woman comes to him and removes his entrails. Aud interprets Án's dream as an evil omen for Kjartan's ride home. Although Kjartan scoffs at her fears, Aud insists that her brothers accompany Kjartan. This they do, only to turn back when Kjartan assures them that he will not need their help. Hope is entirely lost when Thorkel of Hafratindar dissuades his shepherd from warning Kjartan. As surely and swiftly as Kjartan rides so proudly down the valley, fate rides with him and takes its unalterable course. Every condition is accounted for: Án fights bravely on with his entrails coming out; Kjartan does not have Konungsnaut; Bolli stands over Kjartan's dead body, and Footbiter fulfills its curse: " 'ok reyna nú, hversu Fótbítr dugi' " (xlix, 153: " 'And try out now what Footbiter can do' ").

Yet Kjartan's death has not come about merely as a mechanical fulfillment of what was predestined, but also as a result of emotional involvements surrounding Gudrún on the natural, human level. The first inkling of the impending enmity between the house of Óláf and the house of Ósvíf appears in Óláf's presentiment about Kjartan's interest in Gudrún:

> "Eigi veit ek...hví mér er jafnan svá hugstœtt, er þú ferr til Lauga ok talar við Guðrúnu.... *Nú er þat hugboð mitt, en eigi vil ek þess spá, at vér frœndr ok Laugamenn berim eigi allsendis gæfu til um vár skipti"* (xxxix, 112: "I don't know why it always weighs so heavily on my mind when you go to Laugar to talk with Gudrún.... Something tells me — but I don't want to prophesy this — that we kinsmen and the folk over at Laugar may not be exactly lucky in our dealings with one another").

This misgiving heralds the beginning of entanglements between the kinsmen. After the tragic deaths of Kjartan and Bolli, Halldór Óláfsson's summing up of the situation echoes Óláf's foreboding:

"Því at þat er satt at segja, at eptir slíka menn er mestr skaði, sem Bolli var, þó at *vér frændr bærim eigi giptu til samþykkis*" (lvi, 169: "For it can truly be said that it is a great pity to lose such a man as Bolli, even if we kinsmen didn't have the good fortune to get along together").

Previews and hints likewise prepare the reader step by step for Gudrún's destiny. In accordance with her dreams, as Gest predicted, she marries the first time without love and casts off her husband Thorvald. Her second husband is Thórd Ingunnarson, in whom she was interested before her divorce from Thorvald, and who in turn gets a divorce in order to marry her.[6] As was foretold, Thórd loses his life by drowning. We are now ready for Gudrún's third marriage and the fulfillment of her third dream, in which all the hints are given:

"Sá er inn þriði draumr minn, at ek þóttumk hafa gullhring á hendi, ok þóttumk ek eiga hringinn, ok þótti mér bœttr skaðinn; kom mér þat í hug, at ek mynda þessa hrings lengr njóta en ins fyrra; en eigi þótti mér sjá gripr því betr sama, sem gull er dýrra en silfr. Síðan þóttumk ek falla ok vilja styðja mik með hendinni, en gullhringrinn mœtti steini nǫkkurum ok stǫkk í tvá hluti, ok þótti mér dreyra ór hlutunum. Þat þótti mér líkara harmi en skaða, er ek þóttumk þá bera eptir; kom mér þá í hug, at brestr hafði verit á hringnum, ok þá er ek hugða at brotunum eptir, þá þóttumk ek sjá fleiri brestina á, ok þótti mér þó, sem heill myndi, ef ek hefða betr til gætt, ok var eigi þessi draumr lengr" (xxxiii, 89: "This is the third dream I had. I seemed to have a gold bracelet on, and it seemed to be my very own and to make up for my former loss. The thought entered my mind that I would get to enjoy this arm ring longer than I had the other, but it didn't seem as though this costly bracelet suited me that much better, considering that it was gold instead of silver. Then I seemed to stumble and wanted to catch myself with my hand, but the gold bracelet struck against some stone and broke in two, and blood seemed to ooze from the pieces. What I felt then seemed to me more like grief than loss, and it occurred to me that there had been a crack in the bracelet and when I looked at the pieces afterwards, I seemed to see many flaws in them. But yet I had the feeling that it might have remained whole, had I guarded it better. And that was the end of the dream").

Gest interprets the dream as follows:

"Sá var inn þriði draumr þinn, at þú þóttisk hafa gullhring á hendi; þar muntu eiga inn þriðja bónda. Ekki mun sá því meira verðr, sem þér þótti sá málmrinn torugætri ok dýrri, en *nær er þat mínu hugboði*, at í þat mund muni orðit siðaskipti, ok muni sá þinn bóndi hafa tekit við þeim sið, er vér hyggjum, at miklu sé háleitari. En þar er þér þótti hringrinn í sundr støkkva, nǫkkut af þinni vangeymslu, ok sátt blóð koma ór hlutunum, þá mun sá þinn bóndi vera veginn; muntu þá þykkjask glǫggst sjá þá þverbresti, er á þeim ráðahag hafa verit" (xxxiii, 90: "Then there was the third dream of yours, where you thought you had a gold bracelet on. That means that you will have a third husband; this one will not be that much dearer to you, as the one metal is rarer and dearer than the other. And if I don't miss my guess, about that time a change in faith will have taken place, and this husband of yours will have adopted the new faith, which we will deem by far the more exalted. And where you thought the ring broke in two, due somewhat to your own carelessness, and saw blood ooze from the pieces, that means that your third husband will be slain, and it is then that you will see most clearly the flaws which existed in this marriage").

From the gold and silver analogy in the imagery of the dream, it is evident that Gudrún's third husband will be of more worth than her second. He will also have taken on a new faith, one considered the more exalted, just as gold is more precious than silver. Both Kjartan and Bolli are men of accomplishment and more illustrious than Gudrún's second husband Thórd; both Kjartan and Bolli accept Christianity while in Norway. If we consider only these points, the dream could apply to either Kjartan or Bolli. But it is also suggested that Gudrún will not love this third husband proportionately more than the second, as gold is prized over silver. The metal analogy thus functions in triple capacity. The indications in the dream are in perfect accord with the author's intent. Kjartan is Gudrún's greatest love, but is not destined to be one of her husbands. This fact Gudrún herself reveals, when, near the end of the saga, she appraises her four *husbands* but fails to say which *man* she loved best. Pressed for an answer by her son Bolli, she finally says: "'Þeim var ek verst, er ek unna mest'" (lxxviii, 228: "'To him I was worst whom I loved most'").

That blood oozes from both pieces of the broken arm band indicates that two killings will result from that marriage: the slayings of both Kjartan and Bolli. In accordance with both fate and the code of honor and revenge, Kjartan's killing leads inevitably to Bolli's death. The loss of her third husband is in no small part due to Gudrún's own "carelessness": she could have prevented it, had she not instigated the killing of Kjartan. What flaws were in that marriage could not be clearer. With the working out of the third dream (lv, 167-168) and the fulfillment of Gest's prophecy concerning the deaths of Kjartan and Bolli, the central theme comes to a close.

As a carry over from the central to the final section of the saga, revenge for Bolli remains to be executed in accordance with the demands of honor and with Helgi's prophecy made at the time of Bolli's slaying when he wipes his sword on Gudrún's shawl: "Helgi bað hann eigi þat harma, — 'því at ek hygg þat, ... at undir þessa blæjuhorni búi minn hǫfuðsbani'" (lv, 168: "Helgi told him [Halldór] not to let it bother him, — 'for I daresay...that under this sash is nurtured my slayer'"). Gudrún gives birth to Bolli Bollason, who at twelve years of age and carrying Footbiter (lix, 178) is clearly marked as avenger. The deed takes place at Helgi's hut, more as a "quirk of fate," than by Bolli's own planning:[7] "Ok er Bolli sá þetta, þá hleypr hann at Helga ok hafði í hendi Fótbít ok lagði í gegn um Helga" (lxiv, 192: "And when Bolli saw this [that Thorgils was being attacked by Helgi], he made a dash at Helgi, and he had Footbiter in his hand and ran Helgi through with it").

According to Gudrún's fourth dream, she is to marry a chieftain who is rather overbearing and who will ultimately drown in the Hvammsfjord (a branch of the Breidafjord). The execution of this prophecy is brought about through the shrewd planning of Snorri Godi, who sees to it that Thorkel Eyjólfsson becomes a chieftain and marries Gudrún.[8] The ominous portent in the dream is supported by a series of presentiments which prepares the reader for the drowning of Thorkel. The first of these secondary hints occurs in the statement of the outlaw Grím to Thorkel: "'Mun þér annarra forlaga auðit verða en deyja á okkrum fundi'" (lviii, 173: "'A fate other than to die at this encounter of ours is no doubt in store for you'"). The subtle future of probability in which the sentence is cast suits the vagueness of the context and avoids the blunt assertion that Thorkel's fate has already been predicted. Unless he has both good memory and sensitivity, the reader may miss the significance of Grím's apparently casual remark.

After his marriage to Gudrún, Thorkel has a dream in which his beard covers all of Breidafjord. His conceit leads him to interpret the dream as meaning that his power will extend over all the Breidafjord district. Gudrún promptly deflates him by declaring: "'Vera má, at svá sé, ... en heldr mynda ek ætla, at þar myndir þú drepa skeggi í Breiðafjǫrð niðr'" (lxxiv, 215: "'That may be so,...but I am more inclined to believe that one day your beard will be taking a dip into the Breidafjord'"). Gudrún here is playing on the literal and figurative meaning of the idiom at drepa skeggi. Because it cleverly picks up the symbolic language of Thorkel's dream, her interpretation can be taken as a joke on Thorkel and at the same time as a figure of speech

23

meaning "to drown." Gudrún's words thus remind the reader of Gest's interpretation of her fourth dream.

While Thorkel is abroad in Norway getting timber for a church, he again exhibits overweening pride by asserting that he will build a church in Iceland as big as the king's minster in Trondheim. Thereupon the king makes the following prediction: "'En *nær er þat mínu hugboði*, at menn hafi litla nytsemð viðar þessa, ok fari því firr, at þú getir gǫrt neitt mannvirki ór viðinum'" (lxxiv, 217: "'But it is near my guess that people will have little good of this timber, and you will be far from getting anything built with it'"). Upon his return Thorkel postpones transporting the wood home to Helgafell and leaves it with his kinsman Thorstein. Later when he goes to get it, he and Thorstein make Halldór Óláfsson an offer to buy the Hjardarholt lands. As they bargain and argue, Halldór uses an expression which on one level suits the immediate context by implying the height of ridiculousness or improbability, yet on another level echoes the symbolism of Thorkel's dream and the prophecy of Gudrún's dream: "'Fyrr *muntu spenna um þǫngulshǫfuð á Breiðafirði* en ek handsala nauðigr land mitt'" (lxxv, 221: "'Sooner will you be clutching at the tangleweeds in the Breidafjord than I will be pressed into handing over my land for sale'").

As Thorkel is about to sail for home with his wood, Thorstein, fearing that the weather will not hold, tries to dissuade him from going: "'Sá okkar mun nú ráða, er verr mun gegna, ok mun til mikils draga um ferð þessa'" (lxxvi, 222: "'That one of us now gets his way who will be the worse off for it, and something grave is sure to happen on this trip'"). When a storm does indeed break, Thorstein weeps and hears his kinsman's death struggle in the howling of the wind. Thorkel drowns; his beard has taken a "dip," and he is indeed "clutching at the tangleweeds in the Breidafjord." The church timbers drift far and wide about the islands, and it is reported: "Fátt eina náðisk af kirkjuviðinum" (lxxvi, 223: "Only very little of the church wood was salvaged"), as if to confirm the king's prediction.

In subordinate episodes throughout the saga the author also employs the device of prophecy and fulfillment. So, early in the saga when Unn the Deep-minded advises her grandson to marry, she says: "'*Þat er nær minni ætlan*, at vinir várir muni þá mjǫk fjǫlmenna hingat, því at ek *ætla* þessa veizlu *síðast at búa*'" (vii, 11: "'If I don't miss my guess, a great number of our friends will be coming here, for I expect to prepare this feast as my last one'"). Both expectations prove true: a large gathering attends the feast, and it is Unn's last one, for during the celebration she dies. Similarly, Gest's second sight tells him that his and Ósvíf's resting places after death will be closer than they are at present, and he predicts:

> "Ok seg honum þau mín orð, at koma mun þar, at *skemmra mun í milli bústaða okkarra Ósvífrs*, ok mun okkr þá hœgt um tal, ef okkr er þá leyft at talask við" (xxxiii, 91: "And tell him these my words, that there will come a time when the distance between our two dwelling places will be shorter than now, and then he and I can easily have a talk, if we then are permitted to talk").

After both he and Ósvíf have died and odd circumstances bring it about that they are laid to rest in the same grave at Helgafell, the reader is reminded of the ambiguous *leyft at talask við* and of Gest's very words:

> Kom nú fram spásagan Gests, at *skemmra var í milli þeira* en þá, er annarr var á Barðastrǫnd, en annarr í Sælingsdal (lxvi, 196-197: Now Gest's prophecy came true that there would be a shorter distance between them than when the one lived at Bardastrond and the other in Saelingsdal).

The linguistic parallelism, it should be noted, neatly reinforces the prophecy-fulfillment statement.

Direct comment by the author on the realization of what has been forecast is also exemplified by the episode where Hallbjorn Sleekstone-Eye puts a curse on Kambsnes, saying: "'Þat mæli ek um...at Þorleikr eigi þar fá skemmtanardaga heðan í frá, ok ǫllum verði þungbýlt, þeim sem í hans rúm setjask'" (xxxvii, 107: "'This spell I cast that Thorleik will enjoy few happy days there henceforth, and all who settle there in his stead will have neighbor troubles'"), and the author adds: "*Mjǫk þykkir þetta atkvæði á hafa hrinit*" (*ibid.*: "This curse seems very much to have taken effect"), for eventually Thorleik is forced to leave his farm, having had boundary troubles with his neighbor Hrút. Here the omniscient author states that the curse is fulfilled before the events take place later in the saga. The confirmation itself thus points forward as a hint or prophecy.

On another occasion when Audun Festargarm has spoken in a derogatory manner about Ósvíf's sons, Ósvíf retaliates with a prophecy of ill, using Audun's byname disparagingly and in its literal sense: "'En þú, festargarmr, munt fara í trollendr í sumar'" (li, 159: "'And you, Fetter-Hound, will go to the trolls [meet with a bad end] this summer'"). And so it comes about. Festargarm sails from Iceland that summer and is shipwrecked. The author again, and with the same phrase, confirms the prophecy: "Þótti þat *mjǫk hafa á hrinit*, er Ósvífr hafði spát" (*ibid.*: "What Ósvíf had prophesied seemed very much to have come true").

The examples of dreams, curses, prophecies, and premonitions which have been discussed show with what special intent the author has chosen and placed his words.[9] The characters themselves for the most part pay the dreams and prophecies little heed, apparently accepting them as imponderables of life. Yet the author clearly intends the reader to be knowledgeable. Again and again the prophetic statement presupposes the outcome, and when the fulfillment comes, a counter-statement generally recalls the prophecy. Rarely is the reference left to vague association, whether the span between the prophecy and its fulfillment is long or short. Noteworthy also is the frequent occurrence of phrases such as *nær er þat minni ætlan, nær er þat mínu hugboði* (if I don't miss my guess, it's near my guess), *kemr mér þat ekki at óvǫrum* (I wouldn't be surprised), *ætla ek, vænti ek*, or *hygg ek* (I expect, I suspect, I have an idea). So regularly do such phrases occur in premonitions and prophecies that they seem almost like cues for the reader to mark well what is said and to expect a consequence.

Anticipation in Retrospect

In addition to the more obvious anticipatory devices such as those just discussed, the saga contains many clues and hints which are not readily recognized until the thought has been picked up again in a confirming statement. Intimations of this sort might be called hints in retrospect, for generally they are perceived as foreshadowings only when recalled. Superfluous or arbitrary elements in the saga are few, and almost every statement carries with it some significance deeper than the surface meaning of the words. The remark, "'Þú munt þetta eigi fyrr hafa *upp kveðit* en þú munt hugsat hafa, hvar þetta skal *niðr koma*'" ("'You wouldn't have brought this up unless you had thought out what the result would be'"), suggesting premeditated intent on the part of the characters,[10] just as aptly applies to the method of the author. Whatever he brings up is sure to have a generic connection; there are few loose ends or dangling statements. The economy of the saga lies to a great extent in this quality. The author conserves his elements; whatever he introduces has a function and a counteraction. A list of examples would almost equal the saga in length, and each rereading reveals new subtleties. I have therefore chosen one section of the story with which to illustrate types of retrospective cues employed by the author.

Snorri Godi's plan for Gudrún's fourth marriage is an elaborately developed scheme and plays hand in hand with fate. As the first step the reader is introduced to two new characters: Thorgils Holluson and Thorkel Eyjólfsson. Thorgils is the grandson of Gest Oddleifsson on his mother's side; he is therefore a descendant of Bjorn the Eastman and related to Gudrún. On his father's side he is the grandson of Dala-Álf, a descendant of Unn; thus Thorgils is related to Kjartan. Thorkel Eyjólfsson is the great-grandson of Óláf Feilan, who is himself the grandson of Unn. Through these genealogical connections the new characters are put into a familiar context.[11]

We are told further (lvii, 170, 171) that Snorri considers Thorgils somewhat meddlesome and that their relationship is *heldr fátt* (rather cool). The word *heldr* commonly functions as understatement and indicates that this relationship is significant. Thorkel, on the other hand, is *mikill vinr Snorra goða* (a great friend of Snorri Godi). These two succinct characterizations immediately bring Thorgils and Thorkel into opposing relationship with one another as well as with Snorri.

After Thorkel's unsuccessful fight with the outlaw Grím, Snorri advises him to settle down, get married, and become the *chieftain* he was born to be. Up to this point there has been no inkling that Thorkel is a chieftain or indeed may be the chieftain of Gudrún's fourth dream. Yet now the thought is immediately confirmed when Snorri goes on to say to Thorkel that Gudrún is the right match for him. Thorkel, however, finds the suggestion not feasible for two reasons: " 'hon mun vilja hefna láta Bolla, bónda síns. Þar þykkisk í ráðum vera með henni Þorgils Hǫlluson' " (lviii, 174: " 'She will want to have her husband Bolli avenged, and Thorgils Holluson seems to be in on that with her' "). To both objections Snorri has a ready answer:

> "Ek mun í því bindask, at þér mun ekki mein verða at Þorgísli, en *meiri ván* þykkir mér, at nǫkkur umskipti sé orðin um hefndina Bolla, áðr þessi missari sé liðin" (*ibid.*: "I shall see to it that Thorgils won't cause you any trouble. And as for revenge for Bolli, it seems more than likely to me that events will have taken a turn concerning that before the season is out").

Snorri's reassuring reply is a prediction, and the author uses Thorkel's response to foreshadow how it will come about:

> "Vera kann, at þetta sé *eigi orð tóm*, er þú talar nú; en um hefnd Bolla sé ek ekki líkligra nú en fyrir stundu, nema þar *snarisk* nǫkkurir inir stœrri menn *í bragð*" (*ibid.*: "It may well be that these are not just idle words. But as for revenge for Bolli, I don't see any more likelihood of that now than before, unless, of course, some bigger men are drawn into a plan").

The idiom *snarisk i bragð* which Thorkel unwittingly uses indicates how Snorri's prognostication will be made good. If later, in retrospect, the reader recalls the wording, he will become aware of the author's intent and skill. Thorkel is naturally thinking in general practical terms: some bigger men will have to get involved, "join in the plan or scheme." But the literal meaning of the words gives the idiom significance on a second level: *snarisk i bragð*, that is, "snared into a trick"; for it is by a trick, indeed by two tricks, that Snorri accomplishes his objective; and it is none other than Thorgils who is caught in the snare.

Snorri's first task is to get Bolli avenged, and this he achieves through subterfuge. Gudrún tells Snorri that she wants revenge for Bolli, and Snorri suggests Helgi Hardbeinsson (the man slated for death) and Thorgils Holluson (the man who is to lead the raid). Gudrún explains to Snorri that to choose Thorgils is out of the question, for he will carry out the revenge only "'*ef hann næði ráðahag við mik*'" (lix, 178: "'if he gets to marry me'"). Snorri advises her to seem to agree and instructs her to make use of an underhanded stipulation in promising him marriage. She will marry no other *samlendr maðr*. The wording of the stipulation is important, for the expression means first "a fellow countryman, compatriot" and second "one dwelling in the same country." Snorri is confident that the scheme will work, for Thorkel (whom he is reserving for Gudrún) is not then in the country. Gudrún expresses some doubt: "'Sjá mun hann þenna krók'" (*ibid*.: "'He'll see through that twist'"), but Snorri reassures her: "'Sjá mun hann víst eigi'" ("'He'll surely not see through it'").

Gudrún then broaches the subject of revenge to Thorgils; and when he is asked to take part in the raid, he gives the expected answer: "'*ef ek nái ráðahag við þik*'" (lx, 180). So Gudrún does as Snorri has advised and uses the strategic phrase to make the promise. With fine sensitivity the author represents Gudrún as playing with the words almost to the point of divulging the secret:

> "Nú skírskota ek því við vitni yðru, at ek heit Þorgísli *at giptask engum manni ǫðrum samlendum en honum; en ek ætla ekki at giptask í ǫnnur lǫnd*" (lx, 181: "Now with you as witnesses I hereby testify and promise not to marry any other man in the land except Thorgils; and I do not intend to get married in other lands").

The author comments: "Ok sér hann ekki í þetta ("And he did not see through it").

Thorgils leads the raid on Helgi Hardbeinsson and expects his reward. The terms of the agreement are repeated and Gudrún reveals the stratagem. Thereupon Thorgils himself confirms the suggestion given in the beginning that his relationship to Snorri had always been a cool one: " 'Gǫrla skil ek, hvaðan alda sjá rennr undir; hafa mér þaðan *jafnan* kǫld ráð komit; veit ek, at þetta eru ráð Snorra goða' " (lxv, 195: " 'I plainly see whence the wind blows; I have always felt a cold draught from that quarter. I know these are Snorri Godi's counsels' "). Thus Snorri's first trick has been successful: Thorgils has been snared, and the plan for avenging Bolli has been carried out.

Snorri's second *bragð* involves getting rid of Thorgils entirely, and circumstances aid Snorri in bringing this about. A man by the name of Audgísl happens along and is annoyed because of some dealings he has had with Thorgils. Snorri remarks that this would not be the first time such men have been struck down and takes the opportunity to give Audgísl a handsomely decorated axe. Both Audgísl and the reader understand the hint, despite the camouflage (embellishment).

Even as were Kjartan and Thorkel, Thorgils is given forewarnings. His *fylgja* or guardian spirit cautions him through a ditty about Snorri's wiles:[12]

Kosti fyrðar,	Fighters strive onward,
ef framir þykkjask,	If ye deem yourselves forward,
ok varisk við svá	And wary watch for
vélum Snorra;	The wiles of Snorri;
engi mun við varask;	Wary enough no one will be;
vitr es Snorri.	Wise is Snorri.
(lxvii, 198)	

With these words the *fylgja* turns and leaves; Thorgils expresses apprehension: " 'Sjaldan fór svá, þá er vel vildi, at þú fœrir þá af þingi, er ek fór til þings' " (*ibid*.: " 'It seldom happened, when luck was with me, that you went from the Thing when I was on my way there' ").

A second warning comes to Thorgils when one day his blue cloak miraculously begins to speak:[13]

Hangir vǫt á vegg,	Wet it hangs on the wall,
veit hattkilan *bragð*,	Wot the cloak a trick,
þvígit optar þurr,	Ne'er more dry after this,
þeygi dylk, at hon viti tvau.	Nor deny I, it knows of two.
(*Ibid*.)	

It is a riddle, and through it the cloak warns of Snorri's duplicity. Thorgils has been caught by one trick, and the cloak knows of yet another: the plan for Thorgils' death. The use of the word *bragð* at the beginning and again at the end of the episode cannot be coincidence. One day at the Thing Audgísl uses the axe which Snorri has given him to slay Thorgils. Snorri has accomplished both aims, and upon Thorkel's return from Norway informs him of his success:

> "Er nú ok af ráðinn hvárrtveggi hlutrinn, sá er þér þótti torsóttligastr, ef þú skyldir fá Guðrúnar, at Bolla er hefnt, enda er Þorgils frá ráðinn" (lxviii, 200: "And now both obstacles are removed which you felt stood most in the way of your getting Gudrún — Bolli is avenged, and Thorgils has been disposed of").

The statement provides complementary balance to Thorkel's original hesitations, and the episode is closed. What Snorri considered *meiri ván* and his *orð tóm* have proven true. It can be said with Thorkel: " 'Djúpt standa ráð þín, Snorri' " (*ibid.*: " 'Your counsels, Snorri, do indeed run deep' ").

It is now time to consider what means the author has used here to prepare for future events and to achieve the feeling of expectation fulfilled. The warnings of Thorgils' death are direct and supernatural; otherwise, throughout the episode subtle hints and intimations mark the narration. Above all, use of words with intended ambiguity characterizes this passage. Within the frame of the episode expressions such as *heldr fátt, meiri ván, orð tóm, snarisk í bragð* take on added significance. Furthermore, use is made of phrases ambiguous by nature, such as *samlendr maðr*; and that even the word *þurr* in the riddle of the cloak is a pun is not surprising.[14] In addition a hint may be contained in an understatement or in a shift from the figurative to the more literal meaning of an idiom, or vice versa.[15] Repetition of words and phrases (*ef hann [ek] næði [nái] ráðahag við mik [þik]; sjá mun hann [eigi]/sér hann ekki í þetta*) also serves to imply anticipation and fulfillment; what is brought up is confirmed. The equivocal character of the language reflects the subject of the episode, Snorri's duplicity, and so enhances the artistic quality.

Detection of such cues requires close reading, attention to choice of words, and recollection of what has gone before, the more so since the obvious and well-motivated situation camouflages their anticipatory function. Oftentimes even the prophecies are so subtly suggested or occur so naturally that they are passed over, and only later is their full significance realized. Familiarity with the story allows these cues to be recognized as anticipatory.

Like dreams and prophecies, the retrospective cues are literary devices used to foreshadow and to build anticipation. For the most part these devices are distinguished by the following characteristics: (1) parallel statements of preparation and confirmation; (2) words and phrases of added significance or emphasis controlled by ambiguity or repetition; (3) understatement and euphemism; and (4) information about a person or his traits by way of introduction and genealogical lineages. Any one example may illustrate one or several of these features in combination.

(1) How foreshadowing assumes the formal structure of statement and later confirmation of that statement has been evident in many of the prophecies and retrospective cues already discussed. The careful author scarcely makes an idle statement or records an extraneous episode. The description of the relations between Hrút and Thorleik Hoskuldsson affords further example of how such foreshadowing is achieved. Hrút and Hoskuld have settled their quarrel regarding their maternal inheritance. Hoskuld, we are told, is growing old on his farm; his sons are grown; Thorleik has received his share of the family property and has married worthily; Bárd is at home with Hoskuld. All seems prosperous and quiet — or would except for the seemingly unwarranted statement: "*Ekki* lagðisk *mjǫk* á með þeim frændum, Hrúti ok Þorleiki" (xx, 49: "There was not much friendship between the kinsmen Hrút and Thorleik"). Not until several chapters later does the reason for this somewhat euphemistic statement become clear. The author is reminding the reader that Hrút and Thorleik have had their differences before, while preparing at the same time for further trouble between them. Having misgauged the boundary between their lands (xxv, 70), Hrút settled a freedman on property that actually belonged to Hoskuld and Thorleik. Thorleik kills the freedman, and Hrút, although in the wrong, is ill-content with the decision of the lawmen and does not forget the incident. Some time later when Eldgrím finds Thorleik's horses in Hrút's pasture and attempts to steal them, Hrút takes the opportunity to turn the tables in his favor by remarking on Thorleik's habitual laxness in respect to boundaries: "'Þat er satt, at Þorleikr frændi er *jafnan* ómeskinn um beitingar'" (xxxvii, 103: "'It is true that kinsman Thorleik has always been lax about pastures'"). In spite of their latest quarrel and the fact that Thorleik's horses are encroaching on his pasture land, Hrút is not willing to see his kinsman robbed: "'En eigi mun ek láta ræna Þorleik, ef ek hefi fǫng á því, þótt *eigi* sé *mart* í frændsemi okkarri'" (xxxvii, 104: "'But Thorleik is not going to be robbed if I can help it, even if we don't make a lot over our kinship'"). The *eigi mart* confirms the *ekki mjǫk* that introduced the episode.

In a similar manner and through understatement, Óláf Peacock's quarrel with his half brother is first anticipated, then confirmed: "Vel var með þeim brœðrum Óláfi ok Bárði, en *heldr styggt* með þeim Óláfi ok Þorleiki" (xxvi, 73: "The brothers Óláf and Bárd got on well together, but between Óláf and Thorleik there was something of coolness"). Later when their differences are settled, Óláf reaffirms the hint: "'Svá er, frændi, sem þér er kunnigt, at með okkr hefir verit *ekki mart*'" (xxvii, 75: "'As you know, kinsman, there hasn't been much friendship between us'"). Here again the *ekki mart* reechoes the *heldr styggt* and closes the episode.

Another telling example of statement-confirmation occurs in the description of Kjartan's superior qualities. That emphasis is given to his physical prowess is not surprising: "Vel var hann hagr ok *syndr manna bezt*; *allar íþróttir hafði hann mjǫk umfram aðra menn*" (xxviii, 77: "He was very dexterous and the best of swimmers; he outshone other men in all sports"). Yet it is noteworthy that of all the sports in which he is said to excel, swimming alone is mentioned by name. Why swimming — unless as a necessary precondition it is singled out and reserved for a future connection. And so it turns out. When he is in Norway, Kjartan joins in a swimming match with the king and exhibits his ability as a swimmer. Confirmation of the original statement concerning his prowess in sports is found in the king's comment at the end of the contest and in Kjartan's "knowing" reply:

> "Þú ert *sundfœrr vel*, eða ertu at ǫðrum íþróttum jafnvel búinn sem at þessi?" Kjartan svarar...: "Þat var orð á, þá er ek var á Íslandi, at þar fœri aðrar eptir" (xl, 117: "You are a good swimmer. Are you as good at other sports as at this?" Kjartan answered...: "So it was said while I was in Iceland that the others were comparable").

Kjartan's response acts as direct reference to the antecedent statement, and instead of explaining it as apparent knowledge on his part of what had been said about him at home in Iceland, we must rather recognize what it indicates about the precision and necessary structure of the narrative. Numerous other examples could be cited showing similar use of seemingly arbitrary or incidental statements which later evidence predetermined function and tie together the strands of narrative.[16]

(2) With noteworthy consistency the author lends extra weight to ordinary meanings of words, playing on their ambiguous overtones. So, too, emphasis, placement, and repetition regularly serve both to carry veiled hints regarding what probably will happen and also ultimately to fulfill expectations thus aroused. Such practices clearly display the author's interest in language and bear witness to his feeling for its potential beyond the discursive level. We have seen already in passing how full weight must be accorded the *síðast* in Unn's premonition about the wedding feast, or how the emphasis on *jafnan* facilitates connection with Hrút's old complaint about Thorleik and the boundary issue. Deliberate ambiguity characterizes the phrase *ok var þó*

kyrrt [*kyrrt at kalla*] (it was nonetheless quiet or [quiet so to speak]).[17] It occurs throughout the saga almost with the frequency of a refrain and gradually comes to be recognized as signalling the opposite rather than the literal sense. In the beginning, the stereotyped "and now things were quiet" is taken at face value to mean harmony and periods of calm after quarrels. As the saga progresses, however, the falsity of the disguise is perceived, and finally the author by adding *at kalla* himself admits that the calm is really a harbinger of storm.

The repetition of a word like *ambáttarsonr* (concubine's son) over a series of episodes confirms expectations and forcibly brings out the futility of Melkorka's efforts. She sends her son Óláf Peacock to Ireland to claim his noble kinship and thereby to erase the image of *ambáttarsonr*: "'Eigi nenni ek, at þú sér *ambáttarsonr* kallaðr lengr'" (xx, 50: "'I cannot stand having you called a concubine's son any longer'"). Óláf returns with the impressive appellation *dóttursonr Mýrkjartans Írakonungs* (xxii, 61: son of the daughter of Mýrkjartan, king of the Irish). Nonetheless, Egil's daughter Thorgerd rejects his proposal of marriage and tells her father:

> "Þat hefi ek þik heyrt mæla, at þú ynnir mér mest barna þinna; en nú þykki mér þú þat ósanna, ef þú vill gipta mik *ambáttarsyni*, þótt hann sé vænn ok mikill áburðarmaðr" (xxiii, 63: "I have heard you say that you loved me best of all your children; but now it seems to me you disprove it, if you want to marry me off to a concubine's son, no matter how handsome and well decked out he is").

Although Óláf is not informed of precisely what Thorgerd has said to her father in her refusal of marriage, he makes a very good guess: "'Nú er, sem ek sagða þér, faðir, at mér myndi illa líka, ef ek fenga *nǫkkur sviviðingarorð* at móti'" (xxiii, 64: "'Now it is just as I told you, father, that I would take it ill if I got some abusive words in return'"). In spite of the vague plural *sviviðingarorð*, Óláf knows what to say to Thorgerd when he goes himself to Egil's booth to take up the marriage suit: "'Mun þér þykkja djarfr gerask *ambáttarsonrinn*, er hann þorir at sitja hjá þér ok ætlar at tala við þik'" (xxiii, 65: "'You perhaps find it bold of a concubine's son to sit down beside you and presume to talk with you'"). Óláf and Thorgerd reach an understanding and are married. The distasteful epithet, however, continues to follow him. Hoskuld's wife Jórunn harbors a grudge against the bondwoman her husband brought home and against their son. When Óláf moves to Hjardarholt, Jórunn and Hoskuld stand outside their farm on the other side of the river, and Hoskuld wishes his son well: "'Ok *nær er þat mínu hugboði*, at þetta gangi eptir, at *lengi sé hans nafn uppi*'" (xxiv, 68: "'And it is near my guess that his name will long be remembered'"). Jórunn mimics his words, but a shift in emphasis combined with sarcasm and the inclusion of the epithet Melkorka so wished to erase add a sting to Hoskuld's hopeful surmise: "'Hefir *ambáttarsonr* sjá auð til þess, at *uppi sé hans nafn*'" (*ibid.*: "'This concubine's son has enough wealth all right for his name to be remembered'"). Not for his wealth will his name be remembered but, as Jórunn wishes to imply, by the derogatory epithet, and with that she effectively squelches Hoskuld.

Again when Thórd Goddi's wife gives shelter to the outlaw Thórólf, a seemingly careless mention of detail later gains significance through use of a special idiom. The description is explicit: "Eptir þat leiðir Vigdís hann í útibúr eitt ok biðr hann þar bíða sín; *setr hon þar lás fyrir*" (xiv, 31: "After that she led him out to a shed and told him to wait there for her, and she drew a bolt across the door"). Thórd expresses his displeasure at having an outlaw on his farm:

> [Þórðr] kvazk þat víst vita, at Ingjaldr myndi mikit fé taka af honum fyrir þessa bjǫrg, er nú var veitt honum — "er hér *hafa hurðir verit loknar eptir þessum manni*" (xiv, 32: [Thórd] said he knew beyond a doubt that Ingjald would make him pay dearly for the sheltering they had already given him — "seeing that our doors have already been locked after this man").

It is likely that Thórd is using the phrase *hafa hurðir verit loknar* idiomatically in the general sense of "we have given this man shelter, taken him in"; while, unwittingly, on the literal level he underscores Vigdís' action of drawing the bolt, a detail which otherwise might seem but superfluous. It is a case of the characters' being in ignorance whereas the audience is knowledgeable, a contrast which produces the humor or irony here and in many other instances to be noted further on. Note the shift from indirect to direct discourse.

The symbolic and formal dimension in the language furthermore gives clues to Bolli's subordinate position and hence to his resentment over against Kjartan. Note must be taken of the words the author has chosen, their position in the sentence, and even the amount of narrative allotted to each. First the *mjǫk jafngamlir* (xxviii, 75: very nearly the same age) brings into focus the two boys' similarity, then laudatory descriptions of each in practically identical terms appear to assure their equality. Yet appearances are deceptive, for upon exact comparison Bolli falls short of Kjartan. Thirteen lines (in "Íslenzk fornrit," V) give praise to Kjartan:

> Hann var allra manna fríðastr, þeira er fœzk hafa á Íslandi; hann var mikilleitr ok vel farinn í andliti, manna bezt eygðr ok ljóslitaðr;

> mikit hár hafði hann ok fagrt som silki, ok fell með lokkum, *mikill maðr ok sterkr*, eptir sem verit hafði Egill, móðurfaðir hans, eða Þórólfr. Kjartan var hverjum manni betr á sik kominn, svá at allir undruðusk, þeir er sá hann; betr var hann ok vígr en flestir menn aðrir; vel var hann hagr ok syndr manna bezt; *allar íþróttir* hafði hann mjǫk *umfram aðra menn*; hverjum manni var hann lítillátari ok vinsæll, svá at hvert barn unni honum; hann var léttúðigr ok mildr af fé (xxviii, 76-77: He was one of the most handsome men ever to have been born in Iceland. He had a large face with well formed features, the finest of eyes and a light complexion. His hair was long and as fair as silk, and it fell into curls. He was a big man and strong, just as Egil, his mother's father, had been or his uncle Thórólf. Nature had endowed Kjartan with more gifts than most people, and all who saw him marveled at him. He was more skilled in arms than most; he was dextrous, and the best of swimmers; he outshone other men in all sports. At the same time he was more modest than most and was so popular that everyone was fond of him, man or child. He was lighthearted and generous).

Bolli by comparison receives but four lines of lauding:

> Bolli fóstbróðir hans var *mikill maðr*; hann gekk *næst Kjartani um allar íþróttir* ok atgørvi; *sterkr* var hann ok *fríðr* sýnum, kurteisligr ok inn hermannligsti, mikill skartsmaðr (xxviii, 77: His foster brother Bolli was also a big man. He came next to Kjartan in all sports and accomplishments. He, too, was strong and handsome, chivalrous and most warrior-like, a great one for finery).

Aside from the quantitative slight, the expression *næst Kjartani* succinctly sums up Bolli's subordinate position.

That Bolli's name appears second whenever the two are mentioned together should also be noted, as well as his habit of "following" or accompanying Kjartan wherever he goes. Thus literally and figuratively Bolli "comes second": "Þeir Kjartan ok Bolli unnusk mest; fór Kjartan *hvergi þess, er eigi fylgði Bolli honum*" (xxxix, 112: "Kjartan and Bolli loved one another the most, and Kjartan went nowhere without Bolli's going along with him"). The fact that the reader has been cued here to expect Bolli to go with Kjartan "wherever he went" veils the first inkling of Bolli's interest in Gudrún on their visits to Laugar: "Heldr Kjartan teknum hætti um ferðir sínar; *fór Bolli jafnan með honum*" (*ibid.*: "Kjartan continued his usual trips [to Laugar], and Bolli always went with him"). When they go to Norway, Kjartan takes the lead among the Icelanders staying there and chides Bolli for not competing with the best swimmer among the townsmen. In this exchange for the first time

Bolli's reply seems to suggest a slight feeling of resentment: "'Eigi veit ek, hvar kapp þitt er nú komit,' segir Kjartan, 'ok skal ek þá til.' Bolli svarar: 'Þat máttu gera, ef þér líkar'" (xl, 117: "'I don't know what has become of your competitive spirit,' Kjartan said, 'but if you won't, I will.' Bolli answered: 'You can if you like'"). During their stay in Norway, the Icelanders, although heathen, are curious to witness the Yuletide festivities and decide to go to the church: "Gengr Kjartan nú með sína sveit *ok Bolli*" (xl, 122: "Kjartan went now with his following of men, and also Bolli"). Bolli's name falls last here, and so again in the king's invitation: "Síðan bauð konungr Kjartani í jólaboð sitt *ok svá Bolla*, frænda hans" (xl, 123: "Then the king asked Kjartan to his Yule feast, and also Bolli his kinsman").

Parallel statements about the esteem accorded to Kjartan and Bolli at court again prove weighted in Kjartan's favor and reconfirm the inequality noted in the earlier comparison of their talents. Both quantitatively and qualitatively Bolli suffers:

> Konungr *mat* Kjartan *umfram alla menn* fyrir sakar ættar sinnar ok atgørvi, ok er þat alsagt, at Kjartan væri þar svá vinsæll, at hann átti sér engan ofundarmann innan hirðar; var þat ok allra manna mál, at engi hefði slíkr maðr komit af Íslandi sem Kjartan (*ibid.*: The king esteemed Kjartan above all men for his fine lineage and manly accomplishments. It was commonly said that Kjartan was so well liked that he had not a single ill-wisher at the court. It was also generally said that no man such as Kjartan had ever before come from Iceland).

Whereas of Bolli it is simply said: "Bolli var ok inn vaskasti maðr ok *metinn vel af góðum monnum*" (*ibid.*: "Bolli was also a most valiant fellow and esteemed well by good men"). Bolli is merely esteemed *af góðum monnum*; Kjartan by the king. By virtue of its controlled association and contrast with [*mat*] *umfram alla menn*, the weaker [*metinn*] *vel* carries a significance beyond its use outside the saga. It becomes a loaded word designed to bring out a slight. We shall have occasion to note instances where the special *vel* bears similar connotation, a small element whose meaning and interpretation depends entirely on the linguistic framework of the author's world and of his saga.

The sullenness of Bolli's reply to Kjartan's chiding in the episode of the swimming match has been remarked upon. From time to time similar ill-tempered comments hint at Bolli's hidden feelings. So, when Kjartan suggests burning the king in his hall, Bolli with a tinge of sarcasm repeats Kjartan's words and points out how unwise such a move would be. Kjartan, with customary brashness, makes this boast:

> "Engis manns nauðungarmaðr vil ek vera... meðan ek má upp standa ok vápnum valda; þykki mér þat ok *lítilmannligt,* at vera tekinn sem lamb ór stekk eða melrakki ór gildru. ..." Bolli spyrr: "Hvat viltu gera?" "Ekki mun ek því leyna," segir Kjartan, "brenna konunginn inni" (xl, 119: "No one is going to get me under his thumb as long as I can stand on my own two feet and wield my weapons. To my mind it's unmanly to be taken like a lamb out of a fold or a fox out of a trap. ..." Bolli asked: "What do you intend to do?" "I'll make no secret of it," said Kjartan, "to burn the king inside his hall").

To this Bolli replies: "'*Ekki* kalla ek þetta *lítilmannligt*... en eigi mun þetta framgengt verða, at því er ek hygg'" (*ibid.*: "'I don't call that unmanly, but to my mind that can never be carried out'"). In further exchange when they mutually accuse each other of lack of courage, others join in and agree that it is *þarfleysutal* (useless talk). Open hostility has been avoided and tension relieved, for the moment.

When Bolli decides to return to Iceland without Kjartan, his parting from Kjartan affords a significant comment on the relationship between them:

> "Nú em ek búinn til ferðar, ok mynda ek bíða þín inn næsta vetr, ef at sumri væri lausligra um þína ferð en nú, en vér þykkjumsk hitt skilja, at konungr vill *fyrir engan mun þik lausan láta,* en hǫfum þat fyrir satt, at þú munir fátt þat, er á Íslandi er til skemmtanar, þá er þú sitr á tali við Ingibjǫrgu konungssystur" (xli, 126: "I am now ready to depart. I would like to wait for you over next winter, if in the following summer there would be any more chance of your getting away than there is now. But as far as we can see, the king isn't going to let you go on any account, and I hold it for true that you recall very little those pleasures which are to be had in Iceland when you sit talking to Ingibjorg, the king's sister").

The suggestion that even were Kjartan free to go to Iceland, he might prefer to stay in Norway is sly. Kjartan's reply shows that he is aware of the barb: "'*Haf ekki slíkt við,* en bera skaltu frændum várum kveðju mína ok svá vinum'" (*ibid.*: "'Don't be saying such things, but bear my greetings to our kinsmen, and also to our friends'"). By *haf ekki slíkt við* Kjartan not only refers to the idleness of Bolli's suggestion but probably also means it as an injunction against repeating any gossip about him and the king's sister at home. The final position in the sentence of *ok svá vinum* emphasizes that Bolli is to bear greetings to their friends, among whom Gudrún, of course, would be included.

Bolli's withheld resentment comes into the open when he relates to Gudrún the success of his and Kjartan's journey:

> Bolli leysti ofléttliga ór því ǫllu, er Gudrún spurði; kvað allt tíðendalaust um ferðir sínar — "en þat er kemr til Kjartans, þá er þat með miklum ágætum at segja satt frá hans kosti, því at hann er í hirð Óláfs konungs ok *metinn þar umfram hvern mann* (xlii, 127: Bolli replied obligingly to all Gudrún asked about, and said that everything was uneventful as far as his journey was concerned — "but as for Kjartan, one can only report the best about his circumstances, for he is at King Óláf's court and esteemed there above all men").

Taking up the insinuation of his parting words to Kjartan, Bolli significantly goes on to add:

> "En *ekki kemr mér at óvǫrum*, þó at hans hafi hér í landi litlar nytjar ina næstu vetr."...Bolli segir, hvert orðtak manna var á um vináttu þeira Kjartans ok Ingibjargar konungssystur, ok kvað þat *nær sinni ætlan*, at konungr myndi heldr gipta honum Ingibjǫrgu en *láta hann lausan*, ef því væri at skipta (*ibid.*: "And I wouldn't be at all surprised if we saw very little of him here in Iceland for the next few winters."...Bolli told her what rumor there had been about the friendship between Kjartan and Ingibjorg, the king's sister, and said that it was his guess that the king would rather give Ingibjorg to him in marriage than to let Kjartan go, if it came right down to it).

The speech is an important index to Bolli's feelings. Bolli makes little of his own accomplishments and quickly turns the talk to Kjartan. He knew, of course, that news of Kjartan was what Gudrún was most waiting to hear. But as his final departing comment showed, he wanted to make trouble. The shift from indirect to direct discourse is particularly interesting here, since it occurs precisely at the point of shift in subject matter and thus sharpens the comparison-contrast between Bolli and Kjartan. Bolli repeats his parting words to Kjartan about the king's intention of letting him go (*láta hann lausan*) but now changes the emphasis for his own purpose. His repetition of *metinn þar umfram hvern mann*, an echo of the author's statement (*metinn þar umfram alla menn*) concerning the esteem Kjartan enjoyed at court, attests to the structural design in the saga rather than to Bolli's exact knowledge of what was being said at court. The repetition here thus carries the ring of sarcasm. The appearance of the phrases of prediction (*ekki kemr mér at óvǫrum* and *nær sinni ætlan*) lends the impression that the expected will be fulfilled, even though it be surmise. Kjartan has read Bolli's parting speech aright; trouble has been made.

Bolli's insinuations about a possible marriage between Kjartan and Ingibjorg prove well founded when the king indicates his reluctance to let Kjartan go:

> "Vilda ek, at þú fýstisk eigi út til Íslands, þó at þú eigir þar gǫfga frændr, því at kost muntu eiga at taka þann *ráðakost* í Nóregi, er *engi mun slíkr á Íslandi*" (xliii, 130: "I wish your heart were not set on going out to Iceland, even though you have noble kinsmen there, for you could choose a station in life here in Norway such as is not to be had in Iceland").

There is intentional ambiguity in the king's *ráðakostr*, for the word not only means "station in life" but also "marriage." Bolli's surmises about the king's unwillingness to let Kjartan go and about a possible marriage between Kjartan and Ingibjorg are thus both here confirmed. The fact that a position at the court was naturally not to be had in democratic Iceland and the fact that the king conventionally and in similar stereotyped terms (to be discussed later under Recurrence) regrets the departure of visiting Icelanders and offers them any station (*kostr*, *ráðakostr*) they desire, camouflage to some extent the king's offer here. But since such discrepancies between face value and underlying intent are typical of the cast of language in the saga, the alert reader will not be deceived.

The twofold intent in the king's remark is soon further substantiated by an equally subtle reference to Kjartan's marriage with Hrefna. Kjartan's sister Thuríd gives him this advice:

> "Þœtti oss þat ráðligast, at þú kvángaðisk, eptir því sem þú mæltir í fyrra sumar, þótt þér sé *eigi* þar með ǫllu *jafnræði*, sem Hrefna er, því at *þú mátt eigi þat finna innan lands*" (xlv, 137: "We feel the most advisable thing for you to do is to take a wife, just as you said last summer, even if Hrefna isn't an equal match for you in every respect, for you can never expect to find that here in this country").

Since Gudrún, who was said to be *mest jafnræði* (xxxix, 112: most equally matched) with Kjartan, is already married and so cannot come into question, there is no equal match for him in Iceland. The restrictive *innan lands* confirms the *engi mun slíkr á Íslandi* and suggests the possibility of such a match abroad. It is evident from the foregoing examples how parallel statements, ambiguous words, words with special overtones, repetition, and the like have been put into the service of the prediction-fulfillment structure. Many similar instances of perceptive use of words and phrases might be cited.[18]

(3) Even as words and phrases of added significance foreshadow through

hints and suggestions, so understatements, euphemisms, double negatives, and the like represent common rhetorical devices which fit well into the author's schematism of things by conveying hints and different shades of meaning. So, for example, although the quarrel between Hoskuld and Thórd Gellir apparently has been settled by Hoskuld's gifts of appeasement, the words and turn of phrase suggest the real state of affairs: "Ok var þetta *kyrrt* síðan ok *um nǫkkuru færa en áðr*" (xvi, 38: "After that the matter stayed quiet, but the friendship was somewhat cooler than before"). The matter is "quiet" rather than settled; both the ambiguous *kyrrt* and the understatement in *nǫkkuru* foreshadow further developments. Again, when the troublesome Hrapp is dug up and reburied, an understatement hints that not yet has the last been heard from him: "Eptir þetta nemask af *heldr* aptrgǫngur Hrapps" (xvii, 40: "After that Hrapp's ghostwalking more or less let up"). The issue between Hoskuld and Thórd Gellir is indeed brought up again in a confirming statement by Jórunn in talking over with Hoskuld his troubles with Hrút (xix, 47); and Hrapp walks again, is dug up and burned and his ashes carried out to sea: "Heðan frá verðr engum manni mein at aptrgǫngu Hrapps" (xxiv, 69: "After that no man ever came to any harm again because of Hrapp's ghostwalking"). Both episodes thus illustrate again the preparation-fulfillment structure.

Frequently irony or a flash of dry humor characterizes understatements. So, for example, litotes makes an effective introduction to Thorkel Trefil's second scheme to assure his being sole heir to the property left by Thorstein Surt:

> Þorkell trefill grunar *nǫkkut*, hvárt þannig mun farit hafa um líflát manna, sem þeir Guðmundr hǫfðu sagt it síðara sinni. Ekki þóttusk heiðnir menn minna eiga í ábyrgð, þá er slíka hluti skyldi fremja, en nú þykkjask eiga kristnir menn, þá er skírslur eru gǫrvar. Þá varð sá skírr, er undir jarðarmen gekk, ef torfan fell eigi á hann (xviii, 42-43: Thorkel Trefil rather had some misgivings whether the drownings actually had happened in the sequence he and Gudmund had said the last time. Heathen men did not think they had less at stake when they were to go through such tests than Christian men do now when ordeals are performed. Whoever went under the strip of sod stood cleared of guilt provided the strip did not fall down on him).

The understatement in *nǫkkut* contains the key to the ironic tone of the passage. Thorkel has good reason to doubt his own innocence, and since he is sure that the strip of earth will fall down on him, he must devise a way to make the caving-in look like an accident. The comparison of heathen and Christian customs, which has given rise to confusion and misinterpretation, undoubtedly because it represents an anachronism,[19] does stand as an interruption in the continuity of thought, if taken, as obviously intended, to be an author's aside in explanation for Thorkel's serious concern.

A veiled hint may also be conveyed by euphemism, whereby the involuted statement or double negative carries with it a tinge of humor. So, for example, the indirection with which the hostility of the Laugar people is indicated foreshadows the disastrous outcome of Hrefna's visit to Laugar: " 'Margir menn mæla þat, at *eigi sé ǫrvæna*, at ek koma þar, er ek eiga *færi ǫfundarmenn* en at Laugum' " (xlvi, 142: " 'There are those who say that I could find many places to go where I would have fewer ill-wishers than at Laugar' "). This immediately is confirmed when she attends the party at Laugar and her headdress is stolen.

(4) The announcement of characters and their traits before they enter the stage and the inclusion of their names in genealogies ahead of time comprise handy devices for foreshadowing and hence may be incorporated into the design of the saga as necessary rather than adventitious elements. Perfunctory sketches, like the terse descriptions of Thorgils and Thorkel already discussed, set forth temperaments and interrelationships and suggest the part the character is to play in the action. A byname itself often anticipates the personality of a character.[20] Delineation is never introspective. Consistently throughout the saga initial characterizing descriptions are illustrated and confirmed in words and deeds.

The treatment of Gudrún clearly illustrates how her cursorily listed personality traits are later confirmed. Many adjectives are applied to Gudrún: *kvenna vænst, kurteis, vænst at ásjánu ok vitsmunum, kœnst ok bezt orði farin, ǫrlynd kona* (xxxii, 86: most beautiful of women, of courtly manner, foremost in beauty and intelligence, of keenest wit and cleverest tongue, openhanded). And compared to her finery, we are told that other women had only *barnavípur* (childish baubles). All these qualities — beauty, graciousness, keen wit, clever tongue, talkativeness, generosity, and love of expensive things — exhibit themselves on many an occasion. Gest finds her easy to talk to and sits and interprets her dreams with her ("váru þau bæði *vitr* ok *orðig*" [xxxiii, 88: "They were both witty and talkative"]); Thórd rides to the Thing with her in order to chat with her along the way (xxxv, 95). Kjartan, too, likes to go to Laugar to talk to Gudrún ("þótti Kjartani gott at tala við Guðrúnu, því at hon var bæði *vitr* ok *væn* ok *málsnjǫll* [xxxix, 112: "Kjartan liked visiting with Gudrún, for she was both intelligent and beautiful, and had a clever tongue"]).[21] She must own the finest that money can buy — a trait that influences the terms of the marriage contract with Thorvald ("Hann

41

skyldi ok kaupa gripi til handa henni, svá at engi jafnfjáð kona ætti betri gripi" [xxxiv, 93: "He was to buy finery for Gudrún, such that no woman equally well-to-do could boast anything better"]) and which also leads her to divorce him when he refuses to pander to her insatiable wants. Her unbearable jealousy of Hrefna is due in no small part to the fact that Hrefna owns the expensive and elegant headdress (*inn ágætasti gripr*) originally intended for herself:

> Hon tekr þar ór motr hvítan, gullofinn, ok gefr Kjartani ok kvað Guðrúnu Ósvífrsdóttur hølzti gott at vefja honum at hǫfði sér, — "ok muntu henni gefa motrinn at bekkjargjǫf" (xliii, 131: She [Ingibjorg] took out a white headdress, all worked in gold, and handed it to Kjartan and said it was no doubt good enough for Gudrún Ósvífsdóttir to wrap around her head, — "and you can give it to her as a wedding gift").

And when with openhanded generosity she overrules Thorkel in the arrangements for the wedding, Snorri is led to comment: " 'Opt sýnir þú þat, Guðrún,... at þú ert inn mesti kvenskǫrungr' " (lxviii, 201: " 'Often, indeed, you show, Gudrún, that you are the most outstanding of women' "). Finally her sending Thidrandabani off in grand style with ship and goods makes even Thorkel concede: " 'Eigi er þér lítit í hug um mart, Guðrún,... ok er þér eigi hent at eiga vesalmenni; er þat ok ekki við þitt œði' " (lxix, 203-204: " 'You are not smallminded on many a score, Gudrún,... and it would never do for you to have a skinflint for a husband — that would hardly suit your nature' "). Thus all of Gudrún's traits enumerated in a string of adjectives when she is first introduced in the saga are subsequently confirmed one by one.

The chieftain of Gudrún's fourth dream is described as holding a *œgishjálmr* (helmet of terror) over her, implying that he will be overbearing. How well the description fits Thorkel is shown by his overweening confidence in attacking the outlaw Grím (lvii, 172), by his eagerness to provide for his wedding feast (lxviii, 201), by his commandeering attitude regarding the outlaw Thidrandabani (lxix, 203), by his interpretation of the dream about his beard (lxxiv, 215), by his competing with the king in building a church (lxxiv, 216), and by his wilfullness in sailing for home against his kinsman's better judgment (lxxvi, 222). It is amusing, and obviously so intended, that Thorkel fails in each of these endeavors and is put in his place, so that the *œgishjálmr* turns out to be something of a joke. And indeed if we look at Gudrún's dream more closely — in retrospect — we can detect this quality already there.

An example of the ingenuity with which the author has handled a character trait implicit in a byname is the case of Thorbjorn Skrjúp and his son Lambi. In a seemingly innocent and normal statement Lambi is likened to his father: "Hann var *mikill maðr* ok sterkr ok glíkr feðr sínum yfirlits *ok svá at skaplyndi*" (xxii, 61-62: "He [Lambi] was a big man and strong and resembled his father in looks and also in character"). Thorbjorn's byname means "weakling," which is to be understood in its moral rather than physical sense, since he, too, is described as being big and strong (xi, 21: *"mikill maðr* var hann vexti ok rammr at afli"). The final position in the sentence here of *ok svá at skaplyndi* directs our attention especially to the mental and moral make-up Lambi has in common with his father. That Lambi is unreliable and has a weak character like his father is borne out later when he takes part in the raid against his kinsman Helgi, for which his relatives rebuke him: "kváðu hann meir hafa sagzk í ætt Þorbjarnar skrjúps en Mýrkjartans Írakonungs" (lxv, 193-194: "They said he had more in common with the family line of Thorbjorn Skrjúp than with that of Mýrkjartan, King of the Irish"). Although carried over a long span in the story, the statements about Thorbjorn and Lambi prove to have necessary connection; what was "brought up" as preparation "comes down" as fulfillment.

Another method of achieving foreshadowing is the artful — and inconspicuous — naming of characters in genealogies and short introductions, ostensibly, as is generally assumed, for the sake of completeness, or historical interest, or for the artistic purpose of preserving the historical frame of the story and creating its historical illusion.[22] *Laxdœla saga* gives evidence of further purposefulness in introducing a new name or a new character at specific points in the narrative and in selecting certain names for inclusion in the genealogies — a purposefulness that accords with the preparation-fulfillment structure.[23] Snorri Godi, for instance, is mentioned in a genealogy as early as Chapter vii but does not take part in the story until Chapter xxxvi. Gudrún's family line is introduced in Chapter ii and is not picked up again until Chapter xxxii. Thorkel Eyjólfsson's ancestry is given in Chapter vii, but Thorkel does not enter the action until Chapter lvii. Chapter xi presents Vigdís, Thórd Goddi, and Ásgaut, and in so doing prepares for Chapters xiv and xv. Thorbjorn Skrjúp is mentioned in Chapter xi and takes up his part in Chapter xx. Óláf's household servants are all named in Chapter xxiv: Án the White, Án the Black, and Beinir the Strong. Later each plays his role: Án the White in Chapter xlvi; Án the Black in Chapters xlvii, and xlviii; and Beinir the Strong in Chapter lxxv.[24] Hrefna is named in Chapter xl and enters the stage in Chapter xliv.

We have observed how the author uses prophetic statements such as dreams, curses, premonitions or subtly suggested cues to foreshadow subsequent developments and thereby creates a world in which the terms are known and fulfilled as expected. Some of these prophetic statements are direct; others are indicated indirectly through formal means. So well integrated are they in every case with the action and so appropriate are they to the context that they may be passed over. Recognition of the more veiled hints is facilitated through the linguistic fabric. Close observation of the words themselves and of their levels of meaning, placement, repetition, and similarity is required. The foreknowledge which obtains from the use of these anticipatory devices imparts to the saga a form which conceives the end in the beginning, the beginning in the end. Yet interest in what is going to happen is not diminished through this consistent foretelling of coming events. Rather, by presenting incompletely a foreknown completion, the direct and indirect hints serve both to build up a kind of suspense and at the same time to suggest an overall pattern of destiny. The action substantiates the expected. The phrases *sem ván var* (as expected) and *kunnigt* (known) act like refrains and themselves carry the theme.[25]

Since specific statements, not merely vague contextual associations, reconfirm the prophecies and hints, a balanced structure of precise pattern results, setting up a composition of point counterpoint that requires a relating of the complementary elements. Such phrases as *sem fyrr, sem áðr, sem fyrr var ritat* (as before, as previously, as was written before)[26] testify *in this saga* to this intent — an author's cue to his audience. The characters' mention of the time which has elapsed between the event and recalling of it is also suggestive of this structure. It is conspicuous how expressions of remembering and reminding are favored in the saga.[27]

Through anticipation and recollection, a back and forth rhythm is produced in the progress of the action. The fulfillment of destiny does not proceed precipitously to a conclusion, but haltingly, by intervals which are measured by the span between prophecy and confirmation, statement and counterstatement. This progression and regression occasioned by anticipating and recalling is displayed likewise in miniature form in the genealogies that lead forward, while others trace lineages back to the past. The same alternating movement characterizes common incidents such as sea crossings and betrothal scenes where the father passes the decision to the daughter and she in turn refers it to him;[28] in the back and forth dealing representative of the bargainings;[29] and in the frequent mention of how someone lives, turn and turn about, at one place and then at another: "Óláfr ok Þorgerðr váru *ýmisst* þann vetr á Hǫskuldsstǫðum eða með fóstra hans" (xxiv, 66: "Óláf and Thorgerd spent that winter in turns either at Hoskuldsstadir or with Óláf's foster father").³⁰ *Ýmisst* is the catchword that marks these descriptions.

The narrative itself often backtracks, picking up threads that have been temporarily dropped while another action is carried forward. Although not a unique literary device, it is wholly pertinent to the overall design of this saga. Conventional phrases such as *Nú er frá [Ingjaldi] at segja*, and the like, signal the flash-backs.³¹ A singularly good example of this technique and of how the author has combined it with his own original device occurs at the end of Chapter lviii, after Thorkel and Grím have gone to Norway:

> Nú verðr þar frá at hverfa um stund, en taka til út á Íslandi ok heyra, *hvat þar gerisk til tiðenda, meðan Þorkell er útan* (lviii, 175: Now let us turn our attention away from this for a while and take up the story out in Iceland and see what went on there while Thorkel was abroad).

After the happenings in Iceland have been narrated, and upon Thorkel's return from Norway, the careful author closes the flash-back interval with a reminder of the point that has been reached in the story:

> Spurði Snorri tiðenda af Nóregi. Þorkell segir frá ǫllu vel ok merkiliga. Snorri segir í mót *þau tiðendi, sem hér hǫfðu gǫrzk, medan Þorkell hafði útan verit* (lxviii, 199: Snorri asked for news from Norway, and Thorkel gave good account of everything in detail. Snorri in turn told what had happened in Iceland while Thorkel had been abroad).

The parallelism of the content, Thorkel and Snorri each telling of events in turn first of Norway and then of Iceland, mirrors the larger division of the narrative into an account of Thorkel in Norway and the flash-back on happenings in Iceland. This parallelism is reinforced through the identically repeated phrases. The author never forgets what he has brought up and even employs similar vocabulary to facilitate recognition of his own reminders.

Thus foreshadowing and fulfillment with their concomitants, anticipation and recollection, provide a framework according to which the action is developed and made necessary. The comparing back and forth, controlled by this structural feature, is further enhanced through the use of repetitions, as we shall now see.

II

REPETITION

Repetition represents the second of the structural elements which the author uses throughout *Laxdœla saga* to promote unity of composition. With conspicuous frequency words and phrases repeat themselves and so serve to recall to the audience the earlier instance and to point up relationship of episodes. This balancing of expression as well as episode comes very close to suggesting premonition and fulfillment, or clue and effect, except that the examples under Repetition cannot be classified as prophetic in the stricter sense. Repetition, however, is structurally equivalent to Foreknowledge in that the former in building pairs forms a point counterpoint system as does prophecy and fulfillment. The author's practice of employing similar and even identical linguistic components in statement and confirmation has already been incidentally noted under Foreknowledge,[1] and the method is carried further in connection with Repetition. In this present chapter the function of patterned linguistic correspondence will be explored and an attempt made to evaluate Repetition as a formal device.

In order to facilitate the discussion of Repetition, it seems advisable to cite a passage in which specific examples of the various types occur so that the characteristic style may be directly observed. In the following passage the pertinent phrases have been italicized and letters in parentheses supplied to indicate corresponding pairs:

> Þorsteinn rœddi við Þorkel, at þat myndi *vel hent* (a), at þeir fœri í Hjarðarholt; — "*vil ek fala land at Halldóri* (b), því at hann hefir *lítit lausafé* (c), síðan hann galt þeim Bollasonum í fǫðurbœtr; en þat land er svá, at ek vilda helzt eiga." Þorkell bað hann ráða; fara þeir heiman ok váru saman vel tuttugu menn. Þeir koma í Hjarðarholt; tók Halldórr vel við þeim ok var inn málreifasti. Fátt var manna heima, því at Halldórr hafði sent menn norðr í Steingrímsfjǫrð; þar hafði komit hvalr, er hann átti í.

47

Beinir inn sterki var heima; hann einn lifði þá þeira manna, er verit hǫfðu með Óláfi, fǫður hans. Halldórr hafði mælt til Beinis, þegar er hann sá reið þeira Þorsteins: "Gǫrla sé ek ørendi þeira frænda; þeir munu *fala land mitt at mér* (*b*), ok ef svá er, þá munu þeir *heimta mik á tal* (*d*). Þess get ek, at *á sína hǫnd mér setisk hvárr þeira* (*e*), ok ef þeir bjóða mér nǫkkurn ómaka, þá vertu eigi seinni at ráða til Þorsteins en ek til Þorkels; hefir þú lengi verit trúr oss frændum. Ek hefi ok *sent á ina næstu bœi eptir mǫnnum* (*f*); vilda ek, at þar hœfðisk mjǫk á, at lið þat kœmi ok vér slitim talinu." Ok er á leið daginn, rœddi Þorsteinn við Halldór, at þeir *skyldu ganga allir saman á tal* (*d*), — "eigu vit ørendi við þik." Halldórr kvað þat vel fallit. Þorsteinn mælti við fǫrunauta sína, at ekki þyrfti þeir at ganga með þeim; en Beinir gekk með þeim ekki at síðr, því at honum þótti mjǫk eptir því fara, sem Halldórr gat til. Þeir gengu mjǫk langt á brott í túnit. Halldórr hafði yfir sér samða *skikkju ok á nist lǫng* (*g*), sem þá var títt. Halldórr settisk niðr á vǫllinn, en *á sína hǫnd honum hvárr þeira frænda* (*e*), ok þeir *settusk náliga á skikkjuna* (*g*), en *Beinir stóð yfir þeim ok hafði øxi mikla í hendi* (*h*). Þá mælti Þorsteinn: "Þat er ørendi mitt hingat, at ek *vil kaupa land at þér* (*b*). Legg ek þetta því nú til umrœðu, at nú er Þorkell, frændi minn, við; þœtti mér okkr þetta *vel hent* (*a*), því at mér er sagt, at þú hafir *ógnóglig lausafé* (*c*), en land dýrt undir. Mun ek gefa þér í móti þá staðfestu, at sœmilig sé, ok þar í milli, sem vit verðum á sáttir." Halldórr tók því ekki svá fjarri í fyrstu, ok inntusk þeir til um kaupakosti, ok er þeim þótti hann ekki fjarri taka, þá felldi Þorkell sik mjǫk við umrœðuna ok vildi saman fœra með þeim kaupit. Halldórr dró þá heldr fyrir þeim, en þeir sóttu eptir því fastara, ok þar kom um síðir, at þess firr var, er þeir gengu nær. Þá mælti Þorkell: "Sér þú eigi, Þorsteinn frændi, hversu þetta ferr? Hann hefir þetta mál dregit fyrir oss í allan dag, en vér hǫfum setit hér at hégóma hans ok ginningum; nú ef þér er hugr á landkaupi, þá munu vér verða at ganga nær." Þorsteinn kvazk þá vilja vita sinn hluta; bað nú Halldór ór skugga ganga, hvárt hann vildi unna honum landkaupsins. Halldórr svarar: "*Ek ætla, at ekki þurfi* (*i*) at fara myrkt um þat, at þú munt kauplaust heim fara í kveld." Þá segir Þorsteinn: "*Ek ætla ok ekki þurfa* (*i*) at fresta því, at kveða þat upp, er fyrir er hugat, at þér eru tveir kostir hugðir, því at vér þykkjumsk eiga undir oss hæra hlut fyrir liðsmunar sakar; er sá kostr annarr, at þú ger þetta mál með vild ok haf þar í mót vinfengi várt; en sá er annarr, at sýnu er verri, at þú rétt *nauðigr fram hǫndina ok handsala mér* (*j*) Hjarðarholts land." En þá er Þorsteinn mælti svá framt, þá sprettr Halldórr upp svá hart, at *nistin rifnaði af skikkjunni* (*g*), ok mælti: "Verða mun annat, fyrr en ek mæla þat, er ek vil eigi."

"Hvat mun þat?" spyrr Þorsteinn. "*Bolǫx mun standa í hǫfði þér* (k) *af inum versta manni ok steypa svá ofsa þínum ok ójafnaði.*" Þorkell svarar: "Þetta er illa spát, ok væntu vér, at eigi gangi eptir, ok œrnar kalla ek nú sakar til, þóttú, Halldórr, látir land þitt ok hafir eigi fé fyrir." Þá svarar Halldórr: "Fyrr muntu spenna um þǫngulshǫfuð á Breiðafirði, en ek *handsala nauðigr land mitt* (j)." Halldórr gengr nú heim eptir þetta. Þá *drífa menn at bœnum, þeir er hann hafði eptir sent* (f). Þorsteinn var inn reiðasti ok vildi þegar veita Halldóri atgǫngu. Þorkell bað hann eigi þat gera, — "ok er þat in mesta óhœfa á slíkum tíðum, en þegar þessi stund líðr af, þá mun ek ekki letja, at oss lendi saman." Halldórr kvazk þat ætla, at hann myndi aldri vanbúinn við þeim. Eptir þetta riðu þeir í brott ok rœddu mart um ferð þessa með sér. Þorsteinn mælti, kvað þat satt vera, at þeira ferð var in dáligsta, — "eða hví varð þér svá bilt, Þorkell frændi, at ráða til Halldórs ok gera honum nǫkkura skǫmm?" Þorkell svarar: "Sáttu eigi Beini, er *hann stóð yfir þér með reidda ǫxina?* (h) Ok var þat in mesta ófœra, því at þegar *mundi hann keyra ǫxina í hǫfuð þér* (k), er ek gerða mik líkigan til nǫkkurs." Ríða þeir nú heim í Ljárskóga. Líðr nú fǫstunni ok kemr in efsta vika (lxxv, 218-221).

(Thorstein said to Thorkel that it would be a convenient time to ride over to Hjardarholt. "I want to make Halldór an offer for his land, for he hasn't had much livestock since he paid Bolli's sons the indemnity for their father. And that land is just what I would most like to have." Thorkel said he should decide. So they rode from home, a good twenty of them together. They came to Hjardarholt, and Halldór received them well and was very talkative. There were but few men at home, since Halldór had sent some men up north to Steingrímsfjord; a whale had come ashore there in which he had a share. Beinir the Strong was at home; he was the only one still alive of those who had been in Óláf Peacock's household. Halldór had spoken to Beinir as soon as he had seen Thorstein and his men riding up — "I know full well just what business these kinsmen are on. They will want to make me an offer for my land. And if that is so, they will call me aside for a talk. It is my guess that they will sit down, one on either side of me, and if they show signs of giving me any trouble, then you aren't to be any slower in setting on Thorstein than I on Thorkel; you have long been faithful to us kinsmen. I have also sent to the neighboring farms for some men. I am hoping that the two things take place at about the same time, that the help comes just about when we are finishing our talk." And as the day wore on, Thorstein suggested to Halldór that the three of them together should have a talk — "we two have some business to take up with you." Halldór said that was fine with him. Thorstein told his men that they need not come with them, but Beinir went along nonetheless, for things seemed to be going very much as Halldór had guessed. They walked far out into the homefield. Halldór had on a cloak that was fastened by a long clasp, as was the custom then. Halldór sat down on the field, and on either side of him each of the kinsmen, so close that they almost sat down on his cloak. But Beinir was standing over them, and he had a big axe in his hand. Then Thorstein spoke up: "My business in coming here is that I want to buy land from you. I'm bringing this up at this time because my kinsmen Thorkel is on hand. I would think this would be a good arrangement for us both, for I've been told that you don't have enough livestock to run on your valuable land. I will give you property in fair exchange and into the bargain whatever sum we come to an agreement on." Halldór did not take this too adversely at first, and they went on to discuss the terms of the bargain. When they thought Halldór was near to accepting, Thorkel eagerly pushed the bargaining, wanting to bring the deal to a close. Then Halldór started stalling them off, and they tried to push the matter all the harder, and finally it came to this: the harder they pressed him, the further he was from accepting. Then Thorkel said: "You see, kinsmen Thorstein, don't you, where this is leading? He has been stalling the matter for us the whole day, and we have been sitting here while he has made fun of us with his deceit. Now if you are really bent on buying the land, then we will have to press him even harder." At that Thorstein said he wanted to know where he stood and told Halldór to come out into the open now and say whether he intended to sell him the land or not. Halldór answered: "I don't think there's any point in keeping you in the dark about this any longer: you will be going home tonight without a sale." Then Thorstein said: "I don't think there's any point either in our putting off revealing what lies in store: we have thought out two choices for you, as we have reason to believe that the advantage is ours, seeing that you are outnumbered. One is that you go along with us of your own accord and have our good will in return. And the other, clearly the worse one, is that you be pressed into giving me your hand on the sale of the Hjardarholt lands." At these plain words, Halldór jumped to his feet with such sudden force that the clasp tore out of his cloak, and he said: "Something else will happen before I agree to what I don't want to do." "What will that be?" asked Thorstein. "A woodman's axe will lodge in your head, driven by some paltry fellow, and will thus put a stop to your insolence and unfairness." Thorkel answered: "That is ill prophesied, and we trust that it won't be fulfilled. And now I say there's ample reason, Halldór, why you should be made to forfeit your land and get nothing for it." Then Halldór answered: "Sooner will you be clutching at the tangleweeds in the Breidafjord than I will ever be pressed into handing over my land for sale." After that Halldór went home, and now the men he had sent for thronged to the farm. Thorstein was worked up into a rage and wanted to make an attack on Halldór at once. Thorkel told him not to do such a thing — "that would be a most wicked thing in these holy days. But as soon as this season is past, I won't stand in the way of our having an encounter." Halldór said he would make sure he was never caught napping. Thereupon they rode away and had much to say between themselves about this affair of theirs. Thorstein, in speaking of it, said there was no doubt about it, their errand could not have turned out worse — "but why were you, kinsman Thorkel, so afraid of setting on Halldór and putting him to shame?" Thorkel answered: "Didn't you see Beinir standing over you with raised axe? There was no way out, for he would have plunged the axe right into your head, had I made the slightest move." So they rode on home to Ljárskógar. Lent was drawing to a close with only one week left.)

The description of the land sale at Hjardarholt illustrates in a nutshell the formal features of Repetition. The narration moves forth and back, telling first of Thorstein's purpose and of his reception at Hjardarholt, then backing up to relate what Halldór said to Beinir before Thorstein arrived. All Halldór's misgivings are realized; and not only is this fact referred to directly ("því at honum þótti mjǫk eptir því fara, sem Halldórr *gat til*"), but also the very words of Halldór's hunches, formulated with the usual phrases *gǫtla sé ek* and *þess get ek*, are also repeated: *vil ek fala land at Halldóri/ fala land mitt á mér* (b); *heimta mik á tal/ skyldu ganga allir saman á tal* (d); *at á sína hǫnd mér setisk hvárr þeira/ á sína hǫnd honum hvárr þeira frænda* (e). Again Halldór's expectations are fulfilled when the men sent for arrive: *sent á ina næstu bœi eptir mǫnnum/ drífa menn at bœnum, þeir er hann hafði eptir sent* (f). The motif of Beinir and his axe, once brought up, appears again in Thorkel's excuse to Thorstein for his inaction: *Beinir stóð yfir þeim ok hafði øxi mikla í hendi/ hann stóð yfir þér með reidda øxina* (h). And Halldór's ill prophecy directed at Thorstein picks up the theme again; and Thorkel, quite unaware, confirms the words of the prophecy: *Boløx mun standa í hǫfði þér/ mundi hann keyra øxina í hǫfuð þér* (k).

Although not repeated verbatim, the seemingly casual information about Beinir's being the only servant left from Óláf's household ("hann einn lifði þá þeira manna, er verit hǫfðu með Óláfi") proves to have necessary connection in Halldór's remark to Beinir: " 'hefir þú lengi verit trúr oss frændum.'" And stating the number of men in Thorstein's party ("váru saman vel tuttugu menn") and why there were few men at Halldór's are not idly made, for Thorstein brings up the question of their numerical advantage ("'vér þykkjumsk eiga undir oss hæra hlut fyrir liðsmunar sakar'"). Such is the tightness of composition in the passage.

That which may have seemed but arbitrary detail again proves to have necessary function in the motif of the cloak and clasp. The kinsmen sit down, one on each side, as Halldór surmised, and so close *þeir settusk náliga á skikkjuna*. The *náliga* is a euphemistic distractor, for if the kinsmen had not actually sat upon his cloak, the clasp would not have been torn out when Halldór jumped up (*g*). The artistry in the passage consists in the visual and physical image being equivalent to the figurative aspect of the bargaining: a close pressing for the sale.

Parallelisms and equalizations are apparent in other respects. The harder the kinsmen press the sale, the further Halldór is from accepting: *at þess firr var, er þeir gengu nær*. The parallel comparatives *firr-nær* reinforce the back and forth in the bargaining, just as the *vertu eigi seinni at ráða til Þorsteins en ek til Þorkels* sets up an equalization. Each party has devised a plan in case the other does not comply. Halldór finally brings his true intentions into the open, and Thorstein discloses their premeditated alternatives. Two choices are given to Halldór, who in turn makes two ominous predictions, one for each of the kinsmen. Thorstein obviously does not grasp the timeliness of the threat pertaining to Beinir's axe, veiled somewhat through the unspecific *af inum versti manni*; and Thorkel, of course, misses the significance of the *þǫngulshǫfuð* prophecy meant for him. Each of these insinuations carries a specific and a general reference: the one for the audience "in the know," and the other for the participant "in the dark."

Purposeful arrangement also shows up in the dialogue. Halldór picks up Thorstein's very words (*fala land at Halldóri/ fala land mitt at mér* [*b*]), but without having previously heard the talk. Thorstein returns Halldór's *ek ætla, at ekki þurfi* with his *ek ætla ok ekki þurfa* (*i*); and Halldór takes up Thorstein's *nauðigr handsala* (*j*). Thorstein repeats his *vel hent* (*a*) and the *lítit* [*ógnóglig*] *lausafé* (*c*). Repetition in these examples functions as confirmation of something previously known or said; it also decisively distinguishes the dialogue as constructed simulation rather than imitation of natural speech. Through repeated phrases, that which tends to be haphazard and disjointed in nature, becomes organized and tightened in art. The fact that Halldór repeats Thorstein's words without their having been transmitted, suggests the omniscience of author and audience and attests to the structured character of the narrative.

The establishing of a balance between two sides, as epitomized in the bargaining process itself, is structurally and formalistically represented in the grammatical and lexical pattern. There is a certain fitness and neatness about the whole episode — even as Halldór arranged neatly for two things to fall together at the right time. The coming to fruition of a prophecy or hint and the reappearance of a phrase satisfy an aesthetic sensibility for proportion and symmetry that is related to the symbolism of the saga. Repetition coincides with the formal aspects of Foreknowledge, anticipation and retrospect, achieves a special kind of balance marked by formal correspondence, and as a rhetorical device carries out similar purposes.

Accordingly, Repetition will be found to underscore a preparatory statement and its verification, to tie together episodes, and to build a composition of balanced elements. The examples treated in this chapter will include those that are in some way causally related and refer to the same person, fact, or event. For convenience of discussion they have been grouped according to their function as confirming pairs, or as cues to unsuspected subtleties, or as character confirmations.

Repetition tends toward the statement-confirmation structure of Foreknowledge with the additional factor of linguistic parallelisms to strengthen the intended associations, which of necessity are retrospective. Such repetitions have been noted from time to time in a few examples under Foreknowledge: Óláf's foreboding about Kjartan's trips to Laugar (xxxix, 112) and Halldór's commentary on the action taken against Bolli (lvi, 169), for instance, make use of similarity of formulation to give precision to the confirmation and bring the episode to a rounded and fitting close. Furthermore, Halldór's summary evaluation after the killing of Bolli: "'Því at þat er *satt at segja, at eptir slíka menn er mestr skaði, sem Bolli var'*" (*ibid.*: "'For it can in truth be said that it is a great pity to lose such a man as Bolli was'") also contains a substantiation of Thorstein the Black's prior statement deploring the projected killing of Bolli: "'eru nú *fáir slíkir menn í yðvarri ætt, sem Bolli er'*" (liv, 164. "'There are now few such men in your family such as Bolli'").

Illustrative of a precondition is also Hoskuld's statement to Óláf when he discusses with him the advantages of a marriage with Thorgerd Egilsdóttir:

> "Egill á sér dóttur, þá er Þorgerðr heitir; þessarrar konu ætla ek þér til handa at biðja, því at þessi kostr er albeztr í ǫllum Borgarfirði, ok þó at víðara væri; *or þat ok vænna, at þér yrði þá efling at mægðum við þá Mýramenn*" (xxii, 62: "Egil has a

53

daughter whose name is Thorgerd. She is the woman I have in mind to ask in marriage on your behalf, for she is the best match in all Borgarfjord and even farther. It is also more than likely that a marriage tie with the Mýramenn will be an asset to you").

Later on, after the marriage has taken place, reference is made to Óláf's becoming a great chieftain, and the summing up of his assets verifies Hoskuld's surmise: "Óláfi var ok *mikil efling at tengðum við Mýramenn*" (xxiv, 68: "The alliance with the Mýramenn was also a great asset to Óláf"). This statement-confirmation is introduced and cued by the anticipatory *vænna* (likely, to be expected). Repetition, however, underscores the fulfillment of the expected and lends precision and necessity to the lexical units.

Introduced by *jafnan* as a cue, the statement about the support Thórólf Rednose's kinsmen always expected of him: "Þórólfr var hetja mikil ok átti góða kosti; frændr hans gengu þangat *jafnan til trausts*" (xi, 21: "Thórólf was a great fighting man and had means; his kinsmen were always turning to him for help") looks forward to a substantiation, which indeed follows when Vigdís sends the outlaw Thórólf to him for protection: "Ásgautr...sagði honum alla vǫxtu, sem á váru um þeira ørendi, at Vigdís, frændkona hans, hafði þenna mann sent honum *til halds og [sic] trausts*" (xv, 35: "Ásgaut... told him the whole affair leading up to their errand and that Vigdís, his kinswoman, had sent this man to him for help and sheltering"). The repetition of the phrase calls attention to the precondition and its verification, despite the inclusion of the *halds* as increment.

Similarly, Halldór's surmise as to why Gudrún accompanied the men who had attacked Bolli: "'*Hygg ek*, at henni gengi þat meir til leiðiorðs við oss, at hon vildi vita *sem gørst, hverir menn hefði verit í þessi ferð*'" (lvi, 169: "'I think her purpose in chatting with us along the way was rather that she wanted to make sure exactly what men were in on this raid'") prepares, with its predictive *hygg ek*, for Thorgils' remark when he gathers men together for the retaliatory raid on Helgi: "'Nú þó at síðan sé langt liðit, er þeir atburðir urðu, þá ætla ek þeim *eigi ór minni liðit við þá menn, er í þeiri ferð váru*'" (lxi, 182: "'Now even though much time has passed since these events took place, I don't imagine they [Gudrún's sons] have forgotten what men were in on the raid'").[2] The lexical parallelism *hverir menn hefði verit í þessi ferð/ við þá menn, er í þeiri ferð váru* relates the two statements, as does the *eigi ór minni liðit*. Gudrún has not forgotten who the men were, for she noted them *sem gørst*; and through the *eigi ór minni liðit* phrase the reader, too, is given the cue to recall. The foregoing three examples demonstrate how Repetition reinforces the anticipatory devices and cues of Foreknowledge, such as *vænna, jafnan, hygg ek*, and facilitates the relating of statement and confirmation.

Another example of how Repetition marks the precondition and its verification is the episode describing Thorkel's encounter with the outlaw Grím. In their fight by the hut, Grím bests Thorkel but spares his life with the comment that Thorkel may repay him in whatever way he wishes. Together they return to Sælingsdaltunga, where Snorri Godi welcomes them: "Snorri kvað hafa vel orðit, — 'lízk mér *giptusamliga* á Grím; vil ek, at *þu leysir hann vel af hendi*'" lviii, 174: "Snorri said it had turned out well, — 'and it seems to me auspiciously for Grím. I want you to do well by him when you send him off'"). Thorkel answered that many a time Snorri's advice had stood him in good stead; and when the opportunity comes, he gives Grím many trading goods and tells him: "'En at hraustum manni hefi ek þik reynt, ok fyrir þat *vil ek þik svá af hǫndum leysa*, sem ek hafa aldri þungan hug á þér haft'" (lviii, 175: "'I have found you to be a stalwart fellow and for that reason I want to send you off as though I had never borne you any ill will'"). The repetition of phrase calls attention to the fact that Thorkel did precisely as Snorri had surmised and advised, although Thorkel explains his actions as the result of his evaluation of Grím.

In like wise repetitions occur in parallel situations when the neighbors have trouble with Hrapp and then take their complaint to Hoskuld: "En bœndr allir tóku eitt ráð, at *þeir fóru til Hǫskulds ok sǫgðu honum sín vandræði*" (x, 20: "And all the farmers were of one mind: that they go to Hoskuld and tell him their troubles"). After Hrapp is dead, he continues to molest them with his ghostwalking and they go again to Hoskuld: "Nú var enn *sem fyrr, at menn fóru á fund Hǫskulds ok sǫgðu honum til þeira vandræða*" (xvii, 39). Aside from the obvious *sem fyrr*,[3] the author marks the second instance for association with the earlier episode through parallel lexical construction. Repetition in form suggests the parallelism in content: Alive or dead, Hrapp causes the same annoyance.

Parallel phrases also point out the similarity between Óláf's two visits abroad. Orn urges Óláf to go and see King Harald, for "hann gera til þeira góðan sóma, *er ekki váru betr menntir en Óláfr var*" (xxi, 52: "he [King Harald] honored well those who were not as accomplished as Óláf was"). On Óláf's second journey abroad, Geirmund encourages Óláf to visit Hákon the Earl, arguing from the same point of view, and thereby, incidentally, also confirming the high opinion of Óláf's accomplishments, which, no doubt, is the author's purpose in repeating the phrase:

"Ok veit ek víst, ef þú kemr á hans fund, at þér mun sú innar handar, því at jarl fagnar vel þeim mǫnnum, *er eigi eru jafnvel menntir sem þú*, ef hann sœkja heim" (xxix, 78: "And I know for sure that if you go to see him, his forest [for procuring wood] will be at your disposal, for many who aren't nearly as accomplished as you, Óláf, are given good welcome whenever they pay him a visit").

Verification of a precondition is also represented in the episode concerning the Christianization of Iceland. King Óláf Tryggvason suggests to Kjartan that he go out to Iceland and convert his countrymen: " '*annathvárt með styrk eða ráðum*' " (xli, 124: " 'by either force or persuasion' "). Thangbrand goes in Kjartan's stead and carries out the mission according to the king's methods: "ok boðaði mǫnnum trú *bæði með blíðum orðum ok hǫrðum refsingum*" (xli, 125: "And he preached the faith to the people both with persuasive words and severe sourgings"). The parallelism in the content and the intensification of the correlative "either...or" to "both...and" call attention to Thangbrand's having more than fulfilled the king's wishes.[4]

Basically akin to substantiation-type repetition is the consistent practice of attributing to actors in the saga knowledge which they could not have known of themselves but which has previously been presented. Herein again structurally the device is related to Foreknowledge in that it verifies the known and presupposes the omniscience of author and audience. The incident of the Tunga lands affords a telling example of Repetition by omniscience. Gudrún and Bolli have agreed with the owner to buy the lands. The author comments: "En því var kaupit *eigi váttum bundit*, at eigi váru menn svá margir hjá, at þat þœtti vera lǫgfullt" (xlvii, 146: "But since there were not enough people present to make it binding before the law, the sale was not closed by witnesses"). Later Kjartan uses precise knowledge of the situation to further his own advantage:[5] " 'Ekki kalla ek þat landkaup, er *eigi er váttum bundit*' " (xlvii, 147: " 'I don't call that a sale of land when it hasn't been closed by witnesses' ").

Repetition by omniscience again occurs in statements made concerning Thorkel of Hafratindar before and after the ambush against Kjartan. Instead of aiding Kjartan, Thorkel says:

"Sýnisk mér þat betra ráð, at vit komim okkr þar, at okkr sé við engu hætt, en vit megim sem gørst sjá fundinn ok *hafim gaman af leik þeira*" (xlix, 152: "A better plan, it seems to me, would be for us to get ourselves to a place where we will be out of danger but can watch the skirmish to best advantage and have some fun for ourselves out of their sport").

After the fight Thorkel disparages Kjartan, mimicking Kjartan's death with belittling comments. A relative of Thorgerd complains to her of Thorkel's malevolence, and she sympathizes:

> "En Þorkatli hefir alls kostar illa farit þetta mál, því at hann vissi fyrirsát Laugamanna fyrir Kjartani ok vildi eigi segja honum, en *gerði sér af gaman ok skemmtan af viðskiptum þeira*, en hefir síðan lagt til mǫrg óvingjarnlig orð" (lii, 160: "But Thorkel has conducted himself badly at every turn in this affair, for he knew of the ambush the Laugar men had laid for Kjartan and didn't want to warn him, but got instead some fun and sport for himself out of their encounter and has since contributed many unkind remarks").

Not only is Thorgerd aware of Thorkel's present behavior, but she also knows precisely how he acted and what he said at the time of the ambush. Again, this knowledge can scarcely be attributed vaguely to gossip; rather — and the formal similarity and lexical correspondence tell us that that is the case — it is another instance of the author's endowing his characters with knowledge already familiar to the audience.

A similar situation prevails when, after the slaying of Kjartan, Ósvíf sends for support from Snorri:

> *Þeir Þórhǫllusynir váru sendir út til Helgafells* at segja Snorra goða þessi tíðendi, ok þat með, at þau báðu hann senda sér skjótan styrk til liðveizlu á móti Óláfi (xlix, 155: Thórhalla's sons were sent out to Helgafell to tell Snorri Godi this news and ask him to send them immediate aid as backing against Óláf).

Again in accordance with the reader's information, Óláf is allowed knowledge of this when he advises his sons against attacking Bolli: "'En sé ek yðr makligri sýslu; fari þér til móts við *Þórhǫllusonu, er þeir eru sendir til Helgafells at stefna liði at oss'*" (xlix, 155-156: "'But I know a more fitting task that you can do. Go and overtake Thórhalla's sons who have been sent to Helgafell to gather forces against us'").[6]

Several elements in the account of Óláf Peacock's marriage suit illustrate statement-confirmations and the picking up of phrases by omniscience. When first the subject of marriage is broached to Óláf, he declares: "'Máttu svá til ætla, at ek mun *framarla á horfa* um kvánfangit'" (xxii, 62: "'You can be sure that I intend to aim high when it comes to a marriage match'"). Hoskuld approaches Egil with the proposal but does not mention Óláf's high ambitions, of course. Yet when Egil answers Hoskuld, he picks up the phrase and uses it with seeming spontaneity and naturalness: "'Er ok eigi kynligt, at slíkir menn ætli *framarla til,* því at hann skortir eigi ætt né fríðleika'" (xxiii, 63: "'It is also no wonder that such men set their aim high, for Óláf certainly does not lack for lineage or good looks'"). Again, since reference to Óláf's reputation gained from his journey to Norway and Ireland has already been made: *"Óláfr varð frægr af ferð þessi"* (xxii, 61: "Óláf's voyage brought him much fame"), to find this renown referred to in the reply to the marriage proposal accords with the repetition-by-omniscience pattern. Egil's comment confirms the fact of the fame; at the same time it denies casualness to the first phrase: "'Veit ek ok, Hǫskuldr,' segir Egill, 'at þú ert ættstórr maðr ok mikils verðr, en *Óláfr er frægr af ferð sinni'"* (xxiii, 63: "'I also know, Hoskuld,' Egil said, 'that you are a man of noble birth and highly esteemed, and Óláf's voyage has brought him much fame'"). Similarly, the detailing of the slow progress of the marriage suit is marked by use of corresponding phrases. Hoskuld and Egil have a talk together and Hoskuld asks how Óláf's proposal has fared with Thorgerd. Egil tells him all about it and that *"þótti fastliga horfa"* (xxiii, 64: "it looked difficult"). Hoskuld in turn reports back to Óláf: "Hoskuldr kvað *seinliga horfa* af hennar hendi" (*ibid*.: "Hoskuld said it looked slow on Thorgerd's part").[7]

The parallel lexical statements here discussed demonstrate how the author by the formal means of Repetition substantiates the preknown, much as he fulfills prophecies under the aspect Foreknowledge. And likewise, as with some of the devices under Foreknowledge such as understatement, euphemism, and ambiguity, oftentimes Repetition confirms subtly suggested suspicions and reveals unsuspected overtones in the text. An illuminating example occurs when on two separate occasions Bolli makes insinuations which strike too closely to the truth. The passage has been discussed where, upon his departure from Norway, Bolli suggests that Iceland has fewer attractions for Kjartan than does sitting talking to the king's sister. Disconcerted, Kjartan replies: "'*Haf ekki slíkt við*'" (xli, 126: "'Don't be saying such things'"). Bolli is to hear these words again. After he has killed Kjartan, a nervous Gudrún greets him and gloats: "'Hrefna mun eigi ganga hlæjandi at sænginni í kveld'" (xlix, 154-155: "'Hrefna will not be laughing when she goes to bed tonight'"), to which Bolli, exceedingly angry, replies:

> "Ósýnt þykki mér, at hon fǫlni meir við þessi tíðendi en þú, ok þat grunar mik, at þú brygðir þér minnr við, þó at vér lægim eptir á vígvellinum, en Kjartan segði frá tíðendum." Guðrún fann þá, at Bolli reiddisk, ok mælti: *"Haf ekki slíkt við"* (xlix, 155: "I have my doubts that she [Hrefna] will turn any more pale at these tidings than you, and I'm not sure but that it

would have been a lesser shock to you if I [and your brothers] were lying out on the battle ground and Kjartan had brought you the news." Realizing then that Bolli was angry, Gudrún said: "Don't be saying such things").

That the same phrase occurs in each of these passages charged with overtones, speaks for the interpretation that what Bolli has asserted in each instance is not far from the truth.

Insight into Bolli's thoughts and feelings is further provided by a key trait of his which is first anticipated and then repeated throughout several episodes. All of Kjartan's spiteful deeds and words against Bolli and Gudrún have called forth no reaction on the part of Bolli. After Kjartan has outwitted them in the purchase of Thórarin's lands, Gudrún berates Bolli for his easygoing tolerance of Kjartan's acts. Bolli, however, chooses to keep silent: "Bolli *svarar engu* ok gekk þegar af þessu tali" (xlvii, 147: "Bolli did not answer and walked away at once from this talk"). So, too, when Thorhalla Chatterbox's malicious gossip finds Gudrún's ears receptive and moves her to upbraid Bolli again for not taking action, Bolli's lack of response is what we expect: "*Bolli lét sem hann heyrði eigi, sem jafnan*, er Kjartani var hallmælt, því at hann var *vanr at þegja* eða mæla í móti" (xlvii, 148: "Bolli pretended he had not heard, as always, for it was his usual way either to keep silent or contradict when Kjartan was criticized"). The *sem jafnan* and *vanr at þegja* point back to the *svarar engu* and forward to further development. The theme, to be sure, appears again while Bolli waits with the others in ambush: "Bolli var *hljóðr* um daginn ok lá uppi hjá gilsþreminum" (xlviii, 151: "Bolli was quiet throughout the day and lay up on the brink of the gulch"). This might seem normal enough if it were not for Ósvíf's interpretation of Bolli's lying in plain sight of anybody coming along the route as betrayal of the ambush. Indeed, to help Kjartan's cause through inactive participation may represent Bolli's true desire. This is borne out by the next occurrence of the motif. Even after the fighting has begun, Bolli stands quietly by; and to Kjartan's chiding and taunting him for not taking part, Bolli reacts as we have been conditioned to expect: "*Bolli lét sem hann heyrði eigi*" (xlix, 153). The repetition of the familiar phrase confirms the suspicions originally aroused and leads to the interpretation of Bolli's silence as a cover-up for the indecision and pull between love and hate which he feels.

In a similar fashion *hljóðr* (xlv, 137) indicates Kjartan's hidden feelings. Furthermore at Hjardarholt, on two occasions, Kjartan's sharp and quick interjections are pointed at Gudrún, whom he wishes to hurt — a psychologically valid reaction on his part and evidence of the author's fine sensitivity to human nature. The first opportunity for Kjartan to direct his barb is when the question of the seating arrangement comes up:

> Þá mælti Kjartan til konu þeirar, er um kvenna skipunina hafði rœtt, — því at *engi var annarr skjótari til at svara* —: "Hrefna skal sitja í ǫndvegi ok vera mest metin at gǫrvǫllu, á meðan ek em á lífi" (xlvi, 139: Kjartan called out to the woman who had just talked about the seating arrangement — before anyone else had a chance to answer: "Hrefna is to sit in the high-seat and altogether be the most honored as long as I am alive").

And the next day when Gudrún begs Hrefna to show her the precious head-dress, Kjartan again is quicker than anyone else to reply:

> Kjartan var hjá ok þó eigi allnær ok heyrði, hvat Guðrún mælti. Hann varð *skjótari til at svara en Hrefna:* "Ekki skal hon falda sér með motri at þessu boði" (xlvi, 139-140: Kjartan was standing nearby, but not all too close, and heard what Gudrún said: He spoke up before Hrefna had a chance to answer: "She is not to put on the headdress at this feast").

The fact that Kjartan was near but *þó eigi allnær* suggests that he was waiting his chance to direct another rebuff at Gudrún.

Frequently in instances of Repetition, a word or phrase added or a slight change made in the manner of the expression controls even more decidedly the intended correspondence. Gudrún is represented as nurturing hate against the sons of Óláf:

> "Þat er minn vili, at þeir haldi eigi allir heilu Óláfssynir."... "Satt er þat, en eigi má ek vita, at *þessir menn siti um kyrrt allir*" (lix, 177: "I am determined that Óláf's sons shall not all come out of this unscathed."... "That is true, but I cannot stand seeing all of them left to sit in peace").

Later, when Thorgils asks Lambi to join in the raid, Lambi's request that his kinsmen be unmolested echoes Gudrún's words, just as if he knew on what tack Gudrún's mind had been running: "'Vil ek þat til skilja, ef ek geng at þessu, at þeir frændr mínir, *Óláfssynir, siti kyrrir ok í friði*'" (lxi, 183: "'But I want to make this stipulation: if I go along, my kinsmen, Óláf's sons, must be left alone and in peace'"). The example illustrates again the use of omniscience and shows how embellishment in the *ok í friði* phrase strengthens the association between the *um kyrrt* and the *kyrrir*.

Sometimes control of the associations is accomplished by reversal, whereby negative counterparts are formed. This process is particularly apparent in discourse where picking up of the same words is accompanied by negation —

another argument for the artistically chiseled and constructed nature of the dialogue. When, for example, it is reported that the theft of his sword disturbs Kjartan: "*Þetta lét Kjartan á sik bíta* ok vildi eigi hafa svá búit" (xlvi, 142: "This rankled with Kjartan and he did not want to let the matter stand"), Óláf advises him, reversing the phrase: "'Láttu *þetta ekki á þik bíta*'" (*ibid*.: "'Don't let this rankle with you'"). Again the compositional design of the narrative is apparent, as when questioning Bolli about accepting Christianity, Kjartan asks: "'Hversu *fúss* ertu, frændi, at taka við trú þeiri, er konungr býðr?'" (xl, 119: "'How keen are you, kinsman, on accepting this faith which the king is proclaiming?'"). Whereupon Bolli replies: "'*Ekki* em ek þess *fúss*'" (*ibid*.: "'I'm not at all keen about it'"). Another instance of Bolli's turning Kjartan's words negatively and with some sarcasm, as we have seen, immediately follows. Kjartan says that it is "'*lítilmannligt*, at vera tekinn sem lamb ór stekk eða melrakki ór gildru'" (*ibid*.: "'cowardly to be taken like a lamb from a fold or a fox from a trap'") and declares that he intends to burn the king in his hall. Bolli says: "'*Ekki* kalla ek þetta *lítilmannligt*'" ("'I don't call that cowardly'"). Appearance here of the grammatical negatives prepares for Bolli's negativeness *per se* in his relationship with Kjartan and for the sharpened contrasts to follow. In subsequent chapters negative reversal will be shown to play a prominent role as a structural element.

Ingeniously employed, Repetition may illuminate further subtleties in the text, particularly by introducing irony into a confirming statement, and a flash of wit. A case in point is where Gudrún's sons excuse themselves for their procrastination in avenging their father, but Gudrún discredits their reason:

> Þeim brœðrum brá mjǫk við þetta, er Guðrún mælti, en svǫruðu þá á þá leið, at *þeir hafa verit ungir til hefnda at leita* ok forystulausir; kváðsuk hvárki kunna ráð gera fyrir sér né ǫðrum, — "ok muna mættim vit, hvat vit hǫfum látit." Guðrún kvazk ætla, at þeir mundu meir hugsa um hestavíg eða leika (lx, 179-180: The brothers were deeply affected by what Gudrún said, but all the same answered back that they had been too young to carry out revenge and leaderless. They said they had not been capable of devising a plan for themselves, let alone for others, — "but still we might remember what we have lost." Gudrún said she suspected they had been thinking more about horse fights or games).

Immediately thereafter, however, when she attempts to persuade Thorgils to undertake the raid, Gudrún repeats her son's words, turning them now to her advantage:

"Svá þykki mér, Þorgils, sem synir mínir nenni eigi kyrrsetu þessi lengr, svá at þeir leiti eigi til hefnda eptir fǫður sinn; en þat hefir mest dvalit hér til, at *mér þóttu þeir Þorleikr ok Bolli of ungir hér til at standa í mannráðum*" (lx, 180: "I am given to believe, Thorgils, that my sons are no longer content to sit around quietly and do nothing about revenge for their father. But the main reason for the delay has been that Thorleik and Bolli have seemed too young to me to take part in plots against men's lives").

Much as under the aspect Foreknowledge where previously introduced characters and their traits find subsequent confirmation, so by means of Repetition the individual personality of an agent may be defined and confirmed. Unn's proud spirit, for example, is indicated by her replying *reiðuliga* (sharply) when displeased at the pettiness of her brother Helgi's invitation (v, 9) or when asked about her health (vii, 12). Again, repetition of a phrase is used to suggest Queen Gunnhild's partiality toward certain visiting Icelanders. So of Hrút it is said: "En Gunnhildr dróttning *lagði svá miklar mætur á hann*, at hon helt engi hans jafningja innan hirðar" (xix, 44: "And Queen Gunnhild esteemed him so highly that in her opinion no one in the guard could equal him"). And when the phrase is subsequently used in connection with Óláf, association with the former phrase not only tells us something about Gunnhild's fickle character but also narrows the intent, for her real interest is in Hrút: "Gunnhildr *lagði mikil mæti á Óláf*, er hon vissi, at hann var bróðursonr Hrúts" (xxi, 52: "Gunnhild esteemed Óláf highly as soon as she learned that he was Hrút's nephew").

We have noted how the succinct phrases characterizing Thorgils when he enters the saga prepare for his involvement with Snorri Godi and Thorkel Eyjólfsson. Two further characteristics are there presented which are later substantiated when the appropriate circumstance arrives: "þótti Snorra Þorgils *hlutgjarn ok áburðarmikill*" (lvii, 170: "Snorri thought Thorgils meddlesome and puffed up"). Subsequently Thorgils manages to deprive Thórarin of his *goði* title and Thórarin's son Audgísl takes their complaint to Snorri, who repeats what the author has already told us about Snorri's evaluation of Thorgils: "Snorri svarar vel at einu ok tók lítinn af ǫllu ok mælti: 'Gerisk hann Hǫlluslappi nú *framgjarn ok áburðarmikill*'" (lxvii, 197: "Snorri committed himself neither one way nor the other, but said: 'So this gawk of a Halla's son is being pushy and puffed up, is he'"). Thorgils' traits are not only confirmed by his suggested actions, they are confirmed by the formal and lexical parallelism which indicates that the author has not forgotten what he once brought up. Snorri's commitment, at first left indefinite by the *vel at einu ok tók litinn af ǫllu,* becomes explicit when he gives Audgísl the handsome axe.

The author's preference for repeating words and phrases, far from being indicative of lack of imagination on his part, actually serves to best advantage the poetic end. Consistent use of verbal echoes sets up a pattern of confirming statements and brings into focus contextual subtleties implicit in the text. Through underscoring the relationship between antecedent and referent, Repetition can be said to symbolize inevitability of consequence. For the pairs thus formed hold the audience within a world of the expected (*ván*) and known (*kunnigt*). The semblance of a foreknown and predetermined world is produced, to be sure, by direct prophecies and by the more veiled forms of Foreknowledge, but it is also no less made manifest through the reappearance of verbal configurations that one has been conditioned to expect.

By repeating a linguistic pattern the author does not need to state directly that a prophecy has been fulfilled or a prediction has run its course — that the "now" (*nú*) is the same "as before" (*sem áðr*). By repeating words and phrases, by giving knowledge to or withholding it from the actors, and by controlling the choice of words, he has throughout the saga created a semblance of expectation fulfilled. Not only does Repetition confirm what has been presented before, but also the symmetry of the pattern evokes a feeling of poetic rightness — that all is as it should or must be.

Through controlled linguistic choices the author "uses up" his elements as necessary units and realizes a symmetrical formal pattern related to the concept of balance and compensation. Therefore his work can be said to be built upon the idea of inevitable necessity (predeterminism, fate) and equalized balance (moral code of justice), both of which find expression in what he is saying and in how it is being said. Such integration of form and content through consistent use of structural elements and formal devices would seem to point to the creative genius of a single author. Whether such a composition is the result of a conscious or unconscious endeavor cannot be stated apodictically, since one or the other or both may reside in the creative process. Yet it seems more convenient and reasonable to assume an intelligence behind the creation, even if we do not mean to get involved in an ontological argument.

In the foregoing discussion other allied aspects of the basic formal and structural patterns such as omniscience, embellishment, negative counterparts, and irony have been concomitantly recognized. In the next chapter these facets will be further explored in the author's application of Repetition to point up comparisons between different characters and between different episodes that are played off one against the other as likes or unlikes.

III

COMPARISON: PARALLELS AND CONTRASTS

The *Laxdœla* author's consistent use of Repetition encourages contextual association and leads to the third structural and formal device to be considered: Comparison, or the relating of different characters or situations in order to signal resemblances or dissimilarities. In developing this aspect, also, the author makes great use of lexical repetition to point up and emphasize parallels and likenesses or to mark contrasts and balance differences. By bringing together different characters and parts of the saga, by weighing likes against likes, likes against unlikes, evens against odds, the author integrates ever more elements into his grand design of necessary function and compensatory balance.

Instances of Comparison fall, in general, into two groups: the one consisting of examples of comparison of situation or theme; the other, of examples concerned with descriptions and relationship of agents. Since character more often than not is revealed through situation, however, the grouping tends to be somewhat arbitrary.

Many comparisons of situation and theme illustrate the author's preference for using the same or similar expressions in similar circumstances. Indeed, in many of the examples in this category, too, verbal repetition first calls attention in retrospect to the distinguishing characteristic. So, for example, verbal echo points out the comparison between the weakening of both Thórd Goddi and Thorleik when offered tempting bribes: "*Þórði þótti fét fagrt*" (xiv, 32: "The money did look good to Thórd"); "*Þorleikr slæsk nú í málinu, ok þóttu honum fǫgr hrossin*" (xxxvi, 101: "Thorleik now decided to strike the bargain, for the horses did look good to him"). Similarly, Jórunn's advice to Hoskuld and Thuríd's counsel to Kjartan make use of a common formula: Jórunn: "'*Nú þœtti oss hitt ráðligra...*'" (xix, 47: "'Now it would seem more advisable to me...'"); Thuríd: "'*Þœtti oss þat ráðligast...*'" (xlv, 137).

65

And a like verbal pattern also marks the summing-up with which both speeches end: "'Vænti ek þess, at Hrútr *taki því vel ok líkliga*, því at mér er *maðr sagðr vitr; mun hann þat sjá kunna*, at þetta er hvárstveggja ykkar *sómi*'" (xix, 48: "'Hrút, I daresay, will take this well and in good part; I've been told he's a sensible man, and he no doubt will see that this does honor to you both'"); "[Ásgeirr] *tekr því máli líkliga*, því at hann var *vitr maðr ok kunni at sjá*, hversu *sœmiliga* þeim er boðit" (xlv, 137: "Ásgeir took this proposal in good part, for he was a sensible man and could see what an honorable offer was being made them").

In the episodes dealing with Kotkel and his family, phrases succinctly repeated fulfill our expectations as to their undesirability and also draw attention to the similarity of parallel incidents. From their first appearance in the saga, they are looked upon with hostility by their neighbors, first at Skálmarnes: "*ok var þeira byggð ekki vinsæl*" (xxxv, 95: "And their settling there was not popular"); and then in Laxárdal: "*ok var sú byggð óvinsæl*" (xxxvi, 102). Wherever they go, they do evil, and each time their sorcery is directed toward a specific victim: "Því næst laust á hríð mikilli. Þat fann Þórðr Ingunnarson ok hans fǫrunautar, þar sem hann var á sæ staddr, ok *til hans var gǫrt veðrit*" (xxxv, 99: "Presently a violent storm broke loose. Thórd Ingunnarson and his companions felt it out at sea where they were, for the storm was raised against him"); "Kári sofnaði nær ekki, því at *til hans var leikr gǫrr*" (xxxvii, 106: "Kári scarcely fell asleep at all, for the spell was cast against him"). And each time these actions move threats against Kotkel and his family and with the threat the comment that the penalty comes too late. So, after their witchcraft has brought about the drowning of Thórd Ingunnarson, Gest delivers an ultimatum:

> Síðan ferr Gestr Oddleifsson á fund Hallsteins goða ok gerði honum tvá kosti, at hann skyldi reka í brott þessa fjǫlkunnigu menn, ella *kvazk hann mundu drepa þá*, — "*ok er þó ofseinat*"[1] (xxxvi, 100-101: After that Gest Oddleifsson went to see Hallstein Godi and gave him two choices: either Hallstein would have to drive these sorcerers away or else he would slay them — "and it's long overdue").

And when Hrút's son Kári dies as a result of their sorcery, Óláf's demand and comment echo Gest's words: "Óláfr *kvað þá þegar skyldu drepa þau* Kotkel ok konu hans ok sonu, — '*er þó ofseinat nú*'" (xxxvii, 106: "Óláf said Kotkel, his wife and sons should be put to death at once — 'it's now long overdue'"). Parallelism of incident is marked each time by parallelism in expression.

Verbal similarities in other episodes involving witchcraft or ghost tales prompt discussion. So for example, the ghost-walkings of Hrapp and Hallbjorn Sleekstone-Eye exhibit similar elements. Moreover, throughout both descriptions a folkloric tone is preserved. First of all, some phenomenon is provided to aid in the search. Óláf's housecarl has asked for a change of task because of Hrapp's bothering him: "Óláfr tekr í hǫnd sér spjótit gullrekna, konungsnaut, gengr nú heiman ok húskarl með honum. *Snjór var nǫkkurr á jǫrðu*" (xxiv, 69: "Óláf took his gold-chased spear, the king's gift, and he and his servant set out from home. There was some snow on the ground"). Similarly, Thorkel and a servant set out together: "Eitt kveld var vant kýr í Þykkvaskógi; fór Þorkell at leita ok húskarl hans með honum; þat var eptir dagsetr, en *tunglskin var á*" (xxxviii, 109-110: "One evening a cow was missing at Thykkvaskóg; Thorkel and his housecarl set out to look for her. It was after sunset, but the moon was out"). Óláf and the servant find Hrapp at the cow-shed door; Óláf thrusts his spear at Hrapp, but to no avail: "Óláfr vill þá renna á Hrapp, en Hrappr *fór þar niðr, sem hann var kominn*" (xxiv, 69: "Óláf then wanted to make a dash at Hrapp, but he vanished into the ground whence he had come"). And respectively, Thorkel and his servant find Sleekstone-Eye in the woods but no cow: "Þeir runnusk á allsterkliga; fór Hallbjǫrn undan, ok er Þorkel varði minnst, þá *smýgr hann niðr í jǫrðina* ór hǫndum honum" (xxxviii, 110: "They started to fight one another with all their might; Hallbjorn got away, and when Thorkel was least on guard, he slipped out of his reach into the earth"). The end to these ghost-walkings, too, receives set formulation: "*Heðan frá verðr engum manni mein at aptrgǫngu Hrapps*" (xxiv, 69: "After that no man ever came to any harm because of Hrapp's ghost-walking"); "*Ekki varð síðan mein at Hallbirni*" (xxxviii, 110: "After that no one came to any more harm from Hallbjorn").[2]

Again, correspondence can be found in episodes concerning first the promising of a reward and then the granting of it to two obedient slaves. Vigdís says to Ásgaut: "'Með því at þú gerir svá, sem ek býð þér, skaltu nǫkkut eptir taka: *frelsi mun ek gefa þér* ok fé þat, at þú sér fœrr, hvert er þú vill'" (xv, 33: "'If you do as I ask, you shall get something in return. I will give you your freedom and enough money so that you can go anywhere you like'"). When Ásgaut performs his service, Vigdís keeps her promise:

"Hefir þú nú, Ásgautr," segir hon, "vel farit með þínu efni ok trúliga; skaltu nú ok vita skjótliga, til hvers þú hefir unnit; *ek gef þér frelsi*, svá at þú skalt frá þessum degi frjáls maðr heita" (xvi, 36: "You, Ásgaut," she said, "have done your task well and faithfully; you shall now learn immediately the reward you have earned: I give you your freedom, so that from this day forth you may be called a free man").³

A similar promise is made and kept when Óláf makes a bargain with a servant girl to deliver Stígandi into his hands: "Óláfr bauð *at gefa henni frelsi*, ef hon kœmi Stíganda í fœri við þá; ... Óláfr efnir vel við ambáttina ok *gaf henni frelsi*" (xxxviii, 109: "Óláf offered to give her her freedom if she would give them a chance at Stígandi; ... Óláf made good his promise to the bondwoman and gave her her freedom").⁴

The Christianization first of Norway then of Iceland calls forth similar reactions on the part of the people — and use of the same phrase: "*en hinir váru þó miklu fleiri, er í móti váru*" (xl, 118: "but those numbered many more who held out against it" [the new faith]); "*en þó váru þeir miklu fleiri, er í móti mæltu*" (xli, 125). The lexical parallelism focuses attention on the analogous situation in each country respectively.⁵

The marked correspondence between the foregoing pairs of examples suggests, moreover, that although the comparison may appear at first to lie principally in verbal echoes, a deeper relationship or significance may also be traced. Verbal similarity may be used to link different episodes or facts in such a way that the implicit discursive content — balancing of enmities, comparing and contrasting of forces — becomes explicit. So, for example, Vigdís, instead of handing back the bribe money to Ingjald, as was the bargain between the men, rewards Ásgaut with it, declaring: "'*er nú fét betr niðr komit*'" (xvi, 36: "'now the money has fallen into better hands'"). Later, Thórd, to prevent part of his money being confiscated by Vigdís and her kin as divorce settlement, entrusts it to Hoskuld and Óláf, saying: "'*þá sé betr komit fét*'" (xvi, 37). By utilizing the same words the author neatly points up the tit-for-tat between Thórd Goddi and his wife Vigdís.

Another instance of evening the score is contained in the accounts of the divorces of Gudrún and Thórd Ingunnarson. In order to marry one another, each must procure a divorce, and the grounds for these divorces are not merely comparable but even reflect one another in reverse. First, Thórd gives good advice to Gudrún: "'Gerðu honum skyrtu ok *brautgangs hofuðsmátt* ok seg skilit við hann fyrir þessar sakar'" (xxxiv, 94: "'Make him [Thorvald] a shirt with a neck opening so large that his breast nipples show and declare yourself divorced from him for that reason'").⁶ After her divorce, Gudrún, chatting on the way to the Thing with Thórd, asks whether it is true that his wife Aud always wears breeches (xxxv, 95: "*er jafnan í brókum*"). Although he is somewhat slow in catching on, Thórd, during the Thing, sees it Gudrún's way and takes up the hint:

> Einn dag spurði Þórðr Ingunnarson Guðrúnu, hvat konu varðaði, ef hon væri í brókum jafnan svá sem karlar. Guðrún svarar: "Slíkt víti á konum at skapa fyrir þat á sitt hóf sem karlmanni, ef hann hefir *hǫfuðsmátt* svá mikla, at sjái *geirvǫrtur* hans berar, *brautgangssǫk hvárttveggja*" (xxxv, 96: One day Thórd Ingunnarson asked Gudrún what the penalty was for a woman who always wore breeches like the menfolk. Gudrún answered: For that, the same penalty applies to a woman as to a man who wears a shirt with a neck opening so large that his nipples show: grounds for divorce in each case").

Moreover, not only do the grounds for the divorces (unseemly clothing) parallel one another, but also the matching of Aud's retaliation to Thórd's device develops the comparison further. After her divorce, one night before sunup, Aud rides to Thórd's hut where he is asleep in his bed closet: "Hon brá þá saxi ok lagði at Þórði ok veitti honum áverka mikla, ok kom á hǫndina hœgri; varð hann sárr á báðum *geirvǫrtum*" (xxxv, 98: "She drew a short sword and struck Thórd with it, dealing him severe wounds; it cut his right hand and wounded him on both nipples"). The score could not have been evened more fitly than by this "stroke in the dark."

There are other examples. The equalization of power between Óláf and King Mýrkjartan is effectively brought out, for instance, in the "murmur of discontent" that passes through the ranks of the Irish at the sight of Óláf's battle array: "Síðan kemr *kurr mikill* í lið þeira" (xxi, 55) and conversely among Óláf's crew at the sight of the Irish cavalry: "En er Óláfr heyrði þenna *kurr*..." (xxi, 56).

The contrast between Geirmund's evil sword Footbiter and Kjartan's sword Konungsnaut has already been referred to in relation to the curse and the blessing which they respectively bear.[7] As if to draw attention even more to their juxtaposition and equalized roles, the author employs the same phrase in describing the practice of both Geirmund and Kjartan respectively "never to let the sword be far from reach": "Þetta sverð kallaði hann Fótbít ok *lét þat aldregi hendi firr ganga*" (xxix, 79); "Ekki hafði Kjartan haft sverðit konungsnaut í hendi,... en þó var hann *sjaldan vanr at láta þat hendi firr ganga*" (xlvi, 140).

In a similar fashion in the episodes describing Thorkel's experience with the outlaws Grím and Gunnar Thidrandabani, certain elements stand out for comparison. These likenesses not only confirm Thorkel's character, but also focus attention on the relationship between Thorkel and Gudrún, exhibiting to advantage the weakness of the one and the strength of the other. Both times Thorkel is constrained to follow someone else's wishes. Although he feels chagrin at the way his dealings with the outlaw Grím have turned out, he nonetheless, as we have already noted, carries out Snorri's expressed wish that he do well by Grím: "'vil ek, at *þú leysir hann vel af hendi*'" (lviii, 174). In the Thidrandabani episode, it is Gudrún who protects the outlaw and overrules Thorkel. And when the time comes for Gunnar to depart, Thorkel forsees what Gudrún expects: "'Hefir þú tekit þat svá fast, at þér mun ekki at getask, *nema hann sé sœmiliga af hǫndum leystr*'" (lxix, 203: "'You have taken so strong a hand in this matter that probably nothing else will do short of his being sent off honorably'").

As we have observed under Repetition, slight changes in the established pattern may mark a theme even more specifically for comparison. In juxtaposing two situations, the author often makes use of negative reversal or antonyms. Notably, the turning of the same idiom from a negative to a positive or vice versa can neatly image the turn in situation. When Óláf was weighing the possibility of anchoring his ship with safety, the outlook was dark: "'*Ekki eru þau efni í um várt mál*, því at ek sé, at boðar eru allt fyrir skutstafn'" (xxi, 53-54: "'There's no chance for our cause now, for I see that there are breakers all about the stern'"). When the Irish king appeared, however, the outlook brightened and allowed Óláf to reassure his crew: "'*því at nú er gott efni í váru máli*'" (xxi, 56: "'For now there's a good chance for our cause'").

Another case in point is substitution of the negative *þústr* for the positive *kært* within the same linguistic pattern, neatly reflecting the reversal from friendship to enmity which takes place in the relations of the houses of Óláf and Ósvíf. When Kjartan, Bolli, and Gudrún are growing up, the atmosphere is congenial:

> *Vinátta* var ok mikil með þeim Óláfi ok Ósvífri ok jafnan heimboð, ok ekki því minnr, at *kært gerðisk með inum yngrum mǫnnum* (xxxix, 112: There was also great friendship between Óláf and Ósvíf and always partying back and forth, not any the less so now that a fondness was developing between the young people).

Later, the change in the situation is described — and compared: "Þeir Óláfr ok Ósvífr heldu sinni *vináttu, þótt nǫkkut væri þústr á með inum yngrum mǫnnum*" (xlvi, 139: "Óláf and Ósvíf held to their friendship as before, even though some friction had developed between the young people"). Similarly, substitution of *kærleika* for *vináttu* in the same idiom sets up for comparison the rumors of Kjartan's relationship to Ingibjorg and his love for Gudrún: "Bolli segir, *hvert orðtak manna var á um vináttu* þeira Kjartans ok Ingibjargar konungssystur" (xlii, 127: "Bolli told her what sort of talk there hed been about the friendship between Kjartan and Ingibjorg, the king's sister"). Upon Bolli's request for Gudrún's hand, Óláf gives him this reply: " 'Er þér, Bolli, þat í engan stað ókunnara en mér, hvert orðtak á var um kærleika með þeim Kjartani ok Guðrúnu' " (xliii, 128-129: " 'It is no less known to you, Bolli, than to me what talk there has been concerning the love between Kjartan and Gudrún' "). Through this telling substitution the true situation is made clear and the insinuation in the rumor from Norway effectively nullified.

Frequently verbal reduplication would seem to point in the direction of one episode being derived from or modeled upon another, and when this is the case, the former acts as precursor or preparation for the latter, although this may or may not represent the sequence in the creative process. Thus in structure and tone, Vigdís' divorce from Thórd sets the pattern for Gudrún's divorce from Thorvald: "[Vigdís] *sagði skilit við* Þórð godda, ok *fór* hon *til frænda sinna....* Þeir Hvammverjar... ætluðu sér *helming fjár*" (xvi, 37: "Vigdís pronounced herself divorced from Thórd Goddi and went to her kinsmen.... They, the Hvammverjar, intended to get half the money"). Conventional social mores assume conventional literary formulation in the saga, for similar phrases are found again in the account of Gudrún's divorce: "Þat sama vár *segir* Guðrún *skilit við* Þorvald ok *fór heim til* Lauga..., ok hafði hon *helming fjár* alls" (xxxiv, 94).

In another example, Thorleik refuses to sell or trade the stud of horses which he got from Kotkel, declaring: " '*Engi em ek mangsmaðr*' " (xxxvii, 103: " 'I'm no tradesmonger' "). Kjartan in a later incident in the saga rejects Bolli's gift of a stud of horses: "kvazk *engi vera hrossamaðr*" (xlv, 135: "[Kjartan] said he was no horsegroomer"). The similarity in construction and tone is obvious. That the second episode is modeled upon the first is further demonstrated by the descriptions of the horses. Kotkel's stallion is so described: "Hann var bæði *mikill ok vænn ok reyndr at vígi*" (xxxvi, 101: "He was both a large and handsome animal and tried and true in horse fighting"); and the stallion Bolli wished to give Kjartan is likewise portrayed: "Hestrinn var *mikill ok vænn ok hafði aldregi brugðizk at vígi*" (xlv, 135: "The stallion was a large and handsome animal and had never been beaten in a horse fight").

Along with other parallelisms in the saga certain correspondences between elements in Gudrún's dreams and Gest's interpretations of them[8] and the shepherd's description of the circle of riders in the woods outside Helgi's hut and Helgi's interpretations of them prompt speculation.[9] Both are concerned with the solving of a type of riddle. Gest interprets the symbols in Gudrún's dreams, and Helgi guesses the names of the persons in the circle from the clues the shepherd gives him. Gold and silver arm rings occur in the dreams and also in the shepherd's clues. Since their presence in the shepherd's account cannot be explained on grounds of realistic observation of such minutiae, it would appear rather that they merely serve here to establish a formal connection with the earlier "guessing game" and make up part of the clues in a riddle pattern. There are, however, other points of comparison. Although the dreams are told consecutively with the interpretations together at the end and the shepherd's tale has each puzzle solved as it is presented, the interpreters of the signs interject in each case a comment on the seriousness of the matter. So, at a pause in Gudrún's narration, Gest remarks: " 'Ekki fara í þurrð draumarnir' " (xxxiii, 89: " 'Your dreams are not getting any less' "), and Helgi likewise comments on the shepherd's report: " 'Nú versnar mjǫk frásǫgnin' " (lxiii, 188: " 'Now your tale grows much worse' "). Both Gest and Helgi clearly understand the significance of the riddles: Gest says: " 'Glǫggt fæ ek sét, hvat draumar þessir eru' " (xxxiii, 89: " 'I clearly see what these dreams mean' "), and Helgi says: " 'Glǫggt sé ek, hverr þessi maðr er' " (lxiii, 188: " 'I clearly see who this man is' "; lxiii, 189: " 'Gǫrla skil ek, hverir þessir menn eru' ").

Even as some incidents in the first section prepare for similar occurrences later on, sometimes those in the last section act like echoes or reflections of events in the central theme: So, King Óláf Tryggvason reproaches Kjartan for boastfulness: " 'Bæði er, at þú ert gǫrviligr maðr, enda lætr þú allstórliga' " (xl, 118: " 'Two things are certain — you are an accomplished fellow, but too puffed up' "); and King Óláf the Saint uses the same phrase to deflate Thorkel's ego: " 'Bæði er, Þorkell, at þú ert mikils verðr, enda gerisk þú nú allstórr' " (lxxiv, 216-217).

Parallelisms appear in descriptions of and relationships between the agents of the action just as they do in those concerned with situation and theme. The one is generally a reflection of the other, so that the division is an artificial one; and some examples may be considered from either point of view. Any two characters in the saga may have the same name, the same or similar bynames or epithets; and the same personality traits more often that not are shared by more than one agent. The two Víga-Hrapps set themselves up for comparison. The first Víga-Hrapp is so described: "*Mikill maðr var hann ok sterkr; ekki vildi hann láta sinn hlut,* þó at manna munr væri nǫkkurr; ok fyrir þat er *hann var ódæll*..." (x, 19: "He was a big man and strong and never wanted to be worsted, even if the odds were considerably against him. And since he was so hard to deal with..."). His namesake, on the other hand, was a man "small of stature, lively and brisk with darting eyes"; but the second Víga-Hrapp declares that he possesses all the characteristics which the byname Víga (Slayer) implies. So he boasts: "'Hefi ek nafn Víga-Hrapps ok þat með nafni, at ek em *engi dældarmaðr, þó at ek sjá lítill vexti*'" (lxiii, 190: "'I bear the name Víga-Hrapp and have all the name implies, for I am no easy man to deal with, even if I am undersized'"). Through comparison with his counterpart who was *mikill maðr ok sterkr*, this funny little character is made even more comical.

Negative character traits such as those ascribed to the two Víga-Hrapps are also assigned to Thorleik Hoskuldsson: "fálátr ok *óþýðr, engi jafnaðarmaðr, engi dældarmaðr*" (ix, 18),[10] to Vigdís' kinsman Thórólf: "Þórólfr *vildi eigi láta sinn hlut* ok var allstórorðr" (xiv, 29: "Thórólf did not want to be worsted and was given to boasting"); to Geirmund: "*ódældarmaðr* var han...var *fáskiptinn hversdagla, óþýðr* við flesta" (xxix, 77 and 79: "He was a hard man to deal with...usually took little part in things and was unfriendly toward most"); and to Thorgils: "mikill maðr ok vænn ok inn mesti *ofláti*; *engi* var hann kallaðr *jafnaðarmaðr*" (lvii, 170: "a big man and handsome, but a great swaggerer and known for being unfair"). Like Geirmund, Hrút and Thorgerd are said to "take little part in things," and each is described as "liking to have his own way": "Ekki var hann *afskiptinn um flesta hluti*, en *vildi ráða því, er hann hlutaðisk til*" (Hrút, xix, 48); "hon var skǫrungr mikill, en *fáskiptin hversdagliga*; en þar varð fram at koma, er Þorgerðr *vildi, til hvers sem hon hlutaðisk*" (Thorgerd, xxiv, 66).

From the foregoing examples, it can be clearly seen that in depicting his agents, the author has worked within a limited range. By regrouping and redistributing personality traits, by shifting a little here, by changing the emphasis a little there, however, he has achieved variety among the people of the saga. The significance of superlative character traits such as *mikill maðr ok sterkr*, *mikill maðr ok vænn*, or *skǫrungr*, for example, will be discussed under Recurrence. The concern here is to consider how ascribing similar characteristics, attitudes, and actions to different actors through reuse of the same linguistic units brings these agents into relationship without that fact being stated explicitly and to note the tendency to juxtapose both negative and positive qualities.

Even as at times situations or themes in the first part of the saga prepare for episodes in the central part, so, too, characters in the first part regularly act as preparatory figures for the chief protagonists in the main section. Furthermore, counterparts already prepared in the first or central parts may show up in the final section.[11] The resulting effect somewhat resembles duplicate reflections in a tripartite mirror. The earlier agents serve as models; the later ones act as reflections; while the main characters of the central panel, compared and contrasted with the others, gain in stature. One figure throws light on the other, thus deepening and developing the portrayal and controlling the interpretation of the characters and their actions.

One of the most interesting examples of such threefold comparison of agents is contained in a repeated series of pairs of brothers whose dispositions and temperaments are opposite. Early in the saga (v, 8-9) a contrast is drawn between Unn's brothers Helgi Bjólan and Bjorn the Eastman by pointing out how differently they receive their sister. Helgi invites her with only half her company and consequently is called small and stingy (*lítilmenni*); Bjorn, on the other hand, invites her with all her following and entertains her generously (*it stórmannligsta*) and she thanks him for his *stórmennska*.[12] So, too, the sons of Hoskuld, Thorleik and Bárd, are of different temperament and therefore stand in contrasting relationship with each other and with their father:

> Þorleikr var *mikill maðr ok sterkr ok inn sýniligsti, fálátr ok óþýðr*; þótti mǫnnum sá svipr á um hans skaplyndi, sem hann myndi verða *engi jafnaðarmaðr*. Hǫskuldr sagði þat jafnan, at hann myndi *mjǫk líkjask í ætt þeira Strandamanna*. Bárðr Hǫskuldsson var ok *skǫruligr maðr sýnum* ok vel viti borinn *ok sterkr*; þat bragð hafði hann á sér, *sem hann myndi líkari verða fǫðurfrændum sínum*. Bárðr var hœgr maðr í uppvexti sínum ok *vinsæll maðr*; Hǫskuldr unni honum mest allra barna sinna[13] (ix, 18: Thorleik was a big man and strong and very handsome, but close-mouthed and unfriendly. From his disposition most people thought he would be unfair in his dealings. Hoskuld often remarked that Thorleik would likely take very much after the side of the family up at the Strands [his mother's kin]. Hoskuld's other son Bárd was also a fine looking man, strong and intelligent. From his manner it looked as though he would favor his father's kinsmen. He was a good-natured person and popular as he grew up. Of all his children Hoskuld loved Bárd the most).

The comparison of the two brothers presents them as having some features in common: good looks and physical prowess (*inn sýniligsti/ skǫruligr maðr sýnum* and *sterkr*), but there the likeness ends. Their opposition, the one unfriendly and unfair, the other good-natured and popular, is also reflected in the contrastive statements that they take after the two different sides of the house. Thorleik, the least likeable, takes after his mother's side (an oblique criticism of Jórunn) and the good son after his father's side. It is thus natural that Hoskuld favors Bárd.

When the brothers are next mentioned, their personalities conform to our expectations:

> Þorleikr var engi dældarmaðr ok inn mesti garpr...Bárðr, sonr Hǫskulds, var heima með feðr sínum; hafði hann þá umsýslu ekki minnr en Hǫskuldr (xx, 49: Thorleik was no easy man to deal with and very bold....Hoskuld's son Bárd was at home with his father and took no less charge of things than Hoskuld).

It is not surprising that their half-brother, Óláf Peacock, is more attracted to Bárd. Before Óláf's journey to Ireland, Bárd helps Óláf arrange a marriage for his mother Melkorka, and after his return Óláf is welcomed by all his relatives, but he and Bárd felt closest to one another: "Þó var flest um með þeim Bárði" (xxii, 61).

Since in this way the contrast between the brothers has been played up, that Thorleik and Bárd react differently to Hoskuld's wishes regarding Óláf's paternal inheritance,[14] Bárd siding with Hoskuld, comes as foreseeable:

> Bárðr svarar fyrri ok sagði, at hann myndi þetta gera, eptir því sem faðir hans vildi....Þá mælti Þorleikr: "Fjarri er þat mínum vilja, at Óláfr sé arfgengr gǫrr" (xxvi, 72: Bárd answered first and said he would follow his father's wishes....Then Thorleik spoke up: "It is far from my wish that Óláf be made heir").

Hoskuld gives Óláf the twelve ounces allowed an illegitimate son, but in gold instead of in silver as prescribed by law. Again Bárd is agreeable and Thorleik disgruntled: "[Þorleiki] gazk illa at þessu, ok þótti Hǫskuldr hafa haft undirmál við sik....Bárðr kvazk vilja samþykkja ráði fǫður síns" (ibid.: "Thorleik was ill-content with this and thought Hoskuld had dealt underhandedly with him....Bárd said he would comply with his father's wishes"). And after Hoskuld's death the personalities of Thorleik and Bárd are again explicitly juxtaposed in the settlement of the property:

> Þeir Þorleikr ok Bárðr skipta fé með sér; hlýtr Bárðr fǫðurleifð þeira, því at til þess heldu fleiri menn, því at hann var vinsælli. Þorleikr hlaut meir lausafé (xxvi, 73: Thorleik and Bárd divided their father's property between them. Bárd got the estate and lands, for most people favored this because Bárd was the more popular of the two. Thorleik got more of the chattels).

The examples cited of misunderstandings between brothers or half brothers[15] prepare for the next generation and for the central theme of Kjartan and

75

his foster brother Bolli Thorleiksson. As the theme unfolds, some of the personality traits possessed by Thorleik and Bárd, the one ill-content and disgruntled, the other pleasant, amiable, and popular, are somewhat reechoed respectively in Bolli and Kjartan. Meaningful variation on the other hand sets these latter brothers apart from the pattern: in the beginning they are very fond of each other and are by no means opposites. Thorleik and Bárd, though inimical, too, we noted, had some points in common. Aside from their physical likeness and despite their temperamental differences, each, it is said, will be deemed an honorable man. Again lexical parallelism points this out. Of Bárd it is reported: "[Hann] hafði ok verit farmaðr ok var *vel metinn, hvar sem hann kom*" (xxv, 70: "He too had been a traveling merchant and was well esteemed wherever he went"). Some time later when it behooves Thorleik to leave Iceland because of friction with Hrút, Óláf convinces him by saying: "'muntu þar þykkja *sómamaðr, sem þú kemr*'" (xxxviii, 110: "'You will be thought a man of honor wherever you go'"). The similarity is carried despite the varying circumstances under which the judgment is passed. Part of the subtlety of the text lies in the fact that the lexical parallelisms imply rather than state similarities and that they themselves are somewhat camouflaged, imbedded as they are in entirely different contexts. With Kjartan and Bolli the procedure is reversed: their differences are more subtlely hinted, their likenesses and their fondness for one another explicitly expressed.[16] That Kjartan and Bolli loved one another most among all the brothers (xxxix, 112: "Þeir Kjartan ok Bolli *unnusk mest*") is several times underscored and confirmed: "Svá var *ástúðigt* með þeim fóstbrœðrum, at hvárrgi þóttisk nýta mega, at þeir væri eigi ásamt" (xl, 114: "So fond were the foster brothers of one another that neither seemed to be able to enjoy anything if the other was not along") and "'Þú hefir engum manni *jafnmikit unnt* sem Bolla, fóstbróður þínum'" (xliv, 134: "'You have loved no one as much as your foster brother Bolli'"). Establishment of such togetherness makes the final rift all the deeper. The love and friendship they originally had for one another was not enough to prevent Bolli from sensing his subordinate position.[17] Even snatching the bride did not bolster his ego: he was filled with remorse, torn by inner conflict, while Kjartan continued to flaunt his superiority on every hand.

The relationship between Kjartan and Bolli is further highlighted by another pair of opposing brothers in the third and concluding section of the saga. At the same time, interesting facts regarding the structured form of the saga are revealed. Gudrún's sons by her marriage with Bolli Thorleiksson, Thorleik and Bolli Bollason, resemble Thorleik and Bárd Hoskuldsson. As we have seen, Hoskuld loved Bárd the most and Bárd always sided with his father. In the present example Gudrún loves Bolli Bollason best, and he always sympathizes with and supports his mother. When Thorgils is cheated out of marriage with Gudrún, for example, the brothers take opposite sides: "*Þorleiki líkar illa*, er svá var hagat, at Þorgísli var eigi geð á, en *Bolli sampykkisk hér um vilja móður sinnar*" (lxv, 195: "Thorleik was displeased that things had not turned out to Thorgils' liking, but Bolli took his mother's part"). So, too, when Thorkel proposes marriage, Bolli agrees with his mother: "'Móðir mín mun þetta glǫggvast sjá kunna; *vil ek hér um hennar vilja sampykkja*'" (lxviii, 201: "'My mother is no doubt best judge of this, and I am willing to go along with whatever she wishes'"). After Thorkel and Gudrún are married, Gudrún's particular fondness for Bolli is remarked upon: "*Guðrún unni Bolla mest allra barna sinna*" (lxx, 204: "Of all her children Gudrún loved Bolli most"). And when Bolli requests a marriage suit be undertaken on his behalf, Gudrún herself confirms this favoritism and what the audience has seen all along:

> "Þat er skjótt at segja, Þorkell, at ek vil til þessa láta engan hlut spara, at Bolli fái þann ráðakost, sem honum líkar; er þat bæði, at *ek ann honum mest*, enda hefir hann øruggastr verit í því minna barna, *at gera at mínum vilja*" (lxx, 206: "I will say at once, Thorkel, that I'll leave nothing undone so that Bolli gets the marriage match he wants, and that is for two reasons: I love him the most, and he has always been that one of my children who could be relied upon to do my will").

Echoes of Hoskuld's relationship with his two sons and of their respective reactions over the inheritance are unmistakable.

Thorleik and Bolli Bollason, however, also stand in comparable correspondence with the foster brothers Bolli Thorleiksson and Kjartan Óláfsson, and in that order. Bolli Bollason is a second Kjartan, whereas Thorleik Bollason, like Bolli Thorleiksson, plays the secondary role. The two Thorleiks are similar in character and actions, and although the roles of the two Bollis are reversed, they too show some similarities.[18] The following chart lines up the pairs of unlike brothers horizontally, their like counterparts vertically:

Part I:
Preparation   Thorleik Hoskuldsson . . . . Bárd Hoskuldsson
Part II:
Central Theme   Bolli Thorleiksson . . . . . . Kjartan Óláfsson
Part III:
Recapitulation   Thorleik Bollason . . . . . . Bolli Bollason

The opposing natures of the two Bollasons are carried further. When Thorleik Bollason asks for permission to go abroad, he is modest in his demands: "Þorleikr kvazk *ekki mundu hafa mikit fé,* — 'því at ósýnt er, hversu mér gætisk til; em ek ungr ok í mǫrgu óráðinn'" (lxx, 205: "Thorleik said he did not want to have a lot of money along — 'for it is uncertain how well I can manage, young and inexperienced as I am in many things'"). His brother, on the other hand, is self-assured and demanding when he sets out: "Bolli játar því, *at hafa fé mikit,* — 'vil ek,' segir hann, 'engis manns miskunnarmaðr vera, hvárki hér né útanlendis'" (lxxii, 211: "Bolli accepted this and said he wanted to have a lot of money along, — 'I don't want to have to accept anyone's charity, either here or abroad,' he said"). But Thorleik B. and Bolli B. are also not wholly opposite. Just as Thorleik and Bárd Hoskuldsson shared some points, so too the Bollasons exhibit a likeness in that they both have the same reason for wanting to go abroad. When Thorkel hears of Thorleik's plans, he comments: "'Þykki mér þetta *in mesta várkunn, at þik fýsi at kanna siðu annarra manna*'" (lxx, 205: "'It seems most understandable to me that you desire to learn about the ways of other men'"). And when Bolli informs Snorri that he wishes to go abroad, Snorri says: "'Oss þykkir *mikit í hættu, hversu þér teksk*'" (lxxii, 211: "'Much lies at stake in how things turn out for you'"), to which Bolli replies: "'Þykkir maðr við þat fávíss verða, *ef hann kannar ekki viðara en hér Ísland*'" (*ibid.*: "'A man is considered ignorant if he hasn't knowledge of anything farther than Iceland'"). The variation on the same idea is refreshing and witty. But in this regard the two Bollasons have had a precedent set by Kjartan. When Kjartan told Thorstein of his plans to go abroad, Thorstein commended him, saying:

> "Er þat *várkunn mikil,* frændi,...*at þik fýsi at kanna annarra manna siðu*; mun þín ferð verða merkilig með nǫkkuru móti. Eigu frændr þínir *mikit í hættu, hversu þér teksk* ferðin" (xl, 114: "It is quite understandable, kinsman,...that you desire to learn about the ways of other men. Your journey is sure to be remarkable in some way. Your kinsmen have much at stake in how this journey will turn out for you").

Here then is a point of contact between all three, Kjartan and the two Bollasons. The *mikit í hættu* clause is applied only to Kjartan and Bolli B., strengthening the bond there, as might be expected.

In his displeasure over his mother's deception regarding the marriage suit with Thorgils, Thorleik Bollason resembles Thorleik Hoskuldsson, who was disgruntled over his father's deception regarding the inheritance. In his retiring attitude and secondary position Thorleik Bollason corresponds to Bolli Thorleiksson. And Bolli Bollason, always agreeing with his mother and her favorite, is like Bárd Hoskuldsson, but in his pomposity has also something of Kjartan Óláfsson. At one point in the story, the author, as if with a flashback, brings the two Thorleiks again into relationship. When Thorleik Bollason makes his decision to go abroad, Thorkel tells him: "'Þú þykkir vaskr maðr, hvar sem þú kemr'" (lxx, 205: "'You will be thought a man of valor wherever you go'"), just as Óláf once had told Thorleik Hoskuldsson as he set out for abroad. This attribute then is a point of overlap between the two Hoskuldssons and Thorleik Bollason. Thus we see how none of the three pairs is really wholly opposite, how the mixing and matching of attributive elements blurs clear-cut black and white comparison but without destroying the basic pattern. In this way stereotypes are avoided even though stereotyped elements are used, and each character in the sets of inimical brothers is the more effectively illuminated through the tripartite reflection.

Bolli Thorleiksson remains still the most inscrutable, like his silence. And his similarity to Kjartan, stronger than the similarities that exist between the Hoskuldssons or between the Bollasons, only makes the contrast more complex. He would seem to be the sweeter and gentler nature compared with Kjartan, always complying with Kjartan's wishes, more like Bárd and Bolli Bollason, initially, than like the two Thorleiks. But his negativeness fits in with the Thorleiks, for Bolli's compliance takes a different turn, producing rancor and envy. And yet some sort of shift in character seems also to take place in the Bollason pair of brothers. From his agreeableness in doing his mother's will, Bolli Bollason would seem to be the meeker of the two brothers. It is rather surprising to find him so cocky and demanding in his requests upon going abroad, while Thorleik is mild and reasonable. This switch no doubt has something to do with the role that Bolli Bollason now takes up as a second Kjartan.

Even as Hoskuld loved Bárd, and Gudrún loved Bolli Bollason the most, so, too, Óláf's favorite was Kjartan.[19] In his day Óláf represented the pride and brilliance of the family and was "foremost of the brothers": "Var þat brátt auðdsætt, at Óláfr myndi *mjǫk vera fyrir þeim brœðrum*" (xxvi, 73). In the next generation the same is said of Kjartan: "Kjartan var *mjǫk fyrir sonum Óláfs*" (xxxix, 112). And in the next, Bolli Bollason is singled out as foremost: "Váru þeir brœðr miklir menn ok inir knáligstu, ok *hafði Bolli allt fyrir*" (lxx, 204: "These brothers were big men and most stalwart, but Bolli was the foremost in everything"). While in Norway, Kjartan was first in importance and made all the decisions: "Íslendingar váru allir saman um vetrinn í bœnum; *var Kjartan mjǫk fyrir þeim*" (xl, 118: "All the Icelenders stayed together in the town during the winter; and Kjartan took the lead among them"). When Kjartan decides to be baptized a Christian, he assumes that the others will follow suit, and Bolli confirms Kjartan's assumption: "Bolli tók vel undir þetta ok *bað Kjartan einn ráða þeira máli*" (xl, 122: "Bolli fell in with this and said Kjartan alone was to decide their case"). When Bolli Bollason is at the court, he behaves in much the same manner as had Kjartan: "Brátt fannsk þat, at Bolli myndi vera maðr framgjarn ok *vildi vera fyrir ǫðrum mǫnnum*" (lxxiii, 212: "It soon became apparent that Bolli was eager to push himself forward and wanted to be leader"). He and his men have fine weapons and clothes, just as Kjartan had had before him, and when decisions are made, Bolli has his way. Thorleik would like to continue with their journey down to Vík (Oslo fjord), but Bolli prefers to stay in Trondheim: "'Vil ek hér sitja vetrlangt í bœnum....' *Bolli ræðr þessu*" (*ibid.*: "'I want to stay right here in town over the winter....' And Bolli had his way"). When Bolli and Thorleik decide to part company, Thorleik says: "'En þú, Bolli, *munt þessu ráða sem ǫðru*'" (lxxiii, 213: "'And you, Bolli, will have your way in this as in other things'"). The verbally similar statements singled out here, those applying to Kjartan and Bolli Bollason, render the one the like counterpart of the other. The comparisons, we might note, go by pairs, but also link onto one another as a chain reaction from generation to generation. Furthermore, the subordinate position of Thorleik over against his brother Bolli Bollason becomes evident and is presented in much the same tone of resentment as was seen in Bolli Thorleiksson's rejoinders to Kjartan.

There is another point of coincidence. First the Norwegian king is described as honoring Thorleik Bollason: "Er hann með konungi um vetrinn ok gerðisk hirðmaðr hans; *virði konungr hann vel*. *Þótti* Þorleikr *inn vaskasti maðr*" (lxx, 205: "He stayed with the king over the winter and became a member of his guard, and the king esteemed him well. Thorleik was deemed a man most valiant"). But when his brother Bolli appears at the court, Thorleik falls to second place in the king's esteem: "Er konungr *vel* til Þorleiks *sem fyrr, en þó mat hann Bolla miklu meira*, því at konungi þótti hann *mikit afbragð annarra manna*" (lxxiii, 213: "The king treated Thorleik just as well as before, but all the same he esteemed Bolli much more, for in his opinion Bolli was a paragon among men"). Application of the lesser *vel* is again unmistakable (and the *vel sem fyrr* confirms it), for the episode conspicuously suggests comparison with the descriptions of the respective positions Bolli Thorleiksson and Kjartan enjoyed at the court in Norway. There, it will be remembered, Bolli Thorleiksson, in contrast to Kjartan who was *"metinn þar umfram alla menn,"* is deemed *"inn vaskasti maðr ok metinn vel af góðum mǫnnum"* (xl, 123).[20] The fact that *vel* is used in both places and in proximity to the designation *inn vaskasti maðr* leaves no doubt that the author wished to draw the comparison between Bolli Thorleiksson and Thorleik Bollason. Coincidentally, the chiasmus in the names plays neatly and hand in hand with the similarities and differences the author has arranged. The statement that Thorleik Bollason was thought *inn vaskasti maðr* also more than [note the superlative] confirms Thorkel's surmise that he would be thought a *vaskr maðr* wherever he went. The parallel between Kjartan's and Bolli's superior positions is retained by substituting merely one formulaic superlative for another: the *mikit afbragð annarra manna* for the *umfram alla menn*. Thus we see from how many aspects the examples might be considered; associative links and overlappings abound. It would seem that the author is deliberately playing with his units.

The similarities between Kjartan and Bolli Bollason are carried somewhat further, since, in addition, the phrase *mikit afbragð annarra manna* is also once applied to Kjartan (xlv, 136). And both Kjartan and Bolli Bollason are *kurteisligr* (courtly, chivalrous) and take great pride in finery and display upon their respective returns to Iceland. Bolli's pomp at home parallels, if it does not outdo, Kjartan's with his fine weapons, clothes, and *kurteisi*.[21]

In view of the many parallels that have been set up between Kjartan and Bolli Bollason, one might consider one other instance where an echo seems intended. Hrefna says to Kjartan: "'Þat munu menn ætla, at *þú munir eigi kvángask vilja bráðendis*, en geta þá konu, er þú biðr'" (xliv, 133: "'People no doubt expect that you will not want to marry soon, but will get the woman you ask'"). Bolli Bollason, who has just one marriage match in mind, makes a similar statement: "'Kona heitir Þórdís, hon er dóttir Snorra goða; hon er svá kvenna, at mér er mest um at eiga, ok *ekki mun ek kvángask í bráð, ef ek nái eigi þessu ráði*'" (lxx, 205: "'There is a woman by the name of Thórdís, the daughter of Snorri Godi, and she is the one I would most like to have. If I don't get this match, I'll not want to marry soon'"). The latter statement might be said to control the interpretation of the former, for Kjartan, in contrast, did not get the woman he most wanted to have, and thus will not want to marry soon.[22]

The similarity between the two pairs of brothers, Kjartan—Bolli Th. and Bolli Bollason—Thorleik B., is striking, and the chiasmal transference of personality traits enhances the structural significance of the comparison. Through a kind of poetic justice, Bolli Bollason's prowess and gallantry redeem his father's weakness and belatedly compensate for the first Bolli's subordinate position over against Kjartan. Seen in this light, the carefully developed role of Bolli B. becomes clear: the formal structure of the saga is designed in the first place to establish a balance. Each segment, each character must have a counterpart, and Kjartan no less so. Bolli B. functions as a counterpart in a double sense, matching (even outmatching) Kjartan and complementing Bolli Thorleiksson in reverse. Some critics have implied that his magnificence at the end of the saga is contrived and possibly the work of a second compositor who, for family reasons, glorified the lineage.[23] But the saga pictures poetic coherency, not historical probabilities.[24] Bolli Bollason's brilliance accords, in the second place, with the progressive enhancement of the generations — Hoskuld, Óláf, Kjartan, Bolli B. — and must therefore outshine Kjartan's. His position is integral to the form and structure of the saga, serving as he does in this two-fold capacity, and so entirely of stylistic concern.

Comparison of characters and relationships between characters is not limited merely to pairs of brothers, for verbal similarities frequently mark striking parallelisms between many of the agents. Vigdís and Gudrún have already been brought together for comparison through the similarity of their divorces.[25] They are again implicitly juxtaposed in the episodes concerned with the sheltering of the outlaws Thórólf and Gunnar Thidandrabani, respectively. The Thidrandabani episode in Part III of the saga echoes Thórólf's situation in Part I. In the latter Vigdís acts as model or preparatory figure for Gudrún in the former. Thus similarity of agents and circumstances obtains. Of Thórólf we are told: "Þórólfr fekk sér fluting inn til meginlands. Hann ferr *mjǫk hulðu hǫfði*" (xiv, 30: "Thórólf got himself ferried over to the mainland and moved on, keeping under cover"). Gunnar Thidandrabani also "traveled under cover, for many powerful men were following up the prosecution" (lxix, 202: "*Fór hann mjǫk hulðu hǫfði, því at margir stórir menn veittu þar eptirsjár*"). And the reason given for Gunnar's so doing echoes Vigdís' reckoning of the danger inherent in giving Thórólf protection:

> "En þó sýnisk mér svá, sem þeir menn muni veðsetja bæði sik ok fé sitt, er þér veita ásjá, *svá stórir menn sem hér munu veita eptirsjár*" (xiv, 31: "But still it seems to me that anyone who helps you out will be risking both life and property, seeing what powerful men are bound to take up the prosecution of this case").

That Thorgils Holluson and Thorkel Eyjólfsson are from the very first presented as rival figures has already been noted.[26] In the discussions of plans for Gudrún's fourth marriage, the two are again set up one against the other by means of similar grammatical and lexical configurations. When approached by Gudrún for the second time about vengeance for Bolli, Thorgils gives this reply: "*'En allt er mér þat samt í hug ok fyrr, þá vit hǫfum þetta átt at tala'*" (lx, 180: "'I'm of the same mind as before when we talked this over'"). And Thorkel for his part, when marriage with Gudrún is broached for the second time by Snorri, has a like answer: "*'Ok allt er mér slíkt it sama nú í hug, sem þá rœddu vit'*" (lxviii, 199-200). Somewhat more subtle is the comparison implicit in Gudrún's picking up the phrase "*'þá vex mér ekki í augu'*" used by Thorgils (lx, 180) when he was boasting that if he got to marry her he would "not blench at anything." To show that she has the upper hand, Gudrún overrides Thorkel, reiterating Thorgils' boast: "*'Vex mér ekki þat fyrir augum*, at hafa hér kostnað fyrir'" (lxviii, 201: "'I won't blench at having to stand the cost'").

The similarity of the passages in which first Thorgils and then Thorkel in company with Snorri ride out to Helgafell likewise places these contenders in parallel roles:

Of Thorgils:

Þorgils Hǫlluson *ríðr út til Helgafells*, ok með honum synir Guðrúnar ok fóstbrœðr hans, Halldórr ok Ǫrnólfr; þeir kómu síðla um kveldit til Helgafells, svá at allir menn váru í rekkjum. Guðrún ríss upp ok bað menn upp standa ok *vinna þeim beina.* ...*Eptir þat er þeim beini veittr*, ok er þeir váru mettir, var þeim fylgt til rekkna; *sofa þeir af nóttina. Um daginn eptir gengr Þorgils til tals við Guðrúnu ok mælti:* "*Svá er háttat*, sem þú veizt..." (lxv, 194-195: Thorgils Holluson rode out to Helgafell and with him Gudrún's sons and his foster brothers Halldór and Ornólf. They arrived at Helgafell rather late at night, after all were in bed. Gudrún got up and told her people to get up and wait upon the guests.... After that they were served with meat and drink, and when they had had their fill, they were shown to their beds. They slept through the night. Next morning Thorgils went to have a talk with Gudrún and said: "Matters so stand, as you know...").

And of Thorkel:

Snorri var at skipi nǫkkurar nætr; síðan tóku þeir teinært, er flaut við kaupskipit, ok bjuggusk til ferðar, hálfr þriði tøgr manna; *þeir fóru til Helgafells.* Guðrún tók við Snorra ágæta vel; *var þeim veittr allgóðr beini.* Ok er þeir hǫfðu verit þar eina nótt, þá kallar *Snorri til tals við sik Guðrúnu ok mælti:* "*Svá er mál með vexti...*" (lxviii, 200: Snorri stayed at [Thorkel's] ship some nights. Then they took a ten-oared boat which was afloat there beside the merchant vessel and set out, twenty-five of them. They went to Helgafell. Gudrún made Snorri most welcome, and they were served with the best meat and drink. After they had been there one night, Snorri asked to have a talk with Gudrún and said: "This is the way matters stand...").

Whereas Thorgils rides away from Helgafell dissatisfied, Thorkel through Snorri's intercession gets the bride. The more lavish welcome of Thorkel can be detected in the *ágæta vel* and the *allgóðr beini*, whereas Thorgils arrival was inauspicious. Through like linguistic pattern and like situation the meaningful variation and contrast become apparent.

So, too, accounts of the relationship between Melkorka and Thorbjorn Skrjúp and that of Gudrún and Thorgils exhibit elements conspicuously similar. The first, it should be noted, functions as model for the second. Both episodes begin in much the same way. When Melkorka was living alone on the farm, Thorbjorn paid her much attention:

> Þorbjǫrn skrjúpr hafði mest veitt *umsjá um bú* Melkorku; vakit hafði hann bónorð við hana, þá er hon hafði skamma stund búit, en Melkorka *tók því fjarri* (xx, 50: Thorbjorn Skrjúp had given Melkorka the most assistance with her farm; he had made her an offer of marriage when she had been living there only a short time, but Melkorka had coolly refused).

When she wants Óláf to go abroad to claim his royal kinship, however, she is willing to use Thorbjorn's offer to gain her end. So she tells Óláf:

> "Þá mun ek heldr þat til vinna, at giptask Þorbirni, ef þú ræzk þá til ferðar heldr en áðr; því at ek ætla, að [*sic*] hann leggi fram vǫruna, svá sem þú kannt þer þǫrf til, *ef hann nái ráðahag við mik*" (*ibid.*: "I would rather go to the length of marrying Thorbjorn, if that would make you more inclined to this journey than before, for I imagine he will hand over to you as many wares as you think you need, if he gets to marry me").

When Óláf brings the matter up with Thorbjorn, he replies as expected: "'Þat mun því at eins, *nema ek ná ráðahag við Melkorku*'" (*ibid.*: "'On one condition only will I do it, and that is if I get to marry Melkorka'").

Similarly when the widowed Gudrún was living alone, we are told:

> Þorgils gaf sér mart til ørenda út í sveitina; hann kom jafnan til Helgafells ok *bauð sik til umsýslu* með Guðrunu. Hon *tók á því* vel at eins ok *lítit af ǫllu* (lvii, 170-171: Thorgils found all sorts of excuses for errands out to the district and was always coming to Helgafell and offering his help to Gudrún. She took this in good part on the one hand but on the whole committed herself neither one way nor the other).

When the matter of avenging Bolli's death is brought up, Gudrún informs Snorri that Thorgils will do it on one condition:

"Rœtt hefi ek þetta áðr við Þorgils, ok er, sem því sé lokit, því at hann gerði þann einn kost á, er ek vilda ekki á líta; en ekki fór Þorgils undan at hefna Bolla, *ef hann næði ráðahag við mik*" (lix, 178: "I have discussed this with Thorgils before, but that seems to be the end of it, for he stipulated that one thing which I didn't care to consider: he agreed to avenge Bolli if he got to marry me").

When Thorgils is approached a second time concerning the matter of the raid, he gives the expected answer: " 'En allt er mér *þat sama í hug ok fyrr, þá er vit hǫfum þetta átt at tala; ef ek nái ráðahag við þik...*' " (lx, 180: " 'I'm of the same mind as before when we talked this over; if I get to marry you...' ").

The resemblance between the two parallel relationships is obvious. Furthermore, both turn on deception through which each of the women accomplishes her objective.[27] By marrying Thorbjorn and securing Óláf's journey abroad, Melkorka tricks Hoskuld; by beguiling Thorgils by means of a subterfuge, Gudrún makes certain the avenging of Bolli. The word-trick by which Gudrún dupes Thorgils into believing she will marry him has already been discussed, as well as the *ráðahag* repetition,[28] which appears again in the Thorbjorn-Melkorka example. In both instances of its occurrence it functions as a statement-confirmation pair.

As has been noted in discussing pairs of brothers, likenesses frequently exist among members of a family, and resemblances both of character and event often span generations. Repetition so controls the associations that one generation would seem to set a pattern or precedent for the next. So, for example, Hoskuld's journey to Norway is prefaced with the statement: "[Hǫskuldr] *lýsir því, at hann ætlar útan, en Jórunn varðveitir bú hans ok bǫrn*" (xi, 22: "Hoskuld announced that he was going abroad, and Jórunn looked after the farm and children"). A similar statement marks a similar happening in the next generation: "*Þat er sagt eitt vár, at Óláfr lýsti því fyrir Þorgerði, at hann ætlar útan, — 'vil ek, at þú varðveitir bú okkart ok bǫrn'* " (xxix, 77: "One spring Óláf announced to Thorgerd that he was going abroad, — 'and I want you to look after the farmstead and children' "). Careful reading reveals more than a surface likeness and shows Hoskuld to be a preparatory figure for his son Óláf.[29] Kjartan, too, in his turn is an image of his father Óláf. Many details, some of which have already been remarked upon, point up the likenesses between father and son. When he is busy marrying off his mother in order to get means to go abroad, Óláf says he cannot accompany his father to the Thing "because of things to attend to on the farm": "kvazk þat *eigi mega fyrir búsýslu*" (xx, 51). Kjartan uses the same pretext when he declines to go to the party at Laugar: "Kjartan kvazk *mundu heima vera at gæta bús*" (xliv, 134: "Kjartan said he would stay at home to take care of the farm"). Father and son show similar feelings regarding the marriage of Bolli and Gudrún. Óláf is reluctant to take part in the wedding feast: "Bolli bauð Óláfi, frænda sínum, en Óláfr var *þess ekki fljótr ok fór þó at bæn Bolla*" (xliii, 130: "Bolli invited his kinsman Óláf; Óláf was not eager to go but went nonetheless after Bolli's pleading"). After Kjartan has found out about the marriage, he is disinclined to go to Laugar but like his father is persuaded: "Kjartan var *trauðr til ok hét þó ferðinni at bæn fǫður síns*" (xlvi, 142: "Kjartan held back, but nonetheless promised to go after his father's pleading").

Furthermore, the modeling of Bolli Bollason upon Kjartan, already noted, carries the intra-family resemblances into the fourth generation. Both Óláf and Kjartan are something of dandies in their fondness for fine clothes and weapons, and Bolli Bollason carries the ostentation onward. The descriptions of these three heroes (xxi, 55; xliv, 134-135; and lxxvii, 225, respectively) bear striking resemblance, not surprising since Óláf is the model for Kjartan, and Bolli Bollason a second Kjartan. Both Óláf and Kjartan receive a sword as a *konungsnautr* (Óláf, xxi, 59 and xxiv, 69; Kjartan, xliii, 131-132 and xliv, 134) and clothing cut from scarlet (Óláf, xxii, 60 and xxiii, 64; Kjartan, xli, 124 and xliv, 134). The account of Bolli Bollason adds embellishment to the theme since he is described as wearing clothes of scarlet and velvet after his return from Miklagard (Constantinople), where he had received the velvet garments from the king (lxxvii, 225). Óláf, Kjartan, and Bolli Bollason are all asked by the king to remain in Norway at the court, and on departing each is sent off with high praise (xxii, 60; xlii, 130; lxxiii, 213-214, respectively). Upon returning to Iceland, each decks himself out in his finery (xxiii, 64; xliv, 134; lxxvii, 225, respectively).[30]

With so much patent setting up of likenesses between characters, it is not surprising that the author also juxtaposes the main protagonists Kjartan and Gudrún and uses Repetition and marking of their superior qualities to underscore their affinity. From the beginning, for example, it is made clear that both surpass all others in Iceland. Kjartan is described as the "handsomest of all men ever to have been born in Iceland" (xxviii, 76: "Hann var *allra manna fríðastr, þeira er fœzk hafa á Íslandi*"). And Gudrún is said to be "the fairest of all women born and raised in Iceland" (xxxii, 86: "Hon var *kvenna vænst, er upp óxu á Íslandi*"). The recurrent formulas *allra manna friðastr* and *kvenna vænst* carry special advantage in combination with the *fœzk hafa á Íslandi* and *upp óxu á Íslandi* phrases which appear only in connection with these two persons. Furthermore, both Kjartan and Gudrún bear the distinction of being "first" to introduce some of the Christian customs:

> Kjartan fastaði þurrt langafǫstu ok gerði þat at engis manns dœmum hér á landi, því at þat er sǫgn manna, at *hann hafi fyrstr manna fastat þurrt hér innanlands* (xlv, 138: Kjarftan kept the dry fast during Lent; and thus did what no man had ever done before him in this country; for people say he was the first man here in this land to have so fasted).
>
> Guðrún gerðisk trúkona mikil. *Hon nam fyrst kvenna saltara á Íslandi* (lxxvi, 223: Gudrún became a women of great piety. She was the first woman in Iceland to learn the Psalter).
>
> *Hon var fyrst nunna á Íslandi ok einsetukona* (lxxviii, 228: She was the first nun and hermitess in Iceland).

In addition, both Kjartan and Gudrún have the superlative distinction of possessing *kurteisi*.[31]

Kjartan's and Gudrún's equality, however, is not only established through these superlatives. The author explicitly draws a comparison between them, linking it, by the way, with the [*fœzk hafa*] *upp óxu á Íslandi* idea unique to them. So we are told: "Þat var allra manna mál, at með þeim Kjartani ok Guðrúnu þœtti *vera mest jafnræði þeira manna, er þá óxu upp*" (xxxix, 112: "It was common talk that Kjartan and Gudrún seemed to be the most equally matched of all the young people then growing up"). In this connection it is interesting that repetition of the word *jafnræði*, turned negatively, neatly gives a clue to Hrefna's position in the saga and to her relationship with Kjartan: "'Þœtti oss þat ráðligast, at þú kvángaðisk, eptir því sem þú mæltir í fyrra sumar, þótt þér sé *eigi* þar með ǫllu *jafnræði*, sem Hrefna er'" (xlv, 137: "'We feel the most advisable thing for you to do is to take a wife as you said you would last summer, even if Hrefna isn't an equal match for you in every respect'"). Again setting Kjartan and Gudrún up for equal comparison, the author employs the same idiom to describe their suppressed feelings for one another: "því at þat ætluðu flestir menn, at *henni væri enn mikil eftirsjá* [sic] *at um Kjartan, þó at hon hylði yfir*" (xliv, 134: "For most people suspected that she still pined greatly for Kjartan, even though she covered it up"). In this regard Thuríd says to Kjartan: "'Þat er mér sagt, frændi, at þú sér heldr hljóðr vetrlangt; tala menn þat, at *þér muni vera eptirsjá at um Guðrúnu*'" (xlv, 137: "'I've been told, kinsman, that you have been rather glum all winter; and talk has it that you probably are still pining after Gudrún'").

Consideration of how repetition of the same or similar linguistic patterns serves to signal comparable situations or characteristics demonstrates the skill with which the author has used this third structural and formal element to promote unity of composition. By reinforcing, or even at times making first apparent, through the means of this device what is being discursively expressed, he has created a structured whole in which the concepts of matching or compensating underpin the composition.

The compensatory idea behind Comparison finds expression in formal aspects of the saga other than verbal reechoings that compare and contrast characters and events. A preponderance of bargainings, the consistent appearance of grammatical correlatives and balanced syntactical constructions, the preference for the category of words representing evens and odds mirror in themselves the structural idea of the whole. And their meaningfulness within the saga is controlled by this whole, apart from any use they might have outside the saga. The bargaining process, the *kaup*, introduced in detail at the beginning of Chapter II, in particular aptly typifies the idea of comparing and balancing. It is therefore not surprising that bargainings of various kinds occur frequently throughout the saga. When, for example, Hoskuld buys the bondwoman Melkorka, the scales are brought out and the purse weighed against the price set for the concubine (xii, 24). Again, Ingjald makes a bargain with Thórd to hand over the outlaw Thórólf (xiv, 32); Vigdís makes a bargain with Ásgaut (xv, 33); Óláf bargains for the land at Hrappsstadir (xxiv, 67); Kotkel bargains with Thorleik (xxxvi, 101); Hrút tries to bargain with Eldgrím to dissuade him from stealing Thorleik's studhorses (xxxvii, 104); Bolli and Thórarin come to an agreement over the Tunga lands (xlvii, 146); and Snorri and Gudrún give and take in their agreement to exchange property (lvi, 170). Gudrún's underhanded bargain with Thorgils (lxv, 195), Óláf's bargaining with the servant girl in order to capture Stígandi (xxxviii, 109), and Thorstein's attempt to bargain with Halldór for the Hjardarholt lands (lxxv, 218) have already been discussed.

Frequently something is thrown into the bargain to even the trade. So when Eldgrím tries to bargain with Thorleik for the studhorses, he says: "'ek býð þér *jafnmǫrg* stóðhross við ok *meðalauka nǫkkurn*'" (xxxvii, 103: "'I'll offer you equally many studhorses in return and something more into the bargain'"). And Thorstein in trying to bargain with Halldór for the Hjardarholt lands declares: "'Mun ek gefa þér í móti þá staðfestu, at sœmilig sé, ok *þar í milli*, sem vit verðum á sáttir'" (lxxv, 219: "'In exchange I will give you property which would be reasonable and fair, and into the bargain whatever we can come to an agreement on'"). Thus we see that the natural course of bargaining with its concept of evening sides is turned to effective, formal function within the artistic whole.

Again here a negative side makes itself apparent in that frequently bargainings and arguments end in an impasse. An idiom effectively repeated signals these deadlocks: "*ok þótti sinn veg hvárum*" (xiv, 29: "And each would see it only his way.")[32]

In recognition of equalities or inequalities, for example, in compensations and weregild, in consideration of the worth of men, in sales of land, in horse trades, and in marriage agreements, social and legal convention fits into the pattern of equalized balance. This aspect also neatly comes to the fore, as when Snorri and Gudrún meet together for discussion of Bolli's revenge: "Snorri brá skjótt við ok reið þegar *við annan mann*.... Þau kómu þar mjǫk *jafnsnimma. Fylgði ok einn maðr Guðrúnu*" (lix, 176: "Snorri was quick to respond and rode at once with one other man.... They [Snorri and Gudrún] arrived at almost the same time. One other was also in Gudrún's company"). Payment of indemnity for the killing of Bolli is made at a prearranged meeting between representatives of both sides — and again balancing is precise: "Þá kom Snorri goði með þeim Bollasonum, ok váru alls fimmtán saman: *jafnmargir* kómu þeir Steinþórr til mótsins" (lxxi, 210-211: "Snorri Godi came with Bolli's sons in a party of fifteen. Steinthór came to the meeting with equally many"). This type of formulation shows how the legal code and other ethical obligations coincide with the author's purposes. So when Gudrún presses for revenge, one by one are named men whose lives might compensate for the loss of Bolli. And Snorri's comment is significant:

> "Er sǫk við Lamba, þótt hann væri drepinn, en eigi þykki mér Bolla hefnt at heldr, ok eigi mun þeira Bolla *slíkr munr gǫrr í sættum, sem vert er, ef þeim vígum er saman jafnat*" (lix, 177: "There is reason enough that Lambi be killed, but it doesn't seem to me that Bolli will be any the more revenged for that, for in the peace terms there will not be due account taken of the disparity between Lambi and Bolli, if these two killings are equated one with the other").

That a similar approach determines popular comparisons of the worth of men shows up in Queen Gunnhild's estimation of Hrút:

> En Guunhildr dróttning lagði svá miklar mætur á hann, at hon helt engi hans *jafningja* innan hirðar, hvárki í orðrum né ǫðrum hlutum; en þó at *mannjafnaðr* væri hafðr ok til ágætis manna talat, þá var þat ǫllum mǫnnum auðsætt, at Gunnhildi þótti hyggjuleysi til ganga eða ǫfund, ef nǫkkurum manni var til Hrúts *jafnat* (xix, 44: And Queen Gunnhild esteemed him so highly that

in her opinion no one in the guard equaled him, be it in word or deed. And whenever talk ran to the comparison of men and their merits, it was easy for everyone to see that Gunnhild ascribed it to stupidity or envy if any man was said to equal Hrút).

The frequency with which the word *jafn-* in all its compounds and variations appears in the saga affords evidence of the author's intent.[33] The sale of the Hrappsstadir lands is *ekki jafnaðarkaup* (xxiv, 67: not an even trade); Eldgrím offers *jafnmǫrg* studhorses in trade (xxxvii, 103: equally many); Hrút, too, offers to even the bargain since the horses are *ekki jafngóð* (xxxvii, 104: not equally good); Ósvíf reminds Thorvald that he and Gudrún are *eigi jafnmenni* (xxxiv, 93: not an equal match); and, as has been noted, Gudrún and Kjartan are *mest jafnræði* (xxxix, 112: most equally matched), whereas Kjartan and Hrefna are *eigi jafnræði* (xlv, 137: not equally matched). Even the concurrence in time, *jafnsnimma,* fits into the schematism, as we shall presently see.[34]

Even though the saga aims toward a balance, *jafn*-compounds usually combine with a negative to suggest that a balance is not readily attainable. Gudrún herself hints at the futility of the endeavor: "'Vera kann, at vér fáim ekki jafnmæli af þeim Laxdœlum, en gjalda skal nú einhverr afráð, í hverjum dal sem hann býr'" (lix, 177: "'It may well be that we can't even the score exactly with these Laxdalers, but now someone must pay dearly, no matter from what dale he comes'").

In addition to the concept of comparison expressed by *jafn*-words, a preoccupation with instances of weighing the odds and sizing up disparity in numbers is marked by the frequent occurrence of *munr* and *liðsmunr*.[35] How Hrút bolstered the courage of his men in the stand against the Laxdalers is representative: "Fǫrunautar Hrúts sǫgðu, at *liðsmunr* myndi vera. Hrútr kvazk þat ekki hirða; kvað þá *því verrum fǫrum fara skyldu, sem þeir væri fleiri*" (xix, 46: "Hrút's followers said the odds were against them. Hrút replied he did not mind that, declaring that they would fare the worse the more there were of them"). Distinctive in the saga are similar sentences constructed on syntactic parallelisms and grammatical comparatives such as "the more...the better" or "the more...the worse." An almost architectonic symmetry results. The pattern may be clearly observed in the reactions of Jórunn and of Hoskuld when they learn Melkorka's name and background, neatly bringing the two of them into opposition: "var Jórunn *hvergi betr* við hana en áðr, en Hǫskuldr *nǫkkuru fleiri*" (xiii, 28: "Jórunn was in no wise kindlier toward the bondwoman now than before, but Hoskuld somewhat more so"). Óláf's reception by the king and by Gunnhild is formulated according to a similar pattern: "Óláfr Hoskuldsson kom nú til hirðar Haralds konungs, ok tók konungr honum *vel*, en Gunnhildr *miklu betr*" (xxii, 60: "Óláf Hoskuldsson came now to King Harald's court and the king gave him good welcome and Gunnhild an even better one"). Here, too, the lesser value of *vel* is apparent.

The report of Hrapp's ghost-walking balances content with form: "En svá illr sem hann var viðreignar, *þá er hann lifði*, þá jók nú miklu við, *er hann var dauðr*, því at hann gekk mjǫk aptr" (xvii, 39: "But mean as he had been to deal with when he was alive, it got to be even worse now that he was dead, for he walked again a great deal"). Balanced syntax again accentuates the opposition between the brothers Ingjald and Hall:

> Ekki váru þeir brœðr samþykkir optast; *þótti Ingjaldi Hallr lítt vilja sik semja í sið dugandi manna*, en Halli þótti Ingjaldr lítt vilja sitt ráð hefja til þroska (xiv, 28-29: These two brothers were almost always in disagreement. Ingjald thought Hall showed little willingness to conform to the ways of accountable men, and Hall thought Ingjald showed little willingness to help him improve his lot).

Similarly, the party plans of Óláf and Ósvif are counterpoised and the honors paid to each are made equal:

> Þat sumar hafði Óláfr heimboð hálfum mánaði fyrir vetr. Ósvífr hafði ok boð stofnat at vetrnóttum; bauð þá *hvárr þeira ǫðrum til sín* með svá marga menn, sem þá þœtti *hvárum mestr sómi* at vera (xlvi, 139: That summer Óláf held a feast at his farm half a month before winter set in. Ósvíf also had a feast planned for the time of the Winter Nights. Each asked the other with as many guests as would do each of them most honor).

And in Thorgils' arguments for and against Lambi's guilt, parallel syntax weighs and balances social justice:

> "Ferr þat saman, at þú ert sakbitinn í meira lagi, fyrir því at þú eggjaðir mjǫk, at Bolli væri drepinn, *var ok við þik í meira lagi várkunn*, þegar er leið sonu Óláfs" (lxi, 182-183: "You are all the more guilt-laden because you urged strongly that Bolli be slain; on the other hand, next to Óláf's sons, you had the greatest justification for it").

Thorleik's comment when he learns that Hrút has killed Eldgrím syntactically balances cause and effect: "Þorleikr kvað *þat bæði vera, at honum hafði illt til gengit, enda myndi eigi gott í móti koma*" (xxxvii, 105: "Thorleik said two things were certain: something ill had prompted him to do it and nothing good would come of it in return"). And Kjartan's formulation of his eagerness to become a Christian equates the desires of both sides: "'ok fyrir engan mun *má konungi nú tíðara til vera, at ek taka við trúnni, en mér er at láta skírask*'" (xl, 122: "'And now the king by no means can be more eager for me to accept the faith than I am to have myself baptized'").

Frequently, as seen in other places, expressions of balancing are represented by an interchange of antonyms: "[Óláfr] kvað betra vera at fá *skjóta sœmð en langa svívirðing*" (xxi, 59: "Óláf said it was better to have short-lived fame than long-termed shame").

The many instances of sharing and dividing found in the saga also serve to promote the pattern of equilibrium. Half-interest in the ownership of vessels is a frequent motif,[36] and other illustrations such as the following could be cited: Kjartan and Kálf own in common the wares they bring back from Norway (xliv, 133-134); Hall and Thórólf argue over the dividing of a catch of fish (xiv, 29); Hoskuld and Thorkel Trefil both keep all of an inheritance although another person claims half (viii, 16; xviii, 42, respectively); Unn is invited with half her company by one brother and with her whole party by the other (v, 8-9); Hrút drives off twenty head of Hoskuld's cattle and leaves the same number behind (xix, 45).

Also found repeatedly in the saga is a concept of two-ness. Expressions such as *tveimr, tveir kostir* (two reasons, two choices), *annathvárt* (one of two things), *hvárrtveggja* (each of two), *bæði...ok* (both...and), *hvárki...né* (neither...nor) occur with notable consistency. Although these expressions can be found in every saga, their conspicuously frequent appearance in *Laxdœla saga* seems to suggest unusual preference and significance, particularly when considered in combination with the other structural and stylistic elements. As a piece of literature, the saga presents a unified whole, in which the individual elements mutually reflect and control each other. In this instance it is as if the author, consciously or unconsciously, selected the ordinary materials of his language — the stock phrases as it were — which best suited his pattern.

Choice between two alternatives often appears and supports the idea of weighing and comparing. The saga opens with Ketil Flatnose's putting before his family the alternatives open to them in face of King Harald's hostility: "'Lízk mér svá, sem oss sé *tveir kostir* gǫrvir, at flýja land eða vera drepnir hverr í sínu rúmi'" (ii, 4: "'As I see it, we have two choices: to flee the country or be slain, each under his own roof'"). When Kjartan decides that he wants the Tunga lands, he says to Thórarin: "'ger nú *annathvárt*, at þú handsala mér þegar landit at þvílíkum kostum, sem þú hefir ásáttr orðit við aðra, eða bú sjálfr á landi þínu ella'" (xlvii, 147: "'Now you can do one of two things: either give me your hand right here and now on the sale of this land and on the same terms as you have agreed upon with others, or stay put on your land yourself"). When the news of Kjartan's action reaches Laugar, Gudrún also uses alternatives to prod Bolli:

> "Svá virðisk mér, Bolli, sem Kjartan hafi þér gǫrt *tvá kosti,* nǫkkuru harðari en hann gerði Þórarni, at þú munt láta verða herað þetta með litlum sóma eða sýna þik á einhverjum fundi ykkrum nǫkkuru óslæra en þú hefir fyrr verit" (*ibid.*: "It seems to me, Bolli, as if Kjartan were giving you two choices, and somewhat harder ones than he gave Thórarin. Either you will have to leave this district with little honor, or else show yourself somewhat less easygoing in some one of your encounters than you have up until now").

When Án tells his portentous dream before Kjartan's departure from Hól, Aud cautions Kjartan, saying:

> "Eigi þarf at spotta þetta svá mjǫk; er þat mitt tillag, at Kjartan geri *annathvárt,* at hann dvelisk hér lengr, en ef hann vill ríða, þá ríði hann með meira lið heðan en hingat" (xlviii, 149: "There's no call for scoffing at this so much. My advice is that Kjartan should do one of two things: either stay here longer, or if he insists on going, then he should ride away with more men than he came with").[37]

This consciousness of doubleness occurs, as might be expected, whenever two sides are set up for comparison; for example: "Bǫrðusk vel *hvárirtveggju* um hríð" (xix, 46: "Both [each of two] sides fought well for a while"); "'þetta er *hvárstveggja* ykkar sómi'" (xix, 48: "'This would do credit to you both'"); "'brautgangssǫk *hvárttveggja*'" (xxv, 96: "'in either case grounds for divorce'"); "en honum var kært við *hváratveggju*" (xlvii, 146: "And he was friendly to both sides"); "Þeir sá *hváratveggju,* Laugamenn í fyrirsátinni ok þá Kjartan" (xlix, 152: "They saw both sides, the Laugar men in ambush and Kjartan and his companions"); "Urðu þá *hvárirtveggju* sárir, Ósvífrssynir ok Án" (xlix, 153: "Then both sides were wounded, Ósvíf's sons and Án"); "'ok er þá eigi sýnt, *hvárra* vænna er'" (lxiii, 190: "'And then there's no telling which of the two things is the more likely'"); ok þóttu *hvárirtveggju* hafa vaxit af þessum málum" (lxxi, 211: "And both sides were thought to have gained in honor from these affairs").

Many other elements in the saga involve an "either...or," a "both... and," or a "neither...nor," come in pairs or are in some way doubled. When, for example, Jórunn queries Hoskuld about Melkorka, she says:

"Þat mun *tveimr* skipta, at sá kvittr mun loginn, er fyrir mik er kominn, eða þú munt hafa talat við hana jafnmart sem spurt hafa hana at nafni" (xiii, 26: "That will be one of two things: either the rumor that has come to my ears is a lie, or you will have spoken with her enough to have at least asked her her name").

When Melkorka outwits Hoskuld, she gloats because he will be doubly discomfited:

"Er þat ok til kostar, at Hǫskuldi muni þá *tveir hlutir* illa líka, þá er hann spyrr *hvárttveggja*, at þú ert af landi farinn, en ek manni gipt" (xx, 50: "And what will make it even better is that Hoskuld won't be very happy on two scores, when he learns that you have left the country and I am married").

Thorkel Eyjólfsson gives Snorri two reasons for his reluctance to woo Gudrún (lviii, 174), and later Snorri proves to him that "'both obstacles have been removed'" (lxviii, 200: "'Er nú ok af ráðinn *hvárrtveggi* hlutrinn'").[38] Kjartans' stolen sheath is never found, Hrefna's headdress disappears, and Kjartan demands the return of both articles: "'þó vil ek nú hafa *hvárntveggja*'" (xlvi, 143: "'I now want both of them back'"). When Thorkel is shipwrecked, people observe his precarious sailing from "both sides" of the fjord, and the wreckage drifts to "both sides": "Sá menn ferðina af *hvárutveggja landinu*. ... Var þá rekinn víða kominn um eyjarnar ok svá til *hvárrartveggju strandar*" (lxxvi, 222-223).

In addition to these examples of twoness, the lists of correlatives, a pairing up of qualities of all kinds, using *bæði...ok*[39] or its negative counterpart *hvárki* [*eigi, ekki, engi*]...*né*[40] become impressively long. These stylistic preferences, far from revealing the author's private idiosyncracies, support rather the deliberately planned structural pattern of his saga and may or may not be relevant elements in other works that could be attributed to him.

Laxdœla saga might almost be said both in content and form and in larger and smaller units to have been constructed on comparisons, juxtapositions, and equalizations. The author has organized his material and his language to this end, creating similar incidents and similar characters, repeating phrases, introducing contrasts into the same pattern, arranging the dialogues, and even selecting those events and social forms which best develop the idea. Repetition as Comparison, on the one hand, points up a likeness between events and characters, such as the ghost-walkings of Hrapp and Hallbjorn, or the affinity between Kjartan and Gudrún, or emphasizes a gradual enhancement of analogous qualities in the successive generations: Hoskuld-Óláf, Óláf-Kjartan; Kjartan-Bolli Bollason. On the other hand, the comparison may underscore a dissimilarity at the same time it makes the opposites equal: the two swords Footbiter and Konungsnaut, Kjartan's and Mýrkjartan's forces, the pairs of inimical brothers, bargainings, and the like. Substitutions within the patterned idioms, antonyms, negative reversals, syntactically balanced constructions also lend precision to the parallel or contrastive comparisons.

From the consideration of so many likenesses and repetitions, it is but a step to suggesting that the author has created type-scenes and type-characters. Yet descriptions of episodes or characters are marked by an admixture of the linguistic elements they hold in common, so there is rarely a close, point by point correspondence between model and counterpart. Individual elements of a scene appear scrambled, not altogether in the sequence of the preparatory appearance of the linguistic units. Separate motifs in the Eldgrím episode, for instance, appear again in Bolli's presentation of the studhorses and in the bargaining for the Hjardarholt lands.

Personality traits likewise are distributed, most obviously in the mixing and matching of the three sets of brothers, but also in the likenesses to be noted between Melkorka-Vigdís, Vigdís-Gudrún, Gudrún-Thorgerd (the latter to be discussed in the next chapter), and others. The characters in the saga are "gemischte Köpfe," to use Heusler's phrase. Nonetheless, through the limited number of components that have been established, the illusion of stereotypes is created. So Óláf Feilan, Hoskuld, Óláf Peacock, Bolli Bollason all have something of a Kjartan in them; and Unn, Jórunn, Vigdís, Melkorka, and Thorgerd are not much different from Gudrún. The associative bonds extend in multiple directions.

Especially notable within the author's schematism are the verbal similarities that make an earlier situation a model or forerunner for a later one. The likenesses between the persons that run from generation to generation also exemplify this. Such preparatory episodes (or agents) are subsequently recognized as standing in either parallel or contrastive relationship to later incidents. This type of preparation with subsequent counterpart reminds one again of the prophecy-fulfillment, statement-confirmation aspect of the structure.

This characteristic also makes it easier to grant the long introductory portion of the saga its indispensable place. By exhibiting to the audience representative happenings — schemes for marriages and divorces, quarrels over inheritances, piques, umbrages, and resentments — by introducing characters who are difficult, prideful, not wanting to be worsted or who are paragons among men, handsome and accomplished, the first part of the saga sets the pattern and tone for similar motifs and personages in the central theme and for a kind of recapitulation in the third part. It might thus almost be said to function as prophecy.

Structurally and formally the composition presents a fitness and balance in which the word patterns themselves, abstracted from their discursive content, present a concept of determinism and compensation which are wholly analogous to the idea of fateful necessity and the ethical demand for equal revenge. The audience is led into a world of limited and controlled relationships, of exact correspondences, where artistic necessity dictates the possibilities and the word choices. Equalization and compensatory balance are only temporary, however; the lust for vengeance continues in a sequence which also finds its symbolic expression in the structure of the saga.

IV

TRIPLETS AND QUADRUPLETS:
CONTRAPUNTAL VARIATION

Investigation of the structural and formal elements concomitantly has shown how *Laxdœla saga* falls into three distinct parts, and how the action revolves around three central characters. Analysis of the narration readily discloses the tripartite occurrence of other components: first, three parties at which three incidents occur which serve to widen the breach between the families of Óláf and Ósvíf; second, three goadings in which Thorgerd Egilsdóttir and Gudrún Ósvífsdóttir are the protagonists; and third, three slayings which result from the goadings. In addition, three drownings and three sales of land attract particular attention. In the case of the three parties, veiled hints indicate in an ingenious manner the incipient causal connections that set off the chain reaction. And as elsewhere, in all of these series of triplets can be discerned lexical repetitions and repeated motif patterns. The triplet repeatings furthermore often carry with them reversals, variation through increment and embellishment and regroup into parallels and contrasts. These aspects also show up to a marked degree in the set of examples labeled quadruplets. Overlapping of function and integration of the structural elements in the saga will become patent in the course of the discussion of these major components.

The Parties

Partying back and forth was part of the way of life pictured in the saga, and the friendly exchange between the farms of Óláf and Ósvíf represents existent good feeling: "*Vinátta* var ok mikil með þeim Óláfi ok Ósvífri ok *jafnan heimboð*" (xxxix, 112: "There was also great friendship between Óláf and Ósvíf and always partying back and forth"). When Kjartan returns from abroad, there is nothing to suggest that conditions are changed:

Þeir Óláfr ok Ósvífr *heldu inum sama hætti um heimboð*; skyldu sitt haust hvárir aðra heim sœkja. Þetta haust skyldi vera boð at Laugum, en Óláfr til sœkja ok þeir Hjarðhyltingar (xliv, 134: Óláf and Ósvíf kept up their custom of inviting each other back and forth. Every fall one of them was to visit the other. This fall the feast was to be at Laugar, and Óláf and the Hjardholters were to come).

Upon their arrival at Laugar, the semblance of congeniality prevails:

Bolli gekk at Kjartani ok minntisk til hans. Kjartan tók kveðju hans. Eptir þat var þeim inn fylgt. Bolli er við þá *inn kátasti* (xlv, 135: Bolli went toward Kjartan and kissed him, and Kjartan acknowledged his greeting. After that they were seen into the house. Bolli was most gay with them).

Yet the dissimulation implicit in the superlative *inn kátasti* undoubtedly contains a clue that all is not as well as may seem.[1] When Kjartan then refuses Bolli's present of the studhorses, the joviality of the feast is broken, and the Hjardholters go home *með engri blíðu* (in no friendliness, with ill feeling). Throughout the saga the positive *með allri blíðu* (in all friendliness)[2] has so conditioned the audience that the unexpected negative form lends even more serious portent to the incident. Things are quiet, however, *ok er nú kyrrt*, a condition which, as already been noted, is in itself portentous. The tone has been set for the parties which follow.

The next party is at Hjardarholt. Here, Kjartan displays his irritation, first by openly slighting Gudrún in the matter of seating arrangements, and second by denying her request to see the headdress.[3] Later on, however, Gudrún inveigles the guileless Hrefna into letting her see the precious headdress which Kjartan had brought from Norway for his intended bride. She contemplates the headdress without a word. It is a silence that speaks volumes. Clearly she feels cheated of both husband and headdress and at the same time is characteristically envious of anyone's owning finery costlier than hers.[4] The merrymaking of the party continues: "Fór þar fram *gleði ok skemmtan*." As observed above in connection with *kátr*, unmistakably there are undertones.[5]

When Kjartan's prized sword disappears, the situation is not improved:

Síðan gekk hann til rúms síns, þar sem sverðit hafði verit, ok *var þá á brottu*. Hann gekk þegar at segja feðr sínum þessa svipan. Óláfr mælti: "Hér skulu vér *fara með sem hljóðast*" (xlvi, 140: Afterwards he went back to his bed-closet where he had left the sword, and it was gone. Straightway he went to tell his father of this loss. Óláf said: "Let's go about this as quietly as possible").

Án the White recovers the sword in a swamp, but the scabbard is missing and is never found. Kjartan harbors deep resentment; and although "things were left in quiet about this" (xlvi, 142: "Var nú látit *kyrrt* yfir þessu"), hard feelings have been increased and the party spoiled.

What was left unsaid by Gudrún at Hjardarholt sets the stage for the return invitation to Laugar. No sooner had the guests arrived, than the headdress, which Hrefna had reluctantly brought along, disappears:

> En um morgininn, er konur skyldu taka búnað sinn, þá leitar Hrefna at motrinum, ok *var þá í brottu* þaðan, sem hon hafði varðveitt, ok var þá víða leitat ok fannsk eigi.... Hrefna sagði nú Kjartani, at motrinn var horfinn. Hann svarar ok kvað eigi hœgt hlut í at eiga at gæta til með þeim ok bað hana nú *láta vera kyrrt, segir síðan fǫður sínum, um hvat at leika var*. Óláfr svarar: "Enn vilda ek *sem fyrr*, at þú létir vera ok hjá þér líða þetta vandræði; mun ek *leita eptir þessu í hljóði*" (xlvi, 143: But in the morning when the women were to put on their finery, Hrefna looked for her headdress and it was gone from where she had put it away. They searched high and low for it, but it could not be found.... Hrefna now told Kjartan that the headdress had disappeared. He replied by saying it was a delicate matter to attend to with them and bade her keep things quiet. Then he told his father what was afoot. Óláf replied: "I would still like you to let the matter ride as we did before and go on as though nothing had happened. I will look into this on the quiet").

Kjartan, however, is no longer content to let matters rest and delivers an ultimatum to Bolli:

> "Þik kveð ek at þessu, Bolli frændi; þú munt vilja gera til vár drengiligar heðan í frá en hingat til; mun ek þetta *ekki í hljóðmæli fœra*, því at þat er nú at margra manna viti um hvǫrf þau, er hér hafa orðit, er vér hyggjum, at í yðvarn garð hafi runnit" (*ibid*.: "I'm calling on you, kinsman Bolli, henceforth to show yourself more willing to treat us honorably than you have hitherto. I am not going to keep this quiet, for it is now common knowledge that things have been disappearing hereabouts which we believe have found their way into your keep").

The episodes dealing with the thefts are obviously patterned after one another (N. B. the *sem fyrr*). The triple occurrence of *sem hljóðast, í hljóði*, and *ekki í hljóðmæli* represents a type of repetition whereby the first two form a pair of parallels in relationship to which the third stands in contrast. This special type of threefold repetition will be discussed presently.

The Goadings

The marked similarity both in style and wording and also in motifs and progression of the three episodes which depict attempts by Gudrún or Thorgerd to incite actions of vengeance — Gudrún's pressing for the death of Kjartan, Thorgerd's nagging for revenge for Kjartan, and Gudrún's plotting for revenge for Bolli — would indicate that the scenes have been executed according to a pattern. The approach, the development, and the conclusions in each case are much the same. Corresponding themes and arguments in all three goadings will be indicated by letters in brackets.

The series begins with Gudrún's tirade against her slothful brothers:

"Gott skaplyndi hefði þér fengit, *ef þér værið dœtr einshvers bónda* [motif a] ok láta hvárki at yðr verða gagn né mein; en slíka svívirðing ok skǫmm, sem Kjartan hefir yðr gǫrt, þá sofi þér eigi at minna, at hann ríði hér hjá garði við annan mann, ok hafa slíkir menn mikit svínsminni; *þykki mér ok rekin ván* [motif b], at þér þorið Kjartan heim at sœkja, ef þér þorið eigi at finna hann nú, er hann ferr við annan mann eða þriðja, en þér sitið heima ok látið vænliga ok eruð æ hølzti margir." Óspakr kvað hana mikit af taka, en vera illt til mótmæla, ok spratt hann upp þegar ok klæddisk, ok hverr þeira brœðra at ǫðrum. Síðan bjuggusk þeir at sitja fyrir Kjartani. Þá bað Guðrún Bolla til ferðar með þeim. Bolli kvað sér eigi sama fyrir frændsemis sakar við Kjartan ok tjáði, hversu ástsamliga Óláfr hafði hann upp fœddan. Gudrún svarar: "Satt segir þú þat, en eigi muntu bera giptu til at gera svá, at ǫllum þykki vel, ok mun lokit okkrum samfǫrum, *ef þú skersk undan fǫrinni* [motif c]." Ok við fortǫlur Guðrúnar *miklaði Bolli fyrir sér fjándskap allan* [motif d] á hendr Kjartani ok sakar ok vápnaðisk síðan skjótt, ok urðu níu saman (xlviii, 150).

("It would have suited your dispositions just right if you had been daughters of some farmer or other, the way you act, not turning a hand either to help or hinder. Such insult and shame as Kjartan has done to you, and you nonetheless go on sleeping although he is riding right past your door with but one other man in his company. The likes of you have memories about as long as a swine's. As far as I can see there's no hope of your ever getting up enough courage to attack Kjartan on his home ground, if you don't even dare meet up with him now when he is traveling with but a man or two. But you just sit at home making bold talk and are too many for any good use." Óspak said she used very strong language, but that he was hard put for an argument. So he jumped up at once and dressed, as did each of the brothers one after the other. They then laid plans to waylay

Kjartan, and Gudrún asked Bolli, too, to go along. Bolli said it was not right for him to go, because of his kinship with Kjartan, and reminded her with what loving kindness Óláf had brought him up. Gudrún answered: "What you say is true, but it can't be your good fortune to please everybody. And our conjugal life together will be finished if you refuse this." Through Gudrún's persuasions, all the hateful things he had suffered at Kjartan's hands loomed large inside Bolli and he quickly took up his weapons. They were a party of nine altogether.)

A corresponding development characterizes the episode in which Thorgerd, Kjartan's mother, goads her other sons to avenge the slaying of Kjartan. The four themes found in Gudrún's harangue (although not in the same order) and two added motifs *e* and *f* occur in Thorgerd's goadings and in the plans for a raid on Bolli. Thorgerd, like Gudrún, opens her attack by bemoaning the hopelessness of the situation and pointing up the difference in numbers:

> "*Mun yðr fjarri fara brœðrum* [motif *b*], at þér munið þar til hefnda leita, sem ofrefli er fyrir, er þér getið eigi launat sín tillǫg slíkum mannfýlum, sem Þorkell er" (lii, 160: "Far be it from you brothers ever to seek out revenge where the odds are against you, if you can't even pay back scoundrels like Thorkel for what they have done").

Her naggings goad her sons into slaying Thorkel of Hafratindar. Thorgerd, however, will not be quiet until Bolli is killed:

> Þá sneri Þorgerðr hestinum upp at bœnum ok spurði: "Hvat heitir bœr sjá?"⁶ Halldórr svarar: "Þess spyrr þú eigi af því, móðir, at eigi vitir þú áðr; sjá bœr heitir í Tungu." "Hverr býr hér?" segir hon. Hann svarar: "Veiztu þat, móðir." Þá segir Þorgerðr ok blés við: "Veit ek at vísu," segir hon, "at hér býr Bolli, bróðurbani yðvarr, ok furðu ólíkir urðu þér yðrum frændum gǫfgum, er þér vilið eigi hefna þvílíks bróður, sem Kjartan var, ok eigi myndi svá gera Egill, móðurfaðir yðvarr, ok er illt at eiga dáðlausa sonu; ok víst *ætla ek yðr til þess betr fellda, at þér værið dœtr* [motif *a*] fǫður yðvars ok værið giptar. Kemr hér at því, Halldórr, sem mælt er, at einn er auðkvisi ættar hverrar, ok sú er mér auðsæst ógipta Óláfs, at honum glapðisk svá mjǫk sonaeignin; kveð ek þik af því at þessu, Halldórr," segir hon, "at þú þykkisk mest fyrir yðr brœðrum. Nú munu vér aptr snúa, ok var þetta ørendit mest, *at minna yðr á þetta, ef þér mynðið eigi áðr* [motif *e*]. Þá svarar Halldórr: "Ekki munu vér þér þat kenna, móðir, þótt oss líði ór hug þetta." Halldórr svarar hér fá um, ok *þó þrútnaði honum mjǫk móðr til Bolla* [motif *d*] (liii, 161-162).

(Then Thorgerd headed her horse up toward the farm and asked: "What farm is this?" Halldór answered: "You aren't asking this, mother, because you don't already know. This farm is called Tunga." "Who lives there?" she asked. He answered: "That you know, too, mother." Then Thorgerd answered with a sneer: "I do indeed," she said, "there lives Bolli, your brother's slayer. You have certainly turned out very differently from your noble kinsmen, if you don't want to avenge such a brother as Kjartan was. Never would Egil, your mother's father, have acted this way. It's an ill thing to have shirkers for sons. Indeed, to my mind it would have suited you better had you been daughters to your father and were married off. It just goes to prove the old saying: 'there's a black sheep in every family.' The way I see it, Óláf's greatest misfortune clearly lies in the fact that he was cheated when it came to the kind of sons he got. I'm telling this to you, Halldór, because you regard yourself as the foremost of your brothers. Now let us turn back, for the sole purpose of my coming out here was just to remind you of this, in case you didn't remember it before." Then Halldór answered: "It certainly won't be any fault of yours, mother, if it should slip our minds." Other than that Halldór had little to say about it, but all the same a fiery hate against Bolli welled up inside him.)

Thorgerd's barb works: since they can no longer stand their mother's constant egging, the brothers make plans to attack Bolli:

> Nú segir Halldórr Barða í hljóði, at þeir brœðr ætla at fara at Bolla, ok sǫgðusk *eigi lengr þola frýju móður sinnar* [motif *f*]; — "er ekki því at leyna, Barði frændi, at mjǫk var undir heimboði við þik, at vér vildim hér til hafa þitt liðsinni ok brautargengi" (liv, 163: Halldór now told Bardi on the quiet that he and his brothers meant to attack Bolli, saying they could no longer stand their mother's taunts. "It is not to be denied, kinsman Bardi, that a great part of the reason we asked you home with us was that we wanted to have your backing and support in this").

Bardi is reluctant to join them because (like Bolli) he hesitates to break faith with kinsmen, but again, like Bolli, he does not refuse (motif *c*):

> Þá svarar Barði: "Illa mun þat fyrir mælask, at ganga á sættir við frændr sína.... Þykki mér við þetta allt saman óauðsóttligt." Halldórr segir: "Hins munu vér þurfa, at torvelda ekki þetta mál fyrir oss; ...vænti ek ok, frændi, *at þú skerisk eigi undan ferð þessi með oss* [motif *c*]" (*ibid*.: Bardi answered: "People will speak harshly of breaking faith with one's kinsmen.... All in all it strikes me as no easy task." Halldór said: "There's no need

to make this appear more difficult for us than it is;...I expect, kinsman, you won't refuse undertaking this with us").

In the third goading, when Gudrún seeks to spur her sons to avenge Bolli, motifs from the two previous scenes reappear. First, because of hate (motif *d*), Gudrún schemes with Snorri: "'En eigi má ek vita, at þessir menn siti um kyrrt allir, *er ek hefi áðr þenna fjándskap miklat á hendr'*" (lix, 177-178: "'But I can't stand seeing those men against whom I have been nurturing my hate all along left to sit in peace'"). Then she reveals her plans to her sons, and to prod them into action employs a forceful reminder — presenting Bolli's bloody clothes (motif *e*, an alternate to Thorgerd's ride to Tunga); and her sons also cannot stand her taunts (motif *f*):

> Fám nóttum síðar en Guðrún hafði heim komit, heimti hún [*sic*] sonu sína til máls við sik í laukagarð sinn; en er þeir koma þar, sjá þeir, at þar váru breidd niðr línklæði, skyrta ok línbrœkr; þau váru blóðug mjǫk. Þá mælti Guðrún: "Þessi sǫmu klæði, er þit sjáið hér, frýja ykkr fóðurhefnda; nú mun ek ekki hafa hér um mǫrg orð, því at *ekki er ván* [motif *b*], at þit skipizk af framhvǫt orða, *ef þit íhugið ekki við slíkar bendingar ok áminningar* [motif *e*]."...Eptir þetta gengu þeir í brott. Um nóttina eptir máttu þeir brœðr eigi sofa. Þorgils varð þess varr ok spurði, hvat þeim væri. Þeir segja honum allt tal þeira mœðgina ok þat með, *at þeir mega eigi bera lengr harm sinn ok frýju móður sinnar* [motif *f*] (lx, 179-180: A few days after Gudrún had come home, she called her sons for a talk in her kitchen garden. And when they came there, they saw spread out on the ground linen clothes, a shirt and breeches. They were all stained with blood. Then Gudrún said: "These very clothes that you see here challenge the two of you to avenge your father. Now I'm not going to waste my breath on this, for there's not much hope of your being whetted by words, if such tokens and reminders do not impress it on your minds."...After this they walked away. That night the brothers could not sleep. Thorgils noticed this and asked them what was the matter. They told him everything that had been said between them and their mother and added that they could no longer bear their own grief or their mother's taunts).

Thereupon Thorgils gathers men to go along on a raid against Helgi as the victim of revenge, just as Helgi himself had prophesied. Again one member of the group has serious hesitations about joining in:

> Lambi segir: "Illt þykki mér friðkaup í þessu ok ódrengiligt; em ek ófúss þessar farar." Þá mælti Þorsteinn: "Eigi er einsætt,

Lambi, *at skerask svá skjótt undan ferðinni"* [motif *c*] (lxi, 183: Lambi said: "It's an ill price to pay for peace and pardon, and unmanly besides. I'm not at all keen on this undertaking." Then Thorstein spoke up: "It's not all that simple, Lambi, to refuse so hastily to join the raid").

The following schematism indicates the distribution of the motifs and their catch words for each of the three goading episodes. Similar skeletal patterns could be set up for other repeated episodes in the saga. Through ingenuity of arrangement, variation, and application in distinctly individual contexts, the author has avoided rigid repetition and the hollowness of stereotypes. Despite this manner of handling and the fact that not all the motifs appear in every goading scene, it is possible to detect the prototype.

Motif *a*: Disparagement over sons or brothers who act more like daughters.
1. *gott ef þér værið dœtr*
2. *betr at þér værið dœtr*
3. (missing)

Motif *b*: Despair over delay and procrastination in executing revenge.
1. *rekin ván*
2. [*fjarri fara*] (variant)
3. *ekki er ván*

Motif *c*: Persuading an outsider to the group of sons or brothers to join in the revenge; excuses given (ties of kinship); refusal not accepted.
1. *skersk undan fǫrinni* (Bolli)
2. *skerisk undan ferð* (Bardi)
3. *skerask undan ferðinni* (Lambi)

Motif *d*: Building up of hatred.
1. *miklaði fjándskap*
2. [*þrútnaði mjǫk móðr*] (variant)
3. *fjándskap miklat*

Motif *e*: Reminders; key expressions of remembering and reminding.
1. (missing)
2. *at minna; þér myndið* (Thorgerd's ride to Tunga)
3. *íhugið ekki við áminningar* (Gudrún's display of Bolli's bloody clothes)

Motif *f*: Inability to stand mother's taunts.
1. (missing)
2. *eigi lengr þola frýju móður sinnar*
3. *ekki bera lengr harm sinn ok frýju móður sinnar* (N. B. the increment *harm sinn*)

The Killings

The descriptions of the three killings which result from Gudrún's and Thorgerd's proddings likewise show marked similarites. In each of the passages parallel actions and motifs again occur. In each case, for example, the number and names of the men participating are listed. In the ambush against Kjartan there are nine:

> Váru þeir fimm synir Ósvífrs: Óspakr ok Helgi, Vandráðr ok Torráðr, Þórólfr, Bolli inn sétti, Guðlaugr inn sjaundi, systursonr Ósvífrs ok manna vænligastr. Þar var Oddr ok Steinn, synir Þórhǫllu málgu (xlviii, 150-151: There were Ósvíf's five sons: Óspak and Helgi, Vandrád and Torrád, and Thórólf. Bolli made the sixth, and Gudlaug, the son of Óvíf's sister and a most promising man, was the seventh. Then there were Odd and Stein, Thórhalla Chatterbox's sons).

In the raid against Bolli again there are nine in the attacking party; Thorgerd makes a tenth:

> Eptir þetta buaz þeir til ferðar; vóru þeir í ferð fjórir bræðr, Halldórr ok Steinþórr, Helgi ok Höskuldr; hinn fimti maðr var Barði Guðmundarson, hinn setti Lambi, sjaundi Þorsteinn svarti, átti Helgi mágr hans, niundi Ánn hrísmagi. Þorgerðr húsfreyja rézt í ferð með þeim sonum sinum.[7] (After this they prepared to set out; on this trip there were the four brothers Halldór and Steinthór, Helgi and Hoskuld; Bardi Gudmundarson made the fifth, Lambi the sixth, Thorstein the Black the seventh, his brother-in-law Helgi the eighth, and Án Brushwood Belly the ninth. Thorgerd made up her mind to go along with her sons.)

Against Helgi Hardbeinsson there are then ten attackers:

> Þorgils býsk nú heiman, ok ríða þeir upp eptir Hǫrðadal tíu saman. Þar var Þorgils Hǫlluson flokksstjóri. Þar váru í ferð synir Bolla, Bolli ok Þorleikr; Þórðr kǫttr var inn fjórði, bróðir þeira; fimmti Þorsteinn svarti, sétti Lambi, sjaundi ok átti Halldórr ok Ǫrnólfr, níundi Sveinn, tíundi Húnbogi; þeir váru synir Álfs ór Dǫlum (lxii, 184: Thorgils now got ready to go from home. He and his party rode up along Hordadal, ten together. Thorgils Holluson was the leader of the band. In his troop were Bolli's sons, Bolli and Thorleik, and their half brother Thórd Cat made the fourth; the fifth was Thorstein the Black, the sixth Lambi; Halldór and Ornólf made the seventh and eighth, Svein the ninth and Húnbogi the tenth. These last two were the sons of Álf of the Dales).

Events leading up to the attack also show a pattern. A shepherd sees the attackers (motif *a*), but is prevented from giving warning (motif *b*).[8] Prior to the fighting, suspicions are aroused in the attackers or the attacked (motif *c*). There is apprehension that news of the presence of attackers might leak out and be a forewarning (motif *d*). The keen eyesight (motif *e*)[9] of one of the members of the raiding band helps ensure the success of the venture. The following passages describing the three bands of attackers and their preparations will illustrate how these motifs are adapted to each situation. It will be recalled that Thorkel of Hafratindar and his shepherd discover by chance the ambush against Kjartan:

> Þá mælti *smalasveinn* [motif *a*], at þeir myndi snúa til móts við þá Kjartan; kvað þeim þat mikit happ, ef þeir mætti skirra vandræðum svá miklum, sem þá var til stefnt. Þorkell mælti: "Þegi skjótt," segir hann; "mun fóli þinn nǫkkurum manni líf gefa, ef bana verðr auðit?"...Ok varð svá at vera, sem Þorkell vildi [motif *b*]. Þeir Kjartan ríða fram at Hafragili. En í annan stað *gruna þeir Ósvífrssynir* [motif *c*], hví Bolli mun sér hafa þar svá staðar leitat, er hann mátti vel sjá [motif *d*], þá er menn riðu vestan (xlix, 152: The shepherd lad spoke up and said they ought to head off Kjartan and his party, that it was a stroke of luck if he and Thorkel could prevent such great trouble as otherwise was sure to happen. Thorkel said: "Hold your tongue! Are you fool enough to think you can save a man's life if he be doomed to die?"...And so it came to be as Thorkel wished. Kjartan and his companions kept on riding toward Hafragil. Meanwhile Ósvíf's sons began to have their suspicions as to why Bolli sought out such a place for himself where he could easily be seen by anyone riding from the west).

The account of the prelude to the attack on Bolli in his hut begins in much the same way:

> *Smalamaðr* [motif *a*] Bolla fór at fé snimma um morgininn uppi í hlíðinni; hann sá mennina í skóginum ok svá hrossin, er bundin váru; *hann grunar* [motif *c*], at þetta muni eigi vera friðmenn, er svá leyniliga fóru. Hann stefnir þegar heim it gegnsta til selsins ok ætlar at segja Bolla kvámu manna. Halldórr var *skyggn maðr* [motif *e*]. Hann sér, at maðrinn hleypr ofan ór hlíðinni ok stefndi til selsins. Hann segir fǫrunautum sínum, at þat mun vera smalamaðr Bolla — "ok mun hafa sét ferð vára; skulu vér nú gera í móti honum ok *láta hann engri njósn koma til selsins*" [motifs *b*, *d*] (lv, 165-166: Bolli's shepherd went out early that morning to his sheep up on the slope. He caught sight of the men in the woods and also saw the horses which were tied. He suspected

that these likely were no peaceable men who were keeping their travelings so secret, so he headed the straightest way home in order to tell Bolli of the men's presence. Halldór had a sharp eye. He saw the man running down the slope and making straight for the hut. He told his companions it was probably Bolli's shepherd, — "and he must have seen our party. We must now head him off and not let him bring any news to the hut").

Similar circumstances precede the attack on Helgi in his hut:

Helgi rœddi um morgininn við *smalamann* [motif *a*] sinn, at hann skyldi fara um skóga í nánd selinu ok hyggja at mannaferðum eða hvat hann sæi til tíðenda; — "erfitt hafa draumat veitt í nótt...." Hann kvazk sét hafa menn eigi allfá, — "ok hygg ek vera munu útanheraðsmenn."... *Þorgils grunar* [motif *c*], *at njósn muni borin vera frá þeim* [motif *d*], ok bað þá taka hesta sína ok ríða at sem tíðast, ok svá gerðu þeir (lxiii, 186 and 190).... Þeir Þorgils tóku reið mikla, þegar þeir kómu á bak, ok riðu nú fram ór skóginum. Þeir sá fjóra menn ríða frá selinu; þeir hleypðu ok allmikit. Þá mæltu sumir fǫrunautar Þorgils, at ríða skyldi eptir þeim sem skjótast. Þá svarar Þorleikr Bollason: "Koma munu vér áðr til selsins ok vita, hvat þar sé manna; því at þat ætla ek síðr, at hér sé Helgi ok hans fylgðarmenn; sýnisk mér svá, sem þetta sé konur einar." Þeir váru fleiri, er í móti mæltu. Þorgils kvað Þorleik ráða skyldu, því at hann vissi, at Þorleikr var *manna skyggnastr* [motif *e*]; snúa nú at selinu (lxiv, 191).

(That morning Helgi told his shepherd to make the rounds in the woods in the neighborhood of the shiel and to be on the lookout for any comings or goings or anything else he might see worth reporting — "for I have had some bad dreams in the night...." He [the shepherd] said he had seen some men, not all too few either, — "and I think they likely have come from outside the district."... Thorgils suspected that news of them might have reached Helgi and he told his men to take to their horses and be on their way as fast as they could, and they did so.... Thorgils and his men set off at a fast pace, as soon as they got on their horses and rode forth out of the woods. They caught sight of four men riding away from the shed; they too were riding at full gallop. Then some of Thorgils' companions spoke up and said that they should ride after them as fast as they could. Thorleik Bollason answered: "Let us first get to the hut and find out who is there. For I rather doubt that Helgi and his followers are in that group. It looks to me as though they are only women." Most of the men argued against him. Thorgils said Thorleik should decide, for he knew that Thorleik was uncommonly sharp-sighted; they now turned toward the hut.)

Again the motifs of this pattern are unevenly distributed among the examples of the pattern and are in juggled sequence. No one in the group of Kjartan's ambushers, for instance, is "sharp-sighted"; and Helgi's shepherd is not prevented from warning Helgi, but rather because of the latter's dreams is sent out to confirm the bad omen. There are also several interesting modifications by which the motifs are adapted to the needs of the unique situation. In the prelude to the attack on Bolli, preventing of the shepherd from giving warning (motif *b*) merges into one with the closely related motif of preventing news from reaching the attacked (motif *d*). And Thorgils' suspicion that Helgi might have got wind of the impending attack links motifs *c* and *d*. This fact throws light on the proper interpretation of Bolli's lying up on the brink in plain sight. Ósvíf's sons suspect that Bolli might thereby give away the ambush. But the text itself, with the *grunar* expression immediately introducing the *hví Bolli mun sér hafa þar svá staðar leitat, er hann mátti vel sjá* supports the solution to the syntactic reading as rendered.[10] Motifs *c* and *d* are thus also linked together in the second example of this group. The author again shows ingenuity, flexibility, and imagination in the use of his pattern, which despite the variations remains discernible.

In the details of the fighting, there are also marked likenesses. In all three battles, for example, the phrase *í þessi svipan* (at that instant) occurs,[11] as if to call attention to the fact that all are alike or modeled after one another, for the phrase appears nowhere else in the saga. Two accounts correspond respectively regarding the wounds received: an arm is so badly cut that it never completely heals (motif *a*);[12] a leg cut off at the knee results in death (motif *b*); or the viscera are laid open (motif *c*).[13] And there are other parallels. Bolli Thorleiksson, for example, with Footbiter executes the fateful prophecy of Kjartan's death; Bolli Bollason avenges his father with the same sword.[14] Kjartan casts down his weapon and gives up the fight; Bolli Thorleiksson, throwing down his weapons, surrenders to overwhelming odds; and the deaths of both are said to be a "great loss" (*harmdauði*).[15] These similarities also enhance the parallelism already noted between the two Bollis and between Kjartan and Bolli Thorleiksson.[16]

In connection with two of the battles a shameful act takes place, but in the third it is prevented: Kjartan admonishes Bolli that he is about to do a *níðingsverk* (xlix, 154: dastardly deed); Helgi wipes his sword on Gudrún's scarf, to which Halldór says: "'Þetta er illmannliga gǫrt ok grimmliga'" (lv, 168: "'That is a mean and cruel thing to do'"); but twelve-year-old Bolli Bollason prevents twelve-year-old Hardbein Helgason from being killed, saying: "'Skal hér engi maðr vinna klækisverk'" (lxiv, 193: "'No one here is to do a dastard's deed'").

In addition to correspondences of detail in the actual fighting, an interesting parallel also occurs in the descriptions of Gudrún's behavior while Kjartan is being killed and again while Bolli makes his brave defense alone in the hut. When Bolli returns from ambushing Kjartan, we are told:

> Guðrún gekk í móti honum ok spurði, hversu framorðit væri; Bolli kvað þá vera nær nóni dags þess. Þá mælti Guðrún: "Misjǫfn verða morginverkin;[17] ek hefi spunnit tólf álna garn, en þú hefir vegit Kjartan" (xlix, 154: Gudrún went out to meet him and asked him how late in the day it was. Bolli said it was almost noonday. Then Gudrún said: "The morning's tasks have turned out unequal: I have spun yarn for twelve ells of cloth and you have killed Kjartan").

And at Bolli's hut these events take place:

> Guðrún kvazk hyggja, at þau ein tíðendi myndi þar verða, at hon myndi sjá mega, ok kvað Bolla ekki mundu mein at sér, þótt hon væri nær honum stǫdd. Bolli kvazk þessu ráða vilja, ok svá var, at Guðrún gekk út ór selinu. Hon gekk ofan fyrir brekkuna til lœkjar þess, er þar fell, ok tók at þvá lérept sín (lv, 166: Gudrún replied that she did not think anything would happen there which she should not be allowed to see and added that Bolli would not be the worse off for her staying there by him. Bolli said he was the one to decide that, and so it came that Gudrún went out from the hut. She went down the slope to the brook which ran past there and took to washing her linen).

Gudrún's spinning tells us that she was under tension. Might she not also be harboring the hope that Kjartan may come out alive and has killed Bolli instead? Bolli hints as much (xlix, 155). In the parallel activity of washing her clothes in the brook while Bolli is being killed, overtones of tenseness are completely lacking; indeed, she didn't think anything would happen in the hut which she shouldn't see. One wonders just how cryptic that remark is. In any case the scene in contrast to the one when Kjartan is killed tells us a great deal about her feelings without stating them explicitly.

After the slaying first of Kjartan and then of Bolli, the two women who instigated the deeds appropriately have the final word. Thorgerd and Gudrún are here counterpoised as equal matches, just as they were in the prodding scenes. When Bolli returns from killing Kjartan, Gudrún, with calculating cruelty, gloats that "'Hrefna will not be laughing when she goes to bed tonight'" (xlix, 154-155: "'Hrefna mun eigi ganga hlæjandi at sænginni í kveld' "). After Bolli's slaying, the gloating Thorgerd wishes her son "all hale to enjoy the fruits of his labor" (lv, 168: "bað hann heilan njóta handa") and suggests cruelly that "Gudrún would have something to busy herself with for a while — combing Bolli's bloody locks" (*ibid*.: "kvað nú Guðrúnu mundu eiga at búa um rauða skǫr Bolla um hríð").[18] The one malicious remark compensates for the other; with the latter, it is as though revenge had been taken on Gudrún.

The Drownings

Out of the series of three parties, of three goadings, and of three killings, it is possible to derive a patterned prototype for each set according to which the individual examples were executed. Such sets of triple repetitions constitute a structural component that inheres in the saga. That there are three main characters involved in a love triangle, that the saga itself is divided into three main parts cannot be deemed coincidence. If triplicity characterizes a basic structural component, we can expect to find it elsewhere in the saga, and not merely limited to the central action, although the triplet sets just discussed come to the fore here strikingly, corresponding as they do with that part of the saga where the triangular relationship of the protagonists and the results of it are also most fully developed. Threefold incidents based on a schematized concatenation of motifs carries one step further the idea of preparatory figures as models whose echoes reverberate and mingle from one section of the saga to the next. The accounts of the drownings of Thorstein Surt, Thórd Ingunnarson, and Thorkel Eyjólfsson,[19] one for each of the three main divisions of the saga respectively, bear additional witness to the type of schematized repetitions under discussion.

The account of the drowning of Thorstein Surt illustrates the pattern:

> Þorsteinn surtr bjó ferð sína af várþingi, *en smali var rekinn eptir strǫndinni* [motif *a*]. Þorsteinn skipaði ferju ok *gekk þar á með tólfta mann* [motif *b*]; var þar Þórarinn á, mágr hans, ok Ósk Þorsteinsdóttir ok Hildr, dóttir Þórarins, er enn fór með þeim, ok var hon þrévetr. Þorsteinn tók útsynning hvassan; sigla þeir inn at straumum í þann straum, er hét Kolkistustraumr; sá er í mesta lagi þeira strauma, er á Breiðafirði eru. Þeim teksk siglingin ógreitt; heldr þat mest til þess, at þá var komit útfall sjávar, en byrrinn ekki vinveittr, því at skúraveðr var á, ok var hvasst veðrit, þá er rauf, en vindlítit þess í milli. Þórarinn stýrði ok hafði aktaumana um herðar sér, því at þrǫngt var á

skipinu; var hirzlum mest hlaðit, ok varð hár farmrinn, *en lǫndin váru nær* [motif *c*]; gekk skipit lítit, því at straumrinn gerðisk óðr at móti. Síðan sigla þeir á sker upp ok brutu ekki at. Þorsteinn bað fella seglit sem skjótast; bað menn taka forka ok ráða af skipinu. Þessa ráðs var freistat ok dugði eigi, því at svá var djúpt á bæði borð, at forkarnir kenndu eigi niðr, ok varð þar at bíða atfalls; fjarar nú undan skipinu. Þeir sá *sel í strauminum* um daginn, *meira mikilu en aðra; hann fór í hring um skipit* um daginn ok var ekki fitjaskammr; svá sýndisk þeim ǫllum, sem *mannsaugu væri í honum* [motif *d*]. Þorsteinn bað þá skjóta selinn; þeir leita við, ok kom fyrir ekki. Síðan fell sjór at. Ok er nær hafði, at skipit myndi fljóta, *þá rekr á hvassviðri mikit, ok hvelfir skipinu* [motif *e*], *ok drukkna nú menn allir, þeir er þar váru á skipinu* [motif *f*], nema einn maðr; *hann rak á land með viðum;* sá hét Guðmundr; *þar heita síðan Guðmundareyjar* [motif *g*] (xviii, 40-41).

(Thorstein Surt began his moving in spring after the Thing, and his livestock was driven in along the shore. Thorstein fitted out his ferry, and twelve in all went aboard. There was Thórarin, his son-in-law, on board and also Ósk, Thorstein's daughter. Thórarin's daughter Hild was along too; she was then three years old. Thorstein set sail to a stiff southwester. They sailed into the fjord narrows and got into that channel which is known as the Kolkistustraum, the swiftest and strongest of the currents in the Breidafjord. Their sailing was fraught with obstacles. First, ebb tide had set in, and not only that, the wind was unfavorable, for the weather was squally, gusting to a sharp gale when the showers came on, but with scarcely any breeze between times. Thórarin was steering and had the sail braces around his shoulders, because the boat was crowded and tightly packed. It was laden mostly with chests, and the cargo was piled high, and land was close by on either side. The ship made little headway, for a violent countercurrent set in against them. Then they sailed up onto a skerry, but they were not wrecked. Thorstein ordered the men to drop sail as quickly as possible and to take poles and push the ship off. This they tried, but it was to no avail, for it was so deep on either side that the poles could not reach bottom. So they were forced to wait for high tide, and in the meantime the water ebbed out from under the keel. During the day they saw a seal much bigger than any others in the channel. It swam in a circle around the ship throughout the day, and it was uncommonly big-flippered. They all thought it seemed to have human eyes. Thorstein told his men to shoot the seal, and they made a try at it, but that, too, came to nought. Then the tide came in, and just as they were about to get afloat, a sharp gust broke upon them and overturned the boat, and all on board drowned, except

111

for one man. He was washed ashore with the timbers. His name was Gudmund, and the islands where he came to land have been called the Gudmundareyjar ever since.)

In the other parallel accounts of drowning, all or most of the motifs may likewise be noted. The account of Thórd Ingunnarson's drowning (xxxv, 99-100) corresponds to that of Thorstein in all elements:

> (a) *En smala skyldi reka fyrir innan fjǫrðu* (The livestock was to be driven inland along the fjords); (b) [Þórðr] snarask þegar til ferðar við tíunda mann. Ingunn fór ok vestr með honum.... *Tólf váru þau alls á skipi*; þar var Ingunn ok ǫnnur kona (Thórd started out at once with nine men, and Ingunn, too, went west with him.... Altogether there were twelve on board — there was another woman besides Ingunn); (c) Þat sá þeir menn, *er á landi váru*, at hann kastaði því ǫllu, er til þunga var, útan mǫnnum; væntu þeir menn, *er á landi váru*, Þórði þá landtǫku, því at þá var af farit þat, sem skerjóttast var (People who were on shore saw him throw overboard everything that added to the weight, except the men themselves. They had hopes that Thórd would reach land safely, for he had by then passed the place thickest with rocks and reefs); (d) [The sorcerers, Kotkel and his family, cast a spell over Thórd's journey:] Þat fann Þórðr Ingunnarson ok hans fǫrunautar, þar sem hann var á sæ staddr, *ok til hans var gǫrt veðrit* (Thórd Ingunnarson and his companions felt it out at sea where they were, for the storm was raised against him); (e) Síðan *reis boði* skammt frá landi, sá er engi maðr munði, at fyrr hefði uppi verit, *ok laust skipit svá, at þegar horfði upp kjǫlrinn* (Then a breaker rose up a short distance from land, where nobody remembered ever having seen one before, and hit so hard against the ship that it turned keel up all at once); (f) *Þar drukknaði Þórðr ok allt fǫruneyti hans* (There Thórd drowned and all his company); (g) En skipit braut í spán, *ok rak þar kjǫlinn, er síðan heitir Kjalarey; skjǫld Þórðar rak í þá ey, er Skjaldarey er kǫlluð. Lík Þórðar rak þar þegar á land ok hans fǫrunauta; var þar haugr* orpinn at líkum þeira, þar er síðan heitir Haugsnes (And the ship was dashed to splinters. The keel drifted ashore to a place which ever since has had the name Kjalarey [Keel Isle]. Thórd's shield washed up on an island which is called Skjaldarey [Shield Isle]. The bodies of Thórd and his companions also soon washed ashore. There a mound was cast up over them and that place has been called Haugsnes [Mound Ness] ever since).

Variation in the account is achieved principally through altering the circumstances, especially the supernatural happenings that attend each of the drowning episodes and that are ultimately responsible for them. The sequence of motifs in Thórd's drowning undergoes a shift, for in the original text motif *c* follows motif *d*. Noteworthy is the care with which the author ensures the "proper number" of persons being on board.

Except for the detail concerning the livestock (motif *a*), the same elements are found again in the description of the drowning of Thorkel Eyjólfsson (lxxvi, 222):

> (*b*) Þeir sigla om daginn út eptir Breiðafirði *ok váru tíu eða tólf á skipi*[20] (They sailed that day out along the Breidafjord, and there were ten or twelve on board); (*c*) Þeir Þorkell sigla, þar til er þeir kómu at Bjarnarey; — *sá menn ferðina af hvárutveggja landinu* (Thorkel and his men sailed on until they came to Bjarnarey; people on both shores could see his passage); (*d*) Veðrit tók at hvessa mjǫk, ok gerði inn mesta storm, aðr létti (The weather began to blow sharply and turned into a full storm before it let up). [The fateful quality of the storm is carried by recollection of the prophecy and the premonitions that have preceded Thorkel's drowning.[21] And hence Thorstein hears his kinsman's "bane" in the howling of the wind (heyra gnýja bana Þorkels frænda)]. (*e*) *Þá laust hviðu í seglit, ok hvelfði skipinu* (A sharp gust smote the sail and overturned the ship); (*f*) *Þorkell drukknaði þar ok allir þeir menn, er með honum váru* (Thorkel drowned and all the men who were with him); (*g*) Viðuna rak víða um eyjar; *hornstafina rak í þá ey, er Stafey heitir síðan. Skǫfnungr var festr við innviðuna í ferjunni; hann hittisk við Skǫfnungsey* (The timber drifted far and wide about the islands; the cornerstaves drifted ashore at that island which has been called Stafey ever since. The sword Skofnung was stuck fast in the ribbing of the ferry and was found at Skofnungsey).

The motifs of the three drowning episodes can be schematized into a consistent pattern: (*a*) the driving of livestock along the shore; (*b*) twelve persons on board, (*c*) land near or on both sides, providing a danger spot and vantage point for observers; (*d*) the implication that supernatural as well as natural forces are at play; (*e*) the overturning of the boat by a single gust or wave; (*f*) the drowning of all on board (variant: except one man [utilized as substance for the mold of the next motif]); (*g*) the naming of places after whatever is salvaged or washed ashore at that spot; folk etymologies.

The Sales of Land

A schematism also marks the accounts of land sales at Hrappsstadir, Tunga, and Hjardarholt, the themes of which are reechoed, as in the case of the drownings, in each of the parts of the saga respectively. Óláf contemplates buying the lands at Hrappsstadir: "Lendur þær, er Hrappr hafði átt, lágu í auðn, sem fyrr var ritat. *Óláfi þóttu þær vel liggja*" (motif *a*) (xxiv, 66: "Those lands that Hrapp had owned were lying waste, as was said before. Óláf thought the property conveniently situated for him"). It is as though the first note of the theme is sounded here in Part I of the saga as preparation for its development in the succeeding parts.

The land sale at Tunga in Part II is described more fully and indeed occupies two transactions. In addition to the convenience of situation (motif *a*), further reasons for the sale and for the purchase are given. The first reference reports that Thórarin was interested in selling part of his land because, although he had good lands, he had little livestock (motif *b*), whereas Ósvíf wanted to buy for the opposite reason: he was short of land and had much livestock (motif *c*): "[Þórarinn] átti *lendur góðar, en minna lausafé*" [motif *b*]. "Ósvífr vildi kaupa at honum lendur, því at hann hafði *landeklu, en fjǫlða kvikfjár*" [motif *c*] (xxxii, 86). When sometime later Thórarin decides to sell all his land to the people at Laugar, new incentive has been added to the reason for selling: as before, his livestock was dwindling (motif *b*), but also too much friction was developing among the people in the district and he was friend to both sides (increment embellishment as variation). Bolli needed land because the "little land — much livestock" condition (motif *c*) still prevailed at Laugar, and since Tunga was adjacent, it was convenient (motif *a*):

> Þórarinn búandi í Tungu lýsir því, at hann vildi selja Tunguland; var þat bæði, at honum *þurru lausafé* [motif *b*], enda þótti honum mjǫk vaxa þústr milli manna í heraðinu, en honum var kært við hváratveggju. Bolli þóttisk þurfa at kaupa sér staðfestu, því at Laugamenn hǫfðu *fá lǫnd, en fjǫlða fjár* [motif *c*]. Pau Bolli ok Gudrún riðu í Tungu at ráði Ósvífrs; þótti þeim *í hǫnd falla at taka upp land þetta hjá sér sjálfum* [motif *a*] (xlvii, 146).

The episode of the land sale at Hjardarholt (lxxv, 218-219) contains the same ideas.[22] In discussing his intentions, Thorstein tells Thorkel that the time is convenient (*vel hent*) and that the land is just what he would most like to own (motif *a*), and he thinks Halldór might be interested in selling because he does not have much livestock (motif *b*): "hann hefir *lítit lausafé.*" The same reasons are repeated when Thorstein approaches Halldór on his farm: the arrangement would be advantageous (*vel hent*) for both (motif *a*), for Halldór does not have much livestock (motif *b*): " '*þú hefir ógnóglig lausafé, en land dýrt undir*' "[23] (lxxv, 219: " 'You don't have enough livestock, but valuable land for pasturing'"). Repetition of the chiasmal pattern "little livestock — much land" or "much livestock — little land" holds additional interest because it represents in miniature a type of compensatory balancing effected through reversal — and so, in itself, one on the structural ideas of the saga.

The foregoing examples have demonstrated how the motifs are each time recombined and adapted to their individual contexts, how their sequence may be reordered, and how here and there one of the motifs may be missing from the thematic complex, the pattern itself nonetheless remaining discernible and intact. An episode may even at times be sketched in condensed form, almost like a skeletal paradigm of the motifs and their key words. The drowning of Thorkel, which is less detailed and shorter than the corresponding descriptions, borders on this. Depth of interpretation is attained through the fact that the repetitions and formulae mutually elucidate one another. What is not stated is therefore implied.

Flexibility within the pattern is also achieved through variation, substitution of synonyms and antonyms, use of reversal and of increment elements. The uneven distribution of motifs (some appearing twice, others three times) coincides with the formal structure of the saga. Since the basic concept of equal balance and compensation occurs within a tripartite form, motifs are likely to be repeated in duplicate or triplicate. Repetition built upon the unit three contains and includes the unit two. The balance achieved through confirmation or comparison naturally requires readjustment when a third component is present. It has already been noted how from time to time reversals within essentially the same linguistic pattern are used to point up contrasts: *ekki efni / gott efni*; *sjá mun hann / sjá mun hann víst eigi*; *jafnræði / eigi jafnræði*; *ráðagørð / lítla ráðagørð*; *fúss / ekki fúss*; *lítilmannligt / ekki lítilmannligt*, among others. When such reversals occur in triplets, a word, phrase, or theme is repeated two times but is not identically repeated the third time. Instead, one of the three oftentimes presents a negation or reversal, and consequently two of the three units recombine into one unit over against the third.

The prognostication of Óláf, then the substantiation by Halldór of the ill dealings among the kinsmen, discussed earlier in connection with the prophecies,[24] form the first two complementary statements of a triplet: "'at *vér frændr* ok Laugamenn *berim eigi* allsendis *gæfu til um vár skipti*'" (Óláf, xxxix, 112) and "'þó at *vér frændr bærim eigi giptu til samþykkis*'" (Halldór, lvi, 169). Later in the saga Snorri Godi declares: "'En nú vilda ek leita um sættir ok vita, *ef endir yrði á ógiptu yðvarri frænda*'" (lxxi, 209:

"'So now I would like to try for a peaceful settlement and see if there cannot be an end to this ill luck between you kinsmen'").

Another illustration occurs in the comments about Gudrún after Bolli's death. First, we are told: "Þat rœddu þeir fǫrunautar Halldórs, at *Guðrúnu þœtti lítit dráp Bolla*" (lvi, 169: "Talk started up among Halldór's men about how lightly Gudrún seemed to take Bolli's killing"). In expressing his opinion, Halldór reverses their judgment: "'*Ekki* er þat mín ætlan, at *Guðrúnu þykki lítit lát Bolla*'" (*ibid*.: "'I don't believe Gudrún takes Bolli's death so lightly'"), and then substitutes a positive for the *ekki...lítit*: "'Þat er ok eptir vánum, at *Guðrúnu þykki mikit lát Bolla*'" (*ibid*.: "'It is no more than to be expected that Gudrún should take Bolli's death seriously'"). Other examples may be found where the two-and-one pattern results in this same tendency to rebuild pairs in which the confirmation of the positive or the negative element forms a unit.[25]

The following examples, among others, illustrate increment repetitions: Thorgerd's sons, it will be recalled, cannot bear any longer their mother's taunts: *eigi lengr þola frýju móðar sinnar* (liv, 163); the reaction of Gudrún's sons in the same situation is a reecho with increment: *eigi bera lengr harm sinn ok frýja módur sinnar* (lx, 180). Threefold statements concerning availability of aid and support set up likenesses between two related themes. As already noted, the relatives always rely upon Thórólf Rednose for support: "gengu þangat jafnan *til trausts*" (xi, 21); Vigdís confirms this by sending him an outlaw for sheltering: "sent honum *til halds og* [*sic*] *trausts*" (xv, 35);[26] and Gudrún, whose actions parallel Vigdís', also shelters an outlaw: "sendr Guðrúnu *til trausts ok halds*" (lxix, 202). The increment element, with variation through inversion, is retained in the third repetition, bringing the latter two examples into intended closer comparison.

The recruiting of Lambi and Thorstein to take part in avenging Bolli affords another example. Snorri first advises Gudrún: "'Þeir Lambi ok Þorsteinn skulu vera í ferð með sonum þínum, ok er þeim Lamba þat *makligt friðkaup*'" (lix, 178: "'Lambi and Thorstein are to join up with your sons; for the two of them that is a fitting price for peace'"). Next, Thorgils Holluson tells Thorstein the Black: "'Vilju vér þess biðja þik, Þorsteinn, at þú sér í ferð þessi með þeim brœðrum ok kaupir þik svá *í frið ok í sætt*'" (lxi, 182: "'We would like you, Thorstein, to be in on this raid with the brothers and thus buy peace and pardon for yourself'"). And finally Lambi, when asked to join the raid, says: "'*Illt* þykki mér *friðkaup* í þessu ok ódrengiligt'" (lxi, 183: "'It's an ill price to pay for peace, and unmanly besides'"). The increment repetition is contained in the second example, whereas examples two and three form a contrastive pair.

Another case in point is when Thorleik, agreeing to go abroad, says to Óláf: "'Veit ek ok, at þú munt *ekki at verr* gera til Bolla, sonar míns, þó at ek sjá hvergi í nánd'" (xxxviii, 111: "'I know too that you will not treat my son Bolli any the worse for my not being anywhere near'"). Óláf answers: "'Ætla ek mér þat at gera heðan í frá sem hingat til, er til Bolla kemr, ok vera til hans *eigi verr en til minna sona*'" (*ibid.*: "'And when it comes to Bolli, I have every intention of being to him henceforth what I have been hitherto. I shall treat him no worse than my own sons'"). Later on, after Kjartan's death, when Bolli's life is at stake, Óláf says to the force of men that he is sending to Laugar: "'Þat er minn vili, at þér verið Bolla, ef hann þarf, *eigi verr en þér fylgið mér*'" (l, 157: "'It is my wish that you defend Bolli if need be, and no less so than if you were standing by me'"). The *eigi verr* theme applying to Bolli is carried through in triple repetition. Thorleik asked for assurance; Óláf gave his word; and when it became necessary to do so, he made it good. In the last two examples the limiting phrases *en til minna sona* and *en þér fylgið mér* bring increment and variation to the pattern.

Threefold repetitions thus may be grouped under the following categories: all three statements are related to the same person, event, or theme and may or may not show increment or reversal; two of the three are related, the third stands apart (in which case the related two are either confirmations, or parallels or contrasts); or all three are unrelated. For the most part the triplet motifs already discussed belong to the first category. Gudrún's false promise to Thorgils not to marry any other countryman (any other man in the country) is also representative: "'*engum manni samlendum gipt ǫðrum en Þorgísli*'" (lix, 178); "'*at giptask engum manni ǫðrum samlendum en honum*'" (lx, 181); "'*at giptask engum manni samlendum ǫðrum en þér*'" (lxv, 195).

In the second category, two of the statements in the triplet relate to a single referent, the third stands alone. So, for example, the expression *ok heldr seint* (xxxvii, 104: rather reluctantly) occurs first when Eldgrím returns Hrút's greeting and a second and third time in the episode of the swimming match between Kjartan and the king where Kjartan's response to the king's requests is twice given "rather reluctantly" (xl, 117, 118: *ok heldr seint*). The first instance prepares or introduces the motif; the last two are related as confirmation statements and belong to Repetition. Other arrangements of the pattern are possible, as, for example, when Kjartan asks Bolli about accepting Christianity: "'*Hversu fúss ertu*'" (xl, 119: "'How keen are you'"). Bolli replies with a negation: "'*Ekki em ek þess fúss*'" (*ibid.*: "'I'm not at all keen about it' ").²⁷ Later in the saga Eid answers Thorkel's question about pursuing the outlaw Grím with: "'*Ekki em ek þess fúss*'" (lvii, 172). The first two elements in the triplet form a reversed pair, the third picks up the pattern like an echo.

In the third category the circumstances in which the repetitions occur are similar but unrelated. Three times we are told of people making unfortunate choices, and each time similar words are employed. In the first instance, Hrút says to Eldgrím: "'Þat hygg ek, at *þú kjósir þann hlut til handa báðum okkr, er verr muni gegna*'" (xxxvii, 105: "'I think you are making a choice which will prove the worse for both of us'"). In trying to convert the Icelanders, King Óláf Tryggvason tells them they will rue their decision: "Konungr segir, at *þeir myndi þann kost velja sér til handa, er þeim gegndi verr*" (xl, 120: "The king said they were likely making that choice which would be the worse for them"). And a like situation is recognized by Thorstein Thorkelsson: "'Sá okkar *mun nú ráða, er verr mun gegna*'" (lxxvi, 222: "'That one of us who rules now will be the worse off for it'"). From these examples it is again obvious that the author expresses similar ideas in similar fashion.²⁸ He does not innovate, rather he works, consciously or unconsciously, within a limited linguistic field, but always in consonance with the purpose of his composition; always within the conventional and normal idiom, but arranging and repeating his words with precision to form an abstract schematism and pattern of their own.

Quadruplets

This tendency toward triple repetition on occasion develops further into quadruplet repetition. In some respects, such groups of four might be considered transitional and, by virtue of frequency, as falling under Recurrence. But the main distinction to be considered is a qualitative one. Since quadruple repetitions tend to split up into combinations of two pairs, or of a triplet and an odd one, and since structurally and formally they contribute to the preparing, echoing, equalizing, and comparing found everywhere in the saga, it is only proper to consider them here.

Within the quadruplet, combinations are varied and flexible; all the possibilities thus far discussed are also represented here: confirmation-statements, parallels, contrasts, negative reversals, and the like. An example of a quadruplet that re-forms into two pairs, in each of which the repeated words are negated, can be cited. Jórunn asks about Hoskuld's plans (*ráðagǫrð*) and he replies he has made "*'litla ráðagǫrð'*" (xix, 46: "'no plans to speak of'"); similarly, Snorri asks Gudrún's sons about the plans they have been hatching: "'Hvat hafi þit *í ráðagǫrðum?*'" and Bolli replies: "'Þetta eru ekki *ráðagǫrðir*'" (lxxi, 208).

Again two pairs are formed in each of which a comparison is intended. It is stated, for example, that the majority of people held out against Christianity first in Trondheim: "*En hinir váru þó miklu fleiri, er í móti váru*" (xl, 118: "But those numbered many more who were against it"); and then in Iceland: "*En þó váru þeir miklu fleiri, er í móti mæltu*" (xli, 125). With slight variation in form, it is told that the majority argued against Orn's better judgment: "*En mestr hluti manna mælti í gegn*" (xxi, 53) and in another place it is Thorleik who is similarly outnumbered: "*Þeir váru fleiri, er í móti mælti*" (lxiv, 191). The first pair marks a comparison between analogous situations in Norway and Iceland in respect to the conversion, and the second pair describes two episodes in which one man, though outnumbered, overrules majority opinion. All four episodes deal with situations where minority stands against majority or vice versa, thus calling to mind again the concept of weighing evens and odds in the saga — whether it be one man fighting against overwhelming odds, one man's life weighed against another's, one man's worth equalling another's; one man's word against the word of others.

Sometimes a triplet and a lone example will represent a pair in which the components of the triplet relate to a single referent, the odd component serving either to prepare or to recall. So, for example, the reference to Hoskuld's sitting at home on his farm prepares for three subsequent references to Óláf's doing the same: "*Hǫskuldr sitr nú í búi sínu* ok gerisk hniginn á inn efra aldr" (xx, 49: "Hoskuld now sat at home on his farm and was getting bowed down with old age"). And the next generation follows suit: "*Sitr Óláfr nú at búi sínu*, svá at vetrum skipti eigi allfám" (xxviii, 77: "Óláf now sits at home on his farm while quite a few seasons pass"). We have noted before how the author by such subtle and seemingly insignificant repetitions makes Hoskuld the model for Óláf or Óláf the image of his father. The next two references to Óláf, while carrying through the likeness to the others, through an increment element, enhances Óláf over his father: "*Óláfr Hǫskuldsson sat í búi sínu í miklum sóma*, som fyrr var ritat"[29] (xxxi, 83: "Óláf Hoskuldsson sat on his farm with much honor, as was said before"). And in confirmation of this, again it is said: "*Óláfr sat nú í búi sínu með miklum sóma, ok eru þar allir synir hans heima*" (xxxix, 112). One might say, from another point of view, that two pairs are here formed, the one a comparison of Hoskuld and Óláf, the other a confirmation pair relating to Óláf's high esteem. The categories and aspects of the saga overlap, as we have often had occasion to note. In a similar manner, reference to the fine clothes and weapons of Bolli Bollason and his men, like an echo, calls to mind three earlier references to Óláf's fine weapons and clothes and marks a comparison between the generations.[30]

Another example of a quadruplet where one component acts as a preparatory motif and the triplet relates to a single theme but also contains a pair might be cited. In presenting his case to the Irish king, Óláf speaks "both at length and eloquently" (xxi, 57: "*bæði langt ørendi ok snjallt*"). It has been noted at various points how in the episodes concerning the Christianization, first of Norway and then of Iceland, analogous motifs accompany the parallelism.[31] Picking up the motif introduced by Óláf's oration, the Norwegian king, it is twice stated, preached the faith "at length and eloquently" (xl, 118: "*langt ørendi ok snjallt*"; xl, 122: "*bæði langt ørendi ok snjallt*") — a confirmation pair. Then in Iceland Gizur and Hjalti undertake the conversion: "Síðan fara þeir til alþings ok tǫlðu trú fyrir mǫnnum, *bæði langt ørendi ok snjallt*, ok tóku þá allir menn trú á Íslandi" (xlii, 127: "Then they went on to the Althing and preached the faith before the people, both at length and eloquently. Then all the people in Iceland accepted the faith").[32]

We have seen how in both the triplets and the quadruplets the author is working with the units two and three. These factors are occasioned by the saga's structure. And just as there was evidence of preference for the number two and doubles of all kinds, so too the saga shows a predilection for the number three and thirds. Here is a sampling: On three occasions three marks of silver are exchanged: that is the price for Melkorka (xii, 23); Thórd receives that amount as a bribe from Ingjald (xiv, 32); and Óláf pays that sum for the land and property at Hrappsstadir (xxiv, 67). Hild is three years old when she drowns (xviii, 40); Bolli is three years old when Óláf fosters him (xxvii, 75). Hrút lives at Kambsnes for three years (xxx, 80); Óláf lives three years after Kjartan's death (xlix, 159); Kjartan bans exit to the Laugar people for three nights (xlvii, 145); Kjartan asks Gudrún to wait the conventional three years (xl, 115); Thorgils pays one-third and Thorstein two-thirds of the weregild for Helgi Hardbeinsson (lxvii, 197; and Hoskuld's paternal legacy and also the expense of his funeral feast are divided into thirds (xxvi, 72, 73).[33]

The twice and thrice in Eldgrím's bargaining with Thorleik for the stud of horses neatly repeats the idea of doubles incremented to triples. Eldgrím says: "'Munu margir mæla, at ek bjóða við *tvenn verð*'" (xxxvii, 103: "'Many will say I'm offering you twice their worth'"), to which Thorleik replies: "'Þessi hross fær þú aldregi, þóttú bjóðir við *þrenn verð*'" (*ibid.*: "'You'll never get these horses, even if you offer thrice their worth'"). It will be recalled that a type of numerical increment took place when the participants in the three raids increased from nine to ten, with Thorgerd as the extra, and that the increase was retained in the third raiding party where there were also ten. An increment, once introduced, is often repeated: i.e. *í miklum sóma / með miklum sóma* noted above.

The number twelve, too, is given extraordinary preference. Frequently, as the following representative examples show, the reference is marked by similarity of circumstance. So, parties of twelve participate in prosecutions, retaliations, settlements of all kinds, as when Ingjald makes a raid on Thórd Goddi with twelve in his party (xiv, 32) to follow up the prosecution for his brother's killing; or when Hrút makes a cattle raid in retaliation and has twelve in his party (xiv, 45). Drawing-up of a marriage contract, settling a divorce, and witnessing a land sale all involve twelve persons as witnesses (xliii, 129; xxv, 96; xlvii, 146, respectively). Twelve *aurar* of gold (instead of the legally allowable twelve of silver) are given as legacy to an illegitimate son (xxvi, 72). Óláf at twelve rides for the first time to the Thing (xvi, 38); twelve-year-old Kári Hrútsson is killed by witchcraft (xxxvii, 106); twelve-year-old Bolli Bollason goes with Gudrún to meet Snorri (lix, 176); twelve-year-old Bolli Bollason also gives quarter to twelve-year-old Hardbein Helgason, a like image of himself (lxiv, 192); and when he is twelve, Gellir Thorkelsson, goes abroad with his father Thorkel Eyjólfsson (lxxiv, 215).[34]

The legal and social customs that easily could account for the use of the number twelve in the examples cited seem to have attracted the author so strongly that he applies that number to other situations where it would not be obligatory. Óláf, Kjartan, and Bolli Bollason all ride home from their ships upon their return from abroad with twelve in their group (xxii, 61; xliv, 134; lxxviii, 227, respectively), a factor which further strengthens the comparisons between them already noted. Kjartan goes to a feast at Ásbjarnarnes with a party of twelve (xlv, 135) and leaves Hól with like number (xlviii, 149). Twelve are on board at the three shipwrecks and drownings discussed above (xviii, 40; xxxv, 99; lxxvi, 222); there are twelve women in Gilli's tent (xii, 23); and Gudrún spins yarn for twelve ells (xlix, 154).

Although preference for the number twelve and in some cases for the number three may reflect the mores of time and place, and the predilection of the number three may even suggest to some the magical "three times" in folklore, the suitability and re-formation in the individual poetic work are the paramount concerns.

We have seen how themes and phrasing in triplicate and quadruplicate can often be resolved into simple double repetition and serve the same purposes as discussed under Repetition and Comparison. Of particular interest is the manner in which the author has manipulated his thematic patternings of the parties, the incitements, the killings, the drownings, and the land sales, rendering each individual yet preserving the underlying mold. The pattern is so constant that in each case it can be anticipated, thus reinforcing the aspect Foreknowledge through expectation of the known. Since the patterns are predictable and the linguistic variation is kept at a minimum, the reader is held within a sphere of limited and known possibilities. It must be reemphasized here that we are not interested in how commonplace or current in saga literature any given theme, phrase, or technique may be (and this often is an illusion on the part of critics and remains undemonstrated), but rather in the author's special arrangement of these elements within the saga as a closed unit. Provenance is an entirely different question falling outside the scope and purpose of an internal analysis.

The limitations set by the linguistic medium itself enhance the feeling of persistency and predetermination of the world in which the action of the saga takes place. The author has so arranged his linguistic units that a pattern emerges on a grand scale. On an abstract level this pattern is completely analogous to the meaning conveyed behind the events portrayed. That repetition in equalized pairs might be interpreted as expressing symbolically the moral code of compensatory revenge has been suggested. Transition into triplets and quadruplets calls for readjustment within the schematism. That each of the major patterns is used three times coincides with the special form of the saga and gives them importance above double repetitions or multiple appearance. In Gudrún's words, the score cannot be "evened exactly"; the feeling persists that the repetitions, the patterning could run on indefinitely. Equilibrium is but temporarily established and is always on the verge of being upset. Twos run on into threes, threes into fours. Repetition becomes Recurrence. A type of series repetition can be detected in the saga which, like the snowballing of compensatory killings, links together certain special sets of motifs next to be discussed.

V

RECURRENCE

In recounting the progress of events through generation after generation, *Laxdœla* shows the tendency to describe like happenings in like language. These verbal resemblances especially accompany socially set customs that belong to the cultural background and are particularly marked in the cycle of normal life: birth, childhood, betrothal, marriage, career, and death.[1] Such events naturally occur in many other sagas. On occasion, examples of some of the expressions can also be found, yet *Laxdœla*'s formulations are distinctive. Just as some characters appear in major roles in one saga and in another fade into the background, particular linguistic elements which exhibit scantier and less patterned representation elsewhere seem to come to the fore in *Laxdœla*. Also it is not by chance that the *Laxdœla* author has chosen a series of progressive generations and the patterning of each round of life as vehicles for his presentation.

Through premonitions, prophecies, and fated occurrences, the author has established the saga world as being both set and preknown. The sameness of verbal expression in descriptions of the sameness of the round of existence furthers that illusion. This social world, too, is predetermined, in that it follows a prescribed formula. The exactness and infallibility with which the foreknown is fulfilled corresponds to the exactness and inflexibility with which the demands of the code of justice are carried out. Inevitability is the concept which underlies both aspects of life. It is not surprising then that the social order is presented in formalized fashion, couched in set and prescribed terms. If Repetition and Comparison represent through formal means equalization and compensation and so symbolize the retaliatory aspect of justice, Recurrence with its round of social customs and seemingly unlimited repetitions of the formulae accompanying those events presents a poignant reminder of the other ever more disastrous aspect of the moral

123

code. Retaliations can never remain equalized as one-for-one but run on impelling a continuing series. It is an endless cycle.

The examples under Recurrence have not been selected merely because of frequency. This recurring linguistic fabric has its own special quality. First, it presents those events that are common to all, the expected course of life. The similar formulations for each of the phases of the social cycle awaken the feeling that they could run on indefinitely, as often as the situations arise.[2] Seen as a series, Recurrent events form a background for the main events of the narrative with their more unique situations and patternings. The main narrative is most concerned with the retaliatory aspect of justice, with setting up balances and counterbalances (Repetition and Comparison). But this aspect is only part of the total picture. The balancing is temporary, for the retaliatory deeds are ever inclined to continue in a chain reaction. The main agents and the main events belong, naturally, also to the wider social background. It is as though some agents and events, a few links in the chain, had been singled out and their lives and relationships put into center focus on front stage, where the working-out of fate and justice is shown off to advantage by means of the point-counterpoint system established through the abstracted word patterns developed under Repetition and Comparison. Recurrence is the backdrop which shows the larger context of which they are a part, the bigger tragedy. Hence some few of the motifs that pointed out differences and similarities between the agents or events of the main action will be seen also to be part of the recurrent background. In the case of the triplets and quadruplets there was an attempt to hold the equilibrium. In Recurrence there is no check. Yet with certain recurrent phrases, apart from the cycle of life themes, negative and positive formulations momentarily set up a kind of linkage in the chain pulling in equal opposition. Such is the precariousness of the balance and compensating that the author wishes to convey.

Second, some examples under Recurrence represent a group of conventional phrases in which one can sense from their use in *Laxdœla* alone a kind of stereotyped reiteration, verbalisms that ring as clichés of long-standing. This group reflects an idealized heroic tradition with superlative qualities.

Of the descriptions connected with the round of existence some stand out as particularly typical of *Laxdœla*, whereas others, less striking, partake of common Icelandic idiom, yet recur with sufficient frequency to further the illusion of the series. It is, after all, the patterning and repetition of ordinary phraseology that endows any of the words and phrases with unique significance within *Laxdœla*. Such is the case, for instance, with references to the birth of a child, where the conventional procedure is accompanied by verbal formalism: "Sá sveinn *var vatni ausinn ok nafn gefit, ok var kallaðr Hrútr*" (viii, 15: "The boy was sprinkled with water and given a name and was called Hrút").[3]

As children grow up, they are recurrently described as being big and strong and promising at an unusually early age, and the catchword is *snimma* (*snimmendis*): "Hann [Hrútr] var *snimmendis mikill ok sterkr*, er hann óx upp" (viii, 16: "Hrút early grew up to be big and strong").[4] Hoskuld and Bolli Bollason exhibit early maturity and about each of them the same formulaic phrase occurs: "hann [Hǫskuldr] *var fyrr fullkominn at hyggju en vetratǫlu*" (vii, 14: "Hoskuld was mature beyond his years"); "hann [Bolli] var þá tólf vetra gamall, en *fullkominn var hann at afli ok hyggju*, svá at þeir váru margir, er eigi biðu meira þroska, þó at alroskinr væri" (lix, 176: "He [Bolli] was then twelve years old, but just as mature in body and mind as many are after they reach full manhood"). The parallel phrase in reference to Bolli shows an interesting increment *at afli*, for although the formula camouflages it, it is clear from this and from the context that Bolli at twelve is ready to be his father's avenger.[5] He is also already carrying Footbiter.

In making use of another traditional theme, that of one child being "loved most" and so singled out, the *Laxdœla* author has done several things which are unique and which expressly serve the formal concepts in the saga. First, he has consistently employed the motif as a running thread throughout the generations: Unn esteemed Óláf Feilan above all others (vii, 11: "Hann *mat* Unnr *um fram alla menn*"); Thorgerd loved Hoskuld most (viii, 16: "hon *unni* honum *um alla menn fram*"); Hoskuld loved Bárd best (ix, 18: "Hǫskuldr *unni* honum *mest allra barna sinna*"), but afterwards when Óláf was born also showed him great love (xiii, 27: "lagði *ást mikla* við sveininn"); Óláf loved Kjartan most (xxviii, 77: "Óláfr *unni mest* Kjartani *allra barna manna*"); Gudrún loved Bolli Bollason best (lvi, 170: "Guðrún *unni* honum *mikit*"; lxx, 204: "Guðrún *unni* Bolla *mest allra barna sinna*").[6] By virtue of its tone and frequency the motif is rendered commonplace and belongs to Recurrence; yet in addition, the motif is made unobtrusively available for special need (viz. Comparison) at any point in the story, as noted in the relationships among the pairs of inimical brothers. Such double treatment is a characteristic feature of the saga's style throughout.

The conventional procedure in regard to betrothals may be found in most saga literature, but here again the *Laxdœla* author shows greater ingenuity in its presentation. The advice of one kinsman to another *at staðfesta ráð ok kvænask* (to settle down and get married) and other similar formulations of the idea run through the generations: Unn so advises Óláf Feilan (vii, 11); Hoskuld makes the suggestion to Óláf Peacock (xxii, 62); Thuríd to Kjartan (xlv, 137); and Snorri so advises Thorkel (lviii, 174). Significantly, when Bolli wishes to marry Gudrún, he himself makes the suggestion, asking for Óláf's help but using the expected *staðfesta ráð mitt ok kvángask* (xlii, 128). Bolli Bollason in turn also takes the initiative and asks that a woman be wooed on his behalf (lxx, 205). By means of such subtle innovations in the application of the pattern, the author brings out implied differences and likenesses.

In the reply to the suggestion of marriage, the author introduces one of his most ingenious terms, turning normal idiom into poetic imagery. The comment that the question of marriage would not have been "brought up" if it were not already known where it was "to end," (*upp kveðit...niðr koma*) usually accompanies a query regarding the identity of the woman. Óláf's answer to Hoskuld is representative:

> Óláfr svarar: "Lítt hefi ek þat hugfest hér til; veit ek eigi, hvar sú kona sitr, er mér sé mikit happ í at geta;...veit ek ok þat gorla, at *þú munt þetta eigi fyrr hafa upp kveðit en þú munt hugsat hafa, hvar þetta skal niðr koma*" (xxii, 62: Óláf answered: "I haven't given this any serious thought before, and I don't know who or where the woman might be that I would consider myself lucky in getting;...I also am quite sure that you would not have brought this up before you knew were it was to end").

Hoskuld names the woman he has in mind, and Óláf is agreeable: "'En svá máttu ætla, *faðir*, ef þetta mál er *upp borit* ok gangisk eigi við, at mér mun *illa líka'*" (*ibid.*: "'But mind you, father, I will take it very ill if this proposal is brought up and is not carried through'"). Thorgerd Egilsdóttir gives a refusal. Thereupon Óláf reminds his father as follows:

> "Nú er, *sem ek sagða þér, faðir*, at mér myndi *illa líka* ef ek fenga nǫkkur svívirðingarorð at móti; réttu meir, er þetta var *upp borit*; nú skal ek ok því ráða, at eigi skal hér *niðr falla*" (xxiii, 64: "Now it is just as I told you, father, that I would take it ill if I got some abusive words in return. You had your way when this matter was brought up, but now I'm going to have my way and see to it that it isn't dropped here").

The repetition of elements in this episode is like a variation on a theme with rearrangement, substitution, and embellishment. First, the theme *upp kveðit... niðr koma* is sounded in Óláf's surmising the aforethought in Hoskuld's motives. Next, Óláf echoes the *upp kveðit* with his *upp borit*, applying the idea in two contexts, and a new element *illa líka* enters. Confirmation of Óláf's premonition follows with the repetition of *illa líka* and the *sem ek sagða þér*, which latter one points explicitly to the antecedent. It is to be noted that direct address is used in both referent and confirmation. But the *sem ek sagða þér*, as noted in some instances of the *sem fyrr* phrase,[7] refers only to the one clause and not to the *ef ek fenga nǫkkur svívirðingarorð at móti*, which is a new embellishment that on the one hand narrows the meaning of the prior statement *ef þetta mál er upp borit ok gangisk eigi við*, but on the other leaves the association still indefinite by virtue of the plural *svívirðingarorð*. The latter finally becomes specific when Óláf himself selects the abusive word *ambáttarsonr* in his talk with Thorgerd.[8] At the close, repetition of the theme is completed by using the already introduced variation *upp borit* and by substituting *niðr falla* for *niðr koma*. Father and son are brought into comparison and contrast through retention of the antithetical *upp...niðr* and the final apt substitution *falla*. Formal rhetorical devices are thus turned into an image of the discursive content.

According to pattern, the *upp kveðit...niðr koma* construction likewise occurs in Óláf's reply to Bolli's statement that he would like to settle down and get married:

> "Þær eru flestar konur, at vér munum kalla, at þeim sé fullboðit, þar er þú ert; *muntu ok eigi hafa þetta fyrr upp kveðit en þú munt hafa statt fyrir þér, hvar niðr skal koma*" (xliii, 128: "I would say that most women would be getting more than a worthy offer where you are concerned. But you no doubt have not brought this matter up before you had it settled in your own mind where it was to end").

In this illustration of the author's method, it can be seen how one expression serves as a recurrent idea in the proposals, "evens out" a difference between father and son, represents a threefold repetition with confirmation and contrast, and on yet another plane symbolizes in miniature the overall effect the author is seeking to create: of having "upp kveðit" only those components in the narration that also "niðr koma" in necessary correlation.

But to continue with the betrothals. In accordance with normal practice and in conventionalized style, the woman who is to be asked is named with reference to the excellence of the match and oftentimes to the geographic area. The naming of Thorgerd Egilsdóttir is representative:

> "Egill á sér dóttur, þá er *Þorgerðr heitir; þessarrar konu* ætla ek þér til handa at *biðja, því at þessi kostr er albeztr í ǫllum Borgarfirði*, ok þó at víðara væri" (xxii, 62: Egil has a daughter

who is called Thorgerd. She is the woman I have in mind to ask in marriage on your behalf, for she is the very best match in all Borgarfjord and even farther").

The increment *ok þó at víðara væri* adds to the persuasive argument and brings nice variation to the usual naming of her home district: Thorgerd would be the best match even if one included a greater area and looked farther afield.[9]

Next the proposal is broached to the woman's father who in turn speaks of his good knowledge of the suitor and his family and adds that his daughter could not be better married nor the offer better tendered. So when Thorkel presents Bolli Bollason's suit to Snorri, Snorri replies:

"Slíkra mála er *vel leitat*, sem mér er at þér ván; vil ek þessu máli vel svara, því at mér þykkir Bolli *inn mannvænsti maðr*, ok sú kona þykkir mér vel gipt, er honum er gipt" (lxx, 206: "Such a proposal is well tendered, as I would expect of you; and I want to give favorable answer to this suit, for I think Bolli a most promising man, and any woman married to him is well married").[10]

The father presents the suit to his daughter, stating the name of the suitor and praising his qualifications, something like an image in reverse of the presentation given the suitor about the woman to be wooed:

"*Maðr heitir Óláfr* ok er Hoskuldsson, ok er hann nú *frægstr maðr* einnhverr. Hoskuldr, faðir hans, hefir *vakit bónorð* fyrir hond Óláfs ok beðit þín. Hefi ek því *skotit mjok til þinna ráða*; vil ek nú vita *svor þín*; en svá lízk oss, sem *slíkum málum sé vel fellt at svara, því at þetta gjaforð er gofugt*" (xxiii, 63: "There's a man by the name of Óláf Hoskuldsson, and he is now one of the most famous men hereabouts. His father Hoskuld has broached a proposal on behalf of Óláf and has asked for your hand. I have left the matter for your decision, and I would now like to know your answer. However, I would think it easy to answer such a suit, for the match is a very worthy one").

The father and brothers or friend present all urge the match, and as a final step the daughter puts the decision back in her father's hands.[11] The betrothal process thus involves a series of four transactions, three of which give presentations of the proposal in similarly repeated terms. When the woman is a widow or the answer is negative, adjustments in the normal pattern take place.

After the betrothal has been settled, the farmstead where the wedding will be held and the time of the wedding feast are agreed upon,[12] and the bridegroom rides home to await the appointed time.[13] The feast itself is prepared and guests attend from both houses, the *boðsmenn* who come as invited guests and the *fyrirboðsmenn* who, as part of the host's party, receive the others at the farmstead. The guests are described as coming in splendor, dressed in brightly colored clothes (*í litklæðum*), accompanied by a select and handsome company (*valit lið, it skǫruligsta lið*). The feast is always described as being very well attended (*fjǫlmennt*), and the number of guests on both sides is usually about equal so as to pay both sides honor.[14] The reference to specific numbers at the wedding feast of Thorkel and Gudrún, however, prepares the audience for the outcome of the argument which later takes place between Thorkel and Gudrún at the feast.[15] Thus here again the author has veiled his hint through a common convention and seemingly normal formulation of it in order to apply it to his specific purpose later.

The feast is *skǫrulig, virðulig*, or *ágæt* (splendid, worthy, excellent), and the wedding guests depart for home bearing handsome gifts.[16] The bride stays on at the farm where the wedding feast was held or moves to his or her homestead as the case may be, and their married life takes on the typical pattern first introduced with Herjólf and Thorgerd: "*Ok giptisk Þorgerðr Herjólf ok ferr heim til bús með honum; takask með þeim góðar ástir*" (vii, 15: "And Thorgerd married Herjólf and went to his homestead to live and they grew to love one another dearly").[17] Consonant with the author's practice, a reversal or contrastive aspect of the expected pattern is found: "*Vel var um samfarar þeira Hǫskulds ok ekki mart hversdagliga*" (ix, 18: "Hoskuld's and Jórunn's married life went well, but there was not much love day by day"). Note the lesser value of *vel* in comparison to *góðar ástir*. Geirmund's and Thuríd's mismatch is similarly formulated: "*Ekki var mart um í samfǫrum þeira Geirmundar ok Þuríðar; var svá af beggja þeira hendi*" (xxx, 80: "There was not much love in Geirmund's and Thuríd's married life; and that was so on both sides"). The increment element *var svá af beggja þeira hendi* sets the stage for the next occurrence of the situation, namely in Gudrún's and Bolli's marriage where the variant formulation significantly marks the lack of love as being "on Gudrún's part": "*Ekki var mart í samfǫrum þeira Bolla af Guðrúnar hendi*" (xliii, 130).

Before long, children are born to the married couple and the cycle begins again: "*Þau Herjólfr ok Þorgerðr hǫfðu eigi lengi ásamt verit, áðr þeim varð sonar auðit*" (viii, 15: "Herjólf and Thorgerd had not been married long before a son was born to them").[18]

As for the next stage of life, that of attaining a position of power and prestige, a chieftaincy at home, or of becoming liegeman at the Norwegian court comprised the most coveted careers. Historically, in the thirteenth century, the period in which *Laxdœla* was written, prominent Icelanders were increasingly seeking personal honor and prestige at the royal court. The importance attached to gaining recognition at the court in Norway, repeatedly referred to in the saga, undoubtedly reflects this trend,[19] but the particular formulation of these receptions is typical of the saga in that the phrases and repetitions link episodes and make comparisons more obvious. This theme, as in the case of the betrothals, is divided into a series of motifs. Reasons for going abroad usually involve getting timber for building, or are undertaken for the sake of fame and fortune, experience and knowledge.[20]

Descriptions of preparations for the journey abroad and of the voyage itself are likewise stylized and follow a pattern. Wares and goods for trading are assembled; a ship, or more frequently half interest in a ship is purchased; or passage with someone is taken. The crossing generally is said to be a good one with a fair wind (*vel reiðfara, byrjaði vel*); the place of arrival in Norway is usually noted.[21] The account of Hoskuld's journey is representative:

> Nú láta þeir í haf, ok gefr þeim vel, ok tóku Nóreg heldr sunnarliga, kómu við Horðaland, þar sem kaupstaðrinn í Bjǫrgvin er síðan. Hann *setr upp skip sitt* (xi, 22: They put out to sea and got a good wind and made Norway somewhat to the south. They landed at Hordaland, where the town of Bergen is now. Hoskuld laid up his ship).

Within the stereotyped descriptions of smooth and short sea crossings, the author depicts some journeys as arduous or long, thereby setting up a contrast within the series — again the characteristic practice of the *Laxdœla* author. The journey of Thorleik and Bolli Bollason is representative: "Þeir bjuggu nú skipit, ok er þeir váru *albúnir, létu þeir í haf. Þeim byrjaði ekki skjótt, ok hǫfðu útivist langa, tóku* um haustit *Nóreg ok kómu norðr við Þrándheim*" (lxxiii, 212: "They fitted out the ship, and when they were all ready, they put out to sea. They did not get a fair wind and were out a long time, making Norway north at Trondheim in the fall").[22]

Recurrent themes and phrases likewise characterize descriptions of the arrival and stay in Norway. The Icelanders are given good reception (*góðar viðtǫkur*) and a friendly welcome (*með allri blíðu*), wherever they visit abroad. Not uncommonly the king recognizes the leader of the company of Icelanders through his kinsmen and invites him to stay as long as he likes, he and all his followers, and offers him some position at court.[23] The account of Óláf's reception is typical:

> Fara þeir Óláfr ok Ǫrn nú til hirðarinnar ok fá þar *góðar viðtǫkur*; vaknar konungr þegar við Óláf *fyrir sakar frænda hans*

> *ok bauð honum þegar með sér at vera...* en konungr tekr honum þá *með allri blíðu...* "*skal þat ok fylgja, at ek vil þér bjóða til hirðar minnar með alla þína sveit*" (xxi, 52, 57, 58: So Óláf and Orn went to the court and were well received. The king at once recognized Óláf from his kinsmen and invited him to stay... and the king received him in all friendliness... "furthermore I invite you and all your company to my guard").

While at court the Icelander is accorded high honor and esteem (*mikla virðing, miklar mætur, metinn umfram alla menn*).[24] Once again the author has applied this recurrent theme to specific advantage, it will be recalled, in the comparison of Queen Gunnhild's esteem for Hrút and Óláf and in the similarities and contrasts among the pairs of brothers.[25] After a while the Icelander decides to return to Iceland, as he has many noble kinsmen there whom he wishes to go back and see: "*at vitja til Íslands gǫfugra frænda.*"[26] The king expresses regret and more than likely offers a high position at court to entice the Icelander into staying indefinitely. So, when Óláf wishes to depart, King Harald tells him: "'*Þat væri mér næst skapi, at þú staðfestisk með mér ok tækir hér allan ráðakost, slíkan sem þú vill sjálfr*'" (xxii, 60: "'It would be more to my liking if you would settle down here with me and take whatever position you yourself would like'").[27] When King Óláf Tryggvason makes a similar offer to Kjartan, however, the play on words discussed earlier is camouflaged by the recurrent stereotyped phrases: "'*Vilda ek, at þú fýstisk eigi út til Íslands, þó at þú eigir þar gǫfga frændr, því at kost muntu eiga at taka þann ráðakost í Nóregi, er engi mun slíkr á Íslandi*'" (xliii, 130).[28]

Upon the Icelander's departure the Norwegians customarily proclaim that he is worthy and accomplished far beyond their countrymen and indeed the noblest ever to have come from Iceland in their day.[29] Hrút's departure, while rendered individual and specific due to Gunnhild's partiality, is also representative:

> Konungr gaf honum *skip at skilnaði* ok kallaðisk hann *reynt hafa at góðum dreng*. Gunnhildr leiddi Hrút til skips ok mælti: "Ekki skal þetta lágt mæla, at *ek hefi þik reyndan at miklum ágætismanni, því at þú hefir atgǫrvi jafnfram inum beztum mǫnnum hér í landi, en þú hefir vitsmuni langt um fram*" (xix, 44: At parting the king gave him a ship and said he had proved himself a stalwart fellow. Gunnhild saw him off to the ship and said: "It need not be said in a whisper that I have found you to be a splendid man, for in prowess you are equal to the best in the land, and in wits you are far beyond them").

The king and/or queen and courtiers accompany the Icelander to the ship, which has indeed often been given him by the king, or there are some other gifts *at skilnaði* (at parting).³⁰ These gifts are of much value and usually include gold and handsome weapons. Besides, the Icelander may also have received clothes of scarlet at Yule.³¹ Finally, the visit abroad closes with a tribute to the departing guest, and the Icelander expresses his thanks for all the honor bestowed on him, and he and the king part *með inum mesta kærleik* (in kindliest affection). A composite picture of Óláf's departures first from Norway for Ireland, then from Ireland for Norway, and finally from Norway for Iceland will be illustrative of the motifs mentioned and of their key words:

> Haraldr konungr ok Gunnhildr *leiddu* Óláf *til skips*....En er *skip* Óláfs var *albúit*, þá *fylgir* konungr Óláfi *til skips ok gaf honum spjót gullrekit ok sverð búit ok mikit fé annat*...ok *skiljask þeir konungr með allmikilli vingan*....Óláfr *þakkaði* konungi þann *sóma*, er hann bauð honum...Ok er *skipit var búit*, lætr konungr kalla á Óláf ok mælti: "*Þetta skip skaltu eignask*, Óláfr..." Óláfr *þakkaði* konungi með fǫgrum orðum *sína stórmennsku*...ok *skiljask* þeir Haraldr konungr *með inum mesta kærleik* (xxi, 53, 59; xxii, 60-61: King Harald and Gunnhild accompanied Óláf to the ship....And when Óláf's ship was all set to sail, the king saw him off and gave him a spear inlaid with gold and an embossed sword and many other things of value...and he and the king parted in greatest friendship....Óláf thanked the king for the honor he offered him...and when the ship was all ready, the king had Óláf called and said: "This ship is to be yours, Óláf..." Óláf thanked the king with kind words for his generosity...and he and King Harald parted in kindliest affection).³²

A change in the pattern always carries more than surface significance. So, the added detail that Gunnhild after bidding Hrút farewell at the ship "drew her cloak over her head and went swiftly back to town" (xix, 44: "brá síðan skikkjunni at hǫfði sér ok gekk snúðigt heim til bœjar") offers an index to her feelings for Hrút; so also Ingibjorg's refusal to accompany Kjartan to the ship (xliii, 131: "'Hvergi mun ek leiða þik'"). At other times, adherence to conventional form takes precedence over existing relations: so, for example, although the king and Thorkel have quarreled, they are nonetheless said to part *með miklum kærleik* (lxxiv, 217), just as the king for appearance's sake desires — and just as the pattern demands.³³

Accounts of the return journey and the welcome home in Iceland represent the same image in reverse of the sea crossing and reception in Norway. The ship puts out to sea, has a good crossing, reaches Iceland at a specified place, and is laid up on shore. News of the arrival is noised abroad; there is a joyful reunion; and the returned voyager is said to have gained much honor from his journey. The description of Óláf's return affords illustration:

> Eptir þat býr Óláfr ferð sína, ok er hann er búinn ok byr gefr, þá *siglir* Óláfr *í haf*... Óláfi *byrjaði vel* um sumarit; hann *kom skipi sínu í Hrútafjǫrð á Borðeyri. Skipkváma spyrsk* brátt ok svá þat, hverr stýrimaðr er. Hǫskuldr fregn útkvámu Óláfs, sonar síns, ok verðr *feginn mjǫk ok ríðr* þegar norðr til Hrútafjarðar með nǫkkura menn; verðr þar *fagnafundr með þeim feðgum; bauð* Hǫskuldr Óláfi *til sín;* hann kvazk þat þiggja mundu. Óláfr *setr upp skip sitt*...Óláfr varð *frægr at ferð þessi* (xxii, 61: After that Óláf makes ready for his journey, and when all was ready and the wind favorable, he put out to sea...Óláf had good sailing that summer and came into the Hrútafjord at Bordeyr. News of the ship's arrival and also who the master was soon spread abroad. Hoskuld learned of the arrival of his son Óláf and was very pleased and rode straightway north to Hrútafjord with some men. Father and son were very glad to see each other, and Hoskuld asked Óláf home with him, and Óláf said he would come. Óláf laid up his ship... Óláf's voyage brought him much fame).[34]

Hrút's return follows the familiar pattern up to the point of the welcome upon arrival home when, significantly, there is negative reversal. News of Hrút's return was not good news and Hoskuld did not ride to meet the ship:

> En Hrútr stígr á skip ok *siglir í haf. Honum byrjaði vel, ok tók Breiðafjǫrð.* Hann siglir inn at eyjum; síðan siglir hann inn Breiðasund ok lendir við Kambsnes ok bar bryggjur á land. *Skipkváman spurðisk ok svá þat, at Hrútr Herjólfsson var stýrimaðr. Ekki fagnar* Hǫskuldr *þessum tíðendum ok eigi fór hann á fund hans.* Hrútr *setr upp skip sitt* (xix, 44-45: And Hrút boarded his ship and sailed out to sea. He got a good wind and made Breidafjord. He sailed in at the islands, then into the Breidasund and landed at Kambsnes where he put the gangplanks ashore. News of the ship's arrival was noised abroad and also that Hrút Herjólfsson was the ship's master. This news was not welcomed by Hoskuld, and he did not go to meet him. Hrút laid up his ship).

The last theme in the cycle, that of old age and death, also follows a regular form. The most frequent phrases are *til elli, sótti elli, hniginn á inn efra aldr*, and *tók sótt ok andaðisk* (until old age, bowed with age, and took sick and died).[35] A fuller thematic handling is evident in the death bed scenes that

133

follow a stylized pattern: first, old age or sickness makes itself felt; next, relatives are summoned to the bedside; the fact of being sick is remarked upon as being something unusual, and hence interpreted as leading to death.[36] So, of Hrapp it is said:

> Hrappr hafði skaplyndi it sama, en orkan þvarr, því at *elli sótti á hendr honum,* svá at hann lagðisk í rekkju af. Þá *kallaði* Hrappr *til sín* Vigdísi, *konu sína,* ok mælti: *"Ekki hefi ek verit kvellisjúkr,"* segir hann, "er ok þat líkast, at *þessi sótt skili várar samvistur"* (xvii, 39: Hrapp kept his same disposition, but his strength gave out as old age crept up on him, and finally he had to take to his bed because of it. Hrapp then called his wife Vigdís to him and said to her: "I have never been ailing," he said, "so in all likelihood this illness is going to mean the end of our life together").

Consistently, when there is a death, the person who has died is mourned as a great loss (*mikill skaði, harmdauði*).[37]

The important aspect of these events is the emphasis which serial repetition places on their cyclical nature, circumscribing a set world with set formulae. Again in these patterns, not all the motifs are represented in every example of the theme, nor is the first example chronologically in the saga necessarily the most complete, even though it may be termed preparatory or the model for the following ones. The creative process, about which more will be said presently, must not be confused with the critical process.

Another aspect of Recurrence remains to be discussed. The positive and complimentary terms in which many of the activities under Recurrence are depicted permit the epic background to loom in grandiose dimension. In the scenes at the court in Norway, in Ireland, or in Constantinople, the recognized excellence of the Icelanders already remarked upon finds its most exaggerated representation. Yet stylized descriptions also mark references to life at home, and such accounts are also characterized by favorable and superlative treatment. As we have seen, precocity marks the children from birth. A similar heightening is found in the depiction of the people in the saga in general. Most of them are highborn (*stórættaðr*) and of great worth (*mikils verðr*); many are chieftains (*hǫfðingjar*), and although oftentimes their positions are attested to historically, nonetheless to have noble and prominent agents coincides with the author's purpose and with the heroic and epic magnification.[38]

Descriptions of daily life are repeatedly couched in terms of prosperity and magnificence. Gatherings of all kinds — Things, parties, funerals, weddings — are *fjǫlmennt.* Hoskuld's funeral feast offers an example of the importance attached to great numbers and impressive parties, whereas its appeal to historical facts lends veracity and credibility:

> Var þat svá *mikit fjǫlmenni,* at þat er sǫgn manna flestra, at eigi skyrti níu hundruð. Þessi hefir ǫnnur veizla *fjǫlmennust* verit á Íslandi, en sú ǫnnur, er Hjaltasynir gerðu erfi eptir fǫður sinn; þat váru tólf hundruð. Þessi veizla var *in skǫruligsta* at ǫllu, ok *fengu* þeir brœðr *mikinn sóma* (xxvii, 74-75: It is generally said that the number of guests at Hoskuld's funeral did not fall short of nine hundred [1080]. That makes this feast the next largest ever to have been held in Iceland, second only to the funeral feast which the sons of Hjalti gave in honor of their father, where there were twelve hundred [1440] guests. The feast given by Hoskuld's sons was a most splendid one in every respect, and the brothers gained much honor by it).[39]

Such indications of esteem and congeniality contribute to the saga's general tone of splendor and idealization. Receptions and welcomes, like partings, are kind and friendly and such expressions as *fagnar vel, tók vel við [honum], með blíðu* characterize them.[40] The affluence and dignity of the living conditions are mentioned frequently and in stereotyped form. Usually the descriptions contain references to abundance of supplies and handsome housing. Expressions such as *skortir eigi fé [fǫng, hlut]* (there was no lack of supplies); *efni váru gnóg [œrin váru efni], en fé eigi sparat* (supplies were sufficient and no means spared); *risuligr* (stately [used about the dwellings]) are common.[41] There are several references to enlarging or tearing down of houses and building of bigger and better ones.[42] The impression given by the accounts is of life on a grand scale, increasing as the saga progresses along with the increase in magnificence and prestige of the generations. Thorkel's and Gudrún's household represents a climax (lxxiv, 217).

Descriptions of physical beauty and prowess perhaps represent the most stylized element in the saga. Superlative and complimentary designations not only follow a predictable pattern but also represent a stock of clichés which the author no doubt had at his disposal. Here most markedly one can detect the inherited tradition, and even if once derived from an oral technique (which can be questioned), these tags have been used so long already in a literary medium in the narrowest sense that they are all but hollow reiterations. In *Laxdœla* these conventional phrases retain some efficacy and coincide with the heroic magnification. In general the references are marked by such expressions as: *mikill maðr ok sterkr [vaskligr, knáligr]* (a big man and strong [of gallant bearing, hardy]); *atgǫrvimaðr* (a man of great accomplishment); *efniligr, mannvænn, vænligr* (promising); *vænn* (handsome, beautiful);

friðr [skǫruligr] sýnum (of handsome [splendid] appearance); *hraustr* (valiant); *rammr at afli* (strong in body); *merkiligr* (distinguished); *vígr* (skilled at arms); *víkingr* (a viking); *hverjum manni* [plus the comparative: *betr*, etc.] (better than any man in respect to...); *allra manna [kvenna]* [plus the superlative] (of all men [women] the best, most, etc.); and especially the superlatives of many of the above: *allra manna friðastr sýnum; in vænsta kona; friðasta kona,* etc. The description of Hrút is typical:[48]

> Hann var snimmendis *mikill ok sterkr*, er hann óx upp; var hann ok *hverjum manni betr* í vexti, hár ok herðibreiðr, miðmjór ok limaðr vel með hǫndum ok fótum. Hrútr var *allra manna friðastr sýnum, eptir því sem verit hǫfðu þeir Þorsteinn, móðurfaðir hans, eða Ketill flatnefr; inn mesti* var hann *atgǫrvimaðr* fyrir allra hluta sakar (viii, 16: He soon grew up to be big and strong; he had a better build than most: tall, broad-shouldered, slim-waisted, with well-knit arms and legs. He was the handsomest of men, just as his mother's father Thorstein had been or Ketil Flatnose. In all respects he was most accomplished).[44]

It is significant, moreover, that, as a negative variant, some persons are depicted as not handsome. Herjólf is so described: "Herjólfr var *mikill maðr ok sterkr; ekki* var hann *friðr sýnum* ok *þó inn skǫruligsti í yfirbragði; allra mann* var hann *bezt vígr*" (vii, 15: "Herjólf was a big man and strong; he was not handsome, but fine and manly looking; he was the best of fighters"); and so also Aud, Thórd's first wife: "*Ekki* var hon *væn* kona *né gǫrvilig*" (xxxii, 87: "She was neither a beautiful woman nor capable"). Other examples could be found.

Characteristic of saga literature in general is the practice of assigning superlative and positive traits to characters less worthy than the illustrious protagonists. And so in *Laxdœla* outlaws and troublesome persons are given the same complimentary epithets, and slaves are described as equal to freemen. So Stígandi is described by the bondwoman as being "'*mikill...ok sýnisk mér vænligr*'" (xxxviii, 108); the outlaw Grím is said to be *mikill maðr ok sterkr* (lvii, 171); and in addition to being *mikill maðr ok gǫrviligr*, the slave Ásgaut is distinguished by the comment: "en þótt hann væri þræll kallaðr, þá máttu fáir taka hann til jafnaðarmanns við sik, þótt frjálsir héti" (xi, 21: "Even though he was only a slave, there were few men freeborn who could take him on as their equal"). The fact that such clichés as *mikill maðr ok sterkr* are applied without regard for person further attests to their hollowness. At the same time, since these terms for the most part have become meaningless, it is not surprising to find more individual characteristics accompanying the formulae.

The predilection in *Laxdœla* for descriptions of elegance, fine clothes, and weapons is widely acknowledged. In every case these elements exhibit recurrent and predictable patterns and are related to the formal structure. Use of the word *skart*, for instance, attests to this interest in dress and finery. Bolli Thorleiksson is described as being a *mikill skartsmaðr* (xxviii, 77: a great person for show); Gudrún too takes great pride in having finery: "Guðrun var kurteis kona, svá at í þann tíma þóttu allt barnavípur, þat er aðrar konur hǫfðu *í skarti* hjá henni" (xxxii, 86: "Guðrún was a woman of such courtly manner that in her day whatever other women had to boast of in the way of finery seemed but childish trifles compared to hers"); Kjartan dressed himself in finery (xliv, 134: "bjó sik *við skart*"); Hrefna too was fond of fancy clothes (xlv, 136: "helt allmjǫk *til skarts*"); and Bolli Bollason, outdoing them all, "was so given to show when he came back to Iceland from his journey that he would wear no clothes but of scarlet and velvet" (lxxvii, 224-225: "Bolli var svá *mikill skartsmaðr*, er hann kom út ór fǫr þessi, at hann vildi engi klæði bera nema *skarlatsklæði ok pellsklæði*"). It is apparent that this element is used to draw comparisons between the characters, supporting the parallels that have already been demonstrated, mixing and matching the likenesses among them: between Bolli Thorleiksson and Kjartan, Kjartan and Bolli Bollason, Gudrún and Hrefna, etc. Recurrent motifs, it will be remembered, can at any point assume the special function of Repetition and Comparison.

Patterned formulation of gallantry and accoutrements offers another pertinent example of this aspect of the saga. The description of Hrút in battle dress introduces the pattern in more or less skeletal form: "*Hann hafdi hjálm á hǫfði, en sverð brugðit í hendi, en skjǫld í annarri;* hann var vígr allra manna bezt" (xix, 46: "He had a helmet on his head, sword drawn in one hand and shield in the other; he was the best of fighters"). Later in the story we meet Hrút again, attired in battle array as before:

> *ok hafði í hendi bryntroll gullrekit, er Haraldr konungr gaf honum...ok hristi krókaspjótit, er hann hafði í hendi. Hann hafði ok hjálm á hǫfði ok var gyrðr sverði, skjǫld á hlið; hann var í brynju* (xxxvii, 104: [He] had in his hand the gold-inlaid halberd which King Harald had given him...and brandished the barbed spear he had in his hand. He also had a helmet on his head and was girded with a sword and had a shield at his side; he wore a coat of mail).[45]

It is as though the author, once having latched onto the phrase *hafði í hendi*, felt compelled to go on and complete the pattern with all the elements.

137

These descriptions thus would seem to indicate such accoutrements were considered among the proper qualifying characteristics of a hero. The author then applies the pattern repeatedly to echo or re-echo the theme, enhancing and embellishing it through the generations, varying it for special significance, employing it for comparison and contrast at felicitous points in the story. The normal and expected can always be turned into the significant and unexpected, as when at the raid on his hut, Bolli is not dressed as a hero:

> Bolli var nú einn í selinu; hann tók vápn sín, setti *hjálm á hǫfuð sér ok hafði skjǫld fyrir sér, en sverðit Fótbít í hendi; enga hafði hann brynju* (lv, 166: Bolli was now alone in the hut. He took up his weapons, set his helmet on his head, and held his shield before him. He had the sword Footbiter in his hand, but had on no coat of mail).

The detail about the coat of mail, a negative variant to the expected pattern, gives hint of Bolli's doom, for it indicates his vulnerability. And indeed, unprotected, he is stricken by a blow in the abdomen. Lack of part of the equipage provides to some degree (he is also terribly outnumbered) a reason for his defeat (the natural level) in addition to the fact that he is fated to die (the supernatural level). But the break in the pattern (the formal level) even more decisively points to his being an incomplete hero.

The various descriptions of accoutrements of battle are complementary to the *at vápnum ok klæðum* motif briefly dealt with in another context and incorporate other of the related formulae: clothes of scarlet cloth and these or a weapon named as a gift from the king to the Icelander. Hrút, in the example above, has a "bryntroll gullrekit, *er Haraldr konungr gaf honum*," where inclusion of the italicized phrase, due to the very fact that it is inappropriate in this instance (see note 46 below), points up even more its formulaic and patterned nature. It will be recalled also that a gift from the king generally makes up one of the elements in the "career-abroad" pattern and, except for the scarlet clothes, is not infrequently said to be given at the time of parting (*at skilnaði*). Interesting is the tendency for the descriptions themselves to develop progressively with the generations. Even as the attainments of each succeeding hero reach new heights, so, too, the outward signs of his grandeur become more splendid and colorful and the passages describing them more detailed, or rather one can say that it is these pageantry-like descriptions themselves which make it seem as though each new generation had attained more than the former. The description of Óláf Peacock as he rides to his first Thing sets the pattern for his subsequent gallant appearances:

> Þá er hann var tólf vetra gamall, reið hann til þings, ok þótti

þat mikit ørendi ór ǫðrum sveitum, at undrask, hversu hann var ágætliga skapaðr; þar eptir helt Óláfr sik *at vápnabúnaði ok klæðum*; var hann því *auðkenndr* frá ǫllum mǫnnum (xvi, 38-39: When he was twelve years old, he rode to the Thing; people thought it reason enough to have come from other districts just to marvel at how handsome a build he had. To match his natural prowess, Óláf outfitted himself in fine weapons and clothes, so that he was easily distinguished from all other men).

The "weapons and clothes" motif twice again appears in reference to Óláf, functioning like confirmation-statements:

Óláfr Hǫskuldsson er nú ok frumvaxti ok er allra manna fríðastr sýnum, þeira er menn hafi sét. Hann *bjó sik vel at vápnum ok klæðum* (xx, 49: Óláf Hoskuldsson was now also grown up and was one of the most handsome men people had ever set eyes on. He outfitted himself in fine weapons and clothes).
Allir menn hǫfdu á máli, er Óláf sá, hversu fríðr maðr hann var ok fyrirmannligr; hann var *vel búinn at vápnum ok klæðum* (xxii, 62: Everyone who saw Óláf could not help but remark how handsome he was and how noble his bearing. He was well outfitted in weapons and clothes).

When Óláf comes to Ireland to claim kinship with King Mýrkjartan, he decks himself out in finest array and strides forward to the prow to impress the king and gain recognition of his royal kinship:

Óláfr gekk þá fram í stafninn *ok var svá búinn, at hann var í brynju ok hafði hjálm á hǫfði gullroðinn; hann var gyrðr sverði*, ok váru *gullrekin hjǫltin; hann hafði krókaspjót í hendi hǫggtekit ok allgóð mál í; rauðan skjǫld hafði hann fyrir sér, ok var dregit á leó með gulli* (xxi, 55: Then Óláf strode forward to the prow. He wore a coat of mail and had a gilt helmet on his head: he was girded with a sword, its hilts chased in gold. In his hand he carried a barbed spear, embossed and finely wrought, and before him he held a red shield, and on it a lion was traced in gold).

Óláf's showy appearance at the Thing when he was twelve, and again before Mýrkjartan in Ireland prepares for his next ostentatious show — before Thorgerd Egilsdóttir. By this time his splendor has increased through gifts from King Mýrkjartan and from the king in Norway. While at the court in Norway Óláf receives at Yuletide clothes cut from scarlet as a present from King Harald: "Haraldr konungr gaf Óláfi at jólum *ǫll klæði skorin af skarlati*" (xxii, 60). But whereas his fine array convinced Mýrkjartan of his nobility and worth, Thorgerd at first is not swayed by it. Her father's persuasions are

139

to no avail: she will not marry him " 'no matter how handsome and well decked out he is' " (xxiii, 63: " 'þótt hann sé vænn ok mikill áburðarmaðr' "). Óláf then, as might be expected, appears before Thorgerd in all his splendor:

> Óláfr var búinn á þá leið, at hann var í skarlatsklæðum, er Haraldr konungr hafði gefit honum; hann hafði á hǫfði hjálm gullroðinn ok sverð búit í hendi, er Mýrkjartan konungr hafði gefit honum (xxiii, 64: Óláf was dressed in this manner: he had on the scarlet clothes which King Harald had given him; on his head he had a gilt helmet and in his hand the gold chased sword which King Mýrkjartan had given him).

And now, even as King Mýrkjartan, Thorgerd is impressed. These two descriptions of Óláf thus form a confirmation pair. Over against the skeletal hero pattern, noted first in reference to Hrút, the increment embellishment of the later examples stands out particularly well and illuminates the compositional method. The helmet is now *gullroðinn*, the sword has *gullrekin hjǫltin* or is *búit;* the spear, too, is embossed; the shield is *rauðr* and has a tracing in gold; the *brynja* has been replaced with the *skarlatsklæði*; and the illustrious origin of sword and clothes is mentioned. The *at vápnum ok klæðum* motif, the clothes of scarlet, the kingly gifts have become entwined with the motifs of the hero pattern.

In the next generation, Kjartan, like Óláf, shows the same tendency toward ostentation and, like Hrút and Óláf, appears in the typical attire befitting a hero. He also has received clothes of scarlet from King Óláf Tryggvason: "Konungr gaf Kjartani ǫll klæði nýskorin af skarlati" (xli, 124). So, after his return to Iceland, when Óláf urges him to come along to the fall feast at Laugar, Kjartan decks himself out. The formulation of the description is by now familiar:

> Kjartan gerir, svá sem faðir hans beiðisk, ok tekr hann nú upp skarlatsklæði sín, þau er Óláfr konungr gaf honum at skilnaði,[46] ok bjó sik við skart; hann gyrði sik með sverðinu konungsnaut; hann hafði á hǫfði hjálmgullroðinn ok skjǫld á hlið rauðan, ok dreginn á með gulli krossinn helgi; hann hafði í hendi spjót, ok gullrekinn falrinn á. Allir menn hans váru í litklæðum (xliv, 134-135: Kjartan did as his father wished. He took out the scarlet clothes which King Óláf had given him at parting, and dressed himself in all his finery. He girded himself with the sword Konungsnaut [the king's gift] and had a gilt helmet on his head and at his side a red shield with the holy cross traced in gold, and in his hand he carried a spear with a gold-inlaid socket. All his men were in brightly colored array).

The components of this passage fulfill again the basic pattern: on the hero's head a helmet, at his side a shield, in his hand a spear. The embellishments are there too, as well as the scarlet clothes motif and the clause mentioning their kingly origin. The inference that Kjartan has dressed himself up in his finery to cover up his real feelings and at the same time to impress Gudrún, who has married Bolli instead, sets the latter account off as a counterpart to Óláf's decking himself out for Thorgerd — thus again a recurrent pattern takes on qualified function.

The *at vápnum ok klæðum* theme and the distinctive formulation of the accoutrements of a hero culminate in the descriptions of Bolli Bollason. His sojourn in Norway competes, as we have seen, in many respects with Kjartan's:

> Bolli helt sveit um vetrinn í Þrándheimi, ok var *auðkennt*, hvar sem hann gekk til skytninga, at menn hans váru betr búnir *at klæðum ok vápnum* en annat bœjarfólk (lxxiii, 212: Bolli kept a group of followers that winter in Trondheim, and wherever he went to inns for drinking, one could easily see that his men were better equipped with clothes and weapons than the other townsmen).

The familiar motif applies here to Bolli's men — but by mutual inclusion, of course, also to Bolli — and the transposition of the words from their accustomed formulation also brings variation.

These descriptions of gallantry with finery and accoutrements then reach their height in the account of Bolli Bollason's splendor upon his return from his journey:

> Bolli var svá *mikill skartsmaðr*, er hann kom út ór fǫr þessi, at hann vildi engi klæði bera nema *skarlatsklæði ok pellsklæði*, ok ǫll vápn hafði hann *gullbúin*. Hann var kallaðr Bolli inn prúði. ...Bolli ríðr frá skipi við tólfta mann; þeir váru *allir í skarlatsklæðum* fylgðarmenn Bolla ok riðu *í gyldum sǫðlum*; allir váru þeir listuligir menn, en þó bar Bolli af. Hann var *í pellsklæðum*, er Garðskonungr hafði gefit honum; hann hafði ýzta *skarlatskápu rauða; hann var gyrðr Fótbít*, ok váru at honum *hjǫlt gullbúin* ok *meðalkaflinn gulli vafiðr*;[47] hann hafði gyldan hjálm á hǫfði ok rauðan skjold á hlið, ok á dreginn riddari með gulli; hann hafði glaðel í hendi, sem títt er í útlǫndum, ok hvar sem þeir tóku gistingar, þá gáðu konur engis annars en horfa á Bolla ok skart hans ok þeira félaga (lxxvii, 224-225).
> (Bolli was so given to show when he came back from his journey that he would wear nothing but clothes of scarlet and velvet, and all his weapons had gold inlay. He was called Bolli the Magnificent.... He rode from his ship in a party of twelve. They were all dressed in clothes of scarlet, these followers of Bolli, and

rode in gilded saddles, each and everyone of gallant bearing, but Bolli surpassed them all. He wore the velvet clothes which the king of Miklagard [Constantinople] had given him. Outermost he had on a red cloak of scarlet; he was girded with Footbiter, its hilts inlaid with gold and its haft wound in gold. He had a gilt helmet on and a red shield at his side, on which a knight was traced in gold. He had a lance in his hand, as is the custom abroad in foreign lands. Wherever they took lodging, the women could do nothing but gaze at Bolli and his companions in all their finery).

Again the representative elements are present: helmet, shield, spear, sword, or lance, as here. Just as the scarlet clothes took the place of the *brynja*, so now the former have been amplified to include velvet ones, a further enhancement, and these were also given by a king. The spectacle throughout the generations has become greater. The embossed figure on the shield has also undergone transformation from a lion, to a cross, to a knight, paralleling supposedly the historical and cultural progression from viking age, to acceptance of Christianity, to the advent of chivalry,[48] and with it is implied an advancement in value and importance. The *kurteisi*, the *riddari*, the *glaðel* represent the new, the "outlandish," and indicate some of the impact from abroad on thirteenth-century Iceland.

Another recurrent idea attends these patterns, namely the hero's being distinguished (*auðkenndr*), standing out from the crowd, by virtue of his physique or fine appearance in weapons and clothes, or both, which in turn calls forth the admiration of all who see him. Óláf Hoskuldsson, it will be recalled, was the object of awe at his first appearance at the Thing (xvi, 38); the Irish, too, marvel at him when he rides into Dublin (xxi, 57),[49] and upon his return to Iceland his attendance at the Thing is a repeat performance as when he was twelve (xxii, 62). Kjartan's physical appearance, like Óláf's, creates wonder in all who see him: "allir undruðusk þeir, er sá hann" (xxviii, 77); and upon his return from abroad he puts on his finery and all his men were in colored clothes (xliv, 135: *í litklæðum*). But the pageantry of Bolli Bollason and his retinue outdoes Kjartan's, as we have seen. His men are all in clothes of scarlet, but even these are reduced to second place in magnificence over against Bolli, for he is in velvet clothes. His weapons, too, now all have gold inlay. And the attention Bolli and his retinue attract surpasses what has gone before. And well might the people be dazzled by their red and gold array.

Although the pattern of the hero's accoutrements represented here is not of the author's own making (the earliest example being in the *Ágrip*, dated ca.

1190), the handling of the theme is totally individual in *Laxdœla*, where the details, the substitutions, the embellishments are arranged to suit the overall design with its double aspect: namely, the creation of a background of repetitive verbalisms and repetitive thematic patterns, one of which in particular, the theme of the hero's accoutrements, exhibits increasing embellishment that parallels the succession in the chain reaction; and secondly to use these same themes and verbal patterns to draw comparisons implicitly between the actors and events in the foreground.

The account of the physical appearance, accoutrements and so forth of the band of men sitting in a circle outside Helgi's hut (lxii, 187-189),[50] while related thematically, does not follow the motif pattern just discussed. This gives a clue to difference in provenance. It has generally been acknowledged that this passage in particular suggests influence on the author from the courtly literature of the South. Although the rhetorical device of guessing the identity of persons through descriptions of their physical appearance goes all the way back to Homer (*Iliad*, Book III), the *kurteisi* with which the author endows this Icelandic band points to chivalric influence. The naturalistic details of the physical features of the men would almost tempt one to suspect an eye-witness description of contemporary men.[51] Thus both the veneer of chivalry and the more earthy and realistic descriptions point to a thirteenth-century origin, whereas the heroic pattern discussed in connection with the descriptions of Hrút, Óláf, Kjartan, and Bolli Bollason has roots and precedents that go back much further, even though this pattern, too, with its basically old, native, heroic ideals has been colored with contemporary thirteenth-century ones. The author has amalgamated the old and the new.

The foreign *kurteisi*, for instance, has been so thoroughly accepted into the old system of values that it forms a recurrent idea in *Laxdœla*.[52] The superlative and complimentary attributes associated with being *kurteisligr* or having *kurteisi* simply attach themselves to the other praiseworthy qualities ascribed to the saga characters.[53] And *kurteisi*, like *afbragð* or *mikill maðr ok sterkr,* can be lifted from its recurrent use to take on specific function in drawing similarities between characters. The foreground and background actions in the saga are mutually inclusive.

The lapse between the time when the persons in the story lived and the time when they were written about likely has something to do with the magnification of the days of Settlement and the zenith of the Commonwealth. From the point of view of thriteenth-century Iceland the old days might well have appeared ideal. The glorification of the heroic past seems intentional on the part of the author and is of more than passing interest. Such expressions as *mikill maðr ok sterkr, kvenna vænst, friðastr maðr sýnum, mikit afbragð annarra manna [kvenna]*,[54] while indicative of the fact that the saga heroes took the stage at a time when the old formulas had lost their distinctive value and had become flat conventional tags, have in some ways been revitalized by the author of *Laxdœla* and consciously formalized.

Flattening of the recurrent formulae that run through the saga has to some degree been counteracted by introduction of a negative into the familiar pattern, which imparts distinction by virtue of its rarity and unexpectedness. Within the chain of recurrent phrases negative counterparts also effect a type of balancing within the series, as in such phrases: *stórmenni / lítilmenni*;[55] *með allri [mikilli, inni mestu] blíðu / með engri blíðu*;[56] *þeim byrjaði vel / þeim byrjaði illa*;[57] *tók því vel / tók því illa* (took it well, took it ill);[58] *lét vel yfir / /lét illa yfir* (expressed approval, disapproval);[59] and *líkar vel / líkar [unnir] illa* (was well pleased, ill pleased).[60]

The expression *tók af því vel at eins ok lítit af ǫllu*[61] in itself neatly sums up this type of formal balancing between the negative and the positive, between the either-or, neither-nor ideas that are typical of the saga.

This counterpoising within the recurrent chain reveals the author's predilection for composing through contrasts and his sure sense for the unity of the composition. The negative forms are weighted and hence, though for the most part quantitatively fewer, qualitatively of greater import. Recurrence can be said to evidence somewhat the same disposition to act and react which was a functional feature of Foreknowledge, Repetition, and Comparison. Furthermore, the recurrence of the patterns conditions the audience to expect them, in a way similar to the anticipation associated with Foreknowledge. This preconditioning and the commonplace nature of the words and phrases help to camouflage double intentions and to veil the hints. At any time, a Recurrent pattern may be turned to qualified use as Repetition or Comparison. Such double treatment is a characteristic stylistic feature of the saga, there being an ironic tone, a duplicity and ambiguity about many of the devices employed. There is a shift of focus between the foreground and the background, between the surface meaning and the implied meaning throughout the saga.

The round of sameness, the patterning of one generation after the other, bring out most forcibly a formalized ordering of the world. It is *always* (*jafnan*)[62] the same world caught in the endless cycle of retaliations, caught in the social conventions, caught in a fateful destiny. The word *jafnan* is a loaded word. The ethical code is as rigidly prescribed and followed as the fateful prophecies are inevitably fulfilled. This predeterminism apparent also in Recurrence brings us back to Foreknowledge and to the realization that the necessity with which the lexical units and patterns have been applied reflect formally the necessity of the action. Thus all the structural components of the composition have been shown to be but different points of view or aspects that inhere in the formative concept that produced *Laxdœla saga*.

If the words "ok lýkr þar nú sǫgunni" ("and here now the saga ends") did not stand at the close — and indeed the statement is not found in all manuscripts — one would have the feeling that, in some respects, the whole could begin all over again, that the end had run into the beginning. Fittingly enough, too, genealogies open and close the saga, imaging the round of existence in its continuous cycle. Yet the chain has also come *full* circle; the composition has run out; all prophecies have been fulfilled; the motifs and characters neatly played off one against the other; the scales of justice brought to a balance for the time.

The precise completion of prophecies and hints, the matching and patterning of the lexical components that make up the narrative have built a unified structure and integral style, whose formal units abstracted from the discursive content, show the total linguistic fabric to be "all of a piece." What was surmised in the beginning has been demonstrated: the saga is a carefully constructed piece of artistic prose and the plan for its symmetry does indeed "run deep."

LITERARY PERSPECTIVES

In beginning this study, in order to let *Laxdœla saga* speak for itself, I proceeded from a premise which ruled out everything extraneous to the text. The saga was assumed to be a self-contained whole whose purport could be ascertained without recourse to external information. The evidence accruing from the study leaves no alternative but to concede, first of all, that the artistic significance of the saga outweighs, indeed overrules, any claim for historical reliability or pragmatic function. The selecting, ordering, and concentrating of the materials of the composition, both the subject matter and the linguistic components, toward a desired aesthetic end mark the work as an artistic unit. If one were to underline in the original text all the repetitions, formulae, and patterns that have been discussed in this analysis, the staggering number would show the bulk of the saga to be comprised of these elements. What in the face of this manipulation of materials, one can legitimately ask, remains of history? Incontestably the historical ingredient will have to yield its claim to supremacy to the non-historical aspect that places *Laxdœla saga* among the ranks of brilliant literary achievements.

It is evident that a formative concept, which determines the discursive content and the lexical and syntactical choices, equating the "what" and the "how," underpins the total composition. The author not only completes his prophecies, he also fulfills expectations by creating a symmetrical poetic pattern which conveys the ideas of compensation, comparison, and balance against a background of an unending cycle that threatens to upset the delicate equilibrium. The schematism of the total word-pattern conveys this meaning irrespective of the discursive reference. The basic materials of the narrative (agents, events, and lexical components) have been so arranged that every element has a function within the closed system in which these structural associations have been developed. From the larger units down to the smallest linguistic elements the intended poetic meaning is reflected, the whole in the part, the part in the whole. Even single expressions such as *bæði, tveir kostir, ýmisst, hvárki...né, hvárrtveggja,* or *sem áðr, sem ván var, kunnigt, jafn-*, and *jafnan* are bound to all others in a necessary relationship determined by the structure of the whole, a structure and style which controls the associations and lends significance to each of these parts beyond their independent meaning outside the saga. Such tightness of structure, where almost every word is essential to completeness, is not unusual in poetry. In a prose composition of this length it represents an amazing achievement. All the materials of the composition, whatever their provenance — historical figures and events, contemporary happenings, borrowed passages or motifs, universal poetic techniques and rhetorical devices — have not merely been transformed in the sense that they have been accommodated to the new contextual environment of the story, but rather, and more importantly, the author has also given them a formal existence of their own apart from their discursive application. This formal structure he has camouflaged so well that one does not suspect just how ingenious this unknown author was. To appreciate it fully, the saga must virtually be decoded.

Thirteenth-century writers explored a common storehouse of themes and characters and literary devices. Individuality of authorship consisted to a great extent in felicitous and inventive handling of the materials. Anonymity has perhaps been fortuitous in this case in that it has permitted us to focus attention on the work itself rather than on the man. The main concern in appraising a literary work, from whatever century, is not the provenance of the material or of the technique, but what the author has made out of his "givens" in an entirely new and unique composition.

The Historical Illusion

For all his manipulations and poetic handling of the material of his narrative the saga author has managed to keep the illusion of real events and historical truth. What are the means by which he has created such a vivid impression of actuality? First, he has not fabricated completely. The main personages were historical, and some general facts about their lives were known from the *Landnámabók* and the *Íslendingabók*. And these people the author placed in their palpably real setting replete with place names. He knew how to bring the historical figures to life by supplying the happenings in their lives with psychologically plausible motives and reactions. Other persons and events, equally convincing, he totally invented. The rich dialogue also makes the actors seem alive. Upon closer inspection, the true to life narrative, and particularly the discourse, will be found to surpass accounts of real events in vividness. The language is chiseled, the phrases exact, the dialogue filed. All that might be haphazard or superfluous, as it occurs in nature, in real life situations, has been eliminated, and only those elements that perform a necessary function within the work are present.

Second, the author has incorporated genealogies and poems into his narrative, both of which were generally acknowledged sources for history. Snorri Sturluson specifically mentions the skaldic poetry as being one of his sources for the events and battles in the lives of the Norwegian kings. In the purely literary genre, poems may even be invented for the story, merely to give a semblance of tradition.[1] Noteworthy is the fact that the poems often contain archaic word forms, likely deliberate in order to engender belief in their authenticity as handed down from the time of the events described.

Third, the author has made other appeals to authority. Mention of Ari Thorgilsson, the venerable historian, near the beginning and end of the saga puts the story in a historical frame.[2] Phrases such as *svá segja menn, þat er allra manna mál, þat er sǫgn manna* (people say, it is commonly said, that is what men say) were long looked upon as substantiating an oral tradition behind the sagas that told the truth of the matter.[3] Such a literal, face-value interpretation is naive. Originally these expressions no doubt represented nothing but a conventional appeal to authority that placed the storyteller in the line of tradition, offering "proof" that what he was telling was not of his own fabrication; it was based on general knowledge. No storyteller wanted to be just a "teller of tales," a liar. From time immemorial the poet has sought to capture his listener's attention through an appeal to the credibility of his tale. By enlisting the belief of his audience, he drew them into the illusion. In this respect the authors of the Sagas of Icelanders succeeded so well that it has taken critics centuries to recognize the trick.

Fourth, the author preserves the illusion of telling his story in a natural, historical time sequence. Progression of time dominates the action, despite the fact that a back and forth movement has been developed through the abstract formal relationships, but of which one is scarcely aware. Here again the author has subtly concealed his intention. Occasionally he correlates events in the story with historical happenings outside the story.[4] It is significant that in such instances actual dates are never given. Invariably, the time sequence is indicated by designations relative to one another: "the next winter," "the following spring." Passage of time may even be less precise, as with "so the seasons passed," or "he stayed many winters."[5] If the inner chronology of the saga is carefully compared with outside dates from annal tabulations, many irreconcilable discrepancies are found.[6] The author is working not in real time but in poetic time, which can be hastened, collapsed, lengthened, or annuled as he may wish. This aspect of the saga will be dealt with more thoroughly in the subsection Rhythm and Time.

The Oral Heritage Re-evaluated

The adaptability of the saga form to several genres accounts for its popularity in Iceland. The prose style which lent itself to official chronicles and lives of saints proved equally suited for recounting less sedate histories and tales. The Kings' Sagas and the Sagas of Icelanders were created and written during the late twelfth and throughout the thirteenth century. They had several centuries of written training behind them. Turning from didactic and hagiographic literature but under the influence of clerical literature, chronicles, and compendia which the Church brought to Iceland, the authors of the sagas revived native materials and wrote in the vernacular.

The saint's life exhibits a typical formal pattern: marvellous infancy and vocation; struggle and trials by which the saint proved his prowess and virtue; an account of miracles, dreams, and premonitions; perhaps a warning of approaching death; particulars attending his death and the miracles at the tomb and afterward.[7] Somewhere along the line gifted writers were bound to see the connection between these accounts and the motifs characteristic of traditional pagan heroes. Indeed, the saint's life was originally patterned after the ideal hero of the pre-Christian eras. Christianity came late to Scandinavia and to Iceland. The old heroes and heroic ideals were still well in remembrance. At the outset the contact with the hagiographic literature of the Church must have seemed like a secondary borrowing of the heroic concept via the saint's life. This traditional form served as model and inspiration for the writing of the first Kings' Sagas, especially initiating a wealth of sagas about King Óláf Haraldsson, secular hero and saint. The clerical unction of the early versions was gradually shed, witness Snorri Sturluson's rendering of the saga. The earliest purely secular king's saga, the *Sverris saga* (ca. 1185-1188), reveals particularly well the hagiographic origin of the reborrowed heroic motifs: King Sverrir, too, has an unusual birth and infancy; a childhood with marvels; in manhood he performs heroic deeds and tests of courage and prowess; there are premonitions and prophecies connected with his death, pointing both to a fateful concept of life and to

Providence. This saga had much influence on the subsequent sagas that were written in Iceland — sagas about bishops, kings, and Icelanders from the period of Settlement.

Laxdœla saga bears witness to the revival of the heroic tradition on the one hand, and to the merging with chivalric ideals on the other hand. That Kjartan was the first in Iceland to keep the fast, that Gudrún was the first woman to learn the psalter and to become a nun in Iceland shows that the author also took cognizance of the saintly virtues that his characters were to have in addition to the heroic ones, and the chivalric. The three cultural streams merge into one. The appearance of much of the heroic formulae (*mikill maðr ok sterkr*, etc.) no doubt can be traced to the attempt to salvage what was already on the verge of dying out. The courtly knights of medieval Europe were just over the horizon, ready to replace the saints, leaving little time for the upsurge and flowering of the native heroes. The Sagas of Icelanders came into rapid bloom and experienced an equally rapid decline. It is thought by some that the poetic *Edda* was committed to writing as part of an antiquarian revival, and Snorri's prose *Edda* stands witness to the fact that he, for one, felt it behooved him to explain the skaldic forms and devices, since the pagan kennings had fallen into disrepute and their content was no longer understood. We have noted how many Eddic themes have come into *Laxdœla*.[8] These are literary influences. Many of the Eddic lays are demonstrably quite young, while others show evidence of syncretism. They thus can give us only a hazy idea of what the oral poems must have been like. Are there any reflexes of the heroic tradition that might be reminiscent of the themes or techniques of oral poetry, pre-Eddic poetry?

The motif of "early maturity" (e.g. *snimmendis mikill ok sterkr*) hints of the heroic pattern, where typically the youth has a remarkable origin, strength and wisdom beyond his years, and the like. It will be recalled that both Hoskuld and Bolli Bollason are said to be wise and strong beyond their years. In *Laxdœla* this motif, too, is tinged with a chivalric and courtly ideal: beauty is on a par with brawn (e.g. lii, 159; lvi, 170: *snimma...vænn*).

The emphasis placed on the coming of age at twelve years (e.g. Bolli carrying Footbiter at twelve; Óláf's attending the Thing for the first time; Gellir Thorkelsson's accompanying his father abroad for the first time) recalls the tests the Germanic warrior underwent in initiation rites to prove his manhood, but, except for Bolli's bearing a weapon at that age, indicating his readiness to avenge his father, the other instances of the twelve-years-of-age theme are only hollow reminiscences of the original importance which the coming of age carried.

Again in *Laxdœla*, manly virtues are more often ascribed to heroes like Kjartan and Bolli Bollason in words, than demonstrated in deeds. Beauty, popularity, wit, fine clothes have replaced in part the tougher substance of the Germanic hero of ancient times. Fame lies more in gaining favor at the court, in being *handgenginn* to the king, in possessing *kurteisi*. The traditional competition between men (the *flýting*) has become a *mannjafnaður*, almost a courtly pastime where the virtues of the heroes are discussed and compared (xix, 44).

The fabulous origin of weapons, as work of the giants and the like, which endows them with extraordinary power, finds an echo in the supernatural powers of the swords Footbiter and Konungsnaut (King's Gift). Weaponry presented to Icelanders as gifts from the Norwegian king picks up the theme of at least an illustrious origin. The motif of a hero fighting without weapons or protection has been transformed and put to different use in the case of Bolli Thorleiksson who fights without a *byrnja*. Instead of marking great heroism, it is, within the context of *Laxdœla*, a flaw in the heroic pattern, an example of the author's practice of inserting negatives unexpectedly into the pattern.

Interesting to muse upon is whether the author of *Laxdœla* deliberately put the new material in the old forms, or whether he was unable to disengage himself from his cultural milieu so that contemporary values crept in in spite of himself. It is actually more tempting to think that he meant to display the merging of all three cultural strains, collapsing them into one.

The formulation of the accoutrements and trappings associated with the warrior-hero (*hann hafði sverð í hendi, hjálm á hǫfdi, skjǫld á hlið*) is the counterpart in literary form of the archetypal warrior depictions found on weaponry from the period of the Great Migrations at Vendel, Valsgärde, Sutton Hoo, Pliezhausen, and elsewhere in Germanic territory. And also on the church door at Valþjófsstaðir in Iceland (now in the museum in Reykjavík) from the early thirteenth century is found the same typical warrior from a long heritage, in whom ever a new hero can be visualized. The embellishment of weaponry, especially the delight in pageantry noticeable in *Laxdœla*, seems to point to the thirteenth century's increased interest in decorative trappings. Yet traditionally, weapons, particularly those belonging to men of high estate, were richly ornamented, prized and handed-down (*Beowulf* bears earliest witness to this; and the phrase *meðalkaflinn gulli vafiðr*, found in *Laxdœla*, occurs in a verse attributed to skald Sighvat).[11]

In addition, some traditional motifs like sharp-sightedness (*skyggn maðr*), whettings by words and reminders to arouse desire for vengeance, inimical brothers, favoritism toward one child, useless warnings appear in the *Laxdœla saga*. Some of these, as well as all the ghost tales, superstitions, hauntings, the earth being turned inside out by an evil glance, the stuff of dreams, derive from folklore, likely contemporary with the author, or conceivably taken from foreign sources, but this has never been demonstrated. The concept of Fate is, of course, the most obvious hand-me-down from the pagan heroic age. These then are some of the tangible themes in the content that can safely be said to have derived from a preliterate age, or oral transmission existing in the thirteenth century, no doubt in folktales and the like. Apart from these general motifs, inherited from the cultural background, there is not one single fact, event, or character that can demonstrably be said to have come down as the substance from an oral tradition. To the contrary, all the events and persons, except those that can be shown through the aesthetic structure to have been fabricated by the author, will be found to have origins in written sources or in the contemporary scene. There is certainly not much of anything, except the bare skeletal facts about the persons of the saga as given in the *Landnámabók* or derived from an older redaction of the *Íslendingabók* of Ari or from the older sources for the Kings' Sagas that one could call factual.

If the author of *Laxdœla* did not receive substance for his narrative from oral tales as a transmitted substratum, earlier poets and writers can at least be assumed to have used *techniques* of story telling that had been successful in the preceding unlettered age and would continue to employ them as long as they served the purpose of the new medium. Writers would naturally feel, for instance, that the written story should resemble one which was designed to be recited, especially if the practice were to read stories aloud in an age when parchments were scarce. Teller-to-audience directives such as those marking the flash-backs, or abrupt introductions of new persons and the equally curt dismissal of exiting characters[10] are no doubt reflexes of native habits that have found their way into the new lettered age. Once incorporated into literature in the narrower sense, they have become literary devices and even may represent conscious imitation. For by the thirteenth century the accomplished techniques and rhetorical devices of an imported culture, the hagiographic literature of the church, and the foreign example of written chronicles had firmly established themselves.

Some of the phrases which have a hackneyed ring in the sagas can be assumed to have been taken over as traditional forms, early becoming crystallized, conventional tags and mannerisms, hence their fossilized appearance from the beginning in the written literature. Such clichés as *mikill maðr ok sterkr*,

153

kvenna vænst, allra manna fríðastr sýnum seem to be of such long standing that they have lost their original effectiveness and function, being very much "on the autumnal verge," to use W. P. Ker's phrase. The peak of literary creativity in thirteenth-century Iceland already carried with it the seeds of decay. Exploited to the fullest, the literary forms and techniques were bound to lose their meaning and substance. The too succinct turn of phrase, the characteristic stoicism of characters in face of moral obligation or death, all too soon took on the quality of mock heroics.

Rhetorical techniques such as the use of repetitions, increments, antitheses, negative alternatives, litotes, chiasmal relationships; stylistic conventions such as the use of anticipatory devices, contrastives (after gladness, sorrow; e. g., the function of *kátr* as hint of its opposite), incorporation of authoritative names, folk etymologies, poems, dreams; narrative techniques such as interspersing narration with dialogue, mingling of direct and indirect discourse, use of flash-backs are hardly new with the author of *Laxdœla*, and can be shown to be the result of long schooling with classical texts, however much they may have coincided with the devices of native poetry. That the *Laxdœla* author has devised a completely original composition based on these common methods needs no further demonstration. His ingenious application of patterned themes with variation achieved through substitution, reordering and mixing of the motifs, negation, and embellishment draws particular attention. Here he is a master. Comparison with what we know of early poetic techniques where repetitions, patterns, and variation were the favorite devices and with the poetic handling of language as illustrated in deliberate ambiguities, plays on levels of meaning, dual function of idioms as found, for example, in skaldic verse, offers a better basis for evaluating the influence of "tradition" on the ironic prose style of *Laxdœla* than hypothetical oral compositions of which we have not a trace.

Written Sources

The author did not receive the substance of his tale from oral traditions, on the contrary he welded together diverse accounts and themes from a variety of written sources. Rolf Heller has done the most in tracing literary similarities between *Laxdœla* and the Kings' Sagas, *Laxdœla* and the Bishops' Sagas, *Laxdœla* and *Knýtlinga saga*, *Laxdœla* and *Sturlunga saga*, etc. The direction of the borrowings — if indeed it is a matter of borrowing — cannot very well be determined unless one has a better idea of the chronology of the works.

The *Stoffgeschichte* of *Laxdœla* deserves a separate study. Since that would go beyound the scope and purpose of this analysis, a few examples will serve to demonstrate the author's method in handling his materials. Here again it will be seen that he has woven the varied threads so deftly that the seams are nowhere visible. Just as he imbedded the formal arrangement of the lexical components in natural and plausible contexts such that the calculated plan goes by practically unnoticed, so too the diverse origins of his content he cleverly concealed.

The substance of the story, aside from what has been purely invented, the author draws from three basic cultural periods. The Eddic poems (albeit watered down and fragmentary through what might be called a salvage operation) provided an impetus to reenvision the spirit of the old heroic days and provided some motifs. The *Landnámabók* and Ari's original version of the *Íslendingabók* supplied the author with genealogical information and the basic facts about the persons he wanted to use in his saga for the time of Settlement (Gudrún had four husbands; Kjartan was killed in Svínadal; Ósvíf's sons were outlawed for the killing of Kjartan; Hoskuld bought a concubine Melkorka). Interesting in this regard is that the author chose not to include all the names in the genealogies that he could have. The fact that we withheld many substantiates the surmise that the genealogies were not inserted in the saga for the sake of historical completeness or for supplying accurate information, but rather serve an aesthetic function beyond merely an additive to enhance the historical illusion. For some of the basic information about the Norwegian kings the Kings' Sagas (*Heimskringla* and the *Morskinskinna*) were available, and particularly monk Odd's *Óláfs saga Tryggvasonar*, episodes from all of which were incorporated into *Laxdœla*'s characters and events.

The chivalric tastes that began to invade the court in Norway with Brother Robert's translation of *Tristan* in 1226 made themselves also felt in Iceland, but the words *riddari* and *kurteisi* entered the vocabulary long before any specific concepts tinged the attitudes in the sagas. *Laxdœla saga* appears to be one of the earliest sagas to show a shift of interest in this direction to any marked degree. The *Laxdœla* author obviously was receptive to the influences that were in the air. In many respects Kjartan and even more so Bolli Bollason approach the stereotype of the gallant knight, and like Mýrkjartan, each could be *inn vaskligi riddari* and his companions and retinue as they return from abroad a *mikit riddaralið*.[11] The knight on the shield, the loan word *glaðel* in the description of Bolli B. point to acquaintance with the contemporary medieval scene, and the author with his *sem títt er í útlǫndum* gives himself away.[12] The old adjective *vaskligr* combined with the new noun *riddari*, like the *glaðel* being substituted into the pattern for the old sword or spear, is indicative of the process that is taking place and of the author's method of amalgamating.

And not only has this new spirit, whose values have some affinity with the native, Nordic ones, been absorbed into the saga, but so too have contemporary events. To what extent has as yet not been sufficiently researched. The most obvious parallel with a recorded happening is the passage on the fighters at Helgi's hut, which must have some connection with the account in the *Íslendinga saga* about the attack on the Thorvaldssons in 1232.[13] The word *kurteisi*, while sprinkled in less noticeably in the saga in other places, occurs here with some concentration. This fits in with the general increase toward the end of the saga in pomp and pageantry but may also well have something to do with the closer relationship of the passage with the thirteenth century. Content and form would indicate this.

Let us turn briefly to some of the sources for *Laxdœla*. Parallels between it and the *Edda* have already been listed.[14] When it comes to the Kings' Sagas, one must look at both the *Morkinskinna* and the *Heimskringla*. It is at once striking that these two and *Laxdœla* have much phraseology and many themes in common. A small sampling includes: *aptans bida oframs sok* (*Mork.* 29-30;[15] *Lxd.* xxxv, 96); *knif og bellte* (*Mork.* 57; *Lxd.* xx, 51); *ath skilnadi* (e. g.: *Mork.* 57; *Hkr.* II, 219;[16] *Lxd.* xxi, 57); *ath vopnum og klædum* (e. g.: *Mork.* 172; *Hkr.* II, 198; *Lxd.* xxii, 62); *med myklum kærleika* (e. g.: *Mork.* 177, *Hkr.* II, 165; *Lxd.* xxii, 61). Over against the examples from the *Mork.* and *Hkr.*, the *Laxdœla* instances of the formulations take on a more stereotyped tone; not only are they used more frequently, they also belong to structured patterns.

The killing of Bentein Kolbeinsson (*Mork.* 423-424) is also found in the *Heimskringla* (III, 310), and this account together with elements from the attack on Grjótgard as given in the *Óláfs saga helga* (*Hkr.* II, 302-303) form the substance of the narrative about the killing of Bolli Th. in his hut (*Lxd.* lv, 166-168). The description of Magnús berfœtt in his regalia and with his sword Legbiti (*Mork.* 335), the corresponding description of him in the *Heimskringla* (III, 227 and 236), the description of king Óláf Haraldsson in his accoutrements of battle (*Hkr.* II, 367), and the passages about the sword Fótbítr (Footbiter) and Bolli B.'s trappings (*Lxd.* xxix, 79; lxxviii, 224-225) bear striking resemblance among the patterned descriptions of this type.[17] In every instance the *Laxdœla* wording corresponds more closely to the *Heimskringla* over against the source *Morkinskinna*.

Óláf Haraldsson's last battle (*Hkr.* II, 367, 383-384, 385, 387) and that of Kjartan have many similar elements (*Lxd.* xlix, 152-154). The account of

Thorberg's and Ragnhild's harboring of Stein Skaptason (*Hkr.* II, 245-246) and the set-to between Vigdís and Thórd over the sheltering of Thórólf (*Lxd.* xiv, 31-32) offer further striking parallels. Ingigerd's taunting of her father, the king of Sweden, with "'Góð morginveiðr...'" (*Hkr.* II, 132) parallels Gudrún's "'Misjǫfn verða morginverkin...'" after Bolli has killed Kjartan (*Lxd.* xlix, 154). Interesting is the composite picture of Melkorka. The *Landnámabók* relates merely that Hoskuld bought a concubine of that name. The details in that transaction, where and how it took place, as told in *Lxd.* (xii, 22-23), seem to derive from the *Óláfs saga Tryggvasonar* (*Hkr.* I, 301) where the merchant Lodin purchases a concubine in the east at a trade fair, she was ill-clad, and she turns out to be Ástrid the wife of king Tryggvi, who had been sold into slavery. Lodin promises to buy her and take her back to Norway "if she will marry him." All these features are found again in *Laxdœla*: the trade fair in the east, a woman ill-clad who is of royal birth but had been taken into slavery. And the motif "if you will marry me" comes up also in connection with Melkorka (*Lxd.* xx, 50). The tale of Lodin is not in Monk Odd's *Óláfs saga Tryggvasonar* (AM 310), Snorri's source, and would therefore appear to be of the latter's manufacture. Melkorka also shares the woeful service of Herborg, the Hunnish queen, as related in the Guðrúnarkviða I of the *Edda*. Compare the shoes and stockings incident and the fact that the master was friendly whereas the mistress was harsh (Guðrúnarkviða I, vv. 9-10 and *Lxd.* xiii).

To what extent contemporary thirteenth-century events and personages have entered the saga remains one of the knottiest problems to untangle. In the final section of this chapter the attack on the Thorvaldssons in 1232 and other reports from the *Íslendinga saga* which conceivably could have been a source for the *Laxdœla* author are more fully discussed. Chronology here is a decisive factor, and much more detailed investigation must be done before one can assume similarities between *Laxdœla* and any of the saga sources to be borrowings by the *Laxdœla* author, as might so appear at first glance.

From the examples given one can see how the author interwove many strands to develop a composite yet convincingly natural picture of the characters and events in the saga. The substance of the narrative has been so carefully reworked that the multiple origins are disguised. It would not be surprising if further investigation into the sources would reveal that the content as well as the form has its own design, the main episodes and characters being composites from motifs and persons of pre-story time (Eddic lays and heroic themes), from story-time (the eleventh century, the material being provided by the Kings' Sagas), and from the author's own day. The evidence seems to be pointing in that direction.

The conclusion thus remains that *Laxdœla* is a deliberately contrived piece of literary prose, put together from bits and pieces, the patchwork being invisible so that a unified whole emerges. Whatever meager facts the author had, he padded out skilfully with plausible incidents, psychological motives, brilliant dialogue from a storehouse of written material and from his fertile imagination. Of historical truths or of oral traditions it can no longer be a question in the case of *Laxdœla*. It is now easier to grant the literal meaning to Sturla Thórdarson's "setti saman" in reference to the works his uncle Snorri had written (*Íslendinga saga* for the year 1230). The Kings' Sagas and the Sagas of Icelanders, it would seem, are truly "put together."

The Social and Moral Order

Although knowledge of the historical, social, and cultural background of a literary work often contributes appreciably to the better understanding of it, an artistic interpretation may, conversely, illuminate with even greater penetration the vitality of the age which produced it. *Laxdœla* presents the cultural ethos prevailing in Iceland from the time of Settlement to the author's own day. In creating so very real a world in which the characters move and act, the author has set before us the familiar events of that world: births, deaths, wooings, marriage feasts, journeys abroad, business deals and bargainings, ghosts, divinations, dreams, and above all killings and feuds. All the social and moral enactments have been selected in consonance with the saga's overall purpose and design and put into a form that brings out that design most advantageously. Against the backdrop of social conventions, figures move across the landscape in multi-colored array, weapons and shields brightly shining. In spite of its splendor, fate and doom hang over this world; in spite of its variety, the activities contain no real surprises. Everything is caught in a round of formulae, stereotyped scenes, and recurrent phrases. The formulaic character of the language and the predictable patterns in which life in the saga world is depicted mirror the inflexibility of that world.

In the moral order is found the same kind of rigidity and inescapableness as characterizes the social sphere. Here again is formula. Comparison of men and their worth underpins the moral code. Disparities are weighed and counterbalanced; in combat and contests skill is pitted against skill. Snorri

Goði recognizes the disparity between Lambi and Bolli in the compensating of one life with another. In the competitions at Ásbjarnarnes Kjartan is matched against the strongest and best; and at court, talk apparently often runs to the comparison of men (*mannjafnaður*: xix, 44). When king Óláf and Kjartan are measured by the yardstick, they are found to be equally tall: "Þat sǫgðu menn, at þeir hafi *jafnmiklir menn* verit, þá er þeir gengu undir mál, Óláfr konungr ok Kjartan" (xli, 124-125). Doubtless the physical comparison is meant to suggest a sizing-up of their worth as well. Equalizing is basic to the meting out of justice, to the settling of arbitrations, to the paying of indemnities. But perfect atonement, an evened score, can never be attained, for the demands of wounded honor carry the killings onward: "'It may well be that we cannot even the score exactly with these Laxdalers,' Gudrún says, 'but now someone must pay dearly, no matter from what dale he comes.'" A retaliatory system of point counterpoint sets up a measured rhythm within the run-on chain reaction of retribution, from which there is no respite. To be sure, disputes could always be settled peaceably, in a way that would do both sides honor, but efforts in this direction are abortive, even though they stand out as an admirable alternative, an unattainable ideal that is reluctantly relinquished. The aesthetic analysis has shown how the author neatly symbolized this two-edged sword of justice: through Repetition and Comparison, the like-for-like and compensating of likes and unlikes respectively; through Recurrence, the eternal chain.

From the concept of equalization and comparison the saga derives its vital form. Aside from the killings, other activities have been purposely selected to point up the same underlying idea: division of inheritances, marriage contracts, divorce settlements, sharing a catch of fish, making equal trades of horses and land. Bargaining stands out as a particular preoccupation in the saga. Much of the substance of the narrative relates to this equivalent and compensatory aspect of the moral law, as do the lexical, syntactical, and rhetorical preferences.

The round-of-life activities with their repeated patterns lend emphasis to the notion that the enactments of the social code, like those in the moral order, can develop into a vicious cycle. The formal organization of the linguistic materials tells us that this is so. As the tendency toward mutliple repetition presents itself in the triplets and quadruplets, where the balance is preserved, however precariously, through resolution into pairs in varying combinations, so the Recurrent linguistic formulations strive for equilibrium in a sort of check and balance system between negatives and positives. The delicate balance is on the verge of being upset at any moment.

The reappearance of the lexical combinations throughout the saga transmits a sense of necessity and predeterminism. The inner world of the saga is *always* (*jafnan*) the same world, one inextricably caught in its own entanglement, one ethically as well as metaphysically prescribed.

Destiny

The irretractable demand of the code of honor is expressed in the lives of the agents as unavoidable entanglements which lead to misfortune and, ultimately, to death. What is called misfortune by the individual is really part of a larger mysterious doom which pervades life itself; for all things there is an ill-fated destiny. Fate works behind the scenes, yet is manifested primarily in and through the characters. The course of events is determined not only by the will of the characters — and their will is motivated by the ethical code — but also by the will of this inscrutable force. Free and self-determined though the characters may seem to be, there is a power at the core of life itself which motivates both the agents and through them the action. The element of chance is thus all but eliminated. By amalgamating an apparition of destiny with the moral order of things, the author has created a compendious impulse that sets off the dramatic tension.

To represent this supernatural force, the author has made use of the convenient folk belief in dreams, portents, curses, premonitions, and revelations of second sight. These "natural" phenomena, belonging in one sense to the "real" world, were also manifestations of the preternatural. They offered a ready-made device by which a preview of events could be given. But so skillfully has the author couched the will of destiny in the language of dreams and the like — a language characteristically ambiguous — that both agents and audience are left in doubt whether what is suggested will really happen. Ambiguity permits the agents to shrug off prophecies or portents as something puzzling or inexplicable. In any case they pay them no heed, and warnings are deliberately ignored (Án Brushwood Belly's dream, Thorstein's admonishment to Thorkel, for instance), a fact which is again motivated by the characters' own will and stubbornness. Fate is actualized through the agents; it is not a *deus ex machina*. The audience, if alert and atuned to the subtleties of the text, may bear all the long-termed prophetic statements in mind, but somehow also retains doubt concerning the probability of realization. Apprehension aroused increases dramatic anticipation. It is a case of "agents having heard, that still do not hear" and of an "audience having heard, that knows but still plans and hopes." Alternations between fear and hope heighten the excitement. An evil sword comes into the family; but soon a protective one is acquired, an antidote. Hopes are raised, then dampened when the good sword is stolen, raised again when it is found, and again disappointed when it is put aside in a chest. Similarly, we hope that Kjartan will heed Aud's warning, but he refuses to take her brothers along; they go at her insistence, only to turn back before the crucial moment. Finally, the shepherd "by chance" sees the ambush and wishes to head Kjartan off. But the shepherd is overruled by his master, who, along with Thorhalla Chatterbox, is one of the malicious characters in the saga who delights in the misfortunes of others. Thus, Kjartan's destiny overrides all obstacles and takes its course. From the outset it is clear what the end will be.

In addition to vatic pronouncements of various kinds, other elements in the saga contribute to the establishing of a known result. The seemingly perfunctory adjectives used in introducing a character sum up his temperament before it is revealed in the action. Genealogies introduce even the agents themselves long before they come into the story. Ambiguities and rhetorical devices of different kinds aid in transmitting hints ironically veiled by the context, but transparent to the audience "in the know."

Although what the characters experience appears to happen naturally or as chance would have it, the underlying concept is not chance but destiny, a predeterminism which fulfills all that is implicit from the beginning. The inflexibility of fate corresponds associatively and structurally with the inflexibility in the ethical order. In the saga, these two spheres, the ethical and metaphysical (represented by the preternatural), are for all practical purposes amalgamated, and the formal aspects in the saga reflect both. Lexical repetitions set opposing sides against one another in balanced strength and power, either as parallels or antitheses, and hence present a symmetry of their own that has the semblance of an evened score. Furthermore, any given item reappearing underscores the inevitability of what has been intimated or once said and so produces a semblance of function fulfilled. Enactment of the moral law and fulfillment of fate are in each instance binding and necessary. The precision with which the formal elements (i.e. the lexical components and the formalized patterns) reappear shows them to be necessary rather than arbitrary. The whole saga is executed according to a preconceived plan. The author, omniscient and behind the scenes, manipulates his puppets and the actions on stage, much as fate has determined all from the beginning.

The Characters

The foregoing investigation has shown that the *Laxdœla* author worked with a selected number of personality traits and attributive phrases. The character types are not infinitely varied nor are the events and situations of unlimited kinds. Both have been chosen to illustrate a formal concept — either balance and compensation or serial happenings. Both agents and events are subordinate to that function. The inner and outer worlds are thus brought into closest correspondence. The agents in general show those qualities that can best motivate the action and set the ethos in motion — stubborn, hard to deal with, prideful, vain, ready to retaliate when honor is at stake. But despite the patterning, the psychological inner workings of the characters are conveyed by the author with remarkable sensitivity. Here he is a master, somehow capable of working with the stereotyped and with the distinctively individual, the true to life, blending them together.

If any one character can be said to dominate the action, it is Gudrún. She arrests our attention from the moment she appears. High-spirited, beautiful, proud, ambitious, fiercely jealous, quick-witted, sharp-tongued, calculating, and insatiable in vengeance, she of all the characters is the most carefully drawn. We observe her in all four of her marriages: spoiled and petulant in the first; mischievous and self-assured in the second; accepting the third one in spite and ill-humor; and agreeing to the fourth as a means toward gaining revenge. How and when she is moved to remorse or begins to see clearly that the flaws in her third marriage initiated the tragedy is hard to say, for we never look into her heart, except for once and even then briefly. The last words she is represented as speaking suggest that ultimately she has come to see her life for what it was: "To him I was worst whom I loved most." The forces of passion have spent themselves; blind and weary and old she finishes her days as a nun and hermitess. But the fate that is hers has not been imposed upon her by an alien spirit; it has been there inside her all along, forming and shaping her life and finally recoiling upon her. Rather, Christian humility and contrition are the alien elements here; just as medieval gallantry and pageantry comprise, as it were, a light wash over the world depicted in the saga, so, too, Christianity runs thin. The old world order and the fateful conception of life retain their efficacy.

The other women in the saga have something of Gudrún in them: Unn, Jórunn, Melkorka, Vigdís, and of course Thorgerd, — all except the sweet and gentle Hrefna, who is of an entirely different cast and in every respect a foil to Gudrún. Here again the author has brought a contrast into the series, just as a negative element suddenly offsets a preponderance of positives.

The male characters all have something of Kjartan in them: Óláf Feilan, Hoskuld, Óláf Peacock, Bolli Thorleiksson, and Bolli Bollason. Kjartan, as Gudrún's lover, plays the leading male role. He is gallant, self-confident, impetuous, eager for fame and glory, capable in weapons and sports, a born leader, and an extrovert. He comes close to the ideal hero type. When events begin to turn against him, he maintains self-assurance, first through restraint, then by over-compensation, taking especial care to appear gay, flaunting his prowess and authority wherever he can. He is cocky and throws caution to the winds to sport with death. But he, too, has become infected somewhat by Christian ethics: he keeps the fast and Holy Days and in the fight for his life finds it better to receive death than to deal it.[18] Both he and Bolli Bollason with their pomp and weapons and clothes betray the influence of medieval knighthood on the heroic tradition. Nonetheless, both Kjartan and Gudrún are tragic heroes and, like those of old, carry in themselves their fate. In this sense they are like their Eddic counterparts or the classical Greek heroes who are doom-eager. Fate is internalized.

Although Bolli Thorleiksson is said to be closest to Kjartan in prowess and accomplishments, he, like Hrefna, is of a different stamp. What makes the breach between Bolli and Kjartan the more charged with tension is the initial fondness they had for one another. Bolli's passive and introspective nature, his silent, brooding sullenness stand in contrast to Kjartan's outgoing assurance and active retaliation. The first overt act and triumph of Bolli's life, the snatching of the bride, is not enough to bolster his ego; it only brings him inner pain; and his second, the slaying of Kjartan, ultimately is his undoing.

However deft the *Laxdœla* author is in portraying accurately reactions true to life and in suggesting and inferring through the subtlest of means and rhetorical devices psychological truths, his main aim is not character study. Foremost is his achievement in cleverly controlling his verbal units to bring balance, symmetry, and symbolic imagery to his composition. It is through the mixing and correlating of the patterned phrases that most of the characters are "mixed characters" rather than black-and-white types. Even the events surrounding their lives, we have seen, represent an amalgam from various sources. The mixing and matching of the verbal components was particularly evident among the pairs of inimical brothers. When the characters appear, what they say, what is said about them are totally subordinate to the arrangement of the linguistic units with which the author is ultimately concerned. For it is this arrangement that forms an abstract pattern that conveys in itself the notions of comparison, of predetermined necessity, and of a repetitive progression, and these meanings coincide with the structural concepts inherent in the two aspects of the moral code and in a fateful destiny.

Many of the elements appear stereotyped and crystallized even before the *Laxdœla* author employed them, phrases like *mikill maðr ok sterkr*; many others become stereotyped within the saga by virtue of the author's repetitious use of them. However true it may be that the author had precedents for his phraseology or that he used merely ordinary Icelandic idiom or common storyteller's devices, he has nonetheless so organized, concentrated, and repeated them that they have become stereotyped patterns for the first time in *Laxdœla*. Within the overall patterning occasioned by the repeated verbal units, there are thematic patterns or groupings into a complex of specific motifs like the whettings, the drownings, the hero's accoutrements. Characters, too, are modelled after one another. Thorgerd, for instance, represents the stereotype of the prodding woman much more than does Gudrún; Bolli Bollason approaches the stereotype of the gallant much more than does Kjartan. What is intriguing is the author's ability to individualize the elements he has made into stereotypes in the first place, enabling him to conceal his patterns. And here again the author holds the balance.

The Epic Base

The recounting of events in a chronological progression from one generation to the next gives the saga epic scope. The introductory section in particular lays a broader epic base for the central action. The narrative is slow in getting started, halting at intervals to introduce yet another character or episode, looking backward to pick up threads that have been temporarily dropped, rounding out what has been prepared. Chronicling of births, deaths, wooings, marriages, careers, feudings, traffickings between farms, tales of ghosts, gossips and hired hands provide a broader picture of time and place, and supplies, as it were, an epic setting. The terrain and landscape around the Breidafjord Dales, the skerries and channels in the sound, the relationship of the farmsteads to one another and geographical directions, too, set a definite stage, familiar to epic narration. Recurrence, aside from creating the greater tragic aspect of the ethical code through its serial patterning, supplies through its content an epic backdrop for the more dramatic happenings in the foreground.

Many of the trappings and rhetorical devices associated with epic form are also present: backtracking of the action and the use of flash-backs; exaggerations and magnification, a glorification of agents and events. Typical of epic retardation are the incidents prior to the assault on Helgi's hut: the shepherd's account of the band in the woods with the details of dress and appearance; the eating of the *dagverðr* (main meal) by the group of attackers, as if they were in no hurry to get on with the business; the appearance of the comic Víga-Hrapp on the scene. Again epic delay is apparent in the leave-taking scene between Ingibjorg and Kjartan. Pause is taken to describe the expensive headdress, the little chest in which she keeps it, and its velvet case. This scene affords opportunity, too, to convey between the lines what Ingibjorg's feelings are by the fact that she prolongs these moments while in Kjartan is eagerness and expectancy pressing for departure.

Some few descriptions arrest one's attention like vignettes, masterfully presented with a few strokes that catch the eye: Thórólf standing at the landing stage with halberd ready as Hall comes rowing in to shore in high spirits; Vigdís flinging the purse into Ingjald's face, dealing him a bloody nose; Melkorka sitting on a sunny slope talking to her little son; Jórunn lashing Melkorka about the head with a pair of stockings; Óláf all dressed up in battle array striding forward to the prow of his vessel, which is manned from stem to stern, shields and spears studding the gunwales; Óláf again in all his finery marching off to Egil's booth at the heels of his father; Thorstein and Thorkel in the home meadow at Hjardarholt, nudging so close to Halldór that they are sitting on his cloak, while Beinir stands over them with poised axe. In addition, every now and then some small detail of weaponry or clothes is mentioned: shields embossed in gold with a lion, cross, or knight; or Gudrún's bodice and fancy sash of foreign mode. But there is little time to dwell on any of these in the saga. The descriptions are suggested in a minimum of words that form instantaneous pictures.

Although the story is mainly told through dialogue and indirect discourse and through the actions and deeds of the agents, lending an immediate presence to the action, some awareness that the story moves in the memory of bygone days is preserved. Epic time is past time, whereas dramatic time is an imminent future. *Laxdæla* participates in both.

The Dramatic Presentation

All the essential elements of drama are present in the saga: actors, motives turned into action, dialogue, and a limited setting made broader through suggestion. The characters act out their parts, and their words and deeds unfold the plot. But the dramatic quality of the saga runs much deeper than such ordinary histrionic devices. The scene before our eyes is suspended as a theatrical present between the past and the future. What has gone on before is the necessary prerequisite for the present moment, and the present action is, in turn, charged with implication for the future. Herein lies the essence of the dramatic conception of tragedy. The saga is essentially a dramatic presentation in epic form. The central action present before our eyes is always moving against a backdrop of past action.

The prophecies and portents, although more internalized than the oracle or chorus in classical Greek drama, boom forth their doom and disaster and intensify the necessity that is already present as moral obligation. Fate and the code of ethics offered the author ready-made dramatic material in the broadest sense. Both work together toward the same end, and the action fulfills all that was implicit from the beginning.

Tragedy dominates the central theme, and destiny brings the saga to its close. All passions have been spent; the forces of doom have run themselves out; all prophecies have been executed; the demands of justice satisfied. Yet, the saga ends on a different note. The generations continue; the life process goes on. Balance and compensation have been attained momentarily; and so the saga ends on a sort of up-beat. Such a rhythm belongs actually to comedy.[19] Our interest in the story has in a way also remained somewhat disengaged, not because emotions have not been presented, but because they have, without our knowing it, been harnessed in a pattern. Because of this conformity to a mechanical system on all levels in the saga, the tragic impact is not overwhelming. The feeling, however, remains that the closing scenes could easily be as implicitly portentous as the innocent relationships with which the saga opened. It is as if the whole could repeat itself like the round-of-life cycle under Recurrence. The end has run into the beginning. The epic and the dramatic, the comic and the tragic are played off against one another in this two-levelled saga.

Style and Tone

In view of the fact that the structural components, especially Foreknowledge and Repetition and Comparison, are generally so well camouflaged that it requires some sleuthing to detect them, something more should be said about the method of camouflage and the overall style and tone of the saga. The tension produced within the plot through the incompletion of a foreknown conclusion postulates a double audience consisting of some that "hearing shall hear and shall not understand" and others that "when more is meant than meets the ear, [are] aware both of that more and of the outsider's incomprehension."[20] This double treatment penetrates the saga to its core. It is first of all most noticeable in the unawareness of the agents and the omniscience of author and audience. The similarity between the plot structure of *Laxdœla saga* and the dramatic irony of classical Greek drama is obvious. The agents in the saga remain in the dark about the dreams and portents. They accept them on one level, the audience on another, if the latter is "in the know" and can interpret the signs. The language of dreams is by nature ambiguous; and the other vatic statements (in the broader and narrower sense) are likewise veiled through poetic and rhetorical devices such as litotes, euphemism, idioms and expressions of all kinds that show a discrepancy between surface meaning and significant meaning, between specific reference and general reference, between the literal and the figurative meanings (e. g. *kátr; kyrrt; at drepa skeggi; spenna um þongulshofuð; snarisk í bragð; loka hurðir*).

Omniscience is also evident in the attributing to the agents knowledge which has been previously heard only by the audience. Statements made by the author or by other characters are often picked up by one of the agents without their having been transmitted. The audience is again "in the know"; the agents, to all intents and purposes, "in the dark." These passages offer good evidence for the author's method and aim. He, being omniscient, has manipulated his phrases and repetitions, letting them fall at just the right places in the narrative to awaken the sense of necessity and fulfilled function. Some of them (e. g. *siti kyrrir ok í friði; framarla til*) are so pertinent to the situation that the speaker conceivably could have arrived at the idea independently, by chance, so to speak, under the given circumstance. This veils their invented origin and the author's deliberate purpose. Other of these repetitions by omniscience (e. g. *eigi er váttum bundit; Þórhǫllusonu, er þeir eru sendir til Helgafells; gaman ok skemmtun af viðskiptum þeira*) are too good a surmise on the part of the speaker to be coincidental. Rather than resort to pragmatic explanations like neighborhood gossip, which would lead away from the text and outside the poetic illusion, to explain the transmission by real life situations, it is more fitting to see in them part of the total scheme of the author to create structural parallels. Only in some places he has not veiled his method as well as in others. Balanced form and necessary connection are his primary concerns and govern the choice of words and where they occur. He would like to make it all seem as if by chance. Recognition of the reuse of precisely the same words, whether transmitted or untransmitted, discloses their contrivance. The latter type does so more readily since the plausibility for the reappearance of the same words has not been produced.

The irony of the presentation as seen in the double audience also comes out in the contrast between the precise form and the passion and intensity of the events described, causing some disengagement on the part of the reader. Related to this is the objectivity for which the Icelandic sagas have frequently been praised, a generality that needs some qualification. In *Laxdœla*, objectivity consists in a deliberate literary approach where the author disappears behind the scenes, his planning, selecting, contriving, fabricating all so skillfully concealed that the whole action seems to happen through natural motivation and of itself. But the author, like fate, is doing the directing, whether the audience realizes it or not. Again we meet with double treatment and with camouflage.

Camouflage, duplicity, and ambiguity are the keys to much of the substance of the narrative and to the means of its presentation. Snorri Godi's scheming and the play on the word *samlendr* immediately come to mind. But the technique runs much deeper. The author has favored those events, those agents, and those lexical, and syntactical arrangements, those rhetorical and stylistic devices that would play hand in hand with his central concept. Events such as bargainings and their counterpart, impasses; antithetical agents (e. g. inimical brothers; Gudrún-Hefna); parallel agents (e. g. Kjartan-Bolli Bollason; Gudrún-Thorgerd) abound. In the larger and smaller units of the narrative the author has played with all possible arrangements of such architectonics as chiasmus: parallels with opposite actions and effects (e. g. *lendur góðar / minna lausafé; fá lǫnd / fjǫlða fjár*; Án the Black's two dreams) and opposites with same action and effect (e. g. Bolli Thorleiksson and Thorleik Bollason where the chiasmal transposition of the names sets up a kind of opposition but results in their having identical roles; or the two Bolli's despite the same name having opposite roles); or negative reversals (e. g. *jafnræði / eigi jafnræði*; good marriages and bad marriages; smooth sea crossings and difficult sea crossings; *með mikilli blíðu / með engri blíðu*); or antitheses set up through substitution of antonyms (e. g. *kært / pústr; vináttu / kærleik; ekki efni / gott efni*). He also works with parallel comparatives (e. g. *firr / nær; hvergi betr / nǫkkuru fleiri; vel / miklu betri*), as well as with sentences constructed on the basis of parallel syntax (e. g. the sentence about the brothers Ingjald and Hall). Correlatives and duplicates of all kinds abound. Alternations as between the hope and fear discussed above, contrasts between the calm (*kyrrt*) and the storm, between preparatory gaiety and ensuing tragedy, are used by the author to derive the greatest possible effects. So the major enmities grow from incidents which occur at three festive occasions, and an ominous cloud throws its shadow into the jesting and jostling at Hól before Kjartan's fateful ride into Svíndadal, where the comic and the tragic are also juxtaposed. The tension of the tragedy imminent there in the valley is relieved briefly by the pretense of joking when his companions drag Bolli down the slope by his heels. The puny and ludicrous Víga-Hrapp appears on the scene before the attack on Helgi's hut. Likewise the splendor and ennoblement of the social backdrop complements the disastrous events; the most illustrious of the family are doomed to tragic end. Love and hate, a good sword and an evil sword — such contrastive pairs could be enumerated with many more.

One might gather from these remarks that the prose of this saga could easily verge on the trite, almost the euphuistic. But the author has employed his devices so cleverly, making them one with the content, that the trick is well concealed. Besides, the artistic devices are not mere ornaments but are themselves turned into poetic imagery, hence are bearers of meaning. The embellishment of the accoutrements of the hero, helmet, sword, shield, with golden adornments (usually *gullrekit* and the like) is on the formal level also an embellishment (i. e. amplification) of the pattern. Substitution of antonyms also mirrors the content — a turn in the situation described, for instance; or parallel syntax as used about Hrapp dead or alive parallels the discursive idea.

The relationships and comparisons which the repetitions among the verbal units set up are not explicitly or discursively stated, they are implied. Only once in a while does the author himself intrude to give hint of his intent, as with the *þótti mjǫk á hafa hrinit* in the case of two lesser prophecies or with his *sem fyrr* that makes a reference direct. These phrases cue the reader as to what the saga is about: the necessary fulfillment of what has been suggested before; a return of the same situation as obtained before, or, most importantly, the reuse of verbal configurations. The audience must be alert not only to what has been said before but also to how it has been worded.

The repetitions and correlations are first of all masked through integration with the content. Any one phrase can be interpreted at face value within the context where it appears; as soon as its counterpart is found, the co-relationship carries the significance beyond the contextual meaning. Through the arrangement, the language itself becomes an event rather than a medium or vehicle. An abstract pattern emerges that conveys the ideas of necessity, fulfillment, compensatory balance, comparison, reiteration, recurrence.

Another way in which the verbal repetitions are concealed from the casual observer is through subtle variations in the wording itself: e. g. the pair *áttu þáu Guðrún þar mikit traust / þau Ósvífr eiga allt traust*; or the statement referring to Gudrún's remembering exactly what men were in on the raid against Bolli and the corresponding statement that Gudrún's sons hadn't forgotten what men were in on the raid; or the fact that the *at klæðum ok vápnum* phrase is applied to Bolli's men, not specifically to Bolli. These substitutions are practically synonymous, and in every case mutually inclusive by inference so that the correspondence in pattern remains.

Use of vague terms, plurals, or generalities often conceals the specific implication: (e. g. the plurals *nǫkkura, svivirðingarorð*; the vague *af inum versti manni*; or the future of probability *mun auðit verða*; the generality *spenna um þǫngulshǫfuð*). Substitution of synonyms into the same pattern also disguises the parallelism or comparison intended (e. g. *hlutgjarn / framgjarn*; *sómamaðr / vaskr maðr*). Increment embellishment serves the same purpose of making the similarities fuzzier (e. g. "hafim *gaman af leik þeira*" / "gerði sér af *gaman ok skemmtan af viðskiptum þeira*"; "þessir menn *siti um kyrrt allir*" / "Óláfssynir *siti kyrrir ok í friði*"; "jafnan *til trausts*" / "*tils halds og* [sic] *trausts*"; "sitr Óláfr nú *í búi sínu*" / "Óláfr sat nú *í búi sínu með miklum sóma*"; "hafði *sverð í hendi*" / "hafði *í hendi sverð gullrekit*").

In the thematic patterns made up of a concatenation of motifs, the camouflaging is also achieved through variation and substitution, and through rearrangement somewhat of the sequence of the motifs. But above all, camouflaging is accomplished through imbedding the same forms, whether single phrases or whole patterns, in entirely new contexts. Halldór, for instance, is said to take the lead among his brothers ("hann var mjǫk fyrir þeim brœðrum"). The confirmation of the statement is put in a new setting: Thorgerd, in goading her sons to take action, says to Halldór: " 'Þú þykkisk mest fyrir yðr brœðrum' " ("'You consider yourself leader among you brothers'"), which adds a shift of viewpoint to the blanket narrative statement. Despite slight variations and new contexts the designs are never obliterated. The individual motifs in the patterns of the parties, goadings, killings, and drownings offer the best examples of rearrangement and substitution of new substance each time into the same molds. There is no doubt that the author has mastered fully the use of patterns, recognizing established ones, creating new ones.

Many of the themes and well turned phrases can be found elsewhere in saga literature, but their specific and unique form and function in *Laxdœla* make them wholly pertinent to the literary work regardless of their provenance. What has the author done with the materials of his language? He has created formulae out of normal phrases; he has repeated them in accordance with his own structural idea, turning them to new function. He has created patterns and formulae that have become so for the first time within *Laxdœla* alone. Whether any of them are solidified patterns taken over bodily from tradition outside the saga or from other sources, requires further investigation. The hero accoutrements pattern attracts particular attention in this regard.[21] Since with the patterns under Recurrence, as with those in triplicate, not every motif occurs in each repetition of the theme, the archetype of the pattern can only be obtained by building a composite from the specific instances, which I have in effect done in Chapter V. These nucleus patterns must have been the basis for the composition, whether newly invented or borrowed. It is as though the author, visualizing the whole structure, worked, so to speak, from these germinating centers outward, just as the saga is more fully developed in the middle, ripples of its main themes spreading to the periphery as preparation or recapitulation. Indeed, only if one has recognized the patterns, seen the saga as a whole, can one — in retrospect — detect the fact that Hoskuld's not riding to meet Hrút, for instance, is a negative reversal of the expected; or that Bolli's not having on a coat of mail contradicts the pattern, or that Hrút's accoutrements and the descriptive details about them are but iterations of a thematic complex. The chronological order of the saga as preparation, central theme, recapitulation must be distinguished from the sequence of the creative process. The critical analysis has perhaps given us some clues as to the nature of that formative process. The reader (or audience), like the author, must keep the patterns in mind in order to anticipate and recall and thus read the saga from the center outwards. The effect of the patterns and formulae is a cumulative one since ever more elements are introduced and repeated as the saga progresses — which accounts for the concentration of formulae in the last part of the saga. One has the impression toward the end that everything has already been said somewhere, sometime before. The author's method has become all too patent.

The patterns under the round-of-life category are the most readily recognized. Rather than being concealed, they act as distractors and do the concealing, especially in those cases where the more or less stereotyped recurrent phrases take on individual and qualified function (e. g. *ráðakostr*, which is used innocuously enough in the career-abroad offers and then with special intent and double meaning to hint of marriage with Ingibjorg; or the *unni mest*, which is a running theme but also strengthens comparative bonds among the agents: Hoskuld-Óláf, Óláf-Kjartan, Hoskuld-Bard, Gudrún-Bolli B.). Many motifs receive this double treatment. The agents and events of the main action, it must be remembered, also participate in those events which belong to the gackground; thus some of the motifs are bound to show a twofold application, i. e. as Recurrence and as Repetition or Comparison. That both Kjartan and Bolli B. are *kurteisligr* or *mikit afbragð annarra manna*, for instance, would not by itself be enough to establish any meaningful comparison between them. Seen against all the other parallels, these attributes become part of the foreground schematism, being lifted momentarily from the chain, so to speak, to act as comparatives, which accords them greater significance.

The author's schemes (patterns of words) are thus themselves a scheme. This "bragð" of his is equal to any of Snorri Godi's. Without doubt he would hope that his patterns and formulae might be recognized, for his architectonics of matching prophecy and fulfillment, of equalizing events and agents, of comparing and setting up antithetical relationships, of duplicating and doubling are the key to understanding what the saga is really about. But the repeated phrases, like all the veiled hints in the saga, are subtle and apparent only to the knowledgeable reader or audience, whose position must become analogous to that of the author to see through the subterfuge.

After the foregoing analysis and this discussion it is all but a foregone conclusion to say that *Laxdœla* is composed to a great extent, despite the historical frame, of fabricated situations, fabricated dialogues, and when necessary for the composition, of fabricated characters, and that it is a literary work of contrived design. The author has capitalized on a technique, using rhetorical devices, patterns, and formulaic phraseology to set forth his idea complex, whatever their ultimate derivation proves to be. The saga is almost what one could call a self-parody. For after the author produced his patterns and formulae, he reshuffled and recombined them, so that they became unique again, individualized, and thereby camouflaged. His ingenuity is hence twofold. He succeeded so well in his endeavor that his highly stylized composition appears natural and uncontrived to all but the initiated, the ideal audience that has caught on to the tricks involved.

Such self-parody can be witty, consciously or unconsciously, e. g. such as we meet in Gudrún's playing with the term *samlendr* almost to the point of divulging the secret. The author's *sem fyrr, sem ván var* also come close to this type of wit when read with the whole aesthetic design in mind. In the flash-back reminder about the events in Iceland while Thorkel is abroad (lviii, 176; lxviii, 199), the author's repeating of his own sentences would in itself function as a correlative between referent and antecedent apart from the literary convention used. Is the author's allowing Gudrún to turn the excuses of her sons to her own advantage (a kind of antistrophon) deliberate or the result of the system of repetitions, the witticism being incidental or concomitant? Irony is indeed the distinctive quality of this prose.

Rhythm and Time

Circumstances prevalent in thirteenth-century Iceland, when saga writing was at its height, no doubt encouraged interest in the Age of Settlement and the heyday of the Commonwealth. Rise of power politics had brought with it a breaking down of the traditional moral order; political and material aggrandizement superceded personal honor and prestige based on integrity. This century witnessed the outbreak of feuds, vendettas, intrigues, and savageries on a scale hitherto unknown. Times were undeniably crucial.

The turning to historical subjects probably reflects a consciousness that history was in the making. The relentless step by step movement toward relinquishment of freedom and the end of the Commonwealth must have seemed to some, at least, like the machinations of an inscrutable destiny propelling the country toward disaster. *Laxdœla saga* is judged to have been composed about 1250; the Commonwealth came under Norwegian control in 1262. Contemporary events in many ways must have appeared like the disastrous result of the code of vengeance and the fulfillment of a fateful destiny. In a sense it was a turning point where past and future met, a time of precarious balance in the life of the nation.

Laxdœla saga reveals this continuity between time past and time present first of all through the genealogies, some of which follow the names back to a time before the story, while others project the names forward to persons beyond the frame of events in the saga but contemporary with the time of the author and his writing. The author's intrusion into the narrative is minimal and difficult to detect. The few places where he does reveal himself point to his consciousness of the discrepancy between the time of the events he is writing about and the time of the composition, and to the fact that he is writing about the past from the perspective of the present.²² Some of the anachronisms also show that he is comparing the present with the past. The obvious one concerning the fact that "heathen men *then* had no less at stake than Christian men do *now* when ordeals are performed" (xviii, 42-43), which has already been discussed in another connection,²³ explicitly draws the comparison between time "then" and time "now." Two other statements where the author's comment reveals his mediating position between former times and contemporary times carry the comparison implicitly. Halldór is described as wearing a cloak with a clasp that was the fashion *at that time*: "Halldórr hafði yfir sér samða skikkju ok á nist lǫng, *sem þá var títt*" (lxxv, 219). The author herewith gives us a fact about mode of dress in saga times, a small detail that shows an attempt at historical accuracy, keeping his characters appropriate to their times. More importantly, the *þá* tells us that that time and the author's are not the same time. It shows the perspective. But we have met with a similar phrase before, and consideration of the author's general method makes it likely that an association is intended between these two, as is the case with any of the repetitions in the saga. It will be recalled that Bolli Bollason carried a lance "as is the custom in foreign lands": "hann hafði glaðel í hendi, *sem títt er í útlǫndum*" (lxxvii, 225). In contrast to the appropriateness of the clasp to the times about which the author is writing, this reference tells us that a contemporary mode of dress has been superimposed on that past time. The one points to time past, the other to time present; and particularly to be noticed, the one is in past tense, the other in present tense. The similarity of the phrases lexically (*títt* is used only in these two places in the saga), the similarity of the contexts with their references to fashions then and now indicate that a juxtaposition and comparison is being subtly suggested by the author. The natural contexts in which the phrases occur camouflage again the underlying meaning. What the author is hinting is that the fashion is to talk about the present in terms of the past. These inadvertent (I'd rather call them advertent) "slips" on the author's part²⁴ tell us on the discursive level that there is a time discrepancy, and on the formal level that the two times represented are to be compared and contrasted. What structural peculiarities in the saga would further substantiate such a supposition?

We have had many occasions to note that the rhythm in the saga is one of a back-and-forth relating of cause and resultant, of antecedent and referent. Recognition of prophecy and associating it with its fulfillment, or correlating a repeated phrase with its forerunner produce the effect of anticipation and recollection. There is a constant back-and-forth comparing going on within the saga by virtue of its formal structure. The same structural rhythm was found in the bargainings, in the handing of the decision back and forth between father and daughter in the betrothals, in the living alternately first in one place and then in another, in the sea crossings, in the forward-looking and backward-looking genealogies, and in the compositional flash-backs.

The narrative itself, we have noted, shows a mingling and a superimposing of the epic and the dramatic mode of presentation. Epic handling would indicate the remembering of things past and giving an account of them, whereas the dramatic handling renders these past events present and actual. This feeling is transmitted throughout the narrative. The events the author is describing are supposed to be of a by-gone time, yet the action is always vividly present. Time past and time present are merged and blended. The dramatic presentation itself consists in compacting into the present moment the culmination of all that was implicit from the beginning and all that is portentous for the future. Past and future meet in the present moment. The visually present action of the saga, suspended between past and future, is completely analogous to the point in history where Iceland stood in the thirteenth century at the time the saga was composed.

The structure and plot of *Laxdœla saga* are based on a formal conception — that of destiny and dramatic tragedy. The plot is executed through the analogously structured form of the ethical code as necessity and inevitability. The prophecies and the presupposition of rigid fulfillment of the code of honor with its equal retaliations represent that omniscient force in the background which shapes and forms the main action of the drama, action that seemingly takes place naturally and of itself before our eyes. The social order of things, as recognized under Recurrence, serves as the epic backdrop in front of which the drama, the action of the saga, moves as before a screen. This drama itself is also conceived by the author as part of that round-of-existence, part of the whole, the bigger tragedy. Here we discovered the point of contact between the epic mode and the dramatic mode, between the background and the foreground. They are mutually inclusive. And we have seen, too, how on the formal level Repetition and Comparison (used most for the main action) also in places participate in Recurrence. The analogy the author wishes to draw could not be more obvious. The whole saga world, so to speak, was the epic background for the events of the drama taking place in mid thirteenth-century Iceland. Seen against the by-gone days of the Commonwealth as the epic backdrop, the drama of the present represented a culmination of what had been set in motion in Iceland's past and a turning point for the future. What was implicit from the beginning (the social order, the demands of a retaliatory system of justice) was working itself out fatefully in the author's own day. Again we see the author's use of camouflage and pattern. The events of his day supply the new context for the old forms. The background world of the saga represents the same world as that of the thirteenth century — the same social order is implied, the same two-edged sword of justice. Yet the *Laxdœla saga* holds itself up like a mirror to the thirteenth century, in the sense that it gives a positive reflection of the negative contemporary happenings.

The discussion of the *títt* phrases and of the epic and dramatic handling has incidentally also touched upon another closely related problem — that of tenses. The realization that Iceland's historical past has been made actual and the present converted into a semblance of the past throws further light on the mixture of past and present verb forms in the narrative, something which has occasioned much puzzlement in saga research. Use of historical present to enliven action is a well-known storyteller's device. It does not, however, explain the mingling of grammatical tenses found in some sagas, and particularly in *Laxdœla*,[25] a practice which has generally been dubbed as primitive, inept, or a meaningless enigma. Such mixing apparently has an aesthetic function which has evaded critics.[26] The reader is never disoriented in respect to the time of the action; it is always immediately present before his eyes. And, indeed, the shift in tenses is so unobtrusive that it generally passes unnoticed. This in itself should tell us that the author has prepared for us another "bragð." The juxtaposing of the two tenses, past and present, even within the same sentence does not signify that the action in the present tense is the resultant of the action in the past tense in any specific instance — a literary device used by some poets. In *Laxdœla saga* the mingling has broader implication: all the virtually present actions in the saga are the result of those in the past, and by analogy all the present-day events of the author's time, disastrous and portentous as those in the saga, are the culmination and consequence of Iceland's past and the cultural ethos that generated that history. The mixture of tenses is appropriate to the first level — the saga understood as a closed aesthetic unit in which both epic and dramatic handling are inherent to the structure. And the mixture is a clue to the relationship of the saga as a whole to its cultural context — mid-thirteenth-century Iceland. By mixing his tenses the author has confounded the critics and concealed the fact that he was not only writing about the past, but about and for the present. The interspersing and distributing of the two grammatical tenses, like the mixing, distributing and reordering of the patterned phrases and motifs in the saga, camouflage their existence and their function. Like the prophecies and other hints, like the repeated phrases, the tense shifts, too, go by practically unnoticed. The use of tenses, their specific function already indicated in the *títt* phrases, is another camouflaged hint.

We thus see that the saga can be read on two levels. To test this out, one only need apply the categories derived from the aesthetic analysis to the analoguous situation of the thirteenth century. The saga functions as Foreknowledge, the preparation for the events of the author's time. Everything that has happened later is present *in nuce,* as prophecy. The saga events form a Comparison with later times. The author's own day is a Repetition, a parallel to the earlier period of history. But it is also a contrast, for in the saga Repetition and Comparison received the main focus, whereas in the author's day Recurrence is the aspect which has come to the fore. Thus the author's time comprises a negative reversal, a reversed image. The saga as a mirror for the contemporary age gives the positive image. The one historical period is the reversed reflection of the other. Since the analogy the author is drawing is one of formal principles, namely the idea behind the events, it is clear why he attached so much importance to building the formal relationships in the saga. It was through abstract pattern that the analogy could best be conveyed without stating either the function of the pattern or the analogy that he intended.

This supposition can be tested and explored further. The recurrence of the cycle implied at the close of the saga turns out indeed to be the more disastrous one, for the repeat performance in the thirteenth century illustrates the adverse aspect. The structural analysis of the saga showed how the formal aspects tended constantly toward establishing a balance, even when the repetitions threatened to multiply into triplets and quadruplets. The chain reaction itself, illustrated under Recurrence, tended toward setting up its own checks and balances. By contrast, the thirteenth century was not headed toward balance. The concatenation of events had clearly got out of hand; there were no more checks and balances in the system; the nation was headed for disaster. The saga presented an ideal and through it a warning.

The virtual and essential time rhythm of the saga as a comparing back and forth within the saga and between the saga and its contemporary context has also been camouflaged through a semblance of real time and historical progression. The events depicted carry a semblance of history, and with it a semblance of real time. The natural progression of the generations produces a forward movement. The impression is given of a sequence of before, now, and after, corresponding to the three main divisions of the saga; there is a time before the main action, the main action itself, and its sequel. Increment and increase, embellishment and enhancement also accompany the generations. Qualitatively the enhancement stands in contrast to the analogy the author is drawing with his own times. The purpose of what we have called epic magnification, of the grandeur and idealization of saga times becomes apparent. As a contrast with contemporary times, those times appeared as ideal. Quantitatively the series repetitions under Recurrence and the cumulative effect of the patterning toward the end of the saga represent a parallel with the author's times. Increase and increment of the patterns is not only a natural result of all that has been presented and gone before, on the second level it is also meaningful. For the author's own day shows the cumulative effect of all that has gone before, the increased tragedy. Recurrence in the saga represented this larger aspect of the ethical code — there it was the background. For the author's own day, this background has become the foreground. The quantity of the feuds and retaliations has increased, whereas the quality — the honorable reasons for performing the deeds, the ethical demands of equalization and compensation that would do both sides honor (Repetition and Comparison) — has faded into the background.

There is another aspect to this comparing of the present time with the past time. If the agents and situations in the saga are analogous, as has been demonstrated through the repeated patterns and comparisons, the relationship between the "before" in the story, the "now," and the "after" are also for all practical purposes annulled. What is happening now has happened before, and will happen again, or at least so it seems, and it is this seeming that counts. Past and present are one and the same, can therefore be superimposed on each other. Just as one generation is patterned after the former, so the author's generation is derived from the preceding generations and his times are like those times in the saga. But if everything is really like everything else, despite new contexts, substitutions, and negative counterparts, then in effect the happenings are lifted into a time which is like every other time, and hence indefinite in reference to everything except the depicted action. The references to the fall of Óláf the Saint, like mention of Ari, put the saga in a historical frame and help create the illusion of historical reality, whereas actually the saga contains a philosophy of history that is related to the syncretic thinking of the Middle Ages. The events in the saga are merely relative to one another, as the time designations in the story will show. The author is purposely working in poetic time, and that time is a virtual present or eternal time in which repetitive instances can be said to take place "at the same time." The instances in the saga and the analogously repeated instance of the thirteenth century can be interpreted as reenactments of the ethical code, of the pattern of destiny that was common to both. History was therefore envisioned by this poet-author as repetitions of a preestablished pattern — in the history of his country this pattern was based on the cultural ethos, that vital center from which all else sprang. The events of then or now the author saw as taking place *in illo tempore*, in that eternal time of reenactment, synchronic time. The sequence of historical time is thus erased. The likenesses which have been set up within the saga, and the analogy intended with his own time indicate that this is the case. The pattern, this abstraction of the formative principle behind the course of history, was the central nucleus from which all else could be derived. The author employed the same method in miniature with each one of his patterns in the saga: for the goadings, the killings, the drownings, the hero's accoutrements a nucleus pattern could be established from which the specific examples had emanated, in the creative process, as from a center. Substitution of new content in the same forms, displaying of the negative counterpart, the opposites, does not invalidate or obliterate the pattern. Is it any wonder that the *Laxdœla* author was so interested in patterns, repetitions of patterns, and their contrastive aspects? Here the spheres of art and history are brought into closest relationship.

The structural analysis has shown the bigger pattern with which the author was ultimately concerned. The agents and events within the saga are analogous to one another, and these in turn are analogous to those of times before the saga and times after the saga — the happenings of those times and the author's time follow the same pattern, hence can be superimposed on one another. The happenings within the saga and those of the analogy outside the saga can also be drawn together in a simultaneous vision; all and both are immediately present. Indeed, one of the favored expressions in the saga is *mjǫk jafnskjótt*,[27] which indicates that two actions are coincident. The expression is a loaded one and carries several connotations relevant to basic notions in the saga: On the one hand, two events may be taking place concomitantly: "Nú setr Þorkell fram ferjuna ok hlóð. Þorsteinn bar *jafnskjótt* af útan sem Þorkell hlóð ok þeir fǫrunautar hans" (lxxvi, 221-222: "Now Thorkel launched the ferry and started loading. Thorstein carried the timber off just as fast as Thorkel and his comrades loaded it"). On the other hand, two events may converge at the same time: "Eptir þetta ræðr sá til, er skírsluna skyldi af hǫndum inna, ok *jafnskjótt* sem hann var kominn undir jarðarmenit, hlaupask þessir menn at mót með vápnum, sem til þess váru settir" (xviii, 43: "Now the one who was to carry out the ordeal gets started, and just at the moment when he had come under the sod, the men who had been put up to this rush at each other with their weapons"). This situation is, of course, contrived and the audience is aware of the manipulation. Other such incidents in the saga are also "arranged," but the author would like it to seem as if "by coincidence," as for example when Hoskuld and his housecarls arrive home at the same time: "Þat var *mjǫk jafnskjótt*, at húskarlar hans koma heim" (xix, 46); or when Óláf Peacock moves to Hjardarholt: "Þat var *mjǫk jafnskjótt*, at húskarlar hǫfðu ofan tekit klyfjar af hrossum, ok þá reið Óláfr í garð" (xxiv, 68: "Just as the housecarls had got the packs down from the horses, Óláf rode into the farmyard"). The same precision attends the meeting of Gudrún and Snorri: "Þat er í Lœkjarskógs landi; í þeim stað hafði Guðrún á kveðit, at þau Snorri skyldu finnask. Þau kómu þar *mjǫk jafnsnimma*" (lix, 176: "That is on land belonging to Lækjarskóg and at this place Gudrún had arranged to meet with Snorri. They arrived there just at the same time"). This simultaneity is everywhere manipulated by the omniscient author; it is related to the exactness and symmetry of the saga; it is like a contrivance of destiny. Indeed, the fact that Thórólf and Ásgaut escape across the river is attributed to fate, and in this scene significantly the *jafnskjótt* also appears:

> Ok með því at menn váru hraustir, ok þeim varð lengra lífs auðit, þá komask þeir yfir ána ok upp á hǫfuðísinn ǫðrum megin. Þat er *mjǫk jafnskjótt*, er þeir eru komnir yfir ána, at Ingjaldr kemr at ǫðrum megin at ánni ok fǫrunautar hans (xv, 34: And seeing that they were sturdy men and fated to live longer, they got across the river and up onto the pack ice on the other side. Just at the time when they had got across the river, Ingjald and his companions reached the other side of the river).

Much as Halldór expected the men from other farms to arrive just when the sale of the Hjardarholt lands should have been closed, and which they in fact did, the author, too, has neatly prearranged everything. Contemporary time is parallel to saga time, simultaneous with it and also predestined. *Jafnskjótt* is a coded word to be read first on the normal discursive level within the context, second as a clue to the meaning of the time relationships between the events within the saga (what happens in Hoskuld's day can happen in Óláf's day, in Kjartan's day, in Bolli B.'s day), and third as a key to the meaning of the time comparisons the author has contrived with his superimposed images of time present and time past. It reveals also his view of history.

The flash-backs in the saga repeat this structural form. They, too, relate of events in the saga that are taking place simultaneously and produce a back-and-forth comparing. From this new aspect, the whole saga can be said to be a flash-back from the author's time to saga time, a comparing of events "then" and "now" which emphasizes their simultaneity, their parallelism, and their contrast.

Since the present time (thirteenth century) is superimposed on the past time of the saga and simultaneous with it, the saga can be read like a coded message. That is, the structural categories and stylistic devices, the abstracted forms, have double reference. Why the regular occurrence of *bæði...ok* and its negative counterpart *hvárki...né*, why are there always *tveir kostir*, why is *jafnan* a loaded word? The saga is *both* what it seems to be *and* something more; it is also *neither* the one *nor* the other: neither saga time nor contemporary time. The thirteenth century is not wholly analogous to the positive world of the saga; it is the negative counterpart. We have noted, for example, that the positive forms quantitatively outnumbered the negative formulations in the saga, but that the negative reversal in a pattern always carried more than face-value significance. Any one pair of inimical brothers, too, was found not to be a completely opposite pair: Bárd and Thorleik Hoskuldsson overlap in regard to some points, as do Kjartan and Bolli Th., as do Thorleik and Bolli B. The eleventh century and the thirteenth century are the same, yet antithetical. The further import of images in reverse also becomes apparent, as in the betrothals where the pattern is consistently one of presentation of the woman's qualifications to the man and of the man's to the woman; or as in the sea voyages and receptions back and forth in Norway and in Iceland, the one a mirrored image of the other. Then there are reversed images, that is, negative contrasts to a predominantly positive pattern: a bad marriage, a poor sea voyage, a cool reception, an incomplete hero. Án's two dreams are also reversed images of one another, the one negative, the other positive.

It is *always* the same world that is being suggested — the world of the saga shows within itself a repetitive sameness, but beyond this is implied that the Heroic Age is like the Age of the Commonwealth, is like the Age of the Sturlungs, yet the latter also contrasted with the former ones — Parallels and Contrasts are always implied in Comparison. So there are *two* choices for the reader: the one level or the other. The game could go on.

The nonsense riddle of the cloak tells of Snorri's "bragð," and it also explains the riddle of the saga:

> Wet it hangs on the wall,
> Wot the cloak a trick,
> Ne'er more dry after this,
> Nor deny I, it knows of two.

The saga contains one trick — the concealed formal elements; the cloak knows of another, the analogy with contemporary times. The saga is not dry, but wet (filled with significance and knowledge). There seems no limit to the author's ingenuity and to the camouflages that can be unveiled. The language of the saga is ironic beyond anyone's expectation. Its layers are actually threefold. Here is then confirmation of the significance of the structural components based on two and three. The first layer, the normal discursive one, is a camouflage, a coded message, for the second layer, the abstract formal layer that the aesthetic analysis revealed. This layer in turn is the key for the third layer, the analogy with the thirteenth centutry. The first must be decoded to find the second, and the second to find the third. The one hinges on the other. By veiling his patterns, the author has hidden the internal structure, hence the analogy remains concealed, both are hidden by the cloak. And what better image could the author have selected than a hooded cloak for concealment? Could it be that the indictment of his own age he could not state directly and openly, so he spoke in parables much as, for example, Brueghel the Elder dared not speak out against the atrocities, the tragedy of his times but feigning innocence depicted them symbolically through analogy with the remoter times of Biblical happenings? It has taken critics long enough to see through *Laxdœla*'s tricks, something with which we have been confronted all along in this analysis, but which only opened up to myself at the very end. And that is as it had to be, for only after the conclusion of the aesthetic analysis could the next level be unfolded, and that is what has taken place as the sections on Style and Tone and Rhythm and Time were conceived. The saga becomes extremely witty, once the parable is recognized, indeed a self-parody. Some of this wit comes through even if one is not fully "aware." Did the contemporary audience see through it? The saga gives us the author's surmise: Gudrún thinks Thorgils will see through Snorri's first trick: "'Sjá mun hann.'" Snorri answers: "'Sjá mun hann víst eigi'"; and this is confirmed: "ok sér hann ekki í þetta." If the first trick is not discovered, the second will forever remain a secret. The author is telling us throughout the saga what it is all about, but the audience has not been wily enough for this "second Snorri."

    The anonymous *Laxdœla* author can be credited with having produced one of the most remarkable and brilliant prose works of the medieval period. His was a genius of extraordinary power and perception. Significant as literature, significant as a commentary on the age that fostered it, *Laxdœla saga* represents a *tour de force* that few could duplicate. With a sensitivity to the workings of human beings and of history, with a sureness of touch, and with a consciousness of the symbolic import behind the happenings he has selected to depict, the author created not just an account of them on the discursive level, but on the formal level through organization of his linguistic materials a virtual and conceptual image of what he observed. Acutely aware of the irrepressible demands of wounded honor, of the lust for retaliation, of commitments that ever led to further involvement, he perceived a destiny behind the inescapable entanglements of life whether the time was that of the Settlement and the Commonwealth or of the Age of the Sturlungs. In this merging of the cultural reference with the cultural context rests the secret of the saga. If *Laxdœla saga* is a tragedy, it is not one of the human beings but rather of a cultural ethos which had ceased to be constructive. By reason of the selection, arrangement, and organization of all the materials that went into the composition of the saga, it must be conceded that it is a literary monument of the highest order. It stands as a witness to the age that produced it and as a symbol that conveys the meaning of that age more forcibly than any chronicle.

The demonstration should have illustrated sufficiently the nature of the piece of literature here dealt with and, one hopes, it will give an indication of what the solutions to some of the age-old problems discussed in the Introduction might be. It should also have made patently obvious the advantages of the aesthetic method and what can be drawn out of a text through close reading, through an *explication de texte* which needs no outside information to explain the work's purport. Most important it is for readers to return to the saga itself and see it whole, as a masterpiece in creative prose.

The Age of the Sturlungs: Authorship and Date of the Saga

So the exposition of the *Laxdœla saga* was completed. The next day after the pen had been laid down, the thought did not leave me that our anonymous author no doubt had somewhere given hint of who he was, since the work was replete with clues and disclosed a *roman à clef* relationship with the thirteenth century. The farthest from my thoughts in beginning the task of an *explication de texte* was to search for a probable author. My purpose was to demonstrate merely that the *Laxdœla saga*, for one, was a piece of artistic prose, non-historical, non-oral. Now after the last two sections of the Literary Perspectives were finished, the more the conviction grew that my unwitting remark about a "second Snorri" could be taken quite literally. The duplicity of Snorri Godi plays a prominent role in the saga, and the carefully worked out theme arrests the attention of the reader even if he does not know that the duplicity is two-levelled. If the poem about the cloak was a camouflaged riddle in a twofold sense, I reasoned, then one might assume that the other poem connected with the duplicity theme, the one spoken by Thorgils' fetch, also contained a double reference:

> Fighters strive onward
> If ye deem yourselves forward,
> And wary watch for
> The wiles of Snorri;
> Wary enough no one will be;
> Wise is Snorri.

The two Snorri's in the poem are, of course, on the discursive level, the same Snorri Godi mentioned twice. But it is interesting that the name is mentioned twice, for there are indeed two Snorri's involved here. At least one could test out this hypothesis. If the poem is read as an analogy with the thirteenth century, then the second Snorri must have something in common with his eleventh century counterpart. The two are different, yet by analogy also the same. History repeats itself; the actors in it, like the generations in the saga and the characters with their equivalent counterparts, could logically also appear again in new guises in the thirteenth century. We have seen that our author is as wily as Snorri Godi, that he, too, has employed two tricks to confound his audience: a camouflaged aesthetic design and a hidden analogy with his own times. The poem spoken by Thorgils' fetch says that the "fighters" (the word *fyrðar* is a poetic one for "men" or "warriors") will not be wary and wise enough to see through Snorri's tricks. These "fighters" include, of course, Thorgils, who does not see through the first "bragð" involving the word *samlendr* and who then falls prey to Snorri's second wile. But these warriors mentioned in the poem can be taken, as the second meaning of the word implies, as men in general, actually "the living ones" (see *Lexicon poeticum*), that is, the author's contemporaries. And interestingly, the general *engi* ("no one") fits in better with the meaning of the poem as interpreted on its second level (the application to the thirteenth century) than with the literal meaning for the eleventh-century context. So we see here again that the author does not expect any of his contemporaries to see through his wiles either.

What manner of man must this second Snorri of the thirteenth century have been? He must have been thoroughly acquainted with native traditions, the poetry and early writings, as his use of Eddic themes and mastery of rhetorical devices (one could almost say skaldic devices) would indicate. He must have had an extraordinary interest in aesthetics and a gifted sense for history, a person who could make history art, who could look at his own age and himself with some detachment, who observed the trend history was taking and recognized the ambition of the Norwegian kings in their subtle wooing of the favor of Icelanders, getting them to become *handgengnar* (the kings' retainers). He must have felt the breath of chivalry that had swept into the North with the new vogue in literature. This person, logically, could be none other than Snorri Sturluson, writer of the *Heimskringla* (or one should say compiler), author of the prose Edda (a treatise on rhetoric and skaldic poetry which uses illustrations from ancient mythology and the heroic age of the poetic Edda). This revelation came as a great surprise to me, for I had never entertained such a notion about the saga and was not at all preoccupied with pinpointing the man who wrote it. My acquaintance with Snorri Sturluson's works was also cursory. So on the basis of the internal evidence in *Laxdœla saga* alone, of its structure and method of composition, I was forced to the conclusion that the saga is a *roman à clef*, that the two poems about Snorri Godi's wiles should be read on two levels. They tell us what the nature of the saga is and who wrote it.

Rather than go back, armed with this hindsight, and sharpen any of the points in the analysis (the so-called "borrowings" from the *Heimskringla*, etc. discussed briefly under Written Sources, and the note about Leggbítr and Fótbítr would now be more readily clarified), I find it more interesting to leave the aesthetic interpretation as it stands so that the reader may see how the solution gradually emerged. But before we make absolute statements, let us test out the matter of time superimpositions a bit further.

If history represents repetitive examples, then it is from the heroic age of Eddic poetry, from the Age of the Commonwealth, and from the Sturlung Age that the author drew his examples. This we have also seen to be the case in the brief examination of the author's sources. In fact, the time before saga times and the time after saga times converge in the middle, supplying details for the central action, for the lives of the saga characters. The "before," the "now," and the "after," noted in the saga's structure, are again here represented. The two periods, the Heroic Age and the Sturlung Age, are compacted, as it were, in the eternal present of the saga's action. Remember, also, the genealogies go back to a time before the saga and forward to a time after the saga, contemporary time.

Consider first the Heroic Age. The saga characters have something in common with and akin to the legendary figures of the *Edda*. Some of their idealization comes from this perspective, as well as from the backward-looking view that saw the Commonwealth as ideal in contrast with the contemporary age. Gudrún, on the one hand, is like Brynhild in the *Edda*; Kjartan has something of a Sigurd in him, a matchless hero, and as such is somewhat stereotyped, beyond individualized description.[28] This quality we have already detected in him. He and his like counterpart, Bolli B., are idealized, therefore by modern standards somewhat hollow. Gudrún, however, attracted the author's fancy and is more fully drawn. She, on the other hand, has also something of the Eddic Gudrún, whereas Bolli Th. and Hrefna seem to take on the roles of Gunnar and Gudrún in the *Edda*. The saga Gudrún also has counterparts in the Sturlung Age, even if it is the like name that brought some associations to the author's mind.[29] He does not want to tell us again the story of Brynhild and Sigurd or of Yngvild and Thorvald (characters from the *Sturlu saga* from which he borrowed). The repetitiveness, the similarity, the typicalness of what he found in all the time periods fired his imagination. The characters and events are therefore presented scrambled and anachronously. This mixing and matching of characters is typical of the camouflages — his method in regard to the linguistic units is the key to his method in dealing with his sources. He does not intend one-to-one correspondences between his "borrowed" examples. They are amalgams and overlap, an aspect which the structural analysis also brought out.

A brief look at external sources can give us some of the specifics which point to the author and to his probable sources or stimuli for the events in the saga that derive from the Sturlung Age. The most logical place to look for events from Snorri Sturluson's life and times is the *Sturlunga saga*, in particular the *Sturlu saga* (with its immediate prehistory of Hvamm-Sturla's family) and the *Íslendinga saga*. Rolf Heller, in his "Laxdœla saga and Sturlunga saga," has gathered together some of the passages from the two works that look like literary borrowings.[30] It is not possible to evaluate each of his assumptions individually here. Some appear convincing; others are highly questionable; and many important examples are missing. Most intriguing is Heller's statement in regard to the *Íslendinga saga* which throws open the question with some puzzlement as to why the literary parallels with little or no exception involve members of the Sturlung family.[31] If the *Laxdœla* author is a Sturlung himself, it would be no wonder that interest in and knowledge of this family would have drawn him first to use material from the *Sturlu saga* for padding out his characters. The *Sturlu saga* is judged to have been composed in the first quarter of the thirteenth century by someone who stood very close to the events and the family of Hvamm-Sturla.[32]

The author of the *Íslendinga saga,* a Sturlung, Sturla Thórdarson (1214-1284), Snorri's nephew, son of his brother Thórd, would have known much at firsthand about the immediate members of his family. The introduction (Formáli) to the *Sturlunga saga,* written by the compiler of this compendium, but in all probability based on the foreword written by Sturla himself for his *Íslendinga saga,* confirms this. Most scholars are in agreement that Sturla wrote his saga late in life (1275-1284) and left it unfinished. The first part of the work represents the years 1200-1242 and deals mostly with the sons of Hvamm-Sturla as a continuation of the *Sturlu saga.* It is most striking that the phrases and events reminiscent of *Laxdœla* in this part are mostly somehow connected with Snorri and his brothers. If we assume that the *Laxdœla* author used the *Sturlu saga* as source, in which direction did the borrowings from the *Íslendinga saga* go?

The solution that the *Laxdœla* author did the borrowing might suggest itself here as the more natural, and is in fact the assumption made by Heller. Because he entertains the preconception that Sturla Thórdarson is the author of *Laxdœla,* he is forced to find plausible arguments for a rather late date for the saga, 1255 (or even later), and to assume that Sturla had notes for his *Íslendinga saga* that he could use before he started the writing of that saga as we have it.[33] But without going further into his arguments, let us look at a couple of the more striking parallels in the two sagas. The passage regarding the events leading up to Snorri Sturluson's death are so reminiscent of the situation leading up to Kjartan's slaying that the words fairly leap out of the page:

> Ok er Órækju kómu þessi orð, reið hann suðr í Saurbæ, ok riðu þeir Sturla báðir norðr til skips í Hrútafjörð ok ætluðu þaðan til móts við Kolbein.... Þá kómu þeim Órækju ok Sturlu orð sunnan frá Sauðafelli, at Snorri Sturluson var þar kominn ok vildi finna Órækju. Riðu þeir þá suðr þannig, ok var Snorri inn kátasti, ok töluðu þeir í litlustofu Snorri ok Órkækja ok Sturla, en Tumi skenkti þeim. Þar var bjórr heim kominn frá skipinu. Snorri sagði frá skiptum þeira sona Hallveigar. Hann hafði þar ok bréf, er Oddr Sveinbjarnarson hafði sent honum af Álftanesi. Var þar á stafkarlaletr, ok fengu þeir eigi lesit, en svá þótti þeim sem vörun nökkur myndi á vera. Snorri kveðst illa trúa Sunnlendingum, "en þó mun ek suðr fara fyrst ok skipa til búa minna," sagði hann, "ok fara þá vestr ok vera þá hríðum á Hólum, en stundum í Saurbæ." Margt var þar talat, ok riðu þeir allir samt inn í Hjarðarholt.[34]

(And when Óraekja heard this news, he rode south to Saurbae,

187

and he and Sturla both rode north to the ship at Hrútafjord and expected to meet Kolbein there.... Then word came from the south, from Saudafell, that Snorri Sturluson had come there and wanted to see Óraekja. So they rode south then, and Snorri was most gay. They talked together in a little room, Snorri, Óraekja, and Sturla, and Tumi served them with drink. Beer had been brought home from the ship. Snorri told about his dealings with the sons of Hallveig. He also had there a letter which had been sent him from Odd Sveinbjarnarson from Álftanes. There were runic letters on it, and they couldn't read it, but it seemed to them that some warnings were in it. Snorri said he did not trust the Sunnlendings [men from the Southern Quarter], — "but nonetheless I'll ride south first and take care of my homesteads," he said, "and then go west and stay a while at Hólar and a while at Saurbæ." A lot was talked about and they rode all together into Hjardarholt.)

The merry-making immediately reminds one of the situation at Hól before Kjartan's ride into Svínadal, as does the use of *inn kátasti* of several incidents in *Laxdœla* (when Kjartan goes to Laugar to Gudrún's and Bolli's party, for example). The circumstances are telling, both the phrase itself and the idea behind it — psychologically a dissimulation and cover-up for the worries that must have been Snorri's preoccupation, as the whole incident is meant to reveal — and rhetorically as a device which hints of its opposite: after gladness sorrow. The cryptic warnings, Án's dream at Hól and a letter written in runes which no one could read but which were interpreted in any case as a warning, carry the parallels further.[35] The two names Hólar and Saurbæ remind one of where Kjartan went before the ambush took place. The quote ascribed here to Snorri almost gives verbatim the answer Kjartan gave to Thórhalla Chatterbox before he set out (*Lxd.* xlvii, 147-148). Finally it is stated that all of them rode into Hjardarholt — a name immediately associated with Kjartan. Can this be coincidence?

But in regard to borrowings, the similarities between the account of the attack on the sons of Thorvald (March 7, 1232) and the raid on Helgi's hut in *Laxdœla* provide another clue. First it must be stated that Helgi Hardbeinsson is unknown from any historical sources or other sagas. We can safely say, on the basis of the aesthetic analysis, that this Helgi is a fiction created to complete the structure and continue the goadings and killings in triplicate. Again, at first impulse, one would be tempted to assume that the contemporary event was taken from the *Íslendinga saga* and incorporated into *Laxdœla*.[36] But eye-witness to the event was Sturla Sighvatsson (Sturla Thórdarson's cousin and Snorri's nephew), who led the attack. As is told in the *Íslendinga saga*, Hallbjörn Kalason went home to Reykjaholt (Snorri's estate) after the killings and told Snorri the news. Snorri thus could have knowledge of the event and about the participants without recourse to a written source. Sturla Thórdarson, too, probably had some firsthand information and recollection of the event (he would have been eighteen at the time). But curiously, in each of the accounts of this incident we find literary similarities: the *dagverðr* for epic delay (compare the band in the woods eating their meal before they attack Helgi's hut); the device of a bad omen to provide suspense before its fulfillment ("ok kvað Snorri [Þorvaldsson] margt hafa fyrir borit um nóttina" can be compared with Helgi's mention of his dream the night before he was attacked); the phrase *í þessi svipan*; the word *kurteis*.[37]

The *Íslendinga saga* relates that eight men were in the Thorvaldsson group; *Laxdœla* says there were ten in Thorgils' party. But two of these ten are otherwise unknown in saga literature.[38] The *Laxdœla* author needed the number ten for his analogous patterns. If we assume that the *Íslendinga saga* is more or less historical, then it is obvious that a literary work such as *Laxdœla* must be the inventor here. Typical of *Laxdœla* would be the fact that the roles of the attackers and the attacked are reversed. The thirteenth century is, after all, the reversed image of the eleventh. The descriptions of the men are not word for word in the two accounts. The clothes and weapons theme does not appear in Sturla's report. This is the preoccupation of the *Laxdœla* author. Reason for the gold and silver arm rings within this context has already been suggested and would seem hereby confirmed, namely that they serve a poetic function and not a realistic or historical one.[39] The distinctive characteristics in the *Laxdœla* passage point in the same direction — the content, stimulated by a contemporary event, the air of *kurteisi*, and the realistic descriptions derive from the thirteenth century.

The literary function of the elements that these two accounts have in common places the greater plausibility on the historical work's having imitated some of the good style and techniques of a literary work where they are routine than that the literary work borrowed sparsely scattered devices from the historical work. Let us assume then for the argument that Sturla Thórdarson perused *Laxdœla* when looking about for material for the years 1200-1242, for what is telling is that the incidents and phrases which seem to echo *Laxdœla* and which are convincing parallels practically cease after the year 1241, that is after Snorri's death. The much discussed incident at the farm Í Múli in 1244 where Ásbjörn Gudmundarson allegedly dried his sword on the clothing of the wife of the man he has slain (this account is not given in all MSS of the *Þórðar saga kakala* in *Sturlunga saga*) that reminds of the deed Helgi Hardbeinsson committed against Gudrún (lv, 168) could well be coincidental; but also if it is ultimately proven that Sturla knew and borrowed from *Laxdœla*, the similarity could be attributed to *Laxdœla*'s influence. A more definite dating of the sagas would be determinative here. The earliest date for *Laxdœla* is 1228, the death date of Thorvald Snorrason; the latest contemporary named in a genealogy, Ketil, abbot at Helgafell, is mentioned in the past tense; he died in 1220. Ordeals (*Lxd.*, xviii, 42-43) were banned by Cardinal Vilhjálmr who crowned King Hákon in Norway in 1247. Obviously such ordeals were still being performed in Iceland when the saga was written. The law might not have reached Iceland or been implemented until 1248. The oldest fragmentary manuscript of *Laxdœla*, D_2, has been dated ca. 1250. Thus the span for *Laxdœla* falls between 1228-1250. These are in the main the arguments that Sveinsson also advances. Heller's latest arguments for a much later date seem forced in order to lend greater plausibility to his favored candidate, Sturla. Can we venture a closer pinpointing of the saga's date on the basis of internal evidence? If the saga is a *roman à clef*, it may well not only reveal who the author is but also when it was written. The formal elements can again be of help here.

The preponderance of the number twelve, for which we found no explicit structural correspondence, but which was noted as a distinctive element in the saga, can be construed as a hidden reference to the thirteenth century. It must be reemphasized here that all the elements in the saga have internal function that is valid for the literary work as a closed unit, despite any function the words, terms, and expressions may have outside the saga. The saga, as an aesthetic whole, is an organic unit that is self-determinative. The number twelve, its meaning veiled by its use in situations that reflect the normal social and legal customs, represents the year 1200. The next number that comes to mind and which is important in the saga's structure is three: there are three main divisions, three main characters, three parties, three goadings, three killings, three drownings, three main sets of inimical brothers, etc. There are three layers of meaning in the saga and three time periods. The other number of striking importance in the structure is two, representing all the situations of balancing and pairs, correlatives, two choices, equalization and compensation. The number three, as in the triplets in the anlaysis, includes and contains the number two, so I believe that *Laxdœla* was written in 1232. Two of the last mentioned facts in the saga, to be sure without exact dates, are the fall of Saint Óláf (A.D. 1030) and the death of Snorri Godi (A.D. 1031). Since the element ten also plays a part in the saga and even the phrase "tíu eða tólf"[40] appears in one manuscript for a reading on the drowning of Thorkel Eyjólfsson, confirmation of the hypothesis that the saga intends a comparison between the eleventh and thirteenth centuries seems strengthened.

If we look again at the relationship between *Laxdœla* and the *Íslendinga saga* with this date in mind, then Sturla could not possibly be the author of the former. The similarities between the two texts must then be attributed to Sturla's having borrowed from *Laxdœla*. The caliber of *Laxdœla*'s prose in contrast to Sturla's, the difference in the stamp of language, the qualities that cannot be computerized such as structure and style speak against Sturla as author, despite all lexical-statistical counting. In view of the remarkable similarity between the events before Kjartan's death and those before Snorri's, there must be some connection more than literary between Snorri Sturluson and Kjartan. I believe that one would find upon closer inspection that Kjartan has something also from the other time periods embodied in him — something of the Eddic Sigurd, something from Saint Óláf. He is an amalgam of the pagan, Christian, and the contemporary eras. Snorri Godi and Snorri Sturluson also have more in common than just their names. The answer to the dilemma must hinge on the fact that Sturla knew of the author-relationship between *Laxdœla* and his uncle Snorri and that he also understood something of the method of composition. Sturla would then naturally have turned to *Laxdœla* to add color and style to the lives and times of the Sturlungs, since the saga had incorporated as camouflage some of the events and persons from Snorri's own life and times. The attack on Helgi Hardbeinsson takes place in the last part of the saga and must be one of the last events from the contemporary scene that went into the work; that was March 7, 1232. And soon thereafter the saga must have been finished, for its remarkable uniformity and consistency in carrying out the formal design would also suggest that it was written within a short period of time. Might we venture the guess between Yule 1231 and Easter 1232, the two most frequently mentioned times of year in the saga and pivotal points for much of the action?

But what has Sturla done then when it comes to the passage on the events leading up to Snorri's death? He has, it would seem, mixed fact and fiction, allowing himself the superb poetic license of ascribing to Snorri Kjartan's words about his plans and whereabouts. If Snorri actually did go to Hólar and Saurbæ, the similarities in the names Hól and Hólar and the identity of the place Saurbæ must have attracted Sturla to the *Laxdœla* passage. Kjartan's and Snorri's locale of operation coincided. What would be more ironic than Sturla's finding in that work of artistic irony by his uncle

191

Snorri exemplification of Snorri's life. For Snorri's life must have seemed in many ways ironic, as things turned out for him, falling prey as he did to the very type of subterfuges he had been party to and later warned against.

As for the account of the Thorvaldsson attack, Sturla did again what he had done on Snorri's death: he combined what he knew with what he found in *Laxdœla*. As we have shown, Snorri needed no written source for his knowledge of the event and of the men. On the basis of internal evidence and on grounds of the brief examination of external evidence, the argument seems weighted toward Snorri Sturluson as author of *Laxdœla*. If this indeed proves to be the case after further investigation into the sources, then a new look must be taken at this man Snorri, at his *Heimskringla*, and at the reliablity of the *Íslendinga saga*. This investigation I have begun in the article dedicated to Professor Hollander in his forthcoming Festschrift. The conclusions there are the same, based entirely on external rather than internal evidence. I, like Gudrún, stumbled upon a stone; it broke apart and its pieces fell automatically into place in the puzzle. The riddle of one saga seemed solved.

The *Laxdœla* author, dare we now say Snorri Sturluson, was interested in using examples for his saga that were plausible, yet somehow typical. Is it any wonder that the typical and stereotyped can seem so real and natural, so individualized in the saga? The heroic age, the past idealized, met the individual present and combined with it. This characterizes the method of camouflage in general. The Eddic poetry in which Snorri was steeped gave him a sense for the heroic ideals; he must also have been well acquainted with the technique of patterns and archetypes. His keen observation of life, his understanding of the human psyche, his knowledge of history (comprising a view of history representative of the Middle Ages which thought in terms of analogies) enabled him to see the past through the eyes of the present, i.e. anachronously and as a series of repetitive examples. His sharp awareness of the events that were drawing his nation into the clutches of a foreign power lent to the past an air of prophecy — all of these made up the genius of the man.

One might at first be tempted to think that Snorri might have written the saga between 1239 and his death, the work being a kind of culmination of his life and thought and philosophy of history and time bringing the development toward disaster in the political sphere into clearer focus. But would Snorri have had the lightness of touch, the playfulness, the wonderful detachment, the ability to depict the precarious balance which characterizes *Laxdœla* (and the balance is still there) if it had been written during the turbulence and embroilments of the later years?

Snorri had an extraordinary sensitivity to the spirit of the times. His saga shows the preparation, pointing out the perils of a social and ethical system that threatened to engulf his nation like a fateful destiny. Iceland stood at the crossroads — before two choices. The natural and accepted practice of the Icelanders to become *handgengnar* to the Norwegian king could at any moment turn into the unexpected and the disastrous, the negative reversal. The warning is already enunciated in Snorri's *Óláfs saga helga*: "En í þessu vináttumarki, er konungr gerði til Íslands, bjuggu enn fleiri hlutir, þeir er síðan urðu berir" (*Hkr*. II, 214: "But in this sign of friendship which the king showed toward Iceland there dwelt many aspects which became clear later"). Is it any wonder that so much attention is drawn in the saga to relationships between Norway and Iceland, to the voyages back and forth, one a mirror of the other, to the comparison through repeated phrases of the Christianization of Norway and that of Iceland? The Trondheimers, it is said, at first resisted conversion: "En hinir menn váru þó miklu fleiri, er í móti váru" (xl, 118); in Iceland it was the same: "En þó váru þeir miklu fleiri, er í móti mæltu" (xli, 125). But the analogy goes much deeper. When the king asks Kjartan to go out to Iceland and convert his countrymen "annathvárt með styrk eða ráðum" (xli, 124) and it so takes place "bæði með blíðum orðum ok hǫrðum refsingum" (lxi, 125), one cannot help but think of the situation in Snorri's day.

Snorri Sturluson was lawspeaker in Iceland from 1215 to 1218. He then had the opportunity to go abroad and was received at the court of King Hákon IV and by his regent, Earl Skúli. During his stay abroad, an event took place in Bergen in the year 1220 which was determinative for his whole life. The events leading up to this climax are briefly as follows: An argument had taken place in Iceland several years before (1216) at Eyrar between some Icelanders and Norwegian merchants over the circumstance of the death of Pál Sæmundarson in Norway. Pál's father, Sæmund Jónsson (of the Oddaverjar) demanded of the Bergen merchants recompense for his son, and it ended by his taking by force great sums from them. During the next years the dealings between these countrymen worsened to the point where Orm (Sæmund's brother) was killed.[41] Snorri learned of the killing after having arrived in Norway, the year 1218. By 1220 hostilities between the Norwegians and Icelanders had reached a high pitch. Ships and men stood ready to harry Iceland the summer of 1220 when Snorri, on the point of departure for home, used his influence and diplomacy to dissuade the undertaking. He said it was wiser to make friends of the best men in Iceland and so win them

193

over and that by his persuasion the Icelanders would come round to paying homage to Norway's king:

> Hann sagði ok svá, at þá váru aðrir eigi meiri menn á Íslandi en bræðr hans, er Sæmund leið, en kallaði þá mundi mjök eftir sínum orðum víkja, þá er hann kæmi til (He said also that there were no men in Iceland more influential than his brothers, with the exception of Sæmund, and that they would comply with his wishes as soon as he got home).[42]

It was then decided by the king not to send a military expedition to Iceland. While at the court Snorri had been honored with the lesser title of *skutilsveinn* (chamberlain), and now at parting received as reward for his action a ship and fifteen gifts and was given the title of *lendr maðr* (baron).[43] This aroused the suspicion of his countrymen, as they thought he might have been put up by the Norwegians to opposing the prosecution for the slaying of Orm.

Now it had been the custom of Icelanders to keep the connection with the mother country ever since the days of Settlement. They found it an honor to come into the king's service, as *lendr maðr* or *handgenginn* to the king. They, in any case, had always been proud of their noble ancestry, tracing their forefathers back to the chieftains of Norway, so they naturally would feel that they were somehow coming to their own rightful heritage. This practice began, however, to take on sinister and disastrous aspects in the thirteenth century.[44]

Snorri did not keep his promise to the king, which could be construed as betrayal of his duty to his king as a *lendr maðr*. His inaction and the fact that he made no attempt to bring Iceland into the king's power might look from the outside like duplicity or indecisiveness on his part. But something more is involved here, something which perhaps will put his character in better light. We have already seen a parallel to this situation in Kjartan's unwillingness to convert his countrymen to Christianity. In fact, Kjartan's words to King Óláf Tryggvason practically give in substance Snorri's argument to King Hákon:

> Kjartan kaus heldr at vera með konungi en fara til Íslands ok boða þeim trúna, kvazk eigi deila vilja ofrkappi við frændr sína; — "er þat ok líkara um fǫður minn ok aðra hǫfðingja, þá sem frændr mínir eru nánir, at þeir sé eigi at strangari í at gera þinn vilja, at ek sjá í yðru valdi í góðum kostum" (xli, 124: Kjartan chose rather to stay with the king than to go out to Iceland and present the new faith, saying he had no desire to use force against his kinsmen — "and as for my father and other chieftains closely

related to me, it is more likely that they will not be any the more opposed to conforming to your will if I am in your power in honorable service.").

The king's comment to this was that Kjartan had closen wisely and honorably. Both Kjartan and Snorri avoid the use of force against their countrymen. Both argue for the effectiveness of persuasion as the alternative. But in the kings' persuasion, in the promises of friendship, in all the kind words, in the bestowing of titles there were ulterior motives. Just as in the eleventh century the king's promises of friendship in return for payment of church taxes and weregild involved a more tangible hold on Iceland — as it turned out the king requested Grímsey as token of "good faith" — so, too, in the thirteenth the praise and honor bestowed on Icelanders at the court, the gradual wooing of the chieftains into the king's service masked the crown's intentions of territorial annexation. The speech of Einar Thveræing (Eyjólfsson) against forfeiting any piece of land to the king of Norway were to become household words in Iceland (*Hkr.* II, 216). Snorri saw through the subterfuge "then" as "now." And his saga in a way is an exoneration of his own duplicity. He acted under expediency and honorably to save his country from warfare and violence. His promise to the king was never meant to be kept. The second "subjugation" of Iceland by Norway also, nominally at least, had a religious aspect as pretext to political domination. Thus Snorri could well draw the analogy between the Christianization and the machinations of his own century as heading in the same direction. And part of himself he put into Kjartan.

Snorri's nephew Sturla Sighvatsson played for real stakes, making a deal with the king that he would deliver Iceland into his hands on the stipulation that he, Sturla, be made chieftain over the whole of Iceland. But these Sturlungs, father and son (Sighvat and Sturla) were cut down by the intrigues of Gizur Thorvaldsson in the year 1238 at the battle of Ørlygsstadir (*Íslendinga saga*, Chap. 138). Snorri's complicity and duplicity had incurred the displeasure of the king. Because of a falling out with his brother Sighvat and the enemies he had at home, Snorri fled to Norway in the year 1237, where he stayed until news of his brother's killing made it safe for him to return to Iceland in 1239. The king, however, had put an embargo on his leaving. Soon after his return he made fresh enemies by his refusal to pay out an inheritance claim to the sons of Hallveig. The king took advantage of the situation and enlisted Snorri's enemies in his own interest. To one of them, the powerful chieftain Gizur Thorvaldsson, he wrote a letter stating that he was to bring Snorri back to Norway or slay him. Snorri was not given the choice and was slain by Gizur and his men at Reykjaholt, Sept. 23, 1241. The king confiscated all of Snorri's property and wealth and so got a foothold in Iceland. From then on the die was cast. Snorri's own involvements brought about what he had tried to prevent and what he had foreseen and warned against most eloquently in the parable of his saga.

Why did Snorri select the Laxdalers and their farmsteads in the Breidafjord Dales as medium and setting for his camouflage? Snorri was born at Hvamm 1178 or 1179; he was related to Snorri Godi both on his father's and his mother's side, all members of the Laxdœla clan. The Dales were his ancestral home. The actors had changed, but the types of events, the types of people that made up the drama of his own age — members of his own family in part — were moving on the same stage set. The scene remained constant; the pattern remained constant; only new content need be substituted into the old forms. Even the personal names repeated themselves through the generations — all of which suited Snorri's line of thought admirably. The natural mores, the law of the land played hand in hand with the creative process. He even saw in himself the counterpart to his namesake Snorri Godi, famous for diplomacy and shrewdness.

No matter from what angle the problem has been tackled, the evidence accumulates with the same result: Snorri Sturluson. And *Laxdœla* is a key to the man and his works. It was the Sturlung family that gave its name to that turbulent and violent age; it was the Sturlung family that gave Iceland her greatest cultural heritage during the darkest hours. The writing of the major sagas and histories seems to have been very much a family affair — and a family secret. This would explain a lot of things — the anonymity, the sudden flowering, the rapid decline after them. Snorri Sturluson stands like a giant above them all.

> Vögum vér og vögum vér
> með vora byrði þunga.
> Upp er komið sem áðr var
> í öld Sturlunga,
> í öld Sturlunga.[45]

NOTES

INTRODUCTION

[1] The following afford a review of saga scholarship: Otto Springer, *Die nordische Renaissance in Skandinavien* ("Tübinger germanistische Arbeiten," XXII [Sonderreihe 3; Stuttgart-Berlin, 1936]), a good introduction to the trends and influences of the early period; Halldór Hermannsson, *Icelandic Manuscripts* and *Old Icelandic Literature: A Bibliographical Essay* ("Islandica," XIX, 1929; and XXII, 1933), two studies which review, respectively, the history of the Old Icelandic manuscripts from their production to their acquisition by Denmark and other countries, and the history of their editing and publication; Rudolf von Raumer, *Geschichte der germanischen Philologie* (München, 1870), an excellent summary replete with names, dates, and significant quotations on trends and theories in scholarship from the sixteenth century through the height of Romanticism in the nineteenth; Marco Scovazzi, *La Saga di Hrafnkell e il problema delle saghe islandesi* (Arona, 1960), which, beginning with a review of the problems posed by *Hrafnkels saga*, revives the theory that the sagas are based on historical-cultural facts, surveys research on saga literature (especially the controversy between the Free- and Book-prosaists), and, although finding the whole argument rather pointless since the sagas are the collective creation of a nation, expounds again the extreme Free-prose view that *Hrafnkels saga* preserves facts of the Germanic pagan past untainted by Christianity or by the thirteenth century and that the process of transcription did not affect the original oral saga; Theodore Andersson, *The Problems of Icelandic Saga Origins: A Historical Survey* (New Haven and London, 1964), a helpful, middle-of-the-road survey of the controversy surrounding the origins of the Sagas of Icelanders.

[2] Important representative titles include: Rudolf Keyser's *Nordmændenes videnskabelighed og literatur i middelalderen*, Vol. I of his *Efterladte skrifter* (Christiania, 1866), which proposes a Norwegian origin for Icelandic literature; Konrad von Maurer's "Über die norwegische Auffassung der nordischen Literaturgeschichte," *Zeitschrift für deutsche Philologie*, I (1869), 25-88, a rebuttal; Alexander Bugge's "Den islandske sagas oprindelse og troværdighed," *Nordisk tidskrift för vetenskap, konst och industri* (1909), 407-419, which proposes Irish origin and influence; Andreas Heusler's *Die Anfänge der isländischen Saga* ("Abhandlungen der königlich preussischen Akademie der Wissenschaften" [Phil.-hist. Classe, Nr. 9; Berlin, 1914]), which stresses oral origin, historical intent, and artistic excellence and assumes a gradual decline from best to worst in a chronology of saga development; and his *Altgermanische Dichtung* ("Handbuch der Literaturwissenschaft" [2d ed.; Potsdam, 1941]), which presents a slightly less extreme view, emphasizing "das Gradmäßige"; Knut Liestøl's *The Origin of the Icelandic Family Sagas*, trans. A. G. Jayne (Oslo, 1930), which attempts to assess the historic content of the sagas and stresses oral traditions as sources, but which vitiates the folkloristic method by making exceptions for Iceland; Gabriel Turville-Petre's *Origins of Icelandic Literature* (Oxford,

1953), which throws light on literary activity in Iceland before the writing of the thirteenth century; Sigurður Nordal's "Sagalitteraturen," *Litteraturhistorie: Norge og Island* ("Nordisk kultur," VIII: B [København, 1953]), pp. 180-273, which uses aesthetic criteria for establishing a relative chronology and postulates a development from worst to best; and his *Hrafnkatla* ("Studia Islandica: Íslenzk fræði," VII [Reykjavík, 1940]), which points out historical inaccuracies in *Hrafnkels saga* and the artistic powers of a written literature; Einar Ólafur Sveinsson's *Dating the Icelandic Sagas* ("Viking Society for Northern Research: Text Series," III [London, 1958]), a basic essay in methodology; and Walter Baetke's *Über die Entstehung der Isländersagas* ("Berichte über die Verhandlungen der sächsischen Akademie der Wissenschaften zu Leipzig" [Philol.-hist. Klasse, CII: 5; Berlin, 1956]), which comprises the best statement on aesthetic intent of the sagas, demands a literary-aesthetic approach, and discusses *Geistesgeschichte* in relation to the Icelandic literary genre.

[3] Such Romantic postulates as the following found their way, implicitly or explicitly, into saga research: (1) the superiority of primitive poetry over sophisticated poetry; (2) the progressive development from naive "Naturpoesie" to a pretentious "Kunstpoesie," including the related axiom of a declining gradient in the transition from an oral to a written tradition; (3) the presupposition of an oral substratum in smaller units such as songs or tales which were subsequently put together to form larger works; Lachmann's "Liedertheorie" had its counterpart in the *þættir* theory of the origin and composition of the Sagas of Icelanders. Two other issues also played a part: (1) anonymity vs. the gifted redactor or author; (2) the relationship of history to poetry, legend, or *Sage*; i. e., fact vs. fiction. In the nineteenth century, research on the *Nibelungenlied*, the *Poema del Cid*, and the Homeric epics followed these premises with striking consistency. In connection with the Icelandic sagas, the Romantic position has prevailed longer and been more tenaciously asserted.

[4] T. Andersson, *op. cit.*, p. 50.

[5] See above, n. 2.

[6] As early as 1904 with "Landnáma og Egils saga" in *Aarbøger for nordisk oldkyndghed og historie*, pp. 167-247, Ólsen had begun a series of articles correlating the sagas and *Landnámabók*. In his *Om Gunnlaugs saga ormstungu: En kritisk undersøgelse* ("Det kgl. danske videnskabsselskabs skrifter" [7. række, Historisk og filosofisk afd., II: 1; København, 1911]), Ólsen places the saga late in a relative chronology because of its unified composition. Finnur Jónsson, in *Den oldnorske og oldislandske litteraturs historie* (1st ed., København, 1894-1902) II, 422-425, considered the saga to be early for precisely the same reasons. A debate between the two scholars is found in *Skírnir*, LXXXIX (1915), 383-388; XC (1916), 83-84. For Nordal's introduction to *Egils saga*, see "Íslenzk fornrit", II (Reykjavík, 1933), pp. V-CV. For his *Hrafnkatla*, see above, n. 2; an English translation is available: *Hrafnkels Saga Freysgoða: A Study*, trans. R. George Thomas (Cardiff, 1958).

[7] See Nordal, "Sagalitteraturen," pp. 235-239.

[8] T. Andersson, *op. cit.*, pp. 50 and 119, n. 63, seems to feel that the divorce is complete; one need only mention Scovazzi, however, to realize that the more radical views are not completely dead.

[9] See Nordal, "Sagalitteraturen," p. 235; and E. Ó. Sveinsson, *The Age of the Sturlungs* ("Islandica," XXXVI, 1953), pp. 1-7, 117, 152-153.

[10] "Ämnet är i flertalet af dem [sagorna] så väl ordnadt och genomtänkt, att man med rätta kan tala om deras författare" (Bååth, *op. cit.*, p. iii).

[11] *Ibid.*, pp. 57-58: "Den [Kap. 25] börjar liksom de tre närmast föregående afdelningarne *med en upprepning och utfyllning af något förut framdraget*" (emphasis

added). Bååth, close to being on the right track, sees the whole method of the saga author illustrated in a scribal error: "Genom uttrycket: *sem fyrr var ritat*, tjänar dock detta misstag till att än ytterligare belysa författarens hela metod att medels upprepning markera en afdelnings början" (*ibid.*, p. 55; emphasis added). In regard to the author's "mistakes" that illuminate his method, see below, Chap. I, n. 18, Chap. IV, n. 29; Literary Perspectives, n. 24.

12 Johannes van Ham, *Beschouwingen over de literaire Betekenis der Laxdœla Saga* (Amsterdam, 1932).

13 van Ham, *op. cit.*, pp. 11, 17, and 34.

14 *Ibid.*, pp. 97-98, and p. 95 for discussion following the quote.

15 Margrit Schildknecht-Burri, *Die altertümlichen und jüngern Merkmale der Laxdœla Saga* (Luzern, 1945). Heusler's categories are: "(1) Verwirrung der Stammbäume und der Örtlichkeiten; (2) Hinweggleiten über die scharfen Tatsachen des Rechtshandels; (3) Übertreibungen in Waffentaten, leiblichen Vorgängen; das Gedunsene, Barocke, Ruhmredige; (4) Schwarz-Weiß-Zeichnung der Menschen. Wunschbilder an Stelle 'gemischter' Köpfe; (5) Seelische Hochspannung im Sinne des *drengskapr*, der edeln Großmut; anderseits Zunahme schalkhafter Spottlaune; (6) Neigung zu Fabelei, zu Märchenartigem, zu Zauberspuk (wobei zu sondern ist, zwischen ernsthaftem Volksaberglauben und wurzelloser Einbildung); (7) Ausmalung von Abenteurern in der Fremde; (8) Ritterlicher Aufputz, Wappenwesen, Hofzeremoniell; (9) Christliche Züge, die für die Saga-periode einen Zeitverstoß bedeuten; (10) Anteil am Geschlechtlichen, Anflug südlicher Erotik; (11) Neuartiges in der Formgebung; (a) Ausgeglichene Breite, keine jähen Sprünge, (b) Das meiste der Saga gehört zur Sache, (c) Man erzählt Dinge, die keine Zeugen hatten, (d) Vorliebe für Wechselreden; Gesprächigkeit, (e) Glatte Flüssigkeit des Satzbaus; 'ausgeschriebene Feder,' (f) Zunahme der Lehnwörter, besonders der ritterlichen und deutschen" (Heusler, *Die Altgermanische Dichtung*, pp. 217-218). From these characteristics, a negative example of what a saga should be, one can deduce the presuppositions for what Heusler called the "pure saga." The position of the Free-prosaists concerning the standard for the ideal saga, the original oral saga, ranges from the prerogative of simplicity and unity, as with Jónsson, to an appreciation of the disjointed and primitive, as with the "jähe Sprünge" of Heusler, for whom too polished a style and unified composition marked a decline. For Bååth, too, amalgamated wholes indicated later reworkings.

16 Schildknecht-Burri, *op. cit.*, p. 100.

17 *Ibid.*, p. 121. Heusler called it "die buntscheckigste der Sagen," *Die altgermanische Dichtung*, p. 218.

18 Schildknecht-Burri, *op. cit.*, p. 109.

19 *Ibid.*, p. 122; emphasis added.

20 In "Saga: Untersuchungen zur nordischen Literatur- und Sprachgeschichte," Heft 3 (Halle a. S., 1960).

21 *Ibid.*, p. 11.

22 Cf. Heller, "Laxdœla saga und Sturlunga saga," *Arkiv för nordisk filologi*, LXXVI (1961), 112-133.

23 *Laxdœla saga und Königssagas* ("Saga," Heft 5, 1961).

24 *Ibid.*, pp. 8 and 59.

25 "Laxdœla saga und Bischofssagas," *Arkiv*, LXXVII (1962), 90-95; "Laxdœla saga und Knytlinga saga," *Arkiv*, LXXX (1965), 95-122.

26 Peter Hallberg, *Snorri Sturluson och Egils saga Skallagrímssonar; ett försök till språklig författarbestämning* ("Studia Islandica: Íslenzk fræði," XX [Reykjavík, 1962]); *Óláfr Þórðarson hvítaskáld, Knýtlinga saga och Laxdœla saga* ("Studia

islandica," XXII [Reykjavík, 1963]); "Íslendinga saga och Egla, Laxdæla, Eyrbyggja, Njála, Grettla," *Maal og Minne* (1965), pp. 91 ff.

[27] Marina Mundt, *Sturla Þórðarson und die Laxdæla saga* ("Skrifter fra instituttene for nordisk språk og litteratur ved universitetene i Bergen, Oslo, og Trondheim," Nr. 4, 1969).

[28] *Ibid.*, pp. 93-94.

[29] In *Arkiv*, LXXV (1960), 113-167.

[30] *The Laxdœla Saga* (Seattle: University of Washington Press, 1964), pp. xxxix-xlii.

[31] Heller, "Studien zu Aufbau," p. 165.

[32] *Ibid.*, pp. 114 and 130.

[33] The same can be said of the analysis by A. C. Bouman in *Patterns in Old English and Old Icelandic Literature* (Leiden, 1962). Not only does his concept of patterns — in this instance some Eddic borrowings as models — go outside the saga, but so also does his misplaced criticism of the saga as a modern psychological novel — an indication not of the saga author's inability but of Bouman's to understand the saga on its own terms. See my review in *Modern Philology*, LXII (1964-65), 155-158.

[34] Bolton, "The Heart of *Hrafnkatla*," *Scandinavian Studies*, XLIII (1971), p. 51.

CHAPTER I

1 See Genealogical Table I.

2 The *ǫndvegi* was the seat of honor in the family dwelling. Its posts were ornamented with figureheads, usually of Thor, and with carvings and were regarded with religious reverence. "Many of the settlers of Iceland are said to have taken the high-seat posts with them, and when near Iceland to have thrown them overboard to drift ashore, and where they found them, there they took up their abode" (Richard Cleasby, Gudbrand Vigfússon, aud William A. Craigie, *An Icelandic-English Dictionary* [2nd ed.; Oxford, 1957], p. 765). Cf. also Nils Lid, "Gudar og gudedyrking," *Religionshistorie* ("Nordisk kultur," XXVI [1943]), pp. 80-82; also Dag Strömbäck, "Att helga land," *Festskrift tillägnad Axel Hägerström* (Uppsala, 1928), pp. 198 ff.

3 In one instance in the saga fate appears to take its unalterable course without the concomitant predisposition of the characters' motives. Gudrún has heard Helgi's prophecy that the son in her womb will become avenger for his father Bolli. This son, Bolli Bollason, is thus premarked by fate for the deed of vengeance. Yet there is no plan or eagerness on the part of Gudrún or Bolli that he play this role. Following the slaying of Bolli Thorleiksson, Snorri suggests to Gudrún both the object of her revenge, Helgi Hardbeinsson, and the one to lead the raid, Thorgils Holluson. That Snorri, instead of Gudrún, should name Helgi seems an awkward oversight, especially since she carefully noted the participants in the raid and witnessed Helgi's wiping his bloody sword on her scarf while making his prophecy. Yet the saga characters often make statements that have not been transmitted directly from character to character (Gudrún to Snorri in his case), and they also typically ignore prophecy. The reader, however, is always knowledgeable and the author omniscient, an aspect of the saga which we shall have further occasion to discuss. That Gudrún is not thinking of Bolli as avenger of his father is evidenced by the following statements. In Snorri's efforts for conciliation Gudrún shows little interest: "En Guðrúnu var lítit um þat, at játa því *fyrir hǫnd Þorleiks*, at taka fé fyrir víg Bolla" (lvi, 169: "But Gudrún was little minded to agree to accepting payment for Bolli's slaying for Thorleik's sake"). Later when she prevails upon Thorgils to become leader in a raid against Helgi, she remarks: " 'Svá þykki mér, sem *Þorleiki* virðisk engi jafnvel til fallinn at vera fyrirmaðr, ef þat skal nǫkkut vinna, er til harðræða sé' " (lx, 180: " 'I imagine Thorleik will think no one equally well suited to be leader as you, especially if the task requires some courage' "). Just before the band attacks Helgi's hut, some women disguised as men ride off. Thorgils leaves to Thorleik the decision whether to ride after them: "Þorgils kvað *Þorleik* ráða skyldu, því at hann vissi, at *Þorleikr* var manna skyggnastr" (lxiv, 191: "Thorgils said Thorleik should decide, for he knew that Thorleik was the most sharp-

201

sighted of men"). After the successful venture, Thorgils recites this poem which contradicts the idea that he was leader:

Sóttum heim at Helga;	To Helgi's home a raid we led;
hrafn létum ná svelga;	With the corpse the ravens fed:
ruðum fagrrǫðuls eiki,	Stained we all red oaken shield,
þás fylgðum Þorleiki. etc.	Following Thorleik's tracks afield. etc.
(lxv, 194)	

Sveinsson is of the opinion that the verse is neither old nor from *Þorgils saga Hǫllusonar*, see "Íslenzk fornrit," V, Formáli, p. LV. This leaves the possibility that the author created it for the story. By making it *seem* as though Thorleik were taking the lead as elder son to avenge his father, the author was following normal social custom. Did he thereby wish to disguise the machinations of fate and not quite succeed? Previews of the result are present throughout the preparation for the deed. At a previous meeting with Snorri (lix, 176) Gudrún appeared with Bolli Bollason who was then twelve years old and carrying Footbiter. The reader, aware of the prophecy and the fateful role of this sword in the saga, immediately jumps to the right conclusion. The disturbing element in the whole episode is not so much the condensing of time to make Bolli twelve years old — a much discussed "defect" in the saga — but the failure of the author to amalgamate prophecy with the characters' will as with social convention. The working out of what was fated is here mechanical in comparison to the other examples in the saga. As for the other question, a literary work need not adhere to real time, and besides the number of years which passed between Bolli Bollason's birth and the meeting with Snorri is left vague (cf. lvii, 171: where it is stated that Thorleik stayed a long time [*lǫngum*] at Tunga and studied law).

4 The author oftentimes suggests both a natural and a supernatural cause for a happening: cf., for example, where Ásgaut and Thórólf are said to succeed in their undertaking for two reasons: "Ok með því at menn váru hraustir, ok þeim varð lengra lífs auðit, þá komask þeir yfir ána" (xv, 34: "And since they were hardy men and since fate had destined them to live longer, they got across the river"). Also xvii, 40-41, where Thorstein Surt's voyage is described as being made difficult by the weather and current, and the presence of the uncanny seal indicates that another force is also at work against him. Even when in the final fight with Bolli Kjartan throws down his weapons, although fate had ordained the outcome, the author makes it more plausible by giving a natural reason: "Síðan kastaði Kjartan vápnum ok vildi þá eigi verja sik, en þó var hann lítt sárr, en ákafliga vígmóðr" (xlix, 154: "Then Kjartan threw down his weapons and had no will to defend himself, little wounded though he was; but he was, after all, very battle-weary"). The implicit psychological reason is, of course, that he does not want to fight against Bolli; the other reason, Fate. Heller, *Laxdœla Saga und Königssagas*, p. 16, compares this passage with one in *Óláfs saga helga* (Chap. 228) in *Heimskringla* and one in *Knýtlinga saga*, Chap. 58.

5 For triplets of the type: *er mestr er skaði at / at þér er ófalastr / um Kajrtan mun þykkja mest vert*, see below, Chap. IV.

6 For the parallels in means and motives of these two divorces, see below, pp. 68-69.

7 See above, n. 3.

8 See below, p. 27.

9 Many other examples of similar use of premonitions and of their fulfillment might be noted. Although not of central importance, they nonetheless illustrate the author's consistent practice of providing previews through insinuations and hunches and of cuing the reader by means of conventionalized phrases. A few instances are as

follows: King Hákon's prophecy of its being the last time Hoskuld will depart from Norway during his overlordship (xiii, 25: *nær er þat minni ætlan*) turns out to be true; Óláf Tryggvason's prediction of Kjartan's acceptance of Christianity (xl, 120-121: *er þat ok nær mínu hugboði*) is fulfilled when on Kjartan's sailing for home, the king admonishes him to keep his new faith well (xliii, 132) and when at home in Iceland Kjartan fasts and keeps the Holy Days "such as no man had ever done before him" (xlv, 138); after Kjartan's death, Óláf invites the kinsmen from Vídidal to come and foresees that they will be eager for revenge, (l, 157: *nær er þat minni ætlan*) and such proves to be the case, for when the Vídidalers arrive they want to seek vengeance immediately (*ibid.*); after Helgi Hardbeinsson has heard the descriptions of the raiders outside his hut, he makes the obvious guess that they are his enemies (lxiii, 189: *nær er þat minni ætlan*); and Eid's misgivings when Thorkel Eyjólfsson pursues the outlaw Grím (lvii, 172: *ekki kemr mér þat á óvart*) are shown to be justified when Thorkel rues his actions and makes amends to Grím (lviii, 175).

10 For examples of the expression *upp kveðit / niðr koma*, cf. xxii, 62; xxiii, 64; xliii, 128; liv, 163. See below, pp. 126-127.

11 See Genealogical Table II.

12 In ancient Scandinavia a person was thought to have a spiritual double that accompanied him throughout life. This *fylgja* (fetch) sometimes became visible. Thorgils' fetch appears as an unusually large woman. The fact that she departs forebodes death.

13 In preparation, Thorgils' blue cloak has already been mentioned twice; cf. lii, 185 and lxiii, 187.

14 *Þurr* literally means "dry"; the cloak is obviously not "dry" if it is wet. But this nonsense riddle contains in itself a double intention. *Þurr* is used of those fasting without butter and meat products. Thus they are eating "dry" and are empty, not filled and, by transference, "not filled with knowledge." See Johann Fritzner, *Ordbog over det gamle norske sprog* (Kristiania, 1886), III, sv. 1054. Mention of this meaning is also found in Gösta Franzén's "Hangir hattkilan vọt á vegg," *Arv*, XVIII-XIX (1962-1963), 153-158.

15 The reader should compare the two idioms used in connection with Thorkel's drowning: *at drepa skeggi* and *at spenna um þọngulshọfuð*.

16 Compare the statement that Vigdís had been married more for the sake of Thórd's money than for his support (xi, 21: "Vigdís var meir gefin *til fjár* en brautargengis") which prepares for the relatives' attempt to get half of Thord's money in the divorce settlement (xvi, 37: "Þeir Hvammverjar létu fara orð um, at þeir ætluðu sér helming *fjár* þess, er Þórðr goddi hafði at varðveita"); or the fact that Hoskuld did not go to see King Hákon — the opposite of what is generally expected when an Icelander lands in Norway — (xi, 22: "Họskuldr *fór ekki á fund* Hákonar konungs") and the king's later chiding comment with a suggestion of displeasure that Hoskuld could have greeted him earlier (xii, 25: "'Tekit mundu vér hafa kveðju þinni, Họskuldr, þóttú hefðir nọkkuru fyrr oss fagnat, ok svá skal enn vera'"); or Hrapp's insisting on being buried standing beneath his doorsill so that he can keep an eye on his property (xvii, 39: "'ok skal mik niðr setja standanda þar í durunum; má ek þá enn vendiligar sjá yfir hýbýli mín'") and Thorstein Surt's observance of a seal with human eyes keeping a watch out as he attempts to go to Hrapp's farm (xviii, 41: "svá sýndisk þeim ọllum, sem mannsaugu væri í honum"); or Melkorka's foresight in teaching Óláf Irish and her hint that it will not matter where Óláf lands in Ireland (xx, 51: "'Heiman hefi ek þik búit, svá sem ek kann bezt, ok kennt þér írsku at mæla, svá at þik mun þat eigi skipta, hvar þik berr at

Írlandi' ") and how her remark is proven right when Óláf lands in a hostile region and his knowledge of Irish stands him in good stead (xxi, 57: "'Auðsætt er þat á Óláfi þessum,... at hann mælir allra manna bezt írsku' "); or Óláf's statement that it mattered a great deal that his ship's crew appear more like warriors than traders (xxi, 52: "ok kvazk þó þykkja miklu skipta, at þat lið væri líkara *hermǫnnum* en kaupmǫnnum") and the result of this when the Irish see his ship and think it a man-of-war (xxi, 55: "ok þykkir þeim nú auðvitat, at þetta var *herskip*").

17 For occurrences of *kyrrt* and *kyrrt at kalla*, cf. xi, 22; xvi, 37, 38; xxi, 51; xxiii, 65; xxv, 71 (ok var þó samt); xxx, 83; xxxiii, 92; xxxiv, 93; xxxv, 96; xxxvii, 108; xl, 118; xlv, 135; xlvi, 142, 143, 144; xlvii, 147 (2); lii, 161; liii, 162; lvi, 170.

18 Compare the weight given to the word *átti* (Hrút owned half) and how the contrast between *allt* (all) and *hálft* (half) prepares for the quarrel between Hoskuld and Hrút over their maternal inheritance (viii, 16); note the hints given of the bondwoman Melkorka's royal rank: she costs three marks of silver, or three times the price of an ordinary bondwoman (xii, 23: "'því at þetta er þriggja verð'"); fine clothes suit her very well (xii, 24-25: "var þat allra manna mál, at henni semði góð klæði"); people can see that she is high-bred and no simpleton, even though she does not talk (xiii, 27: "Ǫllum mǫnnum var auðsætt stórmennsku-mót á henni ok svá þat, at hon var engi afglapi"); note Kjartan's statement that it is better for Hrefna to *own* the headdress than to display it, with the emphasis on the *eigi* (xlvi, 140: "'því at meira þykki mér skipta, at Hrefna *eigi* ina mestu gersemi, heldr en boðsmenn hafi nú augnagaman af at sinni'") and with the implication that she will no longer own it once she shows it, which is indeed what happens at Laugar; and also how the statement that Thorkel Eyjólfsson *always* stayed with his kinsman Thorstein Kuggason whenever he was in Iceland (lvii, 171: "Hann var ok *jafnan* með Þorsteini Kuggasyni, frænda sínum, þá er hann var út hér") prepares for his next visit when he leaves his timber with Thorstein (lxxv, 218). *Jafnan* frequently receives extra weight in the saga for the purpose of foreshadowing and lending inner necessity to the subsequent action. Other conspicuous, but by no means exhaustive examples include: the reference to Jórunn"s proud-mindedness (ix, 18: "ok *heldr* skapstór *jafnan*"), which with both *heldr* and *jafnan* prepares for her haughty reaction to the bondwoman Hoskuld brings home (xiii, 26, 28); the mention that Thórólf Rednose's kinsmen always go to him for help (xi, 21: "frændr hans gengu þangat *jafnan til trausts*"), which makes Vigdís' elective of sending Hall's slayer to him binding rather than arbitrary (xv, 35: "hafði þenna mann sent honum *til* halds og [sic] *trausts*"), where the repetition also connects the two statements (see below, Chap. II); the statement that Gest made a habit of staying overnight at Hól on his way to the Thing (xxxiii, 87: "ok hafði *jafnan* gistingarstað á Hóli"), which anticipates his next visit there (xxxv, 95: "Þetta sumar fór Gestr til þings ok fór á skipi til Saurbœjar, *sem hann var vanr*. Hann gisti á Hóli í Saurbœ. Þeir mágar léðu honum hesta, *sem fyrr var vant*"). The references to its being "his wont" (*sem hann var vanr*) and to the lending of horses to him as being "the usual custom" (*sem fyrr var vant*) — although this aspect was not mentioned before, so that the *sem fyrr* is somewhat out of place here — relate the episode to the earlier statement. Note the fact that Bolli always goes to Laugar with Kjartan (xxxix, 112: "fór Bolli *jafnan* með honum"), which subtly reveals his own interest in Gudrún and anticipates his visit to Laugar after his return from Norway (xlii, 127; see above); the statement that the partying between Óláf's and Ósvíf's farms was habitual (xxxix, 112: "ok *jafnan* heimboð"), which prepares for the subsequent parties back and forth even after friction develops (xlii, 134 and xlvi,

139); the reference to Bolli's habit of being silent and not answering when Kjartan was criticized (xlvii, 148: "Bolli lét sem hann heyrði eigi, sem *jafnan*, er Kjartani var hallmælt"), which prepares for this repeated motif and renders his actions predictable (see below, Chap. II); and Thorgils' summing up of his relationship with Snorri as being cool (lxiv, 195: "hafa mér þaðan *jafnan* kǫld ráð komit") which exhibits the reversed function, for here *jafnan* is confirmative rather than preparatory.

19 Kristian Kålund prefers to assume that the passage is a face value statement and is forced into hypotheses that contradict the text (Kålund, ed., *Laxdœla Saga* ["Altnordische Sagabibliothek," IV; Halle a. S., 1896], p. 43, n. 12). Hjalmar Alving in his translation (*Laxdalingarnas saga* ["Isländska sagor," I; Stockholm, 1935], p. 205, n. 1) finds all three sentences so "dunkla och störande för sammanhanget" that he leaves them out of the body of the translation and puts them in a footnote.

20 Examples would be Unn the Deep-minded, Óláf Peacock, Thorhalla Chatterbox, Thorbjorn Skrjúp, and Víga-Hrapp and his namesake. For a discussion of the latter two, see below, respectively, pp. 43 and 73.

21 The words *ok væn* have been added in MS M (Möðruvallabók), although Sveinsson does not select this reading for his text. Since this reading would confirm the *kvenna vænst* idea, it would seem to belong to the original text. The alliteration would speak for it, but then the *bæði* would fit only the alliterative pair, which, however, is also stylistically possible within the saga, e. g. xxxvi, 101: *bæði mikill ok vænn ok reyndr at vígi*, where three elements also appear. The only other place where Gudrún's beauty is referred to is when Hrefna insinuates that Gudrún had shown herself in the headdress (xlvii, 145) but the word *væn* is not used there.

22 Although traditionally genealogies have constituted the strongest argument for the chronicle nature of the sagas, critics have repeatedly pointed out discrepancies and errors between the saga account and the authority of the *Landnámabók* or of other sources for early Icelandic family history. It might be well at this point to reemphasize that historical material may always be used freely and even transformed for aesthetic purposes. To the modern reader long genealogies in the narrative may seem tedious and intrusive and the need for untangling family relationships in addition to the complication of events, burdensome. Familiarity with the saga world, however, makes these genealogies more palatable, for the sagas are often complementary; and characters who play major roles in one saga may appear as background or peripheral figures in others.

23 See Genealogical Table II. A separate study of the genealogies in the Sagas of Icelanders with special attention paid to the preannouncement of characters, the forward or backward movement of the various listings, and the purposefulness of their selectiveness for any individual saga would make a fine contribution to saga studies.

24 The author's practice of introducing a character who is to appear later offers the strongest argument in favor of accepting the Y MSS reading for the passage on the theft of Kjartan's sword (xlvi, 140-141). In the Z MSS Beinir the Strong plays the role of scout instead of Án the White, a reading which would leave Án the White functionless in the saga.

25 For instances of *ván* (*vænna*), cf. xiii, 26; xiv, 30 (2), 31; xv, 34; xvi, 38; xviii, 43; xix, 47, 48; xxi, 52, 56; xxii, 62; xxvi, 73; xxx, 82; xxxvii, 105; xlviii, 150; liv, 163; lv, 167 (not in all MSS); lvi, 169; lix, 177, 178; lx, 179; lxiii, 190; lxx, 206. For the frequence of *kunnigt*, cf. ii, 4 (2), 5; vi, 10; xxi, 56, 59; xxii, 61; xxvi, 71; xxvii, 75; xliii, 128; xlix, 152; lviii, 175; lxi, 181; lxviii, 200; lxxi, 209 (3).

26 For instances of the phrases *sem* [*ok*] *fyrr, sem áðr, sem fyrr var ritat* [*sagt*],

cf. iii, 5; x, 19 (2); xvii, 39; xx, 49; xxi, 56; xxiv, 66; xxv, 71; xxxi, 83; xxxiv, 94; xxxv, 95; xlvi, 143; lii, 160; lx, 180; lxxiii, 213; and lxxviii, 228 (sem nú var frá sagt um hríð).

27 Some of the most striking examples of expressions with *minna á, íhuga, ekki ór hug liða, ekki ór minni liðit* include: xlix, 154; liii, 162; lxi, 176-177; lx, 179; lxi, 182; lxv, 195.

28 See below, Chap. V, pp. 125-28.

29 See below, Chap. II, p. 52.

30 Cf. also lix, 176: "Þorleikr var þá *ýmisst* í Þykkvaskógi... stundum var hann í Tungu með Þorgísli"; lxviii, 201: "er hann [Þorkell] *ýmisst* um sumarit í Tungu eða við skip". In another instance ix, 16: "[Hǫskuldr] var jafnan sina vetr *hvárt* með Hákoni konungi *eða* at búi sínu," the same idea is expressed but with *hvárt... eða* instead of *ýmisst*. For *hvárt.. eða* as a formal element, see below, Chap. III, p. 94.

31 The conventional nature of such phrases does not concern us here. Whether it is ultimately derived from oral technique or represents a commonplace of written style does not matter; it plays effectively into the hands of the *Laxdæla* author.

CHAPTER II

[1] See above, Chap. I, especially such examples as: *vér frændr berim eigi gæfu til um vár skipti / vér frændr bærim eigi giptu til samþykkis; ef hann næði ráðahag við mik / ef ek nái ráðahag við þik; mat Kjartan umfram alla menn / metinn þar umfram hvern mann; fyrir engan mun þik lausan láta / láta hann lausan, er því væri at skipta.*

[2] Translators have consistently misinterpreted the second statement because they have not related it to the first and have read the *þeim* and the *við þá menn* as referring to the same persons, whereas the *þeim* is a possessive dative with *ór minni* and pertains to Gudrún and her sons, not to the men who took part in the raid.

[3] Compare also the descriptions of Snorri's kindness and endeavor to do well by Bolli Bollason: first, when he and Thordís Snorradóttir are living at Tunga: *"Snorri lagði ok mikla stund á at veita Bolla vel"* (lxx, 20: "Snorri went to great pains to do well by Bolli"); and then on Bolli's return from abroad: *"Snorri lagði eigi minni stund nú á at veita Bolla með allri blíðu en fyrr,* er hann var með honum" lxxvii, 225: "Snorri went to no less pains now to treat Bolli with the same kindness as before when he was living with him"). The reference is made explicit not only by the repeating of the idiom but also by the addition of *nú* and the comparative *eigi minni en fyrr.* For *sem fyrr* expressions and the like, see above, Chap. I, n. 26.

[4] Cf. also the following occurrences of repetition: the episode where Ingjald demands his money back, asserting that Thórd has acted *ódrengiliga* (xv, 35: dishonorably) and Vigdís picks up the same word in her charge against Thórd (xv, 36); the statement that Gudrún and her family rely on Snorri: *"Áttu þau Guðrún þar mikit traust"* (xxxvi, 100: "Gudrún and her kinsmen had much support from Snorri") and her turning to Snorri for support after Bolli's death: *"því at þar þóttusk þau Ósvífr eiga allt traust"* (lvi, 169); the statement that Halldór Óláfsson is foremost of his brothers: "Hann var *mjǫk fyrir þeim brœðrum*" (lii, 160) and Thorgerd's substantiation of it: "'þú þykkisk *mest fyrir yðr brœðrum*'" (liii, 162).

[5] To make discrepancies and obscurities in a literary work more plausible, critics often seek refuge in real situations outside the work of art. For instance, to explain away the element of omniscience in *Lxd.* through recourse to "neighborhood gossip," a mode of transmission to be read in between the lines, destroys the closed unity of the saga.

[6] Cf. also the following instances of confirmation by omniscience: Óláf's reaction when he learns of Kjartan's decision to go abroad: "þá þótti honum *Kjartan þessu hafa skjótt ráðit*" (xl, 114: "It seemed to him that Kjartan had decided this hastily") and Gudrún's identical comment: "'*Skjótt hefir þú þetta ráðit, Kjartan*'" (xl, 115); and Snorri's mention of what one of the advantages of Gudrún's match with Thorkel would be: "'*skortir hann ok eigi fé*'" (lxviii, 200: "'He doesn't lack for money either'") and Thorkel's own boast to the same effect: "'*mik skortir eigi fǫng*'"

207

(lxviii, 201). No statement is left dangling; nothing is left to chance. As a result the narrative is tightened, the casual made necessary.

7 Here again, consideration of the structure of the saga and the author's working method might well help clarify a textual incongruity between the various MSS readings. Although a younger hand in MS M attributes the *fastliga horfa* to Hoskuld, the Z MSS recast the sentence and attribute it to Egil. So M: "Egill lét lítt yfir, segir allt, hversu farit hafði. Hǫskuldr kvað *fastliga horfa*, — 'en þó þykki mér þér vel fara.' Ekki var Óláfr við tal þeira. Eptir þat gengr Egill á brott. Frétti Óláfr nú, hvat líði bónorðsmálum; Hǫskuldr kvað *seinliga horfa* af hennar hendi" (xxiii, 64: "Egil did not have much good to say of it and told how the whole thing had fared. Hoskuld said the suit looked difficult — 'but anyhow I think you did the best you could.' Óláfr was not present during their talk. After that Egil left and Óláf came and asked how the marriage suit was faring. Hoskuld said the suit was slowed down on Thorgerd's account"). Z MSS read: "Egill lét lítt yfir, segir allt, hversu farit hafði ok *pótti fastliga horfa*. Hǫskuldr sannr þat, en kvað..." ("Íslenzk fornrit," V, 64, n. 1). Since in similar situations characters usually pick up another's words, it would seem more in keeping with the author's style to select the reading of the Z MSS, instead of having Hoskuld repeat his own words.

CHAPTER III

[1] Heller, *Laxdœla Saga und Königssagas*, pp. 54-55, traces this expression to *Þiðranda þáttr ok Þórhalls*.
[2] Other instances of similarities in connection with supernatural happenings might be cited: in the reburying of Hrapp in an effort to end his hauntings and in the reburying of the bones of a witch found under the floor of a church, both are said to have been carried "far away to a place where (livestock or) people were least likely to cross" (xvii, 40: "*fœra hann í brott, þar er sízt væri* fjárgangr í nánd eða *mannaferðir*," and lxxvi, 224: "*fœrð langt í brott, sem sízt var manna vegr*," respectively); or the case of Stígandi and his parents who are "stoned to death and and buried under a heap of stones" (xxxviii, 109: "Síðan *berja* þeir Stíganda *grjóti í hel*, ok þar var hann *dysjaðr*"; xxxvii, 106-107: "Váru þau þar *barið grjóti í hel*, ok var þat gǫr at þeim *dys ór grjóti*," respectively); or the fact that the brothers Hallbjorn Sleekstone-Eye and Stígandi both had skin bags drawn over their heads but nonetheless were able to do a last bit of evil before their deaths (xxxvii, 107 and xxxviii, 109, respectively).
[3] Although the phrase *skaltu nú vita* seems to indicate some forgetfulness on the part of the author, since Vigdís has already indicated to Ásgaut what the reward would be, it is typical of the saga to bring up and then fulfill a statement. Note, however, the *skjótliga*, which perhaps indicates awareness by the author of his previously made statement.
[4] If one compares these two episodes where *frelsi* is first promised, then given, it is likely the reading of the text should follow zpap. MSS, which I have quoted here. Sveinsson's edition has kept the *Möðruvallabók* reading: "Óláfr bauð *at kaupa at henni*, ef hon kœmi Stíganda í fœri við þá." See "Íslenzk fornrit," V, 109 and n. 1.
[5] A certain group of repetitions points to the conscious or unconscious tendency on the part of the author to use similar patterns under similar conditions. No specific comparison (parallel or contrast) would seem intended. Except for the verbal echoes, which carry associations from one section of the saga to the next, always holding the audience within a limited linguistic sphere of "knowns," the instances are not causally connected. Bjorn, for example, wastes no time in expressing his opinion about fleeing Norway: "*'Skjótt mun ek birta minn vilja'*" (ii, 4: "'I'll let my will be quickly known'"), and Ósvíf tells Gudrún in no uncertain (and in the same) terms how he feels about her marrying Bolli: (xliii, 129: "*'Mun ek hér um skjótt birta minn vilja'*"). Hoskuld's regret at his mother's departure: "kvazk þat *mikit þykkja, er þeir skulu skilja*" (vii, 14: "said it was too bad if they had to part") is reechoed in Thorleik's expression of disappointment that Bolli wanted to travel on alone: (lxxiii, 213: "Þorleiki *þótti mikit, ef þeir skulu skilja*"). Hall, before he is felled, "suspects no danger to himself" (xiv, 30: "*uggir ekki at sér*"); and Helgi Hardbeinsson before the raid on his hut likewise feels safe and sound (lx, 180: "*uggir ekki at sér*"). Ósvíf gives his sons permission to cause "whatever

209

harm you see fit to Kotkel and his family" (xxxvi, 102: "'slíkt mein þeim Kotkatli, sem yðr líkar'"), and Óláf similarly approves of whatever punishment his sons would mete out to the sons of Thórhalla (xlix, 156: "'þótt þér skapið þeim slíkt víti, sem yðr líkar'"). Twice in the saga characters are described as shedding tears. A verbal echo points up the fact that in each case the weeping is occasioned by the knowledge that a prophecy will inevitably be fulfilled. Gest divines that Bolli will be Kjartan's slayer: "En nǫkkuru síðar ríðr Þórðr inn lági, sonr hans, hjá honum ok mælti: 'Hvat berr nú þess við, faðir minn, er þér hrynja tár?'" (xxxiii, 92: "A little later his son Thórd the Short rode up alongside and said: 'What causes you to shed tears, father?'"). Thorstein with foreknowledge of his kinsman's impending death lies down to wait, and "the housemaid saw that tears tolled from his eyes down onto the pillow" (lxxvi, 222: "Griðkonan sá, at tárin runnu ofan á hœgendit ór augum honum").

6 A *brautgangs hǫfuðsmátt* is literally "a divorce neck opening." Nowhere in the Icelandic laws is it stated that the wearing of clothing improper to a man or woman is grounds for divorce. In the *Grágás*, where family rights from olden times have undergone influence from the Catholic Church, such habits of dress warranted lesser outlawry and court summons, cf. *Grágás: Islændernes lovbog i fristatens tid*, ed. and trans. Vilhjálmur Finsen (Kaupmannahöfn, 1852-1870, Ib, 203-204. It may well be that the sagas have preserved traces of the older customs, cf. Claudius Freiherr von Schwerin, "Die Ehescheidung im älteren isländischen Recht," *Deutsche Islandsforschung* (Breslau, 1930), I, 283-299.

7 See above, pp. 15, 19.

8 See above, pp. 21-22.

9 The description of the band outside Helgi's hut has occasioned much discussion. Schildknecht-Burri, *op. cit.*, p. 83, finds in it evidence of influence from Southern Romances. Sveinsson, "Íslenzk fornrit," V, Formáli, pp. XXXI-XXXII, weighs the possibility that the passage may have been cut on the pattern of some foreign model, but the only one that comes to mind is the translation of the *Piðreks saga* which contains a description of tents and shields which the author himself identifies, but nonetheless a man is sent out to reconnoitre who the men are that have arrived. The technique of identifying opponents in battle by their trappings and appearance goes all the way back to Homer. The author of *Lxd.* could have arrived at such a universal device independently, but it seems likely that it was transmitted to him via the new courtly literature. And one should not be led astray by the fact that the content is different, being related to an event in Iceland that took place in 1232 and described in the *Íslendinga saga*. See below, Chap. V, p. 143 and Literary Perspectives, pp. 188-89.

10 See below, p. 74.

11 For the main divisions of the saga, see Chap. I, pp. 16-17.

12 The author's practice of substituting antonyms in the verbal pattern in order to establish contrasting or parallel pairs has already been noted. *Lítilmenni / stórmenni* (and their variables *lítilmannligr, stórmannligr, stórmennska*, etc.) is an example of such a pair that runs through the saga, see below, Chap. V, n. 56.

13 A child that is most loved is also a recurrent motif. See below, Chap. V, p. 125.

14 A similar problem involving inheritance rights has already been described in the saga, as preparation, in the episode concerning Hrút Herjólfsson's claiming his share of the maternal inheritance from his half brother Hoskuld (xix, 47). At that time Jórunn tells Hoskuld that Hrút is justified in not wanting to be treated

like a *hornungr* (literally, "one pushed into a corner, but probably to be interpreted as "bastard"), for legally Hrút has birthright to the inheritance. It should be noted also that both quarrels over inheritance take place between half brothers and involve a question of legitimacy.

[15] In addition to Hrút and Hoskuld and Bárd and Thorleik, Ingjald and Hall represent a pair of "inimical brothers": "[Ingjaldr] var auðigr maðr ok mikill fyrir sér. Hallr hét bróðir hans; hann var mikill maðr ok efniligr. Hann var félítill maðr; engi var hann nytjungr kallaðr af flestum mǫnnum. Ekki váru þeir brœðr samþykkir optast; þótti Ingjaldi Hallr lítt vilja sik semja í sið dugandi manna, en Halli þótti Ingjaldr lítt vilja sitt ráð hefja til þroska" (xiv, 28-29: "Ingjald was a wealthy man, prominent and able. His brother's name was Hall. He was a big man and showed promise, but had little means and was considered rather useless by most people. These two brothers were almost always in disagreement. Ingjald thought Hall showed little willingness to conform to the ways of accountable men, and Hall thought Ingjald showed little willingness to help him improve his lot"). The contrasts in *auðigr* and *félítill*, in *mikill fyrir sér* and *engi nytjungr* are obvious, but the parallel syntax in the last sentence even more strikingly emphasizes their parallelism and contrast.

[16] For a discussion of Kjartan's and Bolli's likenesses and differences, see above, pp. 34-35, 36. They are not only *mjǫk jafngamlir* (nearly the same age); each is also *mikill maðr ok sterkr* (although the break in the expression when applied to Bolli — var mikill maðr... sterkr var hann — seems to suggest a distinction); both are conscious of fine dress: Bolli Thorleiksson was *kurteisligr* and *mikill skartsmaðr* (xxviii, 77), and Kjartan dressed in his finery *bjó sik við skart* (xliv, 134) and showed his *kurteisi* (xlv, 136).

[17] See above, Chap. I, pp. 34-38.

[18] Both Bolli's are characterized as *skartsmaðr* and *kurteisligr* [*kurteisi*] (xxviii, 77, and lxxvii, 224-225, respectively). They both carry Footbiter, a natural transference from father to son (xxx, 83 and lix, 176, respectively).

[19] See above, Chap. I, p. 18.

[20] See above, Chap. I, p. 36.

[21] For reference to Bolli Bollason's *kurteisi*, cf. lxvii, 224-225.

[22] It is possible that both *munir* and *vilja* are to be understood with each of the dependent infinitives *kvángask* and *geta*. If this is so, the irony of the situation is sharpened: Kjartan will not want to marry soon, but this time will want to get the woman he asks.

[23] Cf. Schildknecht-Burri, *op. cit.*, p. 25.

[24] The chronological sequence within the saga has been much discussed, and particularly the apparent discrepancy in Bolli Bollason's age between the time of his father's death and the revenge taken for it when he is twelve. At the end of Chap. lvi, it is stated that Thorleik Bollason was four years old when his father Bolli was killed; Bolli Bollason was born the next winter. Chap. lvii relates of Thorgils Holluson, and it is said that Thorleik stayed *a long time* at Tunga and learned law from Thorgils. So it may be assumed that Thorleik was no longer a four-year old. During this period Thorleik Eyjólfsson was on trading voyages. One time, *eitt sinn*, when he was home, Eid's son Ási had been killed. In the spring following, Thorkel has his encounter with the outlaw Grím; thereafter, in summer, he goes abroad to spend the winter. In that same summer Gudrún meets with Snorri to discuss revenge for Bolli. Bolli Bollason is along and is twelve years old. Again, when the events of Chap. lxx take up, time has passed: Bolli is sixteen and Thorleik

twenty. No reader who is "in the story," participating in the illusion, would demand a year by year account.

[25] See above, p. 71.

[26] See above, p. 27.

[27] Parallels between Melkorka and Vigdís can also be discerned, since both are described as giving an opponent a bloody nose (xiii, 28; xv, 36, respectively). Thurid and Aud each get even with their former husbands (xxx, 81 and xxxx, 98, respectively) and carry out their vengeful acts at night toward *sólarupprás* (sunrise). The marked similarities between Gudrún and Thorgerd will be discussed in the next chapter.

[28] See above, Chap. I, pp. 28, 30.

[29] Hoskuld and Óláf exhibit similarity in their reaction to the requests of Thorgerd Thorsteinsdóttir (Hoskuld's mother) and of Thorgerd Egilsdóttir (Óláf's wife), respectively: When Thorgerd Th. expresses her desire to go to Norway, Hoskuld regrets her decision: "kvazk *eigi mundu þetta gera at móti henni heldr en annat*" (vii, 14: "said he would no more oppose her in this than in anything else"); and Óláf respects his wife Thorgerd's wishes regarding their daughter's marriage to Geirmund, even though he finds it unwise (xxix, 80: " '*Eigi skal þetta gera í móti þér, heldr en annat*' ").

[30] These significant passages will be considered more fully in the discussion of recurrent motifs. See below, Chap. V, pp. 138-42.

[31] Cf. xlv, 136 and xxxii, 86, respectively; see also below, p. 143.

[32] For examples of impasses, cf. also xxi, 52; xxiii, 64; xl, 115; xliii, 128.

[33] For the occurrence of the *jafn*-words, cf. iv, 7; ix, 18; xi, 21; xiii, 26; xiv, 30, 31; xv, 34; xvi, 38; xviii, 43; xix, 44 (4), 45, 46; xx, 50; xxi, 51, 55; xxiii, 63; xxiv, 67, 68; xxvi, 72; xxviii, 75; xxix, 78; xxxiv, 93 (2); xxxvii, 103, 104; xxxix, 112; xl, 116, 117 (2), 121; xli, 125; xliv, 134; xlv, 137; xlvii, 148; xlix, 153, 154; lvii, 170; lviii, 175; lix, 176; lix, 177 (2); lx, 180; lxiii, 187; lxxi, 208, 209, 211; lxxvi, 221, 223; lxxviii, 228.

[34] See below, pp. 179-80.

[35] For examples of *munr* and its various compounds, cf. x, 19; xix, 46 (2); xxi, 56; xxxvii, 103; xlviii, 151; xlix, 152.

[36] Concerning half-interest in a ship etc., cf. vii, 14; xl, 114; lxx, 207; lxxii, 211.

[37] Cf. also Thórólf's telling Ásgaut the two choices they have: " 'Vit munim eiga *tvá kosti fyrir hǫndum. Sá er kostr annarr*, at bíða þeira hér við ána ok verjask ... *sá er annarr kostr*, at ráða til árinnar' " (xv, 34: " 'Two choices stand before us. One is to wait for them here at the river and defend ourselves ... the other is to try for the river' "); or Gest's giving Hallstein Godi two alternatives as an ultimatum, discussed elsewhere in another regard: "ok gerði honum *tvá kosti*, at hann skyldi reka í brott þessa fjǫlkunnigu menn, ella kvazk hann mundu drepa þá" (xxxvi, 101); or Thorgils' pointing out of alternatives to Thorstein: " 'Þú munt eiga *tvá kosti fyrir hǫndum*, at ráðask til ferðar eða sæta afarkostum, þegar er þeir megu við komask' " (lxi, 182: " 'You have two choices before you: either you decide to go along or take the consequences as soon as they [Bolli's sons] get the chance' "); or Thorstein's forcing a hard choice upon Halldór in the bargaining for the Hjardarholt lands: " 'at þér eru *tveir kostir* hugðir ... *er sá kostr annarr*, at þú ger þetta mál með vild ... en *sá er annarr*, ... at þú rétt nauðigr fram hǫndina' " (lxxv, 220).

[38] See above, pp. 27, 30.

[39] For *bæði* phrases cf. vii, 13, 14; ix, 16, 18; xiii, 26; xiv, 29, 31; xvii, 40; xxi, 57, 58 (2), 59; xxii, 60; xxxii, 86; xxxiii, 88; xxxvi, 101; xxxvii, 105; xxxix, 112; xl,

118, 118-119 (where curiously the *bæði* is missing), 122; xli, 124; xlii, 127; xlvii, 146; lxx, 206; lxxiv, 216 (2), 216-217.

[40] For *hvárki...né* and the like cf. vii, 11; x, 20; xiii, 27; xix, 44; xxii, 60; xxiii, 63; xxxii, 87; xxxvi, 102; xxxvii, 105; xlv, 136; xlvi, 140; xlviii, 150; lx, 179, 180; lxvi, 197; lxviii, 201; lxxi, 208 (2); lxxii, 211 (2).

CHAPTER IV

1 Other examples with *kátr* are illuminating: When Hall comes rowing to shore with a good catch of fish, he and his men are *kátir*. The term, like a veiled hint, heralds disaster, for Thórólf is standing at the pier with his halberd and strikes Hall his death blow (xiv, 30). When Kjartan returns from the north engaged to Hrefna, he is "*miklu kátari en áðr*" (xlv, 138: "much gayer than before"), and at his wedding feast he was "*svá kátr... at hann skemmti þar hverjum manni í tali sínu*" (*ibid*.: "so gay that he entertained everyone with his talk"). In both instances Kjartan's external gaiety rings false and covers up his inner feelings.

2 See below, pp. 135, 144.

3 See above, pp. 59-60.

4 When Gudrún is first introduced (xxx, 86), mention is made of her great fondness for finery. In the marriage agreement with Thorvald, this stipulation is made: "Hann skyldi ok kaupa gripi til handa henni, *svá at engi jafnfjáð kona ætti betri gripi*" (xxxiv, 93). See above, Chap. II, pp. 41-42.

5 Another example where merrymaking forebodes its opposite follows at Hól before Kjartan's fateful ride into Svínadal: "Var þar *in mesta skemmtan ok gleði*" (xlviii, 149).

6 The elements *hvat heitir bœr sjá* and *hverr býr hér* appear again, like an echo of the earlier theme, in the recapitulation when Thorgils, feigning ignorance and innocence, stops at Helgi's farm to find out if he is at home: "'Þér mun ek þykkja ófróðliga spyrja, félagi, hvar em ek kominn í sveit, eða *hvat heitir bœr sjá*, eða *hverr býr hér?*'" (lxii, 185: "'You will think I am asking a foolish question, my friend, but where have I come to in the district, and what farm is this, and who lives here?'").

7 The passage quoted is taken from Gudbrand Vigfusson and F. York Powell, *An Icelandic Prose Reader* (Oxford, 1879), p. 32, ll. 15-20. The version printed in this Reader is from manuscript C, cf. *Laxdœla saga*, ed. Kristian Kålund (København, 1889-1891), p. 313. The version in MS M, used by Sveinsson in his edition, reads as follows: "Í þessi ferð váru þeir Ólafssynir fjórir, inn fimmti var Barði, — þessir váru Ólafssynir: Halldórr ok Steinþórr, Helgi ok Hǫskuldr, en Barði var sonr Guðmundar, — sétti Lambi, sjaundi Þorsteinn, átti Helgi, mágr hans, níundi Án hrísmagi. Þorgerðr rézk ok til ferðar með þeim" (liv, 164: "On this raid were the four sons of Óláf, the fifth was Bardi, — these were the sons of Óláf: Halldór and Steinthór, Helgi and Hoskuld, and Bardi was the son of Gudmund, — the sixth Lambi, the seventh Thorstein, the eighth Helgi, his brother-in-law, the ninth Án Brushwood Belly. Thorgerd was set on going along with them"). The awkward backtracking in MS M points more to scribal forgetfulness than to structural intent, and so it seems logical to give preference to the C reading which follows the general pattern of the other two lists. See Sveinsson, "Íslenzk fornrit," V, Formáli, p. XXI.

8 The "useless warning" motif is common in folktales. *Laxdœla saga* contains many folklore motifs, evidence of the author's ability to assimilate material from native traditions.

9 Keen-sightedness is also a common motif found elsewhere in heroic literature: for example, Sigurd in the Eddic Fáfnismál (v. 5, l. 4) is described as "hinn fráneygi sveinn" (a sharp-eyed boy); Velleius Paterculus, the long-time comrade in battle of Arminius, describes the latter as "keen-sighted" (cf. Otto Höfler, *Siegfried, Arminius und die Symbolik* [Heidelberg, 1961], pp. 114-115, n. 303). Compare Gering-Sijmon"s *Kommentar zu den Liedern der Edda*, II (Halle a. S., 1931), 187.

10 See "Íslenzk fornrit," V, 152, n. 1: the *hann* should be taken in the accusative.

11 For the phrase *í þessi svipan*: xlix, 153; lv, 167; lxiv, 192. The phrase seems to originate from *Óláfs saga Tryggvasonar* by the monk Odd (MS AM 310). It is also found in the *Heimskringla*. Whatever its provenance, the *Lxd.* author has put it to work in accordance with his own design.

12 For motif *a* (arm / hand), see xlix, 154; lv, 167 (the raids against Kjartan and Bolli, respectively). The motif of the unhealed arm / hand is also found in the episode where Aud wounds Thórd on the breast nipples and hand: "en sú hǫndin varð honum hvergi betr til taks en áðr" (xxxv, 98: "And this hand was never as good in grasping as before") and might be considered as preparation for the motif in the battle scenes.

13 For motif *b* (leg), see xlix, 153; lxiv, 193 (the raids against Kjartan and Helgi, respectively); for motif *c* (viscera), see xlix, 153; lv, 168 (the raids against Kjartan and Bolli, respectively). Án's two dreams about his viscera which parallel one another but show opposite actions and effects are good examples of prophecy-fulfillment as well as parallel with reversal. In the first dream a woman has come to him and removed his entrails and replaced them with brushwood (xlviii, 149). This dream foretells the circumstance that later takes place in the fight. In the second dream the same woman comes to him and removes the brushwood and replaces his bowels, and with this Án gets well (xlix, 155).

14 In the saga there are three swords described as having supernatural powers; in addition to Footbiter and Konungsnaut, which make up an opposing pair, there is Skofnung — another example of a theme being picked up like an echo in the third part of the saga or, stated otherwise, of the two-part structure of balance being accommodated to the tripartite form of the saga. For references to Skofnung, cf. lvii, 172; lviii, 173; lxxvi, 222; lxxviii, 229.

15 For the *harmdauði* expression, cf. lii, 160; lvi, 169. Heller, *Laxdœla saga und Königssagas*, pp. 11-12, attributes Kjartan's "casting away of the weapon" to a borrowing from *Óláfs saga helga* (Chap. 228) in the *Heimskringla*.

16 See above, pp. 76, 77.

17 The version of the text quoted is from manuscript 226 (V). MS M reads: "Mikil verða hermðarverk, ek hefi spunnit tólf álna garn, en þú hefir vegit Kjartan" (*Laxdœla saga*, ed. Kålund, p. 192). Sveinsson has selected the zpap 226 version: "Misjǫfn verða morginverkin..." The word *hermðarverk* is a *hapax legomenon*, interpreted by J. Fritzner (*Ordbog over det gamle norske sprog* [Kristiania, 1886], I, *sv.*, 801) as "an activity which is the fruit of dissatisfaction or embitterment"). The two MSS elucidate one another and help in interpretation of the passage. On the one hand, the morning's tasks are unequal (*misjǫfn*): spinning yarn and killing a man are not comparable. On the other hand, both actions, having grown out of "dissatisfaction and embitterment" (*hermðarverk*), have produced great and grave (*mikil*) results. Gudrún, nurturing her discontent at losing Kjartan for a husband, has goaded Bolli into killing him. Bolli, for his part, also undertook the deed

out of nagging embitterment against Kjartan. Out of her dissatisfaction and the strain of waiting for the outcome, Gudrún turns to activity — a frantic spinning, for undiubtedly twelve ells represents a lot of spinning for one morning. The work that Bolli has done is also "great." Thus, both of the morning's tasks are *mikil*. If one considers the author's preference for *jafn*-expressions, the *misjǫfn* reading sounds more like him, however.

18 It is interesting to note that in both cases the author has used words which echo the poetic Edda. Indeed, throughout *Lxd.* there is considerable evidence of the influence of Eddic poetry, especially in the characters of the women, Melkorka, Thorgerd, and Gudrún. There are also many thematic parallels, in some cases even in the wording, between Brynhild and Sigurd from the *Edda* and Gudrún and Kjartan from the saga. But the saga Gudrún reflects the *Edda* Gudrún as well as Brynhild. Association with the former was probably occasioned by the coincidence of the names. This is no doubt the case in those instances where the saga Gudrún has attracted the author to the Gudrún in *Guðmundar saga dýra* (in *Sturlunga saga*), from which some themes in *Lxd.* may also have been assimilated (cf. Heller, "Laxdœla saga und Sturlunga saga," pp. 112-133). Some of the more striking passages for comparison with the *Edda* are: "Guðrúnarkviða I" (vv. 9 and 10) and *Lxd.* xiii, where Melkorka has been forced to serve the master and mistress of the house (the shoes and stockings episode), and where Hoskuld's relationship to the servant woman improves, whereas Jórunn thinks less of her; "Gríspisspá" (v. 53) and *Lxd.* xxxiii, where Gudrún mentions that Gest could have given her fairer prophecies if the dreams had so warranted; "Guðrúnarkviða II" (v. 30) and *Lxd.* xlii, where Bolli says that Gudrún may be sitting some years husbandless; "Guðrúnarhvǫt" (v. 2) and *Lxd.* xlviii, where Gudrún goads her brothers into attacking Kjartan; "Sigurðarkviða in skamma" (v. 30) and *Lxd.* xlix, where Gudrún gloats over Hrefna's grief (quoted here); "Sigurðarkviða in skamma" (vv. 31 and 32) and *Lxd.* xlix, where Bolli tells Gudrún she would have turned less pale at the news of his death; "Guðrúnarkviða I" (v. 1 and the refrain lines in vv. 2, 5, and 11) and *Lxd.* l, where it is stated that Hrefna died of a broken heart; "Brot af Sigurðarkviðu" (vv. 8 and 10) and *Lxd.* lv, where Thorgerd praises Steinthór for "the work of his hands" in killing Bolli (quoted here).

19 The drownings of Geirmund (xxx, 83) and of Festargarm (li, 159) together form a separate pair outside the pattern.

20 Sveinsson's text, MS M, gives only ten persons on board for this drowning. MS C, however, reads "ten or twelve." From the author's general working method and comparison with the two parallel patterns, where particularly in the one great care is taken to assure the number twelve, the "or twelve" would seem to be correct.

21 See above, pp. 23-24.

22 See above, Chap. II, pp. 47-51.

23 Comparing of the parallel instances leaves no doubt that the author is using *kvikfé* (*fé*) and *lausafé* as synonyms. Since one lexical configuration governs the other and throws light on the author's intent, recognition of the formal patterns in the saga aids in the proper selection of alternate manuscript readings, in the assigning of proper connotations to subtle passages, and in the proper translation and interpretation of the text.

24 See above, pp. 20-21.

25 Cf. also the reversal in relations between Kjartan, Gudrún, and Bolli already discussed as a pair "*kært* gerðisk með inum yngrum mǫnnum / nǫkkut væri *pústr* á með inum yngrum mǫnnum." The confirmation of that reversal is picked

217

up as reason for Thórarin's desire to sell the Tungulands: "mjǫk vaxa þústr milli manna" (xxxix, 112; xlvi, 139; xlvii, 146, respectively); also the formation of two negatives over against a positive in the triad: "*Sjá mun hann* þenna krók / *Sjá mun hann* víst *eigi* / Ok *sér hann ekki í* þetta" (lix, 178 [first two] and lx, 181); see also above, pp. 70, 114 and 28, respectively, and p. 99.

[26] See above, Chap. I, n. 18 and Chap. II, p. 54.

[27] See above, p. 61.

[28] Other illustrations may be found, as in references to someone's being panic-stricken: "*skotit* hefir þér þá *skelk í bringu*" (xvi, 37); "þá *skýtr* þeim *skelk í bringu*" (xxi, 65); "*skaut* þá bóndum *skelk í bringu*" (xl, 119); to the hopelessness of a situation: "'þykki mér ok *rekin ván*'" (xlviii, 150); "'en nú þykki mér *rekin ván*'" (lix, 177); "'en þess er *borin ván*'" (lix, 178). This latter, it will be recalled, is also one of the motifs in the goading pattern; it also functions as a negative counterpart to the *sem ván var* idea that runs like a refrain in the saga affirming the notion of expectation and Foreknowledge; see Chapter I, n. 25.

[29] The *sem fyrr var ritat* can obviously only apply to the first part of the statement, not including the increment element *í miklum sóma*, which appears, to be sure, again in the third reference to Óláf, and one could almost say that the *sem fyrr var ritat* fitted there more properly. This same type of nodding on the part of the author occurs in another example: "Ósk hét in fjórða dóttir Þorsteins rauðs; hon var móðir Þorsteins surts ins spaka, er fann sumarauka" (vi, 10-11: "Thorstein the Red's fourth daughter was called Ósk. She was the mother of Thorstein Surt the Wise, who introduced the summer eke"). The next reference states the following: "Bróðir hennar hét Þorsteinn surtr, er þá bjó í Þórsnesi, *sem fyrr var ritat*" (x, 19: "Her brother was Thorstein Surt, who lived in Thórsnes at the time, as was written before"). In the first citation, Thorstein Surt is mentioned for the first time in the saga. The second reference to him includes the increment element *er þá bjó í Þórsnesi*, which was not stated before, hence the *sem fyrr var ritat* actually can apply only to the first clause and would have to be translated: Her brother was Thorstein Surt, whom we have mentioned before; he was living at that time at Thórsnes. See also above, Chap. I, n. 18.

[30] The quadruplet appears as follows: "helt Óláfr sik *at vápnabúnaði ok klæðum*" (xv, 38); "hann [Óláfr] bjó sik vel *at vápnum ok klæðum*" (xx, 49); "hann [Óláfr] var vel búinn *at vápnum ok klæðum*" (xxii, 62); "betr búnir *at klæðum ok vápnum*" (Bolli Bollason's men: lxxiii, 212). Threefold confirmation of the fame accruing to Óláf from his journey and the comparison of Bolli Bollason's fame with it by virtue of the lexical identities affords another illustration of preparation and echo: "ok er Óláfs *fǫr allfrægr*" (xxi, 59); "Óláfr varð *frægr af ferð þessi*" (xxii, 61); "en Óláfr er *frægr af ferð sinni*" (xxiii, 63); "Bolli varð *frægr af ferð þessi*" (lxxvii, 225). For discussion of the *at vápnum ok klæðum* motif, see below, Chap. V; for Óláf's acquiring fame from his journey, see above, Chap. II, p. 58.

[31] See above, pp. 56, 68. 119.

[32] Other illustrations of quadruplets containing various combinations of pairs and triplets might be cited: "Er nú *fét betr niðr komit*" (xvi, 36); "þá sé *betr komit fét*" (xvi, 37); "þat *fé* væri *vel* komit" (xvi, 38); "Skǫfnung *vel niðr kominn*" (lvii, 172). The first two refer to the tit-for-tat between Vigdís and Thórd over his money (see above, Chap. III, p. 68). Thórd's statement to Hoskuld (example two) is then itself confirmed by Thórd Gellir (example three), namely that Thórd's money has come into good hands now that Hoskuld has it in his keep. The pair develops thus into a triplet, and the fourth reference to Skofnung's having come

into good hands echoes the motif once again. Another quadruplet carries a motif that in each instance relates to Thorkel: "'vil ek, at þú *leysir hann vel af hendi*'" (lviii, 174); "'vil ek þik *svá af hǫndum leysa*, sem ek hafa aldri þungan hug á þér haft'" (lviii, 175). This confirmative pair relating to Thorkel's treatment of the outlaw Grím has been discussed earlier (see above, Chap. II, p. 55). The next time Thorkel has to deal with an outlaw, he anticipates what action will be taken: "'at þér mun ekki at getask, nema hann *sé sœmiliga af hǫndum leystr*'" (lxix, 203), see above, Chap. III, p. 70. And the fourth time Thorkel needs no prompting on how he is to send Bolli off into the world: "Þorkell lézk þat ætla fyrir sér, at *leysa* Bolla *vel af hendi*" (lxx, 206). Thorkel, it would seem, has learned his lesson well.

33 In this connection it should be noted that in addition to Thorleik, Bárd, and Óláf Peacock, Hoskuld had another son, Helgi. The fact that the author chose to include only three in his story indicates that he has used his historical *Stoff* selectively, historical accuracy not being his aim. And not only did he subtract from history, but he also added to it, for there are numerous characters in the saga who are unknown from other sources. This may be coincidence, but more likely these actors have been invented specifically for the story: cf. the references in Sveinsson's edition: xi, 21, n. 1; xiv, 28, n. 2; xxii, 62, n. 1; xxiv, 66, n. 3; xxix, 77, n. 4; xxxvii, 102, n. 5; xxxviii, 109, n. 3; xlviii, 150-151, n. 4; liv, 164, n. 1; lxvii, 197, n. 1.

34 All these examples referring to twelve years of age can naturally be associated with legal and social mores and with the attainment of manhood and the privileges granted youths at that age. The legal aspect is obvious: revenge by killing could not be performed until the youth was of age — in the Icelandic world, twelve. Death of a child at this age (i. e. Kári) would be especially hard to bear. The author's choice of this point in life for some incidents heightens the tragedy, the glory, or the deed of prowess, as the case may be.

CHAPTER V

1 Heller, "Studien zu Aufbau und Stil der Laxdœla Saga," pp. 150-161, catalogues similar examples.
2 The few examples of so-called unrelated pairs and triplets, to which attention was previously called (see above, Chap. III, n. 5 and Chap. IV, n. 28 and p. 118), belong in a sense to the background world of Recurrence. Since, as far as I have been able to detect, they apparently do not set up statement-confirmations or parallels and contrasts, their occurrence only twice or three times would seem to be mere happenstance. As far as tone and purpose are concerned, they might just as well appear any number of times, should the pertinent circumstance arise. Yet the situations they depict are somewhat more unique and do not properly belong to the round-of-life examples, for instance the *skjótt birta minn vilja*; *uggir ekki at sér*; *slíkt mein, sem ýðr líkar*; *mikit þykkja, ef þeir skulu skilja*; *er ekki af sagt hans ferð*; *er verr muni gegna*; *skjóta skelk í bringu*. To these could be added several others: Both Hrapp and Thórd Goddi, for instance, are said to have bought the land they lived on when coming to Iceland (x, 19: "ok [Hrappr] keypti sér þá jǫrð, er hann bjó á"; and xi, 20: "keypta hafði hann [Þórðr goddi] jǫrð þá, er hann bjó á"). Their proximity to one another as neighbors and the fact that Hrapp became involved with Thórd, giving him much trouble, probably led the author to draw this parallel between them. Thórd Goddi is otherwise unknown in saga literature and is not in *Landnámabók*. Setting out after Christmas seems to be the usual practice: xlv, 135: "Þann vetr *eptir jól* býsk Kjartan heiman"; and lxxv, 218: "Þenna vetr *eptir jól* bjósk Þorkell heiman"). The examples show that the author moves in a prescribed lexical domain, consciously or unconsciously, describing like situations in like words, and so holding the saga within its symbolic domain. What has happened once will happen again, what has been brought up once, will appear again — either as double, triple, quadruple, or a series of verbal repetitions according to his purpose.
3 Although throughout the saga references to births and namegiving closely follow a verbal pattern, the references reflect an interesting distinction between pre-Christian and Christian practices. Before Christianization the phrases *var vatni ausinn, ok nafn gefit* [*ok kallaðr*] regularly appear: xxv, 71; xxviii, 75; xxxvi, 100. After Christianization the *vatni ansinn* no longer appears and *var nefndr* (was named) becomes more usual: xlvii, 146; lii, 159; lvi, 170; lxx, 204.
4 For other examples of early promise with the expression *snimma*, cf. xxv, 71; lii, 159-160; lvi, 170; lxx, 204; lxxiv, 215.
5 In the Saga of Icelanders twelve years is generally given as being the age at which a hero performs his first deed of bravery. This legal "coming of age," attested to also in the *Grágás*, no doubt can be traced to tribal customs and warrior cults of the early Germanic period. The motif here and those above with *snimma* echo this tradition, which shows up both in heroic literature and in fairy tales as the

221

"remarkable youth" motif. Óláf's early maturity, twice referred to, is in a similar vein, although the formulations are not stereotyped: "En þá er sveinninn var tvævetr, þá var hann almæltr ok rann einn saman, sem fjǫgurra vetra gǫmul bǫrn" (xiii, 27: "And when the boy was two years old, he ran about alone and could say everything just like children of four years"). As if to confirm this statement about Óláf's early development, King Harald commends the eighteen year old Óláf with these words: " 'Miklir ágætismenn eru slíkt, sem þú ert, því þú ert enn lítit af barns aldri' " (xxi, 53: " 'Men such as you are indeed very exceptional, for you are as yet but little past the years of childhood' "). See also above, Chap. IV, n. 34.

⁶ The motif is picked up again when Thorgerd refuses Óláf's marriage proposal and says to her father: Egil: " 'Þat hefi ek þik heyrt mæla, at þú *ynnir* mik *mest barna þinna*' " (xxiii, 63). No distinction is made between one's own children, an illegitimate, half child, stepchild or foster child, for they are generally loved "no less than one's own" — a motif closely related to the one above and which also receives typical formulation: xvi, 38: "leggr við hann *mikla ást*; xxvii, 75: *"unni honum eigi minna en sínum bǫrnum"*; xxx, 83: *"unni honum eigi minna en brœðrum sínum*; xxxviii, 111: "vera til hans *eigi verr en til minna sona"*; lxx, 204: *"vel* var Þorkatli til stjúpbarna sinna"; lxx, 207: "var til hans hvar *betr en til sinna barna"*; lxxii, 212: "var Guðrún ok *allvel* til hennar." The *eigi verr* motif, while exemplifying this recurrent pattern, also assumes special function under triple confirmation, as discussed earlier. The formulations with *vel* should be noted in view of the controlled meaning this expression has in other places in the saga.

⁷ See above, Chap. IV, n. 29.

⁸ See above, p. 33.

⁹ For examples of the naming of the woman and the *kostr beztr* motif, cf. ix, 17: "Sá [Jórunn] þótti þá *kostr beztr* í ǫllum Vestfjǫrðum'"; lviii, 174: " 'Þeirar skaltu konu biðja, er *beztr kostr* er, en þat er Guðrún Ósvífrsdóttir' "; xliii, 128: " 'Ekki munn ek mér ór sveit á brott biðja konu, meðan *svá nálægir eru góðir ráðakostir.* Ek vil biðja Guðrúnar Ósvífrsdóttur' " (Bolli's action here again constitutes an exception to the normal pattern in the saga: he will not look outside the district when "there are such good matches nearby"); lxx, 205: "Bolli svarar: " 'Kona heitir Þórdís, hon er dóttir Snorra goða; hon er svá kvenna, at mér er mest um at eiga' " (Bolli Bollason does not select the woman who is the "best match" but the one woman "he would most like to have.") This variation in the pattern helps draw the comparison between Bolli Bollason and Kjartan, as the latter did not get the woman he most wanted to have. See above, Chap. III, n. 22.

¹⁰ For the favorable reply of the father and the *vel gipt* motif, cf. ix, 17; xxiii, 63; xxix, 79; xlv, 137. Óláf gives a negative reply to Geirmund, who requests his daughter's hand, but her mother thinks the daughter "could not be better given in marriage" (xxix, 79: " 'muni eigi betr verða gefin' "), since Geirmund has won her over with bribes.

¹¹ For the father's presentation of the suit to his daughter, the urging of the match by him and others, and the daughter's passing the decision back to her father, cf. ix, 17; xxiii, 65; xxix, 79; xliii, 129; xlv, 137; lxviii, 200; lxx, 206. Gudrún, significantly, is overruled by her father even though as a widow she has the right to choose for herself, and accepts Bolli's proposal only reluctantly, xliii, 129.

¹² Examples of the settlement of the betrothal and agreement regarding time and place of the wedding feast include: vii, 11; ix, 17; xx, 51; xxiii, 65; xxix, 80; xxxiv, 93; xxxv, 96; xlii, 129-130; xlv, 137-138; lxviii, 201; lxx, 206-207. Although to have the wedding celebrated at the groom's farmstead is considered a special honor

in one example (xxiii, 65), the number of references to its so being held would indicate that the practice was fairly common.

13 For examples of the groom's awaiting the appointed time, cf. ix, 17; xxiii, 65; xliii, 130; lxviii, 201; lxx, 207.

14 For descriptions of the wedding guests, their clothes and numbers, cf. vii, 11-12; ix, 17-18; xxiii, 65; xxix, 80; xxxv, 96; xliii, 130; lxix, 203; lxx, 207.

15 "Snorri goði sótti þessa veizlu með Þorkatli, ok hǫfðu þeir nær sex tigu manna, ok var þat lið mjǫk valit, því at flestir allir menn váru í litklæðum. Guðrún hafði nær hundrað fyirboðsmanna" (lxviii, 201: "Snorri Godi came to this feast with Thorkel; they had nearly sixty in their company and it was a very select one, for most of the people were in brightly colored array. Gudrún had nearly a hundred and twenty guests there waiting to welcome them"). The number of guests at any given gathering is sometimes remarked upon and so its appearance here, imbedded with the other expected components of the pattern, seems normal, except that Gudrún, in outdoing Thorkel in every way, significantly has twice the number of Thorkel's party instead of the equal number that would show both sides honor.

16 For examples of the excellence of the feast and the honorable gifts, cf. vii, 13; ix, 18; xxiii, 65; xxix, 80; xlv, 138-139; lxix, 203; lxx, 207.

17 For examples of the *takask með þeim góðar ástir* motif, cf. xxiv, 66; xxxv, 96 (variant: Samfǫr þeira Þórðar ok Guðrúnar var góð); xlv, 139; lxix, 203; lxx, 207.

18 For another example of the beginning of the cycle, cf. ix, 18.

19 As liegemen at the Norwegian court, the Icelanders gradually forfeited much of their own freedom. As a result, Iceland came increasingly under the power of Norway and finally fell to the Norwegian crown in 1262; cf. E. Ó. Sveinsson, *The Age of the Sturlungs*, Chap. II, pp. 8-23.

20 For examples of fetching timber, cf. xi, 21; xiii, 25; xxix, 78; lxx, 204; lxxiv, 215. The last two references deal with Thorkel's fetching timber for a church; the first prepares for the second and the episode between Thorkel and the king concerning the minster in Trondheim. For the motif of fame and fortune, experience and knowledge, cf. above, Chap. III, p. 78.

21 Sea crossings from Iceland to Norway, for whatever purpose, are all similarly formulated: cf. v, 8; vii, 14; xx, 51; xxi, 51; xxx, 83; xxxviii, 111; xl, 115; xlii, 127; lviii, 175.

22 Other arduous sea journeys are: xvi, 37; xxi, 53; lxxiv, 215.

23 The theme of warm welcomes and good reception of Icelanders abroad is introduced already with Ketil Flatnose: "Ketil flatnefr... fekk *góðar viðtǫkur* af tignum mǫnnum, því at hann var frægr maðr ok stórættaðr, ok *buðu honum þann ráðakost þar, sem hann vildi hafa*" (iv, 6-7: "Ketil Flatnose... was well recieved by noble men, for he himself was a famous man and high-born. They offered him whatever station in life he chose to have"). Thorgerd Thorsteinsdóttir is well received by her noble relatives and also is offered any status and whatever she will share with them: "Þorgerðr átti í Nóregi mikit ætterni ok marga gǫfga frændr; þeir fǫgnuðu henni vel ok *buðu* henni *alla kosti, þá sem hon vildi með þeim þiggja*" (vii, 15: "Thorgerd had a great number of relatives in Norway and many noble kinsmen. They gave her a good welcome and offered her complete choice of whatever she would accept from them"). References to receptions by kings include: xiii, 25; xxii, 60; xxix, 78 (Earl Hákon); lxx, 205; lxxiii, 213; lxxiv, 215. The fact that Hoskuld did not go to see King Hákon is a negative reversal of the normal pattern: "Hǫskuldr *fór ekki á fund* Hákonar konungs'" (xi, 22), see also above, Chap. I, n. 16.

223

24 For references to the esteem in which the Icelander is held, cf. xix, 44 (*mikla virðing, miklar mætur*); xxi, 52 (*mikil mæti*); xxii, 60 (*mikla virðing*); xl, 123 (*mat umfram alla menn*; *metinn vel*); lxx, 205 (*virði vel*); lxxiii, 213 (*vel* sem fyrr; *mat* hann meira, þótti hann mikit afbragð annarra manna); lxxiv, 215 (*mikils metinn*).

25 See above, Chap. II, p. 62 (for Queen Gunnhild's partiality); Chap. I, p. 36 (for comparison of Kjartan and Bolli Thorleiksson); Chap. III, pp. 80-81 (for comparison of the pairs of brothers).

26 For instances of the *vitja gǫfugra frænda* motif, cf. xix, 44; xxii, 60; xliii, 130. When used in respect to Hrút, the formula shows significant increment: "Hrútr átti *at vitja til Íslands fjárhlutar mikils ok gǫfugra frænda*" (xix, 44: "Hrút had noble kinsmen and a great deal of property out in Iceland, so he desired to go back and see about it"). The *fjárhlutar mikils* sets the stage for the ensuing trouble over Hrút's claim.

27 Cf. also lxxiii, 213: "'Mun ek veita þér þvílíka *nafnbót*, sem ek veitta Þorleiki, bróður þínum.'" The equality of rank with his brother Thorleik is not enough to entice Bolli Bollason into staying with the king; he wants something far better. So here again Thorleik is subtly put in second place.

28 See above, p. 39.

29 For further examples of the visiting Icelander's excellence over his own countrymen or beyond the Norwegians' accomplishments, cf. the following formulations, which, although not stereotyped, indicate a constant theme that is carried through the generations of Icelanders: "'Eigi skal dvelja þik hér með oss lengr en þér likar, en þó þykkir oss vanfengit manns í rúm þitt.... At sómamanni hefi ek þik reyndan'" (Hoskuld: xiii, 25: "'I will not detain you here longer than you wish, but it will not be easy for us get a man in your place.... I have found you to be a man of honor'"); "Þau kǫlluðu engan mann vænligra hafa komit af Íslandi á þeira dǫgum" (Hrút: xxi, 53: "They recalled no man more promising ever having come from Iceland in their day"); "'Virðisk mér Óláfr svá mikill atgǫrvimaðr ok skǫrungr, at vér eigim eigi slíkra manna hér kost'" (xxi, 59: "'I have found Óláf to be a man of such excellence and accomplishment that his equal is not to be found among us'"); "Engi útlendr maðr hafði slíkan virðing af þeim fengit" (Óláf: xxii, 60: "No foreigner before him had ever received such honor from them"); "'Oss sœki eigi heim hversdagliga slíkir menn af Íslandi'" (Óláf: xxix, 78: "'It's not every day we get such men from Iceland'"); "Var þat allra manna mál, at engi hefði slíkt maðr komit af Íslandi sem Kjartan" (xl, 123: "It was the talk of everyone that no man such as Kjartan had ever come from Iceland"); "Konungr kvað svá vera skyldu, en segir sér torfengan slíkan mann ótiginn, sem Kjartan var" (xliii, 130: "The king said it should be so, but that it would be hard for him to find again among men not of princely rank anyone such as Kjartan"); "'Mér þykkir þú, Bolli, hafa komit merkiligastr maðr af Íslandi um mína daga'" (lxxiii, 214: "'You, Bolli, are in my opinion the most noteworthy man ever to have come from Iceland in my day'").

30 For examples of gifts *at skilnaði*, cf. xix, 44 (Hrút: *skip at skilnaði*); xxix, 78 (Óláf from Earl Hákon: *at skilnaði oxi gullrekna*); xliii, 131-132 (Kjartan: *sverð at skilnaði*); lxxiii, 214 (Bolli Bollason: *góðar gjafar at skilnaði*). Gifts at the time of parting but without the *at skilnaði* formula, include: xiii, 25 (Hoskuld: *gullhring, sverð*); xix, 44 (Hrút from Queen Gunnhild: *gullhring*); xxi, 59 (Óláf: *spjót gullrekit ok sverð búit ok mikit fé annat*; see below); xxii, 60 (Óláf: *skip*; see below). Gifts received while at court: lxxiv, 216 (Thorkel: *tíu tigu marka brennds silfrs*); ibid. (Gellir: *at jólum skikkju* [for the motif of scarlet clothes

being given at Yule, see below]); lxxviii, 227-228 (Gellir: *tólf aura gulls ok mikit fé annat*).

[31] See below, pp. 139, 226, n. 46.

[32] Other passages that closely follow this pattern with the motifs of accompaniment to the ship, gift-giving, expression of thanks for the honor received, and parting in friendly affection include: xiii, 25-26; xix, 44; xxix, 78; xliii, 131-132; lxxiii, 214.

[33] The formulaic nature of this phrase is attested by the consistency with which it appears in leave-taking situations: xxii, 61 (Óláf and King Harald [see above]: *skiljask með inum mesta kærleik*); xxix, 78 (Óláf and Earl Hákon: *skilðusk með inum mesta kærleik*); xliii, 132 (Kjartan and King Óláf Tryggvason: *skiljask með miklum kærleik*); lxxiii, 214 (Bolli Bollason and King Óláf Haraldsson: *skilðusk með mikilli vináttu*); lxxiv, 217 (Thorkel and King Óláf Haraldsson [here]). It not only occurs at partings with noble personages; when Óláf takes leave of his brother Thorleik it also appears; xxvii, 75: *skiljask með inum mesta kærleik*, and in alternate form, again when they finally part and go their separate ways: xxxviii, 111: *skilja með mikilli blíðu*.

[34] For other examples of the return crossing and good reception at home in Iceland, cf. xiii, 26; xxi, 59; xxix, 70; xlii, 127, 128; xliv, 132; lxx, 207; lxxiv, 217; lxxvii, 225.

[35] For references to old age in these terms, cf. iii, 6; vi, 10; vii, 12, 13, 14; viii, 16; x, 20; xvii, 39; xix, 48; xx, 49; xxiv, 66; lxvi, 196; lxxviii, 229.

[36] For similarly formulated death bed scenes, cf.: "Hǫskuldr Dala-Kollsson tók sótt í elli sinni; hann sendi eptir sonum sínum ok ǫðrum frændum. Ok er þeir kómu, mælti Hǫskuldr við þá brœðr Bárd ok Þorleik: 'Ek hefi tekit þyngð nǫkkura; hefi ek verit ósóttnæmr maðr; hygg ek, at þessi sótt muni leiða mik til bana'" (xxvi, 71: "Hoskuld Dala-Kollsson took sick in his old age; he sent for his sons and other kinsmen. And when they came, Hoskuld said to his sons Bárd and Thorleik: 'I have taken some sickness, and as I have never been prone to illness, I think it will mean the death of me"); "Á þeim sama vetri fekk sótt Gestr Oddleifsson, ok er at honum leið sóttin, þá kallaði hann til sín Þórð lága, son sinn, ok mælti: 'Svá segir mér hugr um, at þessi sótt muni skilja vára samvistu'" (lxvi, 196: "That same winter Gest Oddleifsson fell sick; and when the sickness came heavy upon him, he called for his son Thórd the Short and said: 'I have a feeling that this illness will mean the parting of our ways'"). Less complete, but reminiscent of one or two of the motifs are: vii, 11; lxxviii, 226.

[37] For the mourning of a death, cf. viii, 16; xiv, 30; xxvi, 72-73; xxxvii, 106; lii, 160; lvi, 169; lxxvi, 196, 223. The recurrent *harmdauði*, it will be recalled, was also specifically applied to the case of Kjartan and Bolli Thorleiksson, see above, Chap. IV. Fostering of children after the death of the father is also expressed in set form: After the drowning of Thórd, Snorri offers to foster Gudrún's child as a consolation to her (xxxvi, 100: "*bauð Guðrúnu barnfóstr til hugganar við hana*") and Thorstein Kuggason, after Kjartan's slaying, offers to foster Hrefna's and Kjartan's son Ásgeir (l, 158: "Þorsteinn Kuggason *bauð Ásgeiri, syni Kjartans, til fóstrs til hugganar við Hrefnu*").

[38] For references to high station, cf. i, 3; iv, 6, 7, 8; vi, 10; vii, 13; viii, 15; ix, 16, 18; x, 20; xiv, 28, 30; xix, 44; xxi, 53, 57, 59; xxiii, 63; xxiv, 66; xxxiii, 87, 92; xl, 122; xlv, 137; lxx, 204; lxxvi, 223.

[39] For examples of gatherings that are *fjǫlmennt* or *skǫrulig*, cf.: v, 9; xii, 22; xiv, 29; xxi, 59; xxii, 62 (2); xxvii, 74 (3); xl, 118; xliv, 135; xlv, 136 (Var þar aukit hundrað manna); l, 157 (2); lii, 161; lxi, 181; lxxiv, 217.

40 The following references are but a sampling to show the preponderance of these expressions in the saga: For *fagnar* expressions, cf. vi, 9; vii, 15; xxi, 52, 57; xxii, 61; xxiii, 64 (2); xl, 115, 116; xli, 124; xlii, 127; xliii, 129, 131; xliv, 132 (2); xlv, 135; xlvii, 146; lvii, 171-172; lix, 179; lxi, 184; lxviii, 201; lxx, 207; lxxi, 208. For *tók vel* expressions, cf. xiv, 32; xv, 35; xxiii, 60; xxix, 78; xxxiii, 88; xli, 125-126; lxvi, 196; lxviii, 200; lxx, 205, 206; lxxi, 209; lxxv, 218. For *blíðu* expressions, cf. xiii, 25; xxi, 52; xxii, 61 (3); xl, 114, 123; xli, 124; xlii, 127; xlv, 135-136; xlv, 136; lviii, 174; lxviii, 199; lxx, 206, 207.

41 For expressions with *eigi skortir*, cf. vi, 10; ix, 18; xxiv, 68; xlv, 137; lii, 159; lxviii, 200, 201. The last reference with its two statements forms a confirmation pair, see above, Chap. II, n. 6. For expressions with *eigi sparat*, cf. v, 9; xxiii, 65; xxxiii, 91. For *risuligr* expressions, cf. xxiv, 66, 68; xxix, 78; xlv, 136 (*in vegligstu*); lii, 159; lvi, 170; lxix, 203.

42 See xxix, 79; lxix, 203; lxx, 204, in particular.

43 References to these qualities include: vii, 11, 14, 15; ix, 16, 18 (2); x, 19, 20; xi, 21 (2); xii, 23; xiii, 27; xiv, 28; xvi, 38; xix, 49; xx, 49 (2); xxii, 61-62, 62; xxiii, 65; xxv, 70, 71; xxviii, 76 (2), 76-77, 77; xxix, 77; xxxi, 83; xxxii, 86 (2), 87 (2); xxxviii, 108, 109; xl, 113; xli, 126; xliv, 133; lii, 159; liv, 164; lvi, 170 (2), 171; lxiii, 189; lxvii, 197; lxx, 204, 206 (2); lxxviii, 226.

44 The similarity between the formulations here and the description of Kjartan (xxviii, 77) is particularly striking, especially the clause containing the likening to relatives. The formula in the case of Kjartan reads: *mikill maðr ok sterkr, eptir sem verit hafði Egill, móðurfaðir hans, eða Þórólfr*. See above, Chap. I, p. 35.

45 Interesting for comparison is the description of Geirmund with its unique variations: "En hann var svá búinn jafnan, at hann hafði skarlatskyrtil rauðan ok gráfeld yztan ok bjarnskinnshúfu á hǫfði, sverð í hendi" (xxix, 79: "And he was always dressed in this way: a scarlet kirtle with a grey cloak over it, a bearskin cap on his head and a sword in his hand"). If one considers Geirmund's role in the saga and compares it with the other hero patterns, this almost seems like a burlesquing; or is it merely realistic in contrast to the idealized pattern?

46 The *skarlatsklæði* were given to Kjartan after his decision to remain in Norway and not attempt to convert his countrymen to Christianity. Óláf received his clothes of scarlet "at Yule"" and Gellir receives a cloak "at Yule." The *skarlatsklæði* motif is nowhere in the saga causally connected with the *at skilnaði* motif. But since parting gifts belong to the scheme of things, it is not surprising that the two formulae have become joined here, albeit erroneously. The fact that the units can be shifted from one pattern to another speaks for the formulaic nature of these motifs and their automatic iteration. Another instance of the author's nodding and use of a formula where it does not apply is Hrút's *bryntroll gullrekit, er Haraldr konungr gaf honum*. It is nowhere stated that Hrút received this weapon from the king. "At parting" King Harald gave him a ship (xix, 44). But again, since the kingly origin of such weapons is recurrently formulated in just such a subordinate clause, its appearance here suggests that the author slipped it in almost automatically. It seems but re-use of the same clause from the heroic description of Óláf (xxiii, 64), since the full development of the hero pattern with this element and with embellishments (N. B. the *gullrekit* here also) does not take place until this later point in the saga. The sequence, together with the fact that the element is used wrongly in the case of Hrút, points to the author's having the total pattern in mind from the beginning, that is, at the center of the creative process, and

that he was working with preformed units, likely of his own making for the most part.

47 Chap. xxix, 79 of *Lxd.* describes Geirmund's sword Footbiter as having a walrus tusk for a hilt: "þat var mikit vápn ok gott, tannhjǫlt at; ekki var þar borit silfr á, en brandrinn var hvass, ok beið hvergi ryð á. Þetta sverð kallaði hann Fótbít ok lét þat aldregi hendi firr ganga" ("It was a large weapon and a good one, with a walrus tusk for a hilt; it was not chased with silver, but the blade was sharp and was never attacked by rust. This sword he called Footbiter and never let it very far out of reach"). Bolli Bollason returns from Miklagard with *all* his weapons chased in gold, Footbiter, of course, included. The transformation is thus made plausible: "hann var gyrðr Fótbít, ok váru at honum *hjǫlt gullbúin ok meðalkaflinn gulli vafiðr*'" (lxxvii, 225). The zpap MSS (C, 226) even add the word *nú* to show the intended difference: "Íslenzk fornrit," V, Formáli, p. XXI. Hint of this intention is given in calling specific attention to the fact that Footbiter had no chased work *in silver*. Mention of silver instead of gold is a substitution — and a distractor. The gold embellishment is reserved for later.

The sword Footbiter in *Lxd.* forms, as we have seen, an antithetical pair with Kjartan"s sword *konungsnautr*. Geirmund the Noisy and his sword are both fictitious, having been created by the author to comply with his schematism of parallels and contrasts. Geirmund is nowhere historically attested and appears only in *Lxd.* ("Íslensk fornrit," V, 77, n. 4.). The sword Footbiter may be fictitious but it is not fabricated totally out of the author's imagination. He has borrowed it from the *Morkinskinna*. In this compendium Magnús Barefoot (in the saga under his name, see edition of Finnur Jónsson [København, 1932], p. 335) carries a sword Legbiti which is described as follows: "voro at tanhiollt. oc vafiðr gvlli medalkaflin oc var allra sverþa bitrast." Snorri Sturluson used this same description of the sword in his redaction of the *Magnúss saga berfœtts* in the *Heimskringla* III ("Íslenzk fornrit," XXVIII, 235: "gyrðr sverði, því er Leggbítr var kallat, tannhjaltat ok gulli vafiðr meðalkaflinn"). He also applies the same adjectives to King Óláf Haraldsson's sword Hneitir in his *Óláfs saga helga*, Chap. 213 (*Hkr.* II, "Íslenzk fornrit," XXVII, 367: "Hann var gyrðr sverði því, er Hneitir var kallat, it bitrasta sverð ok gulli vafiðr meðalkaflinn'"). Sveinsson points out this similarity between the descriptions of Bolli Bollason's sword Footbiter in *Lxd.*, and of Magnús Barefoot's in the *Morkinskinna* and the *Heimskringla* ("Íslenzk fornrit," V, p. XLI, n. 3). But neither he nor Heller (*Laxdœla saga und Königssagas*, p. 13, n. 2) has seen what the *Lxd.* author has done with the sword — and shield — descriptions (see below, n. 48). The description of Legbiti from the *Mork.* has been split up and used in two different places in *Lxd.*: the *tannhjǫlt* used when Geirmund owned it, the *meðalkaflinn gulli vafiðr* reserved for the time when the gold embellishments enter the saga. And furthermore, the *Lxd.* author has not merely borrowed adjectives (note also that the sharpness of the blade appears as *hvass* in the *Lxd.* description of Geirmund's sword, whereas King Óláf's sword in the *Óláfs saga helga* retains the word *bitrast* from the *Mork.*), he has simply taken over the whole sword, substituting *Fót-* (a synonym) for *Leg-*. There is closest correspondence between the form of the name in the *Hkr.* and in *Lxd.* in respect to the last element: Leggbítr and Fótbítr, for the *Mork.'s -biti.* But these swords Legbiti (Leggbítr), Hneitir, and Fótbítr belong, like the shields, to a larger thematic complex. The *Lxd.* author has not just borrowed the sword, he has worked with this whole pattern.

48 Although shields with lions or crosses or knights are anachronisms as far as the time of action in the saga is concerned, the semblance of historical progression is accomplished and the semblance was all the author wanted. Heller, *Laxdœla saga*

und Königssagas, pp. 12-14, cites the *Mork.* and King Magnús' shield as source for the *Lxd.* author's description of Óláf Peacock's shield with a lion; *Óláfs saga helga* in the *Hkr.* with its description of Saint Óláf's shield with a cross as model for Kjartan's shield; and the *Knýtlinga saga*, Chap. 56, as source for the description of Bolli Bollason's shield with a knight on it. A look at the sources reveals at once that it is here a question of a pattern into which new content and embellishments may be substituted, as with so many of the *Lxd.* author's patterns. Both Snorri Sturluson and our anon. author worked with the heroic pattern in this way. The presence of the "scarlet clothes" in the *Knýtlinga* version makes it look suspiciously as if that author or compiler had taken a look at *Lxd*. It is also hard to believe that the compiler of the *Mork.* originated the schematic form, although that text may have been the immediate source for the *Lxd.* author and Snorri. The unadorned version as presented in the case of Hrút in *Lxd.* is a good indication and lead as to what the archetype might have been. See in this connection my article in the forthcoming Hollander Festschrift. It also seems likely now that the deviation from the pattern in the case of Geirmund functions as parody.

The four passages from the sources discussed here read as follows:

Mork. (*Magnúss saga berfœtts*):

> M. konvngr var auþkendr. hann hafþi hialm gylldan ahofþi ok sciolld fire ser. oc var scrifat aleo meþ gvlli. sverþ ihendi er callat var Legbiti. voro at tanhiollt. oc vafiðr gvlli medalkaflin oc var allra sverþa bitrast. Han hafþi dregit silkihivp rauþan vm vtan scyrtvna. oc var þat allra manna mal. at eigi hefþi set vigligra man meþ jafnmorgom vapnom e. tigvligra hofþingia. (p. 335)

Hkr. (*Magnúss saga berfœtts*):

> Hafði Magnús konungr hjálm á hǫfði ok rauðan skjǫld og lagt á með gulli léó, gyrðr sverði, því er Leggbítr var kallat, tannhjaltat ok gulli vafiðr meðalkaflinn, it bezta vápn. Hann hafði kesju í hendi. Hann hafði silkihjúp rauðan yfir skyrtu ok skorit fyrir ok á bak léo með gulu silki. Ok var þat mál manna, at eigi hefði sét skǫruligra mann eða vaskligra. (III, 235)

Hkr. (*Óláfs saga helga*):

> Óláfr konungr var svá búinn, at hann hafði hjálm gylltan á hǫfði, en hvítan skjǫld ok lagðr á með gulli kross inn helgi. I annarri hendi hafði hann kesju, þá, er nú stendr í Kristskirkju við altára. Hann var gyrðr sverði því, er Hneitir var kallat, it bitrasta sverð ok gulli vafiðr meðalkaflinn. Hann hafði hringabrynju. (II, 367)

Knýtlinga saga:

> Benedikt var svo búinn, at hann var í rauðum skallatskyrtili, ok í brynju um utan, yzta hafði hann silkitreyju ermalausa, gullroðinn hjálm, skjöld rauðan ok dreginn á riddari með gulli, sverð búit í hendi, ok var hann allra manna röskligastr. (*Fornmanna sögur* [Kaupmannahafn, 1828], Vol. XI, Chap. 56, p. 272)

[49] Sveinsson's reading for this passage follows MS E and reads: "finnsk þeim Írum nú mikit um, hversu vígligir þessir menn eru." MS M grants only to Óláf the wonderment and admiration of the Irish, not to all his men: "hversu virðuligr þessi maðr er ok vígligr." That some MSS readings would include the whole retinue should not be surprising in view of the fact that this form of the motif is found elsewhere in

the saga. There are arguments on both sides. If the MS M reading is correct, it must be interpreted in relationship to the occurrences of the theme later which show then a progression, an increase in magnificence as the generations continue: Óláf alone was admired, then Kjartan and his men, and finally Bolli Bollason and all his dazzling retinue. This increase would go along with the augmenting and embellishment of the clothing and accoutrements. Nonetheless, I would not rule out MS E as a possible reading. In that case the motif would function as preparation for the ones to come. But I would favor the MS M version for an edition.

50 See above, pp. 71-72.
51 See above, Chap. III, n. 9.
52 For the occurrence of the word *kurteisi* and its derivatives, cf. xiii, 28; xxvi, 73; xxviii, 77; xxxii, 86; xlv, 136; l, 158; lxiii, 187, 188 (3); lxxvii, 225. It perhaps also appeared in reference to Bolli Bollason's following: MS V reads: "allir váru þeir *kurteisir* [instead of *listuligir*] menn" (lxxvii, 225).
53 This same process of assimilation is found in the *Mork.* (*Magnúss berfœtts saga*, p. 329): "En M. Noregs konvngr var af þesom ollom miclo kvrteisastr oc vascligastr oc hermanligastr."
54 For instances of *afbragð*, cf.: iv, 7: "Má af því marka, at hon [Unnr] var *mikit afbragð annarra kvenna*"; xiii, 27: "Óláfr var *afbragð flestra barna*"; xiii, 28: "Brátt sér þat á Óláfi, er hann óx upp, at hann myndi verða *mikit afbragð annarra manna* fyrir vænleiks sakar ok *kurteisi*"; xlv, 136: "Allir menn hǫfðu á máli, hversu mikit *afbragð* Kjartan var *annarra manna*"; lxxiii, 213: "Er konungr vel til Þorleiks sem fyrr, en þó mat hann Bolla miklu meira, því at konungr þótti hann *mikit afbragð annarra manna.*" Again here the assimilation process is evident: the old formula *afbragð* has a new equivalent *kurteisi*.
For the *mikill maðr ok sterkr* [*gǫrviligr, efniligr, vaskligr, vænn, knáligr, rammr at afli*] formula, cf. vii, 11, 15; viii, 16, 18; x, 19; xi, 21 (2); xiv, 28; xvi, 38, xxii, 61-62; xxviii, 76, 76-77, 77; xxxii, 86, 87; liii, 162; liv, 164; lvii, 170, 171; lxvii, 197. References to the other qualities are included in the list for n. 43, above.
55 For examples of the *stór-* combination and its derivatives, cf. ii, 4; v. 9 (2); vii, 12, 13; xiii, 27; xxii, 61; xxiii, 65; xxix, 80 (2); xxx, 81; xlv, 136, 139; l, 156; lviii, 174, 175; lxii, 185; lxix, 202; lxxiii, 213; lxxiv, 207. For variation with *mikil-* note lxii, 185 and lxix, 204. For the *lítil-* combinations, cf. v, 9; xl, 119. Negative reversals as equivalent substitutions are interesting in view of the author''s stylistic predilections: xxxvii, 102: *ekki lítilmenni*; xxxviii, 108: *ekki mikilmenni*; xl, 119: *ekki lítilmannligt*. The positive forms (*stór-* and *mikil-*) far outnumber the negative forms (*lítil-*) and contribute to the general tone of greatness, abundance, generosity — bigness both literally and figuratively.
56 The positive forms with *blíða* are listed above, n. 40. For the negative *með engri blíðu*, cf. xxxvii, 105 and xlv, 135. Also see above, Chap. IV, p. 98.
57 For the positive forms of the *byrjaði* phrase, see above, n. 21 and n. 34. For the negative form, see above, n. 22.
58 For instance of *tók því vel* and its forms, cf. vii, 11, 15; xvi, 37; xix, 48; xxiii, 63; xxvii, 75; xxx, 88; xl, 122, 123; liii, 163; lxxi, 208, 209; [*ekki fjarri*]. For *tók því illa* [*fjarri*], cf. xx, 50; xli, 124.
59 For instances of *lét vel yfir*, cf. ix, 17; xvi, 36; xxxi, 83; xxxiii, 91; xxxv, 98; xlii, 127; xlv, 137; xlix, 154; lii, 161; lxiii, 191. For the negative *lét illa* [*lítt*] *yfir*, cf. xl, 118; liv, 164; lxv, 193.
60 For instances of *líkar vel*, cf. v, 9; xx, 51; lxviii, 201. For *líkar* [*unnir*] *illa*, cf.

xiv, 30; xv, 36; xix, 45; xx, 50, xxi, 51; xxii, 62; xxiii, 64; xxv, 71 (2); xxx, 80; xxxv, 96; xxxvii, 108; xliv, 134; xlvii, 145; li, 158; lxv, 195, 196.

61 Compare lvii, 171: "Hon tók á því *vel at eins ok lítit af ǫllu*" ("She [Gudrún] committed herself neither one way nor the other"); and lxvii, 197: "Snorri svarar *vel at einu ok tók lítinn af ǫllu.*"

62 The frequent appearance of *jafnan* in the saga has double implication, one for the discursive level and applying to the immediate context, another for the formal level, stating in a nutshell the repetitive sameness found throughout the saga: cf. iv, 7; ix, 16, 18 (2); xxi, 53; xxiv, 66; xxxii, 86; xxxv, 96, 97; xxxvii, 103; xxxix, 111, 112 (4); xl, 122; xlvi, 142; xlvii, 148 (2); xlix, 153; lii, 160; lvii, 170, 171; lxv, 195; lxxi, 208 (2); lxxiii, 215; lxxiv, 217. *Jafnan* also takes on special function, hinting and confirming, see above, Chap. I, n. 18.

LITERARY PERSPECTIVES

1 Cf. Nordal, "Sagalitteraturen," p. 250.
2 The two references to Ari read as follows: "Svá segir Ari Þorgilsson inn fróði um líflát Þorsteins, at hann felli á Katanesi" (iv, 7) and "Síðan andaðisk Snorri. Hann hafði þá sjau vetr ins sjaunda tigar. Þat var einum vetri eptir fall Óláfs konungs ins helga; svá sagði Ari prestr inn fróði" (lxxviii, 226). In the extant version of Ari's *Íslendingabók* Snorri's death date is not mentioned, but the *Lxd.* author may well have had an earlier redaction.
3 Theodore Andersson, in his article "The Textual Evidence for an Oral Family Saga" (*Arkiv*, LXXXI [1966], 1-23), categorizes the function of such phrases according to the individual contexts in which they appear. Out of the two hundred and thirty-one instances which he has collected from most of the *Íslendinga sögur*, the majority prove to be empty convention, as suggested here and by Walter Baetke (*Über die Entstehung der Isländersagas, 29-31*). One hundred instances are found alone in *Reykdœla saga*, where they are an obvious mannerism. Literary, stylistic functions include marking a transition to a new topic, where the phrases act as fillers; vouching authority for superlative formulae or other extravagant facts which might seem otherwise dubious to the audience. Some signal a dearth of information, like the phrase "Nothing is said of his journey until he comes to..." which effects the transition to get on with the story without telling about the journey. Andersson considers genuine such alternate traditions as given through the pattern "some say this... others say that" (*sumir... sumir*), but which I would again see as a mannerism taken over from the Kings' Sagas. Snorri Sturluson, in particular, likes to present his material in this way, as does the historian Theodricus when relating how many wounds Saint Óláf received and by whom they were inflicted. Such variants obviously go back to hearsay. The historian either gives the varying versions for completeness or selects the one he considers most reliable. The *Íslendinga sögur*, it would seem, adopted this practice and formulation in order, indeed, for the authors to appear as "artless reporters," as Andersson suggests but rejects on the grounds that it is too bald-faced a conceit. But skaldic verses, too, were no doubt interspersed in the *Íslendinga sögur* for precisely the same purpose — to delude the audience that the tale was based on genuine tradition, whereas Snorri made use of authentic verse to substantiate what he was telling. As for the few instances where an author mentions legal or armed conflicts of which he has knowledge but does not develop in any detail, assuming the audience is already familiar with it, I would propose in contrast to Andersson, who sees in them underlying oral traditions, that they rest on knowledge from written accounts. The reference in *Lxd.*, for example, to Hrút's marriage with Unn Mardardóttir and her leaving him which caused the ill dealings between the Laxdalers and the Fljótshlídings (*Lxd.*, xix, 48), rather, I would think, should be traced to the lost *Fljótshlíðinga saga* which probably contained this material and was also the source for the development of the theme

in *Njáls saga* (see, E. Ó. Sveinsson in his introduction to *Njáls saga*, "Íslenzk fornrit," XII [Reykjavík, 1954], pp. XXIII and XLII. The fact that Sigmund Sighvatsson is not mentioned in any of the genealogies in *Njáls saga* but plays a prominent role in the hypothetical *Fljótshlíðinga saga*, should not be disturbing, as Sveinsson seems to feel, in evaluating the author's use of the latter, since it was not this aspect he wished to develop). In any case I see no reason to prefer oral traditions over against the more likely existence of a written source. References to persons about whom there could be much more told of them or that they are known from other sagas(e. g. *Lxd*., lxxviii, 229: "Gellir Þorkelsson bjó at Helgafelli til elli, ok er mart merkiligt frá honum sagt; hann kemr ok við margar sǫgur, þótt hans sé hér lítt getit") again point in the direction of fuller written sources rather than oral tales about them. Gellir is named in the *Heimskringla, Ljósvetninga s.* and *Bandamanna s.*, in Ari's *Íslendingabók* and in the Annals and *Sturlunga s*. Evidence for the use of written sources in the composition of the *Íslendinga sögur* and for their purely inventive and artistic nature continues to accrue to the disadvantage of the proponents of oral sources for the sagas.

4 Snorri's death one year after the fall of Saint Óláf, for instance, or Thorkel's death four years before Saint Óláf's (lxxvi, 223).

5 See xxviii, 77; xxxix, 112; lxxiii, 214.

6 See above, Chap. I, n. 3; Chap. III, n. 24. Sveinsson, Formáli ("Íslenzk fornrit," V), XLVIII-LX.

7 Cf. André Jolles, *Einfache Formen* (zweite unveränderte Auflage; Darmstadt: Wissenschaftliche Buchgesellschaft, 1958), pp. 23-41; also *Lives of the Saints* (the Voyage of St. Brendan; Bede: Life of Cuthbert; Eddius Stephanus: Life of Wilfrid), trans. J. F. Webb (Baltimore: Penguin Books, 1965), Introduction, p. 17; also my article "The Heroic Pattern: Old Germanic Helmets, *Beowulf* and *Grettis saga*," in *Old Norse Mythology and Literature: A Symposium*, ed. Edgar Polomé (Austin: University of Texas Press, 1969), pp. 165-166.

8 See above, Chap. IV, n. 18.

9 *Heimskringla: Óláfs saga helga* ("Íslenzk fornrit," XXVII), Ch. 224, p. 377, v. 147.

10 The flash-backs usually are signaled by phrases such as "Nú er at segja frá Ingjaldi" (xv, 35); the introduction of a new character takes place without ceremony: "Hrappr hét maðr" (x, 19); and the exit from the story is just as abrupt: "Ok lúku vér þar sǫgu frá Þorleiki" (xxxviii, 111).

11 *Lxd.* xxi, 56.

12 Anachronisms and the foreign words in the saga give evidence for its composition in the thirteenth century.

13 See below, pp. 188-89.

14 See above, Chap. IV, n. 18.

15 The examples here are cited from the *Morkinskinna* according to the edition of Finnur Jónsson (København, 1932), hence the different orthography.

16 The *Heimskringla* is cited after the "Íslenzk fornrit" edition, Vols. I-III, ed. by Bjarni Aðalbjarnarson (Reykjavík: Hið íslenzka fornritafélag,1941, 1945, 1951, respectively).

17 My article in the forthcoming Hollander Festschrift *Saga og språk* deals exclusively with tracing the origin of this pattern and its motifs.

18 Heller compares these words of Kjartan to those of Earl Tostis in Chap. 117 of the *Mork.* (erroneously cited as Chap. 35 in his *Laxdœla Saga und Königssagas*, p. 9). Kjartan's casting away of the weapon he compares with King Óláf Haraldsson's similar act in *Óláfs saga helga*, Chap. 228 (*ibid.*, p. 11).

19 Cf. Susanne Langer, *Feeling and Form* (New York: Charles Scribner & Sons, 1953), pp. 326-350.

[20] H. W. Fowler, *A Dictionary of Modern English Usage* (Oxford, 1958), (*sv.* Irony) pp. 295-296.
[21] See my article in the forthcoming Hollander Festschrift.
[22] The author's consciousness of the difference between conditions obtaining at the time of the saga's events and the time of writing comes to the fore in such passages as: "Ok sér þar tóptina, sem hann lét gera hrófit" (xiii, 26: "And one can see there traces of where he had the shed built"); or where he gives explanation for the men being able to conceal themselves in a woods where in his day there was no longer one: "Skógr þykkr var í dalnum í þann tíð" (lv, 165: "There was a thick woods in the valley at that time"); or in "þar sem Kaupstaðrinn í Bjǫrgvin er síðan" (xi, 22).
[23] For the previous discussion of the passage in connection with the understatement about Thorkel's concern, see above, Chap. I, p. 40. For the help this passage gives in dating the saga, see below, p. 190.
[24] What at first might seem like inadvertant slips or nodding on the part of the author may in fact be deliberate cues for his audience. In any case, it is in these places that we can best detect the trick: e. g. repetitions that appear too pat without a motivating circumstance; seemingly inappropriate uses of *sem fyrr*; misplacement of expected elements in a pattern, like *at skilnaði*; and of course the anachronisms.
[25] How far do other authors or other sagas go in verb-mixing? To answer this the following points will have to be considered first, abbreviations in the MSS and normalizing of editions. Each saga will have to be studied for these aspects individually.
[26] See in this connection the articles by M. C. van den Toorn, "Zeit und Tempus in der Saga," *Arkiv*, LXXVI (1961), 134-152; and by Carl C. Rokkjær, "Om tempusblandningen i islandsk prosa indtil 1250," *Arkiv*, LXXVIII (1963), 197-216.
[27] See above, p. 90.
[28] Cf. Turville-Petre, *Origins of Icelandic literature*, pp. 247-248. W. P. Ker, *Epic and Romance*, p. 209. See also above, Chap. IV, n. 18 on the use of Eddic themes and wording; also Sveinsson, "Íslenzk fornrit, V, Formáli, pp. XLVI-XLVII.
[29] See Heller, "Laxdœla saga und Sturlunga saga," p. 117 (comparison of Gudrún with Yngvild Thorgilsdóttir from the *Sturlu saga*) and p. 123 (comparison of the saga Gudrún with Gudrún Thórdardóttir from *Guðmundar saga dýra*).
[30] Parallels between *Sturlunga saga* and *Lxd.* were noted by Kr. Kålund, *Aarbøger for nordisk oldkyndighed og historie*, 1901, p. 287; by Finnur Jónsson, *Den oldnorske og oldislandske litteraturs historie* (2nd ed.; 1920-1924) II, 551; by Andreas Heusler, *Deutsche Literaturzeitung*, 1932, col. 2469; by Sveinsson, "Íslenzk fornrit," V, Formáli, pp. XXXII-XXXIV and in his *Dating the Icelandic Sagas*, p. 73; and most recently by Heller in "Laxdœla saga und Sturlunga saga," pp. 112-133.
[31] "Laxdœla saga und Sturlunga saga," p. 133.
[32] See *Sturlunga saga*, ed. Jón Jóhannesson, Magnús Finnbogason, Kristján Eldjárn Reykjavík: Sturlunguútgáfan, 1946), Formáli by Jón Jóhannesson, II, pp. xxvi, xxvii. Although the *Sturlu saga* is considered disjointed and poorly written, it comprises one of the best sources concerning the lives of persons living in Iceland in the twelfth century. The author has intimate knowledge of the persons, places, and events he is writing about. B. M. Ólsen ventured a guess that Snorri Sturluson might have written it, but most agree the style is too different to warrant that conclusion. Sturla Thórdarson is assumed to be too far from the events in time to have the intimate and close knowledge which the saga contains. I would venture a guess that Sturla Thórdarson's father, Thórd Sturluson, had begun a history of the family and that his son carried on the family tradition, especially since the *Íslendinga saga* takes up where *Sturlu saga* leaves off (*Sturlu saga* covers

the years 1148-1183; *Islendinga saga* takes up with the death of Hvamm-Sturla 1183). If Thórd Sturluson did write the *Sturlu saga*, this could explain the intimate details he would have known about his father Hvamm-Sturla (Sturla Thórdarson, son of Thórd Gillsson), the ineptness of style, the homely qualities.

33 Heller, "Das Alter der Laxdœla saga," *Zeitschrift für deutschen Altertum und deutsche Literatur*, XCVII (1968), 143-145.

34 *Islendinga saga*, Chap. 150, pp. 452-453, in *Sturlunga saga, op. cit.*

35 Interesting is a further parallel with *Laxdœla* where a ship arrives with drink on board and it was served and there was a lot of talk: "Þorkell hafði ok mikinn drykk á skipi sínu; var veitt allkappsamliga; varð þeim ok mart talat'" (lxviii, 199). And one of Thorkel's ships comes into Hrútafjord, just as does the one Óraekja and Sturla rode to meet. Interesting, too, is that Snorri Godi comes into this passage. Did Sturla Thórdarson puruse *Laxdœla* and use those places where he found Snorri Godi mentioned to fill in the account in the *Islendinga saga* about Snorri Sturluson? This is a hypothesis that would be worth testing out. Many questions about the *Islendinga saga* still need to be resolved. B. M. Ólsen felt that the saga ended with the year 1242; there is a break of three years between chapters 190 and 191; and there is the question of interpolation from other sagas into the text by Sturla or by the compiler of the *Sturlunga saga*.

36 There are varying opinions as to the direction of borrowing: Ólsen felt that *Lxd.* stood under the influence of the *Islendinga saga*: *Um Sturlunga* in "Safn til sögu Íslands," III (København, 1902), 427 ff. Sveinsson is more cautious: *Lxd.* could be the giver rather than the recipient: "Íslenzk fornrit," V, Formáli, p. XXXII.

37 *Islendinga saga*, Chap. 84, pp. 348, 350; Chap. 85, pp. 353, 355.

38 Sveinsson, "Íslenzk fornrit," V, 184, n. 1.

39 See above, p. 72.

40 The "ten or twelve" (*tíu eða tólf*) reading from MS C for the number on board at the drowning of Thorkel Eyjólfsson (see above, Chap. IV, n. 20) might be the right choice after all. The numbers ten and twelve alternate in the saga in any case — ten in raiding parties, twelve riding out together (*tólf saman*). If Snorri used the *tíu eða tólf* as a variation in his pattern of the drownings, then it must be a hint: the saga is the eleventh century and the thirteenth, it is *both* this *and* that. The expression appears to be a normal and frequent one used particularly about the number on board a vessel depending on its lading (see *Islendinga saga*, Chap. 142, p. 443). Normal usage of such expressions in everyday speech veils their secondary meaning within the saga. This is part of Snorri's method of camouflage, as we have seen. There is another place in the saga where alternate readings might be considered in this connection: when Bolli rides to Laugar to sue for Gudrún's hand, he rides there *tólf saman* (MS M). MS V has *tíu saman*, and zpap. MSS have *tíu saman eða tólf*. It looks as though the zpap. reading might be correct in view of the other instance of this sort and that the different scribes, not understanding why there should be any uncertainty about the number, selected the one or the other.

41 *Sturlunga saga*, I, (*Islendinga saga*), Chap. 35, pp. 269-271.

42 *Ibid.* Chap. 38, pp. 277-278.

43 *Ibid.*

44 See Jón Jóhannesson, *Sturlunga saga*, II, ix.

45 According to folk tradition, the poem was first recited in the graveyard at Síðumúli (possibly at the burial lot of the Sturlungs) just at the beginning of the great plague, 1402-1404. This is the first recorded instance of the use of the term Age

of the Sturlungs: see Jón Jóhannesson, *Sturlunga saga*, II, vii. The poem might be so rendered:

> Stagger we and stagger we
> with our heavy burden.
> Up has come the same as of yore,
> in the Sturlung age,
> in the Sturlung age.

APPENDIX I
Genealogical Table I
The Two Branches of Ketil's Family

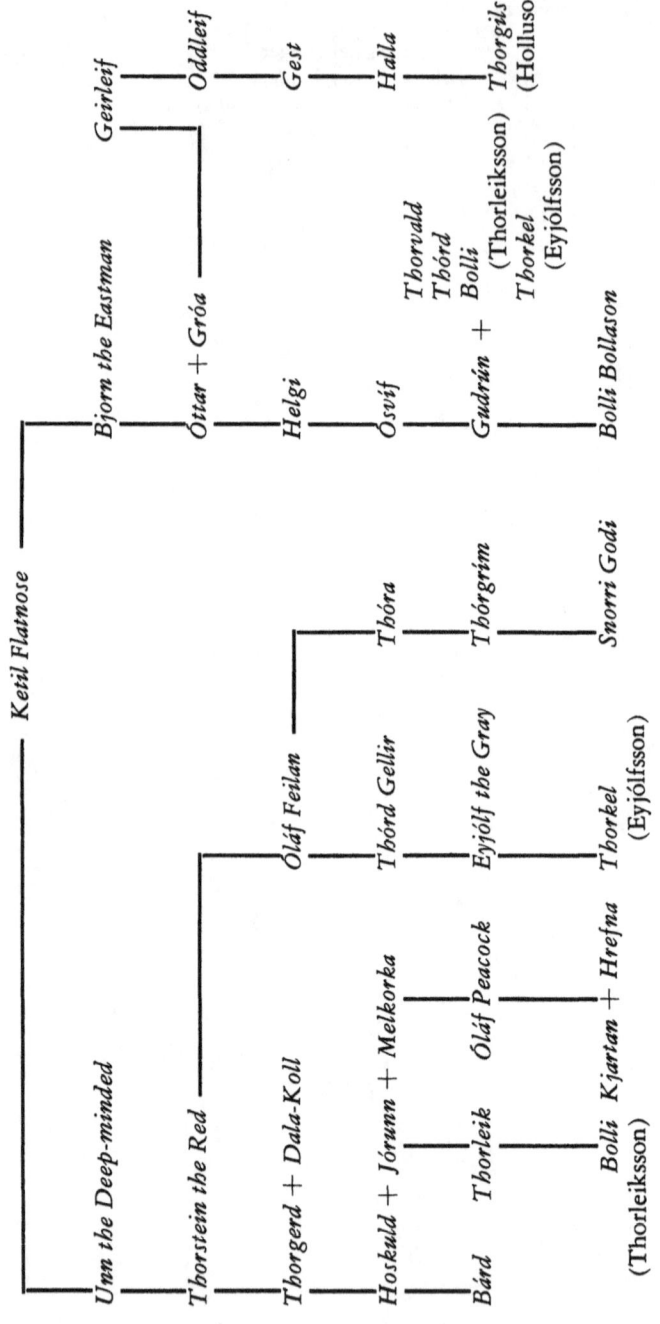

APPENDIX I
Genealogical Table II
Interrelationships between the House of Óláf and the House of Ósvíf

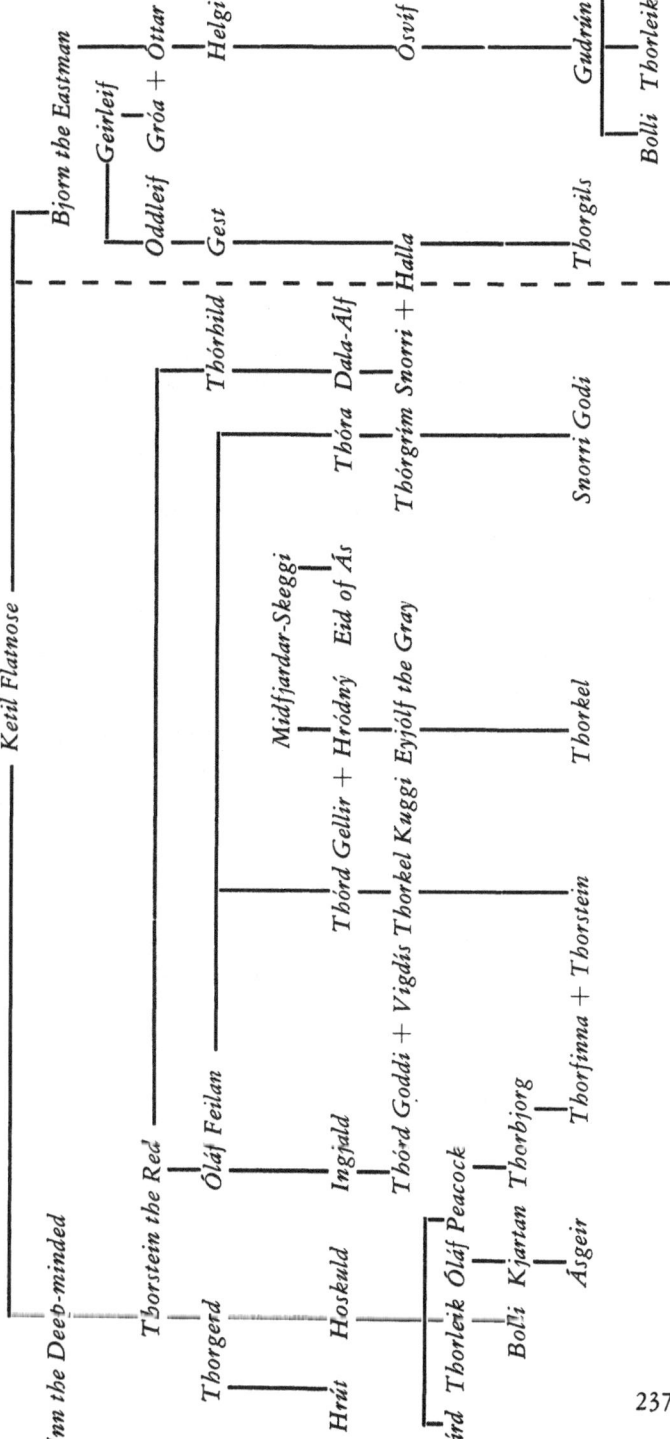

APPENDIX II

Manuscripts of *Laxdœla saga* and Abbreviations

Y-Class includes:

- M: Möðruvallabók, AM 132, fol. (Complete text on parchment; 1st half of 14th C.)
- D_1: AM 162 D_1, fol. (Fragment of 5 leaves; ca. 1300.)
- V: Vatnshyrna copy, ÍB 225, 4to. (Original text on parchment, dated ca. 1400 and based on D_1, burned in the fire of 1728. V is a reliable copy on paper done by Árni Magnússon's scribe, Ásgeir Jónsson.)

Z-Class includes:

- D_2: AM 162 D_2, fol. (Fragment of one parchment leaf, considered to be the oldest sample of the text, ca. 1250.)
- E: AM 162 E, fol. (Fragment of 5 parchment leaves, dated near close of 13th C.)
- S: Stockholm (Fragment of two parchment leaves from close of 14th C., preserved in Stockholm.)
- C: AM 309, 4to. (Fragment, derived apparently from E; written 1498.)
- zpap: paper MSS of the Z-class. (The four best, complete MSS in the group bear the numbers 158, 226, 123, 124. Sveinsson's edition usually notes the variants from 226; when the whole class is referred to as zpap, the wording follows 158.)

Other Abbreviations:

- *Hkr.*, I, II, III: *Heimskringla* in 3 vols., corresponding to "Íslenzk fornrit," XXVI, XXVII, XXVIII, ed. Bjarni Aðdalbjarnarson, (Reykjavík, 1941, 1945, 1951).
- *Lxd.*: *Laxdœla saga,* "Íslenzk fornrit," V, ed. E. Ó. Sveinsson, (Reykjavík, 1934).
- *Mork.*: *Morkinskinna*, ed. Finnur Jónsson, (København, 1932).

BIBLIOGRAPHY

Editions of the Laxdœla saga

Laxdœla saga. Kristian Kålund (ed.). København, 1889-1891.
—. Kristian Kålund (ed.). ("Altnordische Sagabibliothek," Heft 4.) Halle a. S., 1896.
—. Einar Ólafur Sveinsson (ed.). ("Íslenzk fornrit," V.) Reykjavík, 1934.

Translations of the Laxdœla saga

ALVING, HJALMAR (trans.). Laxdalingarnas saga. ("Isländska sagor," I.) Stockholm, 1935.
ARENT, A. MARGARET (trans.). The Laxdoela Saga. Seattle, 1964.
LARSEN, THØGER (trans.). Laksdøla saga. ("De islandske sagaer," I.) København, 1960.
MAGNÚSSON, MAGNÚS and PÁLSSON, HERMANN (trans.). Laxdaela Saga. Penguin Book, 1969.
MEISSNER, RUDOLF (trans.). Die Geschichte von den Leuten aus dem Lachswassertal. ("Thule," VI.) Jena, 1923.
PRESS, MURIEL A. C. (trans.). Laxdæla Saga. London, 1899.
PROCTOR, ROBERT (trans.). The Story of the Laxdalers. London, 1903.
SEIP, DIDRIK A. (trans.). Sagaen om Laksdølene. ("Íslandske ættesagaer," III.) Oslo, 1953.
VEBLEN, THORSTEIN (trans.). The Laxdæla Saga. New York, 1925.

Primary Sources

ARI ÞORGILSSON. Íslendingabók. Finnur Jónsson (ed.). København, 1930.
Eyrbyggja saga. Einar Ólafur Sveinsson (ed.). ("Íslenzk fornrit," IV.) Reykjavík, 1935.
Grágás: Islændernes lovbog i fristatens tid. Vilhjálmur Finsen (ed. and trans.). Vols. I-II, text; Vols. III-IV, trans. København, 1852-1870.
Heimskringla. Bjarni Aðalbjarnarson (ed.). Vols. I-III. ("Íslenzk fornrit," XXVI, XXVII, XXVIII.) Reykjavík, 1941, 1945, 1951.
Knýtlinga saga. ("Fornmanna sögur," XI.) Kaupmanhahöfn, 1828.

Landnámabók Íslands. København, 1925.
Morkinskinna. Finnur Jónsson (ed.). København, 1932.
Sæmundar-Edda. Finnur Jónsson (ed.). Reykjavík, 1926.
—. Gustav Neckel (ed.). 2d. ed. Heidelberg, 1927.
Sturlunga saga. Jón Jóhannesson, Magnús Finnbogason, Kristján Eldjárn (ed.). Vols. I-II. Reykjavík, 1946.

Secondary Literature

ANDERSON, SVEN AXEL. "The Origin of the Old Norse Sagas: A Brief Review of the Controversy," *Scandinavian Studies,* XIV (1935-1937), 25-30.

—. "The Attitude of the Historians toward the Old Norse Sagas," *Scandinavian Studies,* XV (1938-1939), 266-274.

ANDERSSON, THEODORE. *The Problems of Icelandic Saga Origins: A Historical Survey.* New Haven and London, 1964.

—. "The Textual Evidence for an Oral Family Saga," *Arkiv,* LXXXI (1966), 1-23.

—. *The Icelandic Family Saga: An Analytic Reading.* ("Harvard Studies in Comparative Literature," XXVIII.) Cambridge, 1967.

BÅÅTH, A. W. *Studier öfver kompositionen i några isländska ättsagor.* Lund, 1885.

BAETKE, WALTER. "Zum Erzählstil der Isländersagas," *Mitteilungn der Islandfreunde,* XVII (Heft 3/4, 1940), 63 ff.

—. *Über die Entstehung der Isländersagas.* ("Berichte über die Verhandlungen der sächischen Akademie der Wissenschaften zu Leipzig: Philologisch-historische Klasse," CII, No. 5.) Berlin, 1956.

BOLTON, W. F. "The Heart of *Hrafnkatla,*" *Scandinavian Studies,* XLIII (1971), pp. 35-52.

BOUMAN, A[RI] C. *Patterns in Old English and Old Icelandic Literature.* ("Leidse germanistische en anglistische reeks, van de Rijksuniversiteit te Leiden," I.) Leiden, 1962.

BUGGE, ALEXANDER. "Entstehung und Glaubwürdigkeit der isländischen Saga," *Zeitschrift für deutsches Altertum,* LI (1909), 23-38.

EKBO, SVEN. "Nordiska personbinamn under vikinga- och medeltid," *Personnamn.* ("Nordisk kultur," VII.) Stockholm, 1948. Pp. 269-284.

EINARSSON, STEFÁN. *A History of Icelandic Literature.* New York, 1957.

FALK, HJALMAR. *Altwestnordische Kleiderkunde.* ("Videnskapsselskapets skrifter II: historisk-filosofiske klasse," 1918, No. 3.) Kristiania, 1919.

—. *Altnordische Waffenkunde.* ("Videnskapsselskapets skrifter II: hist.-filos. klasse," 1914, No. 6.) Kristiania, 1914.

HAECKEL, MARGARETE. *Die Darstellung und Funktion des Traumes in der isländischen Familiensaga.* Hamburg, 1934.

HALLBERG, PETER. *Den isländska sagan.* ("Verdandis skriftserie," VI.) Stockholm, 1956.

—. *Snorri Sturluson och Egils saga Skallagrímssonar; ett försök till språklig författarbestämning.* ("Studia Islandica: Íslenzk fræði," XX.) Reykjavík, 1962.

—. *Óláfr Þórðarson hvítaskáld, Knýtlinga saga och Laxdæla saga.* ("Studia islandica," XXII.) Reykjavík, 1963.

—. "Óláfr Þórðarson hvítaskáld, Knýtlinga saga och Laxdæla: en motkritik," *Arkiv för nordisk filologi,* LXXX (1965), 123-156.

—. "Íslendinga saga och Egla, Laxdæla, Eyrbyggja, Njála, Grettla," *Maal og Minne* (1965), pp. 91 ff.

HAM, JOHANNES VAN. *Beschouwingen over de literaire Betekenis der Laxdœla Saga.* Amsterdam, 1932.

HELLER, ROLF. *Literarisches Schaffen in der Laxdœla Saga.* ("Saga: Untersuchungen zur nordischen Literatur- und Sprachgeschichte," Heft 3.) Halle a. S., 1960.

—. "Studien zu Aufbau und Stil der Laxdœla Saga," *Arkiv,* LXXV (1960), 113-167.

—. "Laxdœla saga und Sturlunga saga," *Arkiv,* LXXVI (1961), 112-133.

—. "*Laxdœla saga und Königssagas.* ("Saga,'" Heft 5.) Halle a. S., 1961.

—. "Laxdœla saga und Bischofssagas," *Arkiv,* LXXVII (1962), 90-95.

—. "Droplaugarsona saga, Vápnfirðinga saga, Laxdoela saga," *Arkiv,* LXXVIII (1963), 140-169.

—. "Studien zu Aufbau und Stil der Vápnfirðinga saga," *Arkiv,* LXXVIII (1963), 170-189.

—. "Laxdœla saga und Knytlinga saga," *Arkiv,* LXXX (1965), 95-122.

—. "Neue Wege zur Verfasserbestimmung bei den Isländersagas und ihre Anwendung auf die Laxdoela saga," *Forschungen und Fortschritte,* XLI (1967), 239 ff.

—. "Das Alter der Laxdœla saga," *Zeitschrift für deutsches Altertum,* XCVII (1968), 134-155.

—. "Der Verfasser der Laxdœla saga und sein Verhältnis zur Sturlubók," in *Afmælisrit Jóns Helgasonar: 30. júní 1969.* Jakob Benediktsson et al. (eds.). Reykjavík 1969. (Not available to me.)

HEUSLER, ANDREAS. *Die altgermanische Dichtung.* ("Handbuch der Literaturwissenschaft.") 2d ed. Potsdam, 1941.

—. *Die Anfänge der isländischen Saga.* ("Abhandlungen der königl. preuss. Akademie der Wissenschaften, philos.-historische Classe," 1913, No. 9.) Berlin, 1914.

HRUBY, ARTHUR. *Aufsätze zur Technik der isländischen Saga: Die Kategorien ihrer Personencharakteristik.* Wien, 1929-1932.

JOLLES, ANDRÉ. *Einfache Formen.* 2nd ed. Darmstadt, 1958.

JÓNSSON, FINNUR. *Den oldnorske og oldislandske litteraturs historie.* Vols. I-III. 1st ed. København, 1894-1902. 2nd ed. København, 1920-1924.

KELCHNER, GEORGIA D. *Dreams in Old Norse Literature.* Cambridge, 1935.

KER, WILLIAM PATON. *Epic and Romance.* London, 1931.

KERSBERGEN, ANNA CORNELIA. "Frásagnir in de Laxdœla Saga," *Neophilologus,* XIX (1934), 65-67.

LID, NILS. "Magiske fyrestellingar og bruk," *Folketro* ("Nordisk kultur," XIX.) Stockholm, 1935. Pp. 1-76.

—. "Gudar og gudedyrking," *Religionshistorie.* ("Nordisk kultur," XXVI.) Stockholm, 1942. Pp. 80-153.

LIESTØL, KNUT. *The Origin of the Icelandic Family Sagas.* Translated by A. G. Jayne. Oslo, 1930.

MAURER, KONRAD. "Die unächte Geburt nach altnordischem Rechte," *Sitzungsberichte der philos.-philolog. und historischen Classe der königl. bayer. Akademie der Wissenschaften, 1883.* München, 1884. Pp. 3-86.

MÜLLER, PETER ERASMUS. *Sagabibliothek.* Vols. I-III. Kiøbenhavn, 1817-1820.

MUNDT, MARINA. *Sturla Þórdarson und die Laxdæla saga.* ("Skrifter fra instituttene for nordisk språk og litteratur ved universitetene i Bergen, Oslo og Trondheim," Nr. 4.) Universitetsforlaget: Bergen, Oslo, Tromsö, 1969.

NORDAL, SIGURDUR. *Hrafnkatla.* ("Studia islandica," VII.) Reykjavík, 1940.

—. *Hrafnkels Saga Freysgoða: A study.* Translated by R. George Thomas. Cardiff, 1958.

—. "Sagalitteraturen," *Litteraturhistorie: Norge og Island.* ("Nordisk kultur," VIII: B.) København, 1953. Pp. 180-273.

—. *The Historical Element in the Icelandic Family Sagas.* Glasgow, 1957.

ÓLSEN, BJÖRN M. "Landnáma og Laxdœla saga," *Aarbøger for nordisk oldkyndighed og historie,* XXIII (1908), 151-232.

—. *Om Gunnlaugs saga ormstungu: en kritisk undersøgelse.* ("Det kgl. danske videnskabsselskabs skrifter, hist. og filos. afd.," 7. række, II: 1.) København, 1911.

Origines Islandicae. Gudbrand Vigfusson and F. York Powell (ed. and trans.). Vols. I-II. Oxford, 1905.

PHILLPOTTS, BERTHA S. *Edda and Saga.* New York, 1931.

RAUMER, RUDOLF VON. *Geschichte der germanischen Philologie.* ("Geschichte der Wissenschaften in Deutschland," IX.) München, 1870.

ROKKJÆR, CARL C. "Om tempusblandningen i islandsk prosa indtil 1250," *Arkiv,* LXXVIII (1963), 197-216.

RUBOW, PAUL V. "The Icelandic Sagas," *Two Essays.* Copenhagen, 1945. Pp. 30-64.

SCHACH, PAUL. "The Anticipatory Literary Setting in the Old Icelandic Family Sagas," *Scandinavian Studies*, XXVII (1955), pp. 1-13.

SCHILDKNECHT-BURRI, MARGRIT. *Die altertümlichen und jüngeren Merkmale der Laxdœla Saga*. Luzern, 1945.

SCHNEIDER, HERMANN. "Die altnordische Literatur in ihrem Werdegang," *Euphorion*, XLVII (1953), 1-15.

SCHWERIN, CLAUDIUS FREIHERR VON. "Die Ehescheidung im älteren isländischen Recht," *Deutsche Islandsforschung*, I (Breslau, 1930), 283-299.

SPRINGER, OTTO. "Style in the Icelandic Family Sagas,'" *Journal of English and Germanic Philology*, XXXVIII (1953), 107-128.

STRÖMBÄCK, DAG. "Att helga land," *Festskrift tillägnad Axel Hägerström*. Uppsala, 1928. Pp. 198-220.

—. "Von der isländischen Familiensaga," *Beiträge zur Geschichte der deutschen Sprache*, LXVI (1942), 117-133.

SVEINSSON, EINAR ÓLAFUR. *Verzeichnis isländischer Märchenvarianten*. ("Folklore Fellows Communications," LXXXIII.) Helsinki, 1929.

—. *The Age of the Sturlungs*. ("Islandica," XXXVI.) Ithaca, N.Y., 1953.

—. *Dating the Icelandic Sagas*. ("The Viking Society for Northern Research: Text Series," III.) London, 1958.

TOORN, M. C. VAN DEN. "Zeit und Tempus in der Saga," *Arkiv*, LXXVI (1961), 134-152.

—. "Erzählsituation und Perspektive in der Saga," *Arkiv*, LXXVII (1962), 68-83.

TURVILLE-PETRE, GABRIEL. *Origins of Icelandic Literature*. Oxford, 1953.

VRIES, JAN DE. *Altnordische Literaturgeschichte*. Vols. I-II. 1st. ed. Berlin, 1941-1942.

—. *Altnordische Literaturgeschichte*. ("Grundriß der germanischen Philologie," XV-XVI). 2nd ed. Vols. I-II. Berlin, 1964, 1967.

INDEX OF TOPICS AND CONCEPTS

Aesthetic method, 11, 12, 36, 88, 122, 147-48; need for, 1, 4, 5, 10; results of, 145, 147-48, 154, 172, 183. *See also* Language, provenance of, irrelevant; *Laxdœla saga*, as aesthetic unit.

Alternation. *See* Rhythm; Stylistic devices, contrastives

Ambiguity, 30, 39, 144, 154, 167, 168. *See also* Camouflage, means of; Double treatment; Rhetorical devices
— in idioms: *at drepa skeggi*, 23-24, 167; *hurðir loknar*, 34, 167; *spenna um þonguls-hofuð*, 24, 49, 52, 167; *snarisk í bragð*, 27-28, 29, 167
— in words with double intent: *fyrðar*, 29, 184; *kyrrt*, 32-33, 40, 98, 167; *ráðakostr*, 39, 131; *samlendr*, 28, 168, 172-73; *þurr*, 30, 203 n. 14 (See also *Laxdœla saga*, coded words in)

Anachronism: chivalric fashion (*glaðel, sem títt er í útlondum*), 155, 174; ordeals "then" and "now," 40-41; shield insignias (lion, cross, knight), 142, 227-28 n. 48. *See also* Author, time consciousness of; Time, discrepancies in

Analogy. *See also* Simultaneity, of time; Superimpositions, of time
— between "before" and "now," 63, 181
— between "before," "now," and "after," 178, 179
— between Christianization of Norway and of Iceland, 68, 119, 120, 193, 195
— between eleventh and thirteenth centuries, 174, 175-77, 179, 184, 234 n. 40; as coded message based on formal principles, 172, 177, 181, 182; as a parable, 182
— between generations, 79, 80, 85, 94, 119-20, 120, 125, 125-26; of saga times and author's time, 178, 184
— between gold and silver, 22
— between precarious balance and suspended time of saga and point of time in Iceland's history, 173, 175

Anticipation: direct means of presenting (*See* Prophecy); indirect means of presenting (*See* Retrospective cues)

Antonyms, 92, 169. *See also* Reversals

Ari Thorgilsson, function of, 149, 178

at skilnaði: as motif, 132, 138, 224-25 n. 30, 226 n. 46

Author:
— analogous to fate, 161, 168
— and his audience, 26, 169, 171, 172, 182, 184 (*See also* Omniscience, of author and audience)
— creative process of, 71, 134, 171, 179, 226-27 n. 46
— identification of, 8-10, 183-85, 187, 190, 191, 192
— intrusion of, 25, 40-41, 169, 173

245

— as man of his times, 152, 192
— method of, general, 26, 31, 45, 62, 127, 155-56, 161, 168-73
— method of, in handling materials of language, 94, 154, 171, 186; in handling patterns, 148, 154, 164, 170-71, 192, 226-27 n. 46; in handling sources, 155, 157-58, 186; in handling tenses, 176-77, 186
— nodding of, 138, 167-68, 174, 199 n. 11, 201-2 n. 3, 204 n. 18, 209 n. 3, 218 n. 29, 226 n. 46, 233 n. 24
— preferences of, deliberate, 63, 94
— talents of, 182-83, 184-85, 192
— time consciousness of, 40-41, 155, 174-75, 233 n. 22

Balance (equalization). *See also* Comparison, formal symbolism of; Recurrence, formal symbolism of; Repetition, formal symbolism of
— attained through bargaining, 53, 88, 159
— compensatory, 68-69, 88, 96, 115, 159
— through grammatical-lexical pattern, 52, 53, 88, 90-91, 159, 161
— through legal-social mores, 88, 89-90, 158-59
— numerically expressed, 92-94
— between positives and negatives, 73, 124, 144, 159, 163
— precariousness of, within the saga, 90, 96, 122, 124, 159, 177, 192
— precariousness of, in thirteenth-century Iceland, 173, 177
— between stereotypes and individuals, 164, 192
— through structure, 44, 63, 82, 96, 115, 177

Bargaining: examples of, 88-89; for Hjardarholt, 47-51 (text), 51-53 (discussion); negative aspect of, 89; significance of, 88-89, 159, 168

Book-prosaists, 4, 11

Camouflage, means of producing, 23, 30, 39, 76, 141, 144, 147-48, 167-71, 172, 174, 176-77, 192, 234 n. 40

Characters, 162-64 (*See also* Stereotypes vs. individuals); as composites of linguistic units, 73, 81, 95, 163; as composites from various sources and times, 157, 163, 185-86; as counterparts, 77, 80, 82, 162, 163, 168, 191, 195, 196. (*See also* Comparison, examples of; Inimical brothers); negative vs. positive traits of, 73, 162; similarity of, 72-73 (*See also* Generations); subordinate to formal concept, 162, 163-64; traits of, confirmed, 41-42, 62

Christianization, 56. *See* Analogy, between Christianization of Norway and of Iceland

Clichés: effectiveness of, 135, 136, 143-44, 153-54; examples of, 135-36; origin of, 124, 135, 151, 153-54. *See also* Superlatives

Comparison: compensatory aspect of, 65, 88; examples of, 65-73, 74-82 (inimical brothers), 82-87; as foreground 124, 177; related to Foreknowledge, 95; formal symbolism of, 88, 123, 159; function of, 65, 94-95; grammatically expressed in *jafn*-words, 90; implied in *títt* phrases, 174; retrospective nature of, 65

Cultural influences: chivalric, 142, 143, 151, 152, 155-56, 162, 163; Christian, 87, 151, 162, 163; contemporary Icelandic, 130, 143, 156, 157 (*See also* Norwegian court, Iceland's relationship to); heroic, 151, 152, 162 (See also *Edda*, poetic or Sæmundar)

Cultural periods: analogy of, 181; merging of, 142, 151, 152, 155-56, 183; as source material, 155, 157-58, 185-86; 186-89

Destiny, 44, 160, 160-61, 166. *See also* Fate

Determinism. *See* Fate; Inevitability

Dialogue. *See* Discourse

Discourse, 34, 38, 52, 60-61, 127, 148-49, 165

Double treatment, 125, 144, 167, 168, 172. *See also* Ambiguity; Duplicity; Overlapping; Recurrence, qualified function of; Shift of focus

Dramatic presentation, 166; as comedy, 166, 169; as imminent future or theatrical present, 165, 166, 175; as foreground, 124, 165, 175; material for, ready-made, 160, 166; as tragedy, 166, 175, 178, 183

Dreams: as ambiguous, 17, 26, 160, 167; examples of Án's, 20, 181, 216 n. 13; of Gudrún's, 16, 21-22, 23, 42; of Óláf's about ox Harri, 16; of Thorkel Eyjólfsson's 23; as foreshadowing device, 18, 160

Drownings: of Geirmund and Festargarm, 217 n. 19; of Thórd Ingunnarson, 112; of Thorkel Eyjólfsson, 113; of Thorstein Surt, 110-12; schematized pattern for, 113

Duplicity: of Gudrún, 28-29, 85; of Hoskuld, 75, 78; of *Lxd.* author, 172, 176, 184; of Melkorka, 85; of Norwegian kings, 195; of Snorri Godi, 28-30, 168, 183-84; of Snorri Sturluson, 195

Edda, poetic or Sæmundar, 151, 155, 156, 185; themes of, in *Lxd.*, 109-110, 151, 157, 185-86, 217 n. 18

Edda, prose or Snorri's, 151, 185

Embellishment: double function of, as adornment and formal increment, 86, 140-41, 169; as camouflage, 29. *See also* Increment; Recurrence, progressive enhancement of

Epic: background, 16, 124, 134, 164-65, 175; devices, 165; magnification, 134, 135, 143, 178; time (past time), 165, 175

Ethical code: amalgamated with destiny, 17, 63, 160, 161, 164, 175, 193; significance of, 179; symbolically expressed, 12, 89, 122, 123-24, 159, 161, 163-64

Evens and odds, 88, 90, 119

Fate: as determinism, 17, 18; as foreshadowing device, 6, 15, 16, 17; implied in *ǫndvegissúlur*, 15; as inheritance from pagan past, 153; and will of characters, 17, 20, 160, 163, 201-2 n. 3

Folklore: theories of, applied to sagas, 2, 3, 4, 198 n. 3; influences from, 67, 121-22, 151, 152, 152-53, 216 n. 8, n. 9, 221-22 n. 5

Foreknowledge: *See also* Prophecy; Retrospective cues
— as an apparition of destiny, 15-18
— direct means of presenting, 18-26
— formal function of, 44;
— reinforced through controlled linguistic choises, 26, 63, 122; through repetition, 20-21, 25, 28, 30, 53, 53-54, 54-55
— relationship of, to Comparison, 95; to Recurrence, 144-45; to Repetition, 47, 53
— structural features of: anticipation-recollection rhythm, 44, 45; point-counterpoint precision, 26, 31, 44, 45, 47, 53
— veiled forms of (anticipation in retrospect), 26-45

Free-prosaists, 3, 4

Genealogies: as literary device, 41, 43, 155, 205 n. 22; historical function of, 43, 149, 155, 219 n. 33; as evidence of time relationships, 44, 173, 185

Generations: as analogous to one another, 79, 80, 85, 94, 119-20, 120, 125, 125-26, 178, 184; progressive enhancement of, 82, 94, 135, 138, 142, 144, 177-78, 178; as related to Recurrence, 123, 224 n. 29

Geographical setting, 164, 196

Goadings, 100-104; archetypal pattern for, 104

247

Gold and silver, role of: in band at Helgi's hut, 72, 189; in Gudrún's dream, 22; in inheritance claim, 75; in regard to sword Footbiter, 227 n. 47

Hagiography, influence of, 5, 150

Heimskringla, as source for *Lxd.*, 8, 9, 155, 156-57, 185

Helgi's hut, attack at, 71-72, 143, 156, 188, 210 n. 9; thirteenth-century origin of, 143, 156, 189, 191

Hero's accoutrements:
— descriptions of, 139-40 (Óláf Peacock), 140-41 (Kjartan), 141-42 (Bolli Bollason)
— origin of, 142, 152, 171
— related motifs: *auðkenndr*, 139, 141, 142; gift from a king (*er ... konungr gaf honum*), 86, 138, 140, 142, 226-27 n. 46; scarlet clothes, 86, 139, 140, 142; *at vápnum ok klæðum*, 120, 138, 138-39, 140, 141, 218 n. 30
— sources for, 142-43, 156, 171, 227 n. 47, 227-28 n. 48

Historical: background in thirteenth century, 129-30, 173, 177; illusion, 134-35, 148-50, 177, 227-28 n. 48; reliability in sagas, 2, 3, 4; in *Lxd.*, 7-8, 82, 148, 153, 155, 158, 172, 189, 219 n. 33, 227 n. 47

History: and art, 179, 185; author's view of, 178-79, 180; philohophy of, in Middle Ages, 178, 192

Increment: as compositional method, 140; examples of, 54, 60, 104, 105, 114, 116, 116-17, 117, 119, 120-21, 121, 125, 128, 129; as related to thirteenth-century analogy, 178. *See also* Embellishment, double function of; Rhetorical devices, general

Inevitability (inflexibilitay, predeterminism), as concept underlying ethical, social, metaphysical spheres, 17, 63, 123, 144, 158-60, 160, 161, 175

Inimical brothers, 74-82, 152, 181, 211 n. 15; as composites of verbal components, 163; likenesses of, 74, 76, 77, 78, 79; opposition of, 74-75, 76, 77, 78; not wholly opposite, 76, 78, 211 n. 15; shift in character of, 79; significance of, for analogy, 181; tripartite arrangement of, 73-74, 77, 79

Irony: defined, 167; distinctive quality of saga, 144, 173, 182, result of implied discrepancies, 34, 40, 61, 144, 168, 173; of double audience and omniscience, 160-61, 167, 168. *See also* Ambiguity; Omniscience; Wit

Íslendinga saga, relationship of, to *Lxd.*, 9, 10, 156, 157, 186-90, 191. *See also* Thorvald, attack on sons of

jafnan: as anticipatory device, 35, 54, 54-55, 59, 95, 204-5 n. 18; as confirmative, 29, 31, 32, 59, 205 n. 18; related to Foreknowledge and inevitability, 144, 181, 230 n. 62 (See also *Laxdœla saga*, coded words in)

kátr, as literary device to signal its opposite, 98, 154, 167, 188, 215 n. 1. *See also* Stylistic devices, contrastives

Killings, three main: motifs in, 106-8; participants in, 105, 215 n. 7; sources for pattern of, 156

kunnigt: examples of, 205 n. 25; as related to Foreknowledge, 44, 63 (See also *Laxdœla saga*, coded words in)

Language. *See also* Ambiguity; *Laxdœla saga*, overall style of; Rhetorical devices
— formal dimension of: abstracted word-pattern (schemes), 12, 63, 96, 118, 122, 147, 148, 161, 163-64, 170, 172; unity of form and content, 30, 45, 53, 55, 63, 70, 122, 127, 147, 159, 169
— potential of, beyond discursive content, 30, 32, 34; examples of, 19, 24, 34—35, 37, 39, 45, 55, 126-27, 204-5 n. 18

— precision and necessity of, vs. arbitrariness, 15, 26, 31, 32, 34, 44, 51-52, 52, 54, 63, 148, 161
— provenance of, irrelevant, 12, 88, 92, 122, 124, 147-48, 164, 171, 190, 206 n. 31, 216 n. 11 (See also *Laxdœla saga*, as aesthetic unit)

Laxdœla saga:
— as aesthetic unit, 13, 88, 92, 96, 122, 145, 147, 176, 183, 190
— as analogy with thirteenth century, 174, 175-77, 179, 184, 190-91, 234 n. 40
— as coded message, 148, 181-82
— coded words in: *bæði... ok*, 92, 94, 147-48, 181; *hvárki... né*, 92, 94, 144, 147-48, 181; *hvárrtveggja*, 92, 93-94, 144, 147-48; *jafnan*, 144, 147-48, 131, 230 n. 62; *jafnskjótt*, 180; *jafn*-words, 90, 147-48; *kunnigt*, 44, 147-48; *sem áðr* [*fyrr*], 44, 55, 63, 99, 147-48, 173; *tíu eða tólf*, 190-91, 234 n. 40; *tólf* (twelve), 190; *tveir kostir*, 92-93, 147-48, 181; *upp kveðit... niðr koma*, 26, 127; *ván*, 44, 147-48, 173; *ýmisst*, 44-45, 147-48
— comparison with Greek drama, 17, 163, 166, 167
— cultural sources for, 143, 151, 155, 157-58, 185-86
— dating of, 189-91, 232 n. 12
— economy of, 26, 31, 63
— oral sources for, 153
— overall structure of, 63, 65, 88, 94; based on twos (balance, preparation-fulfillment, symmetry, comparison, equalization, juxtaposition), 43, 44, 47, 53, 63, 82, 88, 94, 95-96, 115, 159; based on threes (triple repetitions, three parts), 97, 110; as merger of two-ness and three-ness, 115, 120, 122, 166, 182 (*See also* Tripartite form)
— overall style of, 125, 144, 154, 167-73 (*See also* Ambiguity; Irony; Stylistic devices)
— as a parable, 177, 182, 196
— as parody, 172, 182
— parts of, 16, 17, 95-96
— plot structure of, 15-17, 175
— studies on: Bååth, 5-6; van Ham, 7-8; Heller, 7-8, 11-12; Hallberg, 8-9; Mundt, 9-10; Schildknecht-Burri, 7
— written sources for, 8, 10, 153, 154-58, 186-89

misjofn verða morginverkin, 109, 157, 216-17 n. 17

Models (modeling), 71, 73-74, 95, 164; distribution in parts of saga, 72, 73-74, 82, 110, 113-14; examples of 71, 72, 74-82, 82-85, 85-86, 99, 100, 108, 119, 162; preparatory, not most complete, 95, 134; as prototypes, 95, 162-63; in sequence of generations, 85, 86, 95, 138; scrambled, 95. *See also* Patterns

Moral code. *See* Ethical code

Morkinskinna, as source for *Lxd.*, 8, 155, 156, 227 n. 47, 227-28 n. 48

MSS, 217 n. 23, 238; variant readings from, 205 n. 21, n. 24, 208 n. 7, 209 n. 4, 215 n. 7, 216 n. 17, 217 n. 20, 228-29 n. 29, 234 n. 40

Norwegian court, Iceland's relationship to, 129 30, 130-31 (offer of position at court), 131 (wooing of favor), 185, 193, 194, 195

Omniscience, 167-168; of author and audience, 25, 53, 56, 57, 161, 167, 168, 180, 201 n. 3; as evidenced by double audience, 26, 34, 51, 52, 160-61, 167-68 (*See also* Ambiguity; Irony); as evidenced by untransmitted statements, 32, 38, 52-53, 56, 56-57, 57, 57-58, 58, 60, 207 n. 5, 207-8 n. 6; related to objectivity, 168

Oral tradition, 150-54; motifs of, 151, 152, 152-53, 154, 158 (*See also* Folklore); techniques of, 4-5, 149, 153-54, 231-32 n. 3; as substratum, 2-5, 153

Ordeals (heathen and Christian); as evidence of anachronism, 40-41; as evidence of author's intrusion, 41; as means for dating the saga, 190; as evidence of time comparison, 174

Overlapping: of characters, 73, 78, 79, 81, 95, 157, 163, 185-86; of comic and tragic, 166, 169; of epic and dramatic modes, 165, 166, 175; of ethical and metaphysical spheres, 17, 160, 164, 175; of functional categories, 78, 79, 95, 97, 120, 127, 144-45, 172; of time periods, 143, 174, 175, 178, 179

Parties: at Hól, 20, 188, 215 n. 5; at Laugar and Hjardarholt, 97-99; as precondition for tragedy, 98, 169, 215 n. 5 (See also *kátr*; Stylistic devices, contrastives)

Patterns: archetypal nature of (nucleus patterns), 99, 104, 106, 108, 110, 113, 137-143 (hero's accoutrements), 171, 179; change in, significant, 76, 98, 126, 132, 138, 144, 181; compelling force of, 132, 137, 138, 226-27 n. 46 (*See also* Author, nodding of); concealment of, 76, 164, 167, 169-71, 172, 174, 182; constancy of, despite variation, 79, 108, 115, 122, 134, 170, 179; cumulative effect of, 171, 178; formulaic (stereotyped) nature of, 138, 164, 171, 226 n. 46; means of varying, 60, 70, 73, 79, 95, 104, 108, 112-13, 115, 126, 134, 141, 143, 154, 170-71; mutual elucidation of, 79, 81, 115, 211 n. 22, 217 n. 23; predictability of, related to Foreknowledge, 122, 144; significance of, for analogy, 177, 179; used to do the concealing, 39, 125, 129, 131, 144, 171-72, 223 n. 15, 234 n. 40

Poems: as riddles, 29, 181-82, 184; to further historical illusion, 149

Prophecy: as anticipatory device, 18, 43-44, 160; examples of direct type of, 18-26, 202-3 n. 9; examples of indirect type of (anticipation in retrospect), 26-30, 30-43; fulfillment of, precise, 24, 25, 26, 31, 44; Part I of saga as, 95-96; prediction-fulfillment structure of, 25, 26, 39, 40, 44, 45, 47; progression-regression rhythm of, 44, 45, 174; as representing supernatural power (fate, destiny), 15, 160; signalled by phrases of prediction, 26, 38, 51, 202-3 n. 9; subtlety of, 17, 30, 44, 160, 167; suspense not compromised by, 17, 18, 44, 160; whole saga as, 177

Quadruplets: defined, 118; examples of, 118-20, 218 n. 30, n. 32; structurally related to Repetition and Comparison, 97, 120, 122

Recurrence, 122-23, 123-24;
— balance in, 124, 144, 159, 177
— background for Repetition and Comparison, 124, 143-44, 175
— cyclical nature of, 123-24, 134, 145, 177
— as epic base, 164-65
— as foreground in thirteenth-century analogy, 177, 178
— formal symbolism of, 123-24, 144, 159
— magnification of, 124, 134-35, 143, 178
— motifs of: abundance, 135; congeniality, 135; early maturity, 125, 151; favorite child, 79, 126-27, 152; numerical greatness, 134-35; scarlet clothes, 139, 140, 142; *skart*, 137; superlative designations, 135-36; weapons and clothes, 138, 139-42 (hero's accoutrements)
— progressive nature of: temporally expressed through forward movement of generations, 123; qualitatively expressed in increased enhancement (pageantry-like descriptions of hero), 82, 135, 138, 139-42
— qualified function of (overlap with Repetition and Comparison), 86-87, 124, 125, 131, 137, 138, 141, 143, 171-72, 175
— quality and quantity of, 124, 178
— exemplified by round of life: 124-25, 129 (births), 125-28 (betrothals), 128-29 (wedding), 129-33 (career abroad), 133 (old age and death); by round of sameness, 144

— structurally related to Foreknowledge, Repetition, and Comparison, 144, 144-45
— uncamouflaged (used to conceal), 39, 125, 129, 131, 144, 171-72

Repetition. *See also* Omniscience
— examples of, 53-54 ,54, 55-56, 59-60, 60, 61-62, 62
— as foreground, 124, 175
— formal symbolism of, 63, 96, 122, 123, 124
— as leitmotif, 33-34, 59
— as reinforcement for Foreknowledge, 25, 28, 30, 37-38, 53-54, 54-55
— as reinforcement in a flash-back, 45
— retrospective nature of, 53
— structural features of: forth-and-back rhythm occasioned by comparing antecedent and referent, 51, 52; precise parallelism of statement and confirmation, 47, 52, 53, 56
— structurally related to Foreknowledge, 47, 53, 56, 58, 63, 161

Retrospect, 26, 30, 53, 65; as general point of view in *Lxd.*, 26, 174, 180-81; as substantiated in phrases of recalling, 44, 54

Retrospective cues (veiled hints):
— defined, 26, 43-44, 161
— distinguishing features of, 30-31
— examples of, in Snorri Godi's scheme, 26-30
— function of, as camouflage, 170
— ambiguities (double intent): *fylgði*, 35; *hurðir loknar*, 34; *kyrrt*, 32, 33, 40; *næst Kjartani*, 35; *snarisk í bragð*, 27-28; *ráðakostr*, 39 (*See also* Ambiguity)
— by-names, 41, 43
— euphemism, 41 (*See also* Rhetorical devices)
— future of probability, 23
— generalities for specifics (vague plurals, vague terms): *af inum versti manni*, 52; *nǫkkura*, 33, 127; *svívirðingarorð*, 33, 127 (*See also* Ambiguity)
— litotes, 27, 31, 40 (*See also* Rhetorical devices, litotes)
— pre-introduced character traits, 27, 41-42, 42, 62, 161
— pre-introduction of characters (mainly in genealogies), 27, 43, 161
— quantitative slights, 34-35, 36
— repetitions (statement-confirmations), 27/29, 28, 30, 31/32, 32, 33/34, 36/38, 39
— weighted words: *eigi orð tóm*, 27; *jafnan*, 31, 32, 33, 54; *meiri ván*, 27; *vel*, 36 (See also *jafnan*; *vel*)

Reversals (reversed images): in dialogue, 37, 60-61, 116, 117-18, 119; as contrast within a series, 98, 129, 130, 132, 133, 136, 138, 152, 162-63, 171, 203 n. 6, 223, n. 23; as negative counterpart, 60, 82, 90, 94, 129, 144, 218 n. 28; as negative or positive substitution within a pattern, 39, 43, 70, 70-71, 87, 92, 95, 115, 116, 118, 119, 168-69, 210 n. 12, 216 n. 13, 217-18 n. 25; qualitatively of greater import, 98, 132, 138, 144; significance of, for thirteenth-century analogy 171, 176, 177, 181, 189, 193

Reverse, images in (mirrored images):
— like-reflections: betrothals, 128; divorces, 68; sea-crossings, 132-33, 181
— opposite reflections: Án's dream, 216 n. 13
— significance of, for thirteenth-century analogy, 176, 177, 181, 193

Rhetorical devices: general 30-31, 40, 44, 58, 63, 95, 97, 115, 118, 127, 143, 154, 168-69; antistrophon, 34, 38, 55, 61-62, 173; balanced comparatives, 52, 90-91, 169; balanced syntax, 91-92, 169; chiasmus, 81, 115, 168; correlatives, 56, 94,

251

169, 181; euphemism, 31, 41, 52; litotes, 6, 27, 31, 31-32, 40; weighted words, 19, 24, 32, 39, 204-5 n. 18. *See also* Ambiguity; Increment; Reversals

Rhythm, alternating (back and forth): expressed in form and content, 44-45, 174-75, 181; expressed in the narrative form, 45, 51, 52, 180; as result of structure, 44, 149, 159, 174-75, 177; significance of, for thirteenth-century analogy, 174-75, 177, 180-81, 181; subtlety of, 149, 177

Riddles, 71-72, 143. *See also* Poems

Romantic School, 2, 198 n. 3

Sagas of Icelanders: chronology of, 2, 4, 154, 157; composition of, 158; as thirteenth-century literary works, 4, 150; sources for, 8, 11, 150

Saint's life. *See* Hagiography

Sales of land, 113-115; function of chiasmus in, 115. *See also* Bargaining, for Hjardarholt

Scarlet clothes, motif of, 86, 132, 138, 139, 140, 222 n. 46

Schemes: the author's, 168, 172, 176, 181-182, 183-84; use of word *bragð*, 27-28, 29, 167; Snorri Godi's, 28-30, 168, 181, 183-84; of words, 172 (*See also* Language, formal dimension of)

Sea crossings, 130-132; as mirrored images (like reflections), 181; as reversed image (opposite reflection), 181; rhythm of, 44, 175

Shields, insignias on: as anachronisms, 142, 155, 227-28 n. 48; descriptions of, 139 (Óláf Peacock's), 140 (Kjartan's), 141 (Bolli Bollason's); sources for, 227-28 n. 48

Shift of focus: between foreground and background, 124, 143, 144, 172, 175, 177, 178; between the implicit and the explicit, 68, 73, 76, 109, 115, 144, 169, 177

Simultaneity: of depiction, 165; of time, 89, 90 (*jafnsnimma*), 178-80, 179-80 (*jafnskjótt*)

Skaldic: devices, 154, 185; poetry, 149, 151

Snorri Sturluson, 149, 150, 151, 158, 185, 186, 187-88 (prelude to his death, account in *Íslendinga saga*), 189, 191-92, 193-96 (life and times of)

Social and Moral Order, 158-60; inevitability of, 144, 159; significance of, 175-76, 178-79, 179; symbolically expressed, 123-24, 144, 159. *See also* Epic, background; Ethical code; Inevitability

Statement-confirmation (anticipation-fulfillment), examples of, 18-25, 26-30, 31-39, 40, 43, 51-63

Statistical studies of *Lxd.*, 8-10; evaluated, 9-10

Stereotypes vs. individuals, 6, 7, 79, 95, 104, 136, 155, 162, 163, 164, 192. *See also* Characters, as composites of linguistic units, from various sources and times

Sturla Thórdarson, 9, 10, 158, 187, 189, 191, 192

Sturlu saga, 186, 187, 233 n. 32

Stylistic devices, 154;
— contrastives: between calm and storm, 32-33, 169 (*See also* Ambiguity, *kyrrt*); between gaiety and ensuing tragedy, 20, 98, 169, 215 n. 5 (See also *kátr*); between hope and fear, 19-20, 20, 161, 169; between splendor and tragedy, 16, 158, 169
— narrative techniques, 154; flash-backs, 45, 79, 165, 173, 175, 180-81

Subterfuge. *See* Duplicity

Superlatives, 6, 73, 81, 134, 136, 143. *See also* Clichés; Recurrence, magnification of

Superimpositions: of epic and dramatic, 175; of present on the past, 174; of time-periods, 178, 179; of sources, 185. *See also* Overlapping; Time, superimpositions of

252

Supernatural happenings, 66, 67, 111, 112, 113, 209 n. 2; amalgamated with natural causes, 20, 112-13, 138, 202 n. 4

Suspense, 17, 18, 44, 160

Sverris saga, 150-51

Swimming match, 32, 35-36

Swords: Footbiter, 15, 19, 23, 69, 161; Konungsnaut, 15, 19, 69, 161; as part of hero's accoutrements, 227 n. 47; Skofnung, 216 n. 14

Ten (*tíu*), as coded word, 190; as increment, 105, 121; as numerically important in saga, 190, 234 n. 40

Tenses, 176-77; camouflaged use of, 176-77; method of handling, 176-77, 186; in *títt* phrases, 194

Thorvald, attack on sons of, in *Íslendinga saga*, 156, 157, 188-89, 192, 210 n. 9. *See also* Helgi's hut, attack at; *Íslendinga saga*, relationship of, to *Lxd*.

Time: discrepancies in, 143, 149-50, 173-74, 202 n. 3, 211-12 n. 24, 233 n. 22 (*See also* Anachronism; Ordeals, as evidence of anachronism); compacted, 185, 192; present ("now") and past ("before") compared, 63, 173-74, 174 (*títt* phrases), 174-75, 177-78, 180-81, 195; epic and dramatic, 165, 166, 174-75, 178; equivalent to three cultural periods, 155, 157-58, 185; as historical sequence, 142, 149-50, 177, 227 n. 48; poetic, 150, 202 n. 3; relativity of, 149-50, 178; superimpositions of, 174, 175, 178, 179, 180; suspended, 150, 166, 175, 178; synchronic, 90, 179-80. *See also* Overlapping, of time periods

tíu eða tólf, 190, 217 n. 20, 234, n. 40

Tripartite form. *See also Laxdæla saga*, parts of, overall structure of

— characterized by two within three, 77, 79, 115, 120, 216 n. 14; exemplified in comparisons of "before" and "now," (two time periods), 63, 174, 180-81; in comparisons of "before," "now," and "after," (three time periods), 177, 178, 181, 185; in distribution over parts of saga, 73-74, 76, 77, 181, 216 n. 14; in layers of meaning (two-levelled and three-levelled), 166, 167, 177, 182; in numerical preferences, 92-94, 120, 120-21; important for dating the saga, 190-91

— reflected in themes in triplicate, 97 (*See also* Drownings; Goadings; Killings; Parties; Sales of land)

— reflected in triple repetitions, 110 (*See also* Triplets)

— relationship of, to convention and folklore, 120, 121-22

Triplets: examples of, 99, 108-9, 115-118, 217-18 n. 25, 218 n. 28; formally related to Repetition and Comparison, 99, 122, 159; types of, 117

Twelve (*tólf*); numerical preference for, 121; significance of, for analogy, 190; social and legal mores associated with, 121-22, 151, 219 n. 34, 221-22 n. 5

Understatement. *See* Rhetorical devices, litotes

upp kveðit... niðr koma: in betrothals, 126-27; symbolic function of, 26, 127

ván: as coded word, 44, 147-48, 173; as signifiying Foreknowledge, 44, 63; examples of, 205 n. 25

vel, lesser value of, 36, 80, 81, 91-92, 129. *See also* Language, provenance of, irrelevant

Weaponry, 152. *See also* Hero's accoutrements; Shields; Swords

Weapons and clothes (*at vápnum ok klæðum*). *See* Hero's accoutrements, related motifs

Wit, 34, 40, 41, 42, 61-62, 78, 172, 172-73, 182, 226 n. 45, 228 n. 48

þættir theory, 4, 5-6, 11, 198 n. 3

253

INDEX OF PERSONAL NAMES

Álf of the Dales (Dala-Álfr), 27
Án the Black (Brushwood-Belly) (Án svarti, hrísmagi), 20, 43, 93, 160, 188
Án the White (Án inn hvíti), 43, 99
Ásgaut (slave) (Ásgautr), 43, 67-68, 88
Aud (of Hól; first wife of Thórd Ingunnarson) (Auðr), 20, 68, 69, 93, 136, 161
Audgísl (Auðgísl Þórarinsson), 29, 62, 63
Audun Festargarm (Auðunn festargarmr), 25
Bárd Hoskuldsson (Bárðr Hǫskuldsson), 31; compared with brother Thorleik, 74, 76; with Kjartan, 76; with Thorleik Bollason, 79; favored by Hoskuld, 74, 77; reaction over inheritance claim, 75
Bardi (Barði Guðmundarson), 102-3
Beinir the Strong (Beinir inn sterki), 43, 51 *passim*
Bjorn the Eastman (Bjǫrn inn austrœni Ketilsson), 15, 27; compared to brother Helgi, 74
Bolli Bollason, 23, 125, 126, 128, 130, 137, 142; compared to Bárd, 76, 76-77, 79; to Bolli Thorleiksson, 108; to brother Thorleik, 77, 78; to Kjartan, 77, 79, 80, 81, 121; to Óláf Peacock, 121; counterpart for father, 81-82; foremost, 79, 80; in hero's accoutrements, 141-42; marriage plans of, 81; ostentation of, 86, 137; shift in character of, 79; as stereotype, 164; superiority of, 80; at twelve years of age, 121
Bolli Thorleiksson (Bolli Þorleiksson), 15, 16, 17, 19, 22, 88, 89, 93, 99, 102, 105, 106, 109, 120, 126; compared to Bárd, 79; to Bolli Bollason, 79, 108; to Kjartan, 76, 79, 108, 163; to Thorleik Bollason, 79, 81; as Eddic counterpart, 186; insinuation of, 37, 39, 58; negativeness of, 61, 79, 117; relationship to Gudrún, 35, 71, 129; resentment of Kjartan, 35-36, 36-37, 38, 61, 117; showiness of, 137; in hero's accoutrements, 138; silence of, 59, 79; subordinate position of, 34-35, 35-36, 80
Egil Skalla-Grímsson (Egill Skalla-Grímsson), 57-58
Eid (Eiðr Skeggjason), 118
Eldgrím (Eldgrímr), 31, 88, 91, 117, 118, 120-21
Geirmund the Noisy (Geirmundr gnýr), 18, 19, 55, 69, 73, 129
Gellir Thorkelsson (Gellir Þorkelsson), 121
Gest (Gestr Oddleifsson), 15, 16, 19, 27, 41; dream interpretations of, 21-22, 72; prophecies of, 17, 24-25; threat against Kotkel, 66
Gizur (Gizur hvíti Teitsson), 120
Grím (outlaw) (Grímr), 23, 27, 55, 69-70, 118, 136

255

Gudrún Ósvífsdóttir (Guðrún Ósvífrsdóttir), 15, 16, 17, 20, 22, 26, 27, 28, 29, 37, 38, 68, 89, 93, 94, 126, 128, 135; uses an antistrophon, 61-62, 173; character traits of, 41-42, 98, 137, 162; compared to Kjartan, 86-87; to Melkorka, 85; to Thorgerd, 100-104, 109-10; to Thorgils, 83, 84; to Vigdís, 82, 116; as composite, 186; as contrast to Hrefna, 39; cruel remarks of, 58-59; divorce of, 68, 71; dreams of, 21, 72; favoritism toward Bolli Bollason, 77, 125; introduced in genealogy, 43; goadings of, 100, 103; marriage with Bolli Thorleiksson, 129; nurtures hate, 60; observes men on raid, 54; as prototype, 95, 162-63; rebuffed by Kjartan, 60; spinning and washing of, 109

Gunnar Thidrandabani (Gunarr Þiðrandabani), 42, 69-70, 82

Gunnhild (queen) (Gunnhildr), 62, 89, 91, 131, 132

Hákon the Earl (Hákon jarl), 55

Hallbjorn Sleekstone-Eye (Hallbjǫrn slíkisteinsauga Kotkelsson), 25, 67

Hall (brother of Ingjald) Hallr, bróðir Ingjalds Sauðeyjargoða), 91, 92, 115, 116

Halldór (Halldórr Óláfsson), 20, 51 *passim*, 54, 88, 114

Harald (king) (Harald Gunnhildarson Noregskonungr), 55, 131

Hardbeiń (Harðbeinn Helgason), 121

Helgi Bjólan (Helgi bjólan Ketilsson), 74

Helgi Hardbeinsson (Helgi Harðbeinsson), 17, 23, 28, 71-72, 105, 106, 120

Herjólf (Herjólfr Eyvindarson), 129, 136

Hild (Hildr Þorarinsdóttir), 120

Hjalti (Skeggjason), 120

Hoskuld Kollsson (Dala-Kollsson), 31, 33, 34, 40, 88, 90, 92, 93, 94, 120, 126, 129, 130, 133, 134; compared to son Óláf Peacock, 85, 119; favoritism toward Bárd, 75, 77, 79, 125; division of inheritance, 75; love for Óláf Peacock, 125; broaches marriage proposal to Egil, 57; counsels neighbors, 55

Hrapp (Víga-Hrappr, I; Sumarliðason), 40, 55, 67, 72, 91

Hrapp (Víga-Hrappr, II), 73

Hrefna (Ásgeirsdottir œdikolls), 81, 94, 99; as composite, 186; as contrast to Gudrún, 39, 162-63; Gudrún's jealousy of, 42; pre-introduced, 43; showiness of, 137

Hrút (Hrútr Herjólfsson), 25, 31, 32, 40, 120, 121; cattle raid of, 92; character traits of, 73; early maturity of, in hero's accoutrements, 137; relationship of, to Eldgrím, 88, 91, 117, 118; to Gunnhild, 89, 131; return of, to Iceland, 133; superlative description of, 136

Ingibjorg (the king's sister) (Ingibjǫrg Tryggvadóttir), 39, 70, 132

Ingjaldr (Sauðeyjargoði), 88, 91, 120, 121

Jórunn (Hoskuld's wife) (Bjarnardóttir), 40, 65-66, 93, 119, 129; opposition of, toward Hoskuld, 33-34, 90

Kálf (Kálfr Ásgeirsson), 92

Kári Hrútsson, 66, 121

Ketil Flatnose (Ketill flatnefr), 15, 92

Kjartan Óláfsson, 15, 16, 17, 18, 19, 20, 22, 27, 92, 93, 94, 97, 109, 117, 120, 126, 131, 142, 161; character traits of, 36-37, 163; compared to Bolli Bollason, 78, 80, 81, 86, 121; to Bolli Thorleiksson, 34-35, 76; to Guðrún, 86-87; to Óláf Peacock, 85-86, 121, 140; to Óláf Tryggvason, 159; to Thorleik Bollason, 78; as composite, 186, 191, 195; favor of, at court, 36, 38; foremost, 79, 80; in hero's accoutrements,

140; receives king's offer of *ráðakostr*, 39; has knowledge of Tunga sale, 56; marriage plans of, 81; as prototype, 163; reaction to Bolli's insinuation, 37, 58; relationship of, to Bolli Thorleiksson, 37, 58, 61, 75-76; to Gudrún, 41, 59-60, 98; to Ingibjorg, 70; showiness of, 137; receives stud of horses, 71; superior position of, 80; superior qualities of, 32; and his sword Konungsnaut, 61, 69, 98-99

Kotkel (sorcerer) (Kotkell), 66, 71, 88

Lambi (Þorbjarnarson skrjúps), 43, 60, 91

Melkorka (Mýrkjartansdóttir), 33, 34, 75, 88, 90, 93, 94, 120; compared to Gudrún, 84-85; as a composite, 157

Mýrkjartan (king of the Irish), 69, 139

Óláf Feilan (Óláfr feilan Þorsteinsson rauðs), 27, 125, 126

Óláf Peacock (Óláfr pái Hǫskuldsson), 16, 17, 84, 88, 90-91, 91, 97, 114, 115, 117, 120, 126-27, 131, 133; 142; as *ambáttarsonr*, 33-34; compared to Bolli Bollason, 121; to Hoskuld, 85, 119; to Kjartan, 86, 121; to Mýrkjartan, 69; favoritism of, toward Kjartan, 79, 125; foremost, 79; inheritance quarrel of, 31-32, 75; in hero's accoutrements before Mýrkjartan, 139; before Thorgerd, 140; has knowledge about Thorhalla's sons, 57; marriage of, into Mýramenn, 54, 57; premonitions of, 18, 19, 20; prestige abroad, 55-56; promises a reward, 68; relationship to Bárd, 75; showiness in weapons and clothes, 138-39; threat against Kotkel, 66; at twelve years of age, 121

Óláf, the Saint (Haraldsson, king of Norway), 72 (deflates Kjartan)

Óláf Tryggvason (king) (Óláfr Tryggvason), 118, 131; blesses Kjartan's sword, 19; deflates Thorkel, 72; method of Christianization, 56; makes a prophecy, 18

Orn (helmsman) (Ǫrn), 55, 119

Ósvíf (father of Gudrún) (Ósvífr Helgason), 25, 91, 97

Snorri Godi (Snorri goði Þorgrímsson), 17, 23, 26, 28, 29, 30, 42, 70, 88, 89, 94, 115-16, 126; advice of, to Thorkel Eyjólfsson, 62; pre-introduced, 43; relationship of, to Thorgils, 27, 62; to Thorkel, 27; to Snorri Sturluson, 182, 183-84, 191, 196; scheming of, 28-30

Stígandi (Kotkelsson), 68, 88, 136

Thangbrand (Þangbrandr), 56

Thórarin (Þórarinn, father of Audgísl), 62

Thórarin (Þórisson), 20, 59, 88, 92; accompanies Halldór to bargain for Hjardarholt, 114 *passim*

Thorbjorn Skrjúp; compared to Thorgils Hǫlluson, 84-85; meaning of by-name, 43; pre-introduced, 43

Thórd Goddi (Þórðr goddi), 34, 69, 88, 120, 121; bribed, 65; divorce of, 71; evens score with Vigdís, 68; pre-introduced, 43

Thórd Ingunnarson (Þórðr Ingunnarson), 21, 41; divorce of, 68; drowning of, 112-13

Thorgerd Egilsdóttir (Þorgerðr Egilsdóttir), 33; character traits, 73; compared to Gudrún, 100-104, 109-10; goading of, 101-2; knowledge of Thorkel of Hafratindar's behaviour, 57; marriage to Óláf Peacock, 53-54, 126-27, 127-28; reaction to Óláf's finery, 139-40; as stereotype, 164

Thorgerd (wife of Dala-Kolli) (Þorgerðr Þorsteinsdóttir), 129; favorite son Hoskuld, 125

Thorgils Holluson (Þorgils Hǫlluson), 28, 29, 30, 77, 88, 91, 116, 120; character traits, 73; compared to Gudrún, 83; to Thorbjorn Skrjúp, 84-85; relationship to Thorkel Eyjólfsson, 27, 82-83, 83-84; to Snorri Godi, 27, 62

257

Thorhalla Chatterbox (Þorhalla málga), 59, 161, 188

Thorkel Eyjólfsson (Þorkell Eyjólfsson), 24, 28, 30, 42, 72, 77, 94, 114, 118, 121, 126, 128, 132, 135, 160; character trait, 42; compared to Gudrún, 69-70; dream of, 23; drowning of, 113; experience with outlaws, 55, 69-70, 218-19 n. 32; pre-introduced, 43; relationship to Thorgils Holluson, 27, 82-83, 83-84

Thorkel of Hafratindar, 18, 20, 56-57, 101, 106

Thorkel Skalli of Thykkvaskóg (Þorkell skalli á Þykkvaskógi), 67

Thorkel Trefil (Þorkell trefill Rauða-Bjarnarsonar), 40-41, 92

Thorleik Bollason (Þorleikr Bollason), 119, 130; compared to Bolli Bollason, 77, 78; to Bolli Thorleiksson, 77, 79, 81; to Thorleik Hoskuldsson, 76-77, 77, 78, 79; subordinate position of, 80, 224 n. 27.

Thorleik Hoskuldsson (Þorleikr Hǫskuldsson), 88, 91, 117; bribed, 65; character traits of, 73; compared to Bárd, 74-75, 76; to Bolli Thorleiksson, 76; reaction to inheritance claim, 75; relationship to Hrút, 25, 31; bargains for stud of horses, 71

Thórólf (outlaw) (Þórólfr), 54, 82, 88, 92

Thórólf Rednose (Þórólfr rauðnefr), 54, 73, 116

Thorstein the Black (Þorsteinn svarti), 116

Thorstein Kuggason (Þorsteinn Þorkelsson kugga), 24, 88, 114, 118, 120; admonishes Thorkel, 160; takes part in Hjardarholt bargaining, 51 *passim*

Thorstein Surt (Þorsteinn surtr inn spaki Hallsteinsson), drowning of, 110-12

Thorvald (Gudrún's first husband) (Þorvaldr Halldórsson), 21, 41-42

Thuríd Óláfsdóttir (Þuríðr Óláfsdóttir), 18, 19, 39, 65-66, 87, 126, 129

Unn the Deep-minded (Unnr in djúpúgða Ketilsdóttir), 15, 16, 24, 27, 32, 92, 126; character trait, 62; favoritism toward Óláf Feilan, 125

Vigdís (Ingjaldsdóttir), 34, 54; 88; evens score with husband Thórd, 67-68; compared to Gudrún, 71, 82, 116; pre-introduced, 43

www.ingramcontent.com/pod-product-compliance
Lightning Source LLC
Chambersburg PA
CBHW020748160426
43192CB00006B/278